STATE BEHAVIOR AND THE NUCLEAR
NONPROLIFERATION REGIME

 STUDIES IN SECURITY
AND INTERNATIONAL AFFAIRS

SERIES EDITORS

William W. Keller
Professor of International Affairs, Center for International Trade and Security, University of Georgia

Scott A. Jones
Director of Export Control Programs, Center for International Trade and Security, University of Georgia

SERIES ADVISORY BOARD

Pauline H. Baker
The Fund for Peace

Eliot Cohen
Paul H. Nitze School of Advanced International Studies, Johns Hopkins University

Eric Einhorn
Center for Public Policy and Administration, University of Massachusetts, Amherst

John J. Hamre
The Center for Strategic and International Studies

Josef Joffe
Hoover Institution, Institute for International Studies, Stanford University

Lawrence J. Korb
Center for American Progress

William J. Long
Sam Nunn School of International Affairs, Georgia Institute of Technology

Jessica Tuchman Mathews
Carnegie Endowment for International Peace

Scott D. Sagan
Center for International Security and Cooperation, Stanford University

Lawrence Scheinman
Monterey Institute of International Studies, CNS-WDC

David Shambaugh
The Elliott School of International Affairs, George Washington University

Jessica Stern
FXB Center, Harvard School of Public Health

STATE BEHAVIOR AND THE NUCLEAR NONPROLIFERATION REGIME

Edited by Jeffrey R. Fields

The University of Georgia Press
Athens

Paperback edition, 2018
© 2014 by the University of Georgia Press
Athens, Georgia 30602
www.ugapress.org
All rights reserved
Set in 10/14 Minion Pro by Graphic Composition, inc., Bogart, Georgia

Most University of Georgia Press titles are
available from popular e-book vendors.

Printed digitally

The Library of Congress has cataloged the
hardcover edition of the book as follows:

State behavior and the nuclear nonproliferation regime /
edited by Jeffrey R. Fields.
xv, 321 pages ; 24 cm pages cm. — (Studies in security and international affairs)
Includes bibliographical references.
ISBN 978-0-8203-4729-5 (hardcover) — ISBN 0-8203-4729-9 (hardcover)
1. Nuclear nonproliferation—international cooperation.
2. Treaty on the non-proliferation of Nuclear Weapons (1968)
I. Fields, Jeffrey R.
JZ5675.S75 2014
327.1'747—dc23

2014015865

Paperback ISBN 978-0-8203-5479-8

publication of the proliferation
is made possible via grant by
Figure Foundation

CONTENTS

Acknowledgments   xi

Abbreviations and Acronyms   xiii

Introduction
Jeffrey R. Fields   1

Theoretical Approaches

CHAPTER 1. Explaining Dynamics and Stasis in the Nuclear Nonproliferation Regime: The Challenges of a Multiplicity of Public Goods
Jason Enia   19

CHAPTER 2. Glass Half Full? Evaluating the Impact of New U.S. Policy on the Legitimacy of the Nuclear Nonproliferation Regime
Nina Srinivasan Rathbun   40

CHAPTER 3. Construction of Threat and Nuclear Nonproliferation Measures: Considerations on Theory and Policy
Maria Rost Rublee   84

CHAPTER 4. Nuclear Disarmament and Nonproliferation: Examining the Linkage Argument
Jeffrey W. Knopf   106

Country and Regional Explorations

CHAPTER 5. How Supportive of the Nonproliferation Regime Are the United States and Its Allies? U.S. Security Guarantees and the Free Rider Problem
Lowell H. Schwartz   149

CHAPTER 6. The Nonproliferation Motivations of the Non-Aligned Movement
Deepti Choubey   169

CHAPTER 7. Russia, Iran, and the Nuclear Nonproliferation Regime
Robert J. Reardon   190

CHAPTER 8. Brazil and Mexico in the Nonproliferation Regime: Common Structures and Divergent Trajectories in Latin America
Arturo C. Sotomayor   218

CHAPTER 9. The Additional Protocol in the Middle East and North Africa: Explaining Lag in Adoption
Jim Walsh   251

CHAPTER 10. Conclusion
Jeffrey R. Fields   276

Bibliography   283

Contributors   315

Index   319

ACKNOWLEDGMENTS

It has been quite satisfying to be a part of this volume, working in partnership with scholars, researchers, and practitioners on the very important topic of nuclear nonproliferation, and I am grateful to a number of people. The idea for this project was due in large part to the thinking of my friend and colleague Edward Lacey, deputy director of Policy Planning at the State Department. While working at State, I frequently had informal discussions with Ed on any number of topics, and the direction of this book emanated from one of those conversations. Then acting assistant secretary of state Vann Van Diepen played a similar role in a casual conversation about forward-looking projects I might undertake in motivating me to include a chapter on the Non-Aligned Movement.

All of the essays here began their lives at a workshop I held at the University of California, San Diego in March 2011, and I am indebted to the Institute on Global Conflict and Cooperation there for providing space for us and for their overall support. Particular thanks goes out to Laura Martin and Sara Sheffer for their help with the logistics. All of the participants of the workshop provided helpful comments and suggestions to improve and move the project forward. In particular I would like to thank Robert English and Scott Sagan for their thoughtful comments as discussants.

In the long road to publication, versions of two of the essays here appeared in the journals *Nonproliferation Review* and *International Security*, further indicating the salience and timeliness of this book, and we thank those publishers for allowing us to include versions here. I would also like to thank for help along the way Jonathan Snider, Meena Singelee, Jack Boureston, Sara Kutchesfahani, Tim McCarthy, Zachary Zwald, Stephanie Young, Rebecca Loewenstein, Geoffrey Wiseman, Rebecca Gibbons, and Patrick James. The authors' workshop was made possible with funding from the U.S. Department of Defense, where I worked during the early stages of this project. The views here are my and the authors' own opinions and do not represent those of the Department of Defense or the U.S. government. My final thanks and appreciation go to the authors here who worked hard and stuck with this project through many ups and downs along the way to publication.

Jeffrey R. Fields
Los Angeles

ABBREVIATIONS AND ACRONYMS

ABACC	Argentine-Brazilian Agency for Accounting and Control of Nuclear Materials
ABM	anti-ballistic missile
AP	Additional Protocol
BWC	Biological Weapons Convention
CANFWZ	Central Asian Nuclear-Weapon-Free Zone
CBW	chemical and biological weapons
CD	Conference on Disarmament
CNEN	National Nuclear Energy Commission
CPPNM	Convention on the Physical Protection of Nuclear Material
CSA	Comprehensive Safeguards Agreement
CTBT	Comprehensive Nuclear-Test-Ban Treaty
CTBTO	Comprehensive Test-Ban Treaty Organization
DTRA-ASCO	Defense Threat Reduction Agency/Advanced Systems Concepts Office
ENR	enrichment and reprocessing
EU-3	United Kingdom, France, and Germany
FMCT	Fissile Material Cut-off Treaty
FSB	Federal Security Service
HEU	highly enriched uranium
IAEA	International Atomic Energy Agency
ICBM	intercontinental ballistic missile
IMS	International Monitoring System
INFCIRC	Information Circular
INSPP	Integrated Nuclear Security Support Plan
INSServ	International Nuclear Security Advisory Service
INTELSAT	International Telecommunications Satellite Organization
IO	international organization
ISI	import substitution industrialization

ISSS-ISAC	International Security Studies Section/International Security and Arms Control Section
LEU	low-enriched uranium
LTBT	Limited Test Ban Treaty
LWR	light-water nuclear reactors
MENA	Middle East and North Africa
Minatom	Ministry for Atomic Energy
MLF	multilateral force
NAC	New Agenda Coalition
NAFTA	North American Free Trade Agreement
NAM	Non-Aligned Movement
NDP	National Democratic Party
NGO	nongovernmental organization
NNWS	nonnuclear weapons state
NPR	Nuclear Posture Review
NPT	Treaty on the Non-Proliferation of Nuclear Weapons
NSG	Nuclear Suppliers Group
NSOI	Nuclear Smuggling Outreach Initiative
NWFZ	nuclear-weapons-free zone
NWS	nuclear weapons state
OAS	Organization of American States
OECD	Organisation for Economic Co-operation and Development
P-5	permanent members of the UN Security Council (China, France, Russia, United Kingdom, and United States)
P5+1	China, France, Russia, United Kingdom, United States, and Germany
PATN	Autonomous Program of Nuclear Technology
PD	Prisoner's Dilemma
PSI	Proliferation Security Initiative
Pu	plutonium
RevCon	Review Conference
ROK	Republic of Korea
SORT	Strategic Offensive Reductions Treaty
SQP	Small Quantities Protocol
START	Strategic Arms Reduction Treaty

UAE	United Arab Emirates
UNAEC	UN Atomic Energy Commission
UNSC	United Nations Security Council
WMD	weapons of mass destruction
WTO	World Trade Organization

STATE BEHAVIOR AND THE NUCLEAR
NONPROLIFERATION REGIME

INTRODUCTION

Jeffrey R. Fields

WHAT EXPLAINS COUNTRIES' variable support for global nonproliferation efforts? More than two decades after the end of the Cold War, the spread of weapons of mass destruction (WMD)—nuclear, chemical, biological, and radiological weapons—continues to be a concern for the international community. A multidimensional regime has evolved over many years to help check the spread of these deadly weapons. The nuclear regime in particular has become an important line of defense. Anchored by the Treaty on the Non-Proliferation of Nuclear Weapons (NPT), the nuclear nonproliferation regime is a constellation of agreements, initiatives, and norms aimed at regulating the use and spread of nuclear material and technology. Among both scholars and practitioners, the health of this regime is a much-discussed topic.[1] The nuclear nonproliferation regime, like other regimes, whether trade or security oriented, relies on cooperation and coordination between states. And while the NPT is its cornerstone, the regime comprises many other instruments, initiatives, and arrangements working in concert. This book is about how states make decisions concerning their support for or resistance to those components that make up the nuclear nonproliferation regime.

What explains states' behavior once they have nominally or formally joined a regime? Often the focus of regime studies—particularly those studies on WMD regimes—has been on explaining the decision to join or not. But international regimes are dynamic forms of governance. We need to be able to explain behavior beyond the point where countries make the initial yes or no decision. That is the focus of this book. As such, the basic issue it addresses is why states behave in certain ways regarding principles of nonproliferation—that is, *within* the regime. One very important aspect of this issue is better understanding why states are sometimes unsupportive and obstructionist. The authors of the essays that follow take varied approaches—some theoretical, some empirical, some hybrid—to tackle the issue of state behavior in the nonproliferation regime.

When analysts, scholars, and policymakers think and talk nuclear proliferation, they are generally referring to state acquisition of nuclear weapons. Nonproliferation in this sense is the mirror image of proliferation in that it means preventing a particular ambitious country, like Iran for example, from achieving nuclear weapons capability. Thus, nonproliferation involves measures targeted at preventing specific state actors from achieving nuclear capacity or capability. This book is not simply about *why* states acquire or do not acquire nuclear weapons. Our approach to nonproliferation focuses not simply on one component of the regime, such as the NPT. Rather, we broaden our scope to include other aspects of and perspectives on nonproliferation as we try to better understand states' thinking about support for the various individual instruments that comprise the regime.[2]

Nonproliferation refers to limiting or preventing the spread of nuclear weapons. Conceptually and in practice it concerns the prevention and dissuasion of states from acquiring a nuclear explosive capability—focused on *individual* state acquisition. However, nonproliferation also refers to multilateral activities designed to prevent the diffusion of nuclear material and technology in general. (Increasingly, especially since the terrorist attacks of September 11, 2001, the concern is that weapons or weapons-usable material could fall into the hands of nonstate actors.) The latter does not necessarily focus on any specific actor. The difference derives from the term "proliferation" used to mean both the decision to acquire nuclear weapons and also the spread of nuclear weapons, material, and technology. The distinction is important for the theme of this book.[3] The nonproliferation regime here refers to the totality of efforts to prevent the transnational spread of nuclear weapons and material, including restrictions on and regulation of states with civilian or military nuclear programs (i.e., efforts to detect diversion and prevent breakout). In sum, the regime is much more than just the NPT, and nonproliferation decision making involves considerations on many levels—both systemic and domestic—and on differing efforts. The strength and health of the regime is not only a function of individual states' actions to acquire or abjure nuclear weapons for themselves but also a function of efforts to prevent *other* states from acquiring weapons (or efforts to make doing so more difficult). We know of no other published book-length treatments that explore why states cooperate with or undermine global nonproliferation efforts.[4]

It is indeed important to measure the relative success of global nonproliferation efforts. However, perceptions of the health or strength of the regime are often reduced to the number of states that have nuclear weapons and the number that want them or are actively seeking them. This reflects an overly narrow view of what regimes are and how they operate.[5] When states explore a nuclear weapons option or when NPT-member nuclear states share technology with other states in violation of NPT commitments, analysts tend to reflexively remark on the crumbling of the regime. This reduces the regime to one constituted by only supplier states and recipient states. But since the health of the regime is determined by much more than a simple count of how many states have nuclear weapons combined with how many are actively pursing them, understanding states' motivations for supporting regime components is essential. The regime comprises formal treaties like the NPT, multilateral agreements, and initiatives, as well as less formal instruments intended to restrain the flow of nuclear material and technology. How states make decisions about their participation in these *individual* efforts is surprisingly underexplored by scholars and policymakers. This book is an effort at filling the lacuna.

Practitioners can make better and more effective policy when they better understand the motivations and interests of other actors and the challenges of getting countries to cooperate on nonproliferation efforts. A delineation of the specific aspects of behavior is important, even necessary, to both better frame the issue of "nonproliferation" and yield actionable policy recommendations. Knowing *why* states tend to play spoiler at NPT review conferences or refuse to sign an Additional Protocol can only help make better policy. That specific knowledge, however, is quite distinct from why states may resist better domestic antismuggling efforts or fail to implement robust export controls. While policymakers are quick to note uncooperative behavior, they often give little consideration to its sources (or have scant time to do so).

Better understanding the sources of these behaviors also contributes to the scholarly study of nonproliferation. A substantial literature exists that seeks to answer the question of why states pursue nuclear weapons—the demand side of proliferation.[6] Are states motivated by threats to security, prestige, or other factors in deciding to build nuclear weapons? A subsequent and emerging literature has begun to explore the inverse: Why do states abjure nuclear weapons (especially when they have the technical ability to do so and face existential security threats)? This "new demand-side research" focuses on what restrains states in potential nuclear pursuits, whether the reasons are self-imposed (e.g., economics, domestic politics) or external (e.g., security assurances, coercive threats).[7] Whereas that research concerns motivation for individual proliferation, this book is about motivations for restraining other states' proliferation.

This introduction characterizes the theme of the book as state behavior in the regime. A more explicit articulation asks the question: Why do some states ignore, oppose, or undermine global efforts to prevent the proliferation of nuclear weapons?[8] This may include transferring sensitive nuclear technology to other states.[9] Or it may take the form of states' reluctance or refusal to take steps to strengthen other global efforts. While most states view nonproliferation as a good thing, a puzzle exists as to why there is differentiated support for various components of the regime. For example, why do states with no purported interest in nuclear weapons resist signing an International Atomic Energy Agency (IAEA) Additional Protocol? Brazil, for example, is constitutionally prohibited from having a nuclear weapons program, which would seem to indicate a firm commitment to nuclear nonproliferation. However, it has steadfastly refused to conclude an Additional Protocol.[10] Despite almost universal membership in the NPT, there is variable state support for any number of specific measures like the Convention on the Physical Protection of Nuclear Material (CPPNM) and more normative and informal arrangements like the Proliferation Security Initiative (PSI). Why do some states support while others undermine sanctions regimes designed to punish and hamper would-be proliferators?

In a 2010 article Andrew Grotto begins to explore this issue, and this book is in part an extension of his thinking and questioning. Several of the chapters explicitly incorporate and reflect on Grotto's thinking on this subject. His argument of state reluctance breaks down along three lines: "regime symbolism"—that is, the equity/inequality of the NPT; security and relative power; and distributive economic effects. Grotto writes:

> The picture of nonproliferation decision-making that emerges from this more comprehensive accounting of the national interests that may be implicated by nonproliferation policies is that states may have as many reasons to oppose NPT-plus measures as they do to support them. Normative factors may push some countries to resist NPT-plus measures and others to endorse them; security concerns about the balance of power can create both incentives and disincentives to support nonproliferation; and the economic stakes implicated by nonproliferation policies often have distributional consequences that benefit some constituencies and burden others. A state may have a normative interest rooted in concerns about the fairness of the NPT's bargain in pressuring the NWS to pursue disarmament, but also have countervailing security and economic interests in denying adversaries access to

nuclear weapons technology and sustaining important relationships with key countries and institutions that may outweigh disarmament concerns. On the other hand, a state may perceive marginal security or economic benefit in NPT-plus measures, or even view them as affirmatively costly, as well as harboring normative objections to additional nonproliferation measures.[11]

Grotto's thesis is one about NPT-related measures. This is a somewhat circumscribed issue of norms vis-à-vis what he characterizes as resistance to "NPT plus" measures.[12] There is a considerable range of global nonproliferation efforts to be accounted for in states' policy formulations. In this book the authors consider many different aspects of nonproliferation and do not confine their analyses solely to efforts that are extensions of and adjuncts to the NPT.

APPROACH OF THE BOOK

States' decision making concerning nonproliferation measures, whether proactive or punitive, is the crux of this project. As Grotto reminds us, "NPT parties are under no general legal obligation to support measures intended to bolster basic [nonproliferation] norms, such as the IAEA's Additional Protocol, modern export controls, economic sanctions against norm violators, and constraints on national fuel cycle activities."[13] There are a multitude of other efforts, agreements, and measures that states choose or decline to support, including signing and ratifying the Comprehensive Nuclear-Test-Ban Treaty (CTBT), support for a Fissile Material Cutoff Treaty (FMCT), concluding an Additional Protocol agreement, implementing robust export controls, honoring United Nations Security Council Resolution (UNSCR) 1540 commitments, supporting international sanctions regimes designed to compel and punish would-be proliferators, or signing amendments to the Convention on the Physical Protection of Nuclear Material. There are also a host of other informal agreements in which states can participate including the Nuclear Smuggling Outreach Initiative (NSOI), Wassenaar Arrangement, and PSI, to name a few.

When considering these additional aspects, it becomes more challenging to think about state decision making in a parsimonious way. Different regime components address different aspects of proliferation. The various initiatives also impose different requirements on individual states. At once we are considering how states willfully constrain their own nuclear ambitions by agreeing to restrictions and monitoring of their fuel cycle activities, for example. At the same time, how should we think about their efforts to constrain others' activities, especially those that do not represent security threats to them?

In our initial approach to thinking about this question we considered broad motivators of state behavior: free riding; security and self-interest; discrimination, hegemony, and legitimacy; and norms. Several of the chapters explore in detail one or more aspects of these motivators, whereas others demonstrate how they are manifested through empirical work. The eclectic approach of this volume is a function of the intersection of norms and rationality in the various analyses. Here I briefly discuss the motivators before laying out the structure of the rest of the book.

In this book we are considering both cooperation *and* resistance to certain nonproliferation efforts. One line of reasoning for resistance (a normative-legitimacy argument) might follow that the inherent bias of the NPT makes non-nuclear weapons states (NNWS) reluctant to take measures that would seem to accept and validate the perceived discriminatory nature of the treaty. A related line of reasoning contends that lack of progress on disarmament on the part of nuclear weapons states (NWS) serves as a disincentive for NNWS to take an active role in nonproliferation efforts. Another could be that differential threat perceptions militate against robust nonproliferation policies. And as such, some states may view proliferation/nonproliferation as an "American" or superpower issue.[14] Thus, some states may find discomfort with the notion of taking direction from Washington for a "problem" that does not concern them directly. And though states may be sympathetic to nonproliferation efforts, there may also be a reaction to the overwhelming multitude of efforts initiatives (some of which are costly) they are asked to support, leading to what one analyst referred to as "recipient fatigue." Another possibility for reluctance to actively support nonproliferation efforts is free-riding or moral hazards—that is, superpower safety may yield a sense of luxury of inaction.

Threat Perception

Differential threat perceptions may lead states to pursue nonproliferation policies that coincide with the level of threat, particularly by another nuclear power. In a straightforward sense, states facing external threats may be more likely to pursue nuclear weapons if they are in an enduring rivalry, the threatening states have nuclear arms, or they are inferior conventionally.[15] Conversely, states that are relatively secure have greater leeway in decisions to forego nuclear weapons. A similar dynamic may exist regarding other nonproliferation efforts. States facing few external threats may perceive nonproliferation efforts as a low priority. That is, there is a low probability of blowback if they do not implement or vigorously support nonproliferation measures. Many governments in Europe and elsewhere were aware (vaguely or better) of the intentions of Pakistan and A. Q. Khan in the late 1970s and 1980s and later. Yet, low threat perception from a nuclear-armed Pakistan may have helped economic interests (Khan sometimes paid beyond asking price for equipment and technology) subvert rigorous enforcement of export controls.[16] An alliance (e.g., NATO) or a security assurance from a stronger, nuclear power such as the United States may have the effect of reducing threat *and* sensitivities to nonproliferation efforts. Alternatively, it may make the country even more attuned to the perils of proliferation, as with Japan.

Free Riding

Free riding may be an element that underpins multiple (or perhaps all) measures of the nonproliferation regime. The costs (whether economic, political, or other) a state is willing to incur in support of some aspect of the regime may be less than those of the strongest state in the "alliance"—the alliance in this case being supporters of the nonproliferation regime. Smaller states as with other alliances recognize that the bigger NWS not only can afford to expend more resources maintaining the regime, but they also have a greater incentive to do so.[17] Thus, they can enjoy either the effect of fewer costs or the luxury of not having to worry about maintenance of the regime. In sum, as in the original economic/alliance conception, regime members can rest safely with the knowledge that the stronger state will continue to provide the public good.

Hegemony, Legitimacy, and Discrimination

States may not explicitly resist nonproliferation efforts or the notion that they are important. Rather they may resist being pressured to pursue certain policies. For example, though Brazil for the most part has solid nonproliferation credentials, it has resisted signing an Additional Protocol in part because it views the measure as an additional burden difficult to swallow on top of a discriminatory NPT. Other countries are reluctant to be seen as taking direction from the United States on issues related to shoring up customs practices, border security, and antismuggling efforts even when they see the importance of such measures.[18]

As Nina Srinivasan Rathbun contends in an earlier article (which she revisits in this book), "States are more likely to join and comply with regimes they regard as legitimate."[19] At the core of the regime stands a treaty that was conceived to be inherently discriminatory. Over forty years after it came into force many countries still resent this reality. Their calculations of whether to support efforts that in effect bolster a discriminatory dynamic have to be considered, but how much this is a factor is difficult to assess. States frequently rail against this reality, but are these true motivations for specific nonproliferation policies? India cited the discriminatory nature of the NPT as part of its rationale for not signing the treaty at its inception. Similarly, Brazil takes the inherent discrimination a step further. The Lula administration refused to sign an Additional Protocol in part because Brazil had already signed on to the NPT and would thus not further constrain itself. Brasilia felt that its nonproliferation credentials were solid and that the burden should not be on it to prove this but rather on the NWS to demonstrate their commitment to disarm.[20]

Disarmament

Related to the legitimacy argument is one of unfulfilled commitments. Does the perceived reluctance of the NWS to live up to their disarmament commitments serve as motivators for resistance to nonproliferation efforts or merely convenient excuses for accusatory rhetoric? Certain Non-Alignment Movement (NAM) states, NNWS, and states from the global South at times allege lack of progress on Article VI and commitment to deep reductions and disarmament.

In turn, they question why they should be asked to take measures to strengthen the regime or be accused of lack of enthusiasm for nonproliferation efforts when in their minds the NWS are equally culpable for failing to take significant steps to disarm. In essence, states may view the NPT bargain as being neglected by the NWS. The "bargain" includes good faith negotiation to nuclear disarmament by all signatories. However, inherent power disparities place most of the burden on the NWS to disarm. As Andrew Grotto writes, "many states [may] resist proposals to strengthen the nonproliferation end of the NPT bargain largely because America and other nuclear-weapon states haven't made satisfactory progress towards nuclear disarmament.... [T]his consensus rests primarily on an argument about the role of norms in international affairs: some states oppose NPT-plus measures not necessarily because they fear the nuclear-weapon states will use nuclear weapons against them, but because of what accepting those measures would symbolize."²¹ The issue of the NWS fulfilling their Article VI commitments has been a frequent point of contention at NPT review conferences.²²

Security Guarantees

A state may face potential existential security threats from nuclear or nonnuclear states. However, their nonproliferation policies may be influenced by external security guarantees. In much the same manner as security assurances have in influencing state decisions on nuclear weapons acquisition, those guarantees may play a similar role in state nonproliferation policies. The logic may be thus: when external threats are mitigated by a third-party security guarantee, states may become more risk acceptant regarding other states' proliferation. An alliance member, who still bears responsibility for supporting the regime, might shirk those responsibilities because of a feeling of relative security. Even if the state is not fully implementing nonproliferation measures, there is little chance of blowback. Security guarantees might work in the other direction as well. Countries like Japan—that are in regions with nuclear-armed competitors but are under the nuclear umbrella of a superpower—may be freer to pursue policies in *support* of the nonproliferation regime. If a state can remove potential nuclear threats from its security worries, it has more flexibility in security policymaking. The Obama administration incentivized compliant nonproliferation policies by making explicit in the 2010 Nuclear Posture Review (NPR) a promise that states in good standing with their NPT commitments would receive negative security assurances from the United States: "the United States will not use or threaten to use nuclear weapons against non-nuclear weapons states that are party to the Nuclear Non-Proliferation Treaty (NPT) and in compliance with their nuclear non-proliferation obligations."²³

Resource Constraints and Economic Interests

Many nonproliferation efforts require states to expend or forego economic revenue. Implementing export controls, tightening and enforcing customs and border security, supporting sanctions, and so forth have economic consequences for the implementing country.²⁴ States may "rationally calculate the material costs and benefits and find that the benefits (such as market access and potential for technology transfers) outweigh the costs."²⁵ There may be "pressure to relax nonproliferation standards to pursue export opportunities, or to debase a disarmament standard in order to provide business to local industries."[26] Resulting policies may reflect not only the economic burden a state is prepared to accept (or not accept) but also its security situation—that is, the threshold for participation might be lowered if the state faces a threat and regime-strengthening measures mitigate it or make it more sensitive to the importance of implementing nonproliferation measures in general.

Implementing measures like UNSCR 1540 may prove to be a challenging endeavor for "many of the world's developing states, some of which, even if they have the will to [implement the resolution], lack resources. States particularly affected are those which are not already parties to the relevant WMD treaties and do not therefore already have the appropriate measures in place—and those which, although parties, have not fully implemented their obligations."[27] States may also be unwilling to take punitive actions toward other states that do not threaten them and whose goods and services they need. This is often cited as a reason for why countries like China and Russia oppose strong punitive actions against Iran for its failure to fully cooperate with the IAEA and abide by United Nations resolutions. How economic interests affect state decision making is an important question. Whereas a poor country like North Korea might be expected to profit any way it can from proliferation of WMD technology, what can we make of wealthy countries like Germany and Switzerland who have done so as well?[28] Several questions are extant. How do we assess the economics of nonproliferation policies? Are economics epiphenomenal of some of the other factors discussed here?

Self-Interest

Political scientists and scholars of international relations generally prefer parsimonious, far-reaching theories and explanations for dynamics in international relations. Realists might consider the overarching question this book seeks to explore as quite facile and simply answered. States will act in ways that best protect their own security interests. And self-interest might often explain variability in policy choices because different aspects of initiatives constituting the regime differentially affect states' own interests. When considering nuclear weapons, states have only two self-interested routes—acquisition or restraint. However, self-interest as it relates to support for global nonproliferation efforts produces many different (and sometimes conflicting) options and paths states can follow for the simple reality that there are so many initiatives and instruments that constitute the regime. As Jayantha Dhanapla writes, threats to the regime "are as many as they are deceptive—since they come clothed in the seductive garb of national interest and realism."[29]

STRUCTURE OF THE BOOK

I began this project by proposing the above explanatory factors and motivators not as certain, driving forces for state behavior, but simply as catalysts to deeper thinking about this issue. The authors then took their own approaches to address the book's overall research question. The first part of the book consists of four chapters that take theoretical approaches to gain leverage on the issue at hand. The chapters in the second part tease out motivating factors after considering specific regional and country cases.

The first four chapters consider broad themes concerning states' cooperation in and support for the regime. In the first chapter, Jason Enia observes that because the regime provides a multiplicity of public goods, there will be a variety of collective action challenges. He hypothesizes that a high ratio of private to public provision may explain a good bit of willingness to participate in regime-strengthening activities and initiatives. The NPT is by design a discriminatory treaty, which affects attitudes of member states not only concerning that treaty but also other regime instruments. Considering the Obama and George W. Bush administrations, Nina Srinivasan Rathbun next examines the impact of discrimination and how various policy positions affect legitimacy of the nonproliferation regime. States proliferate for different reasons. One is threat perception. In chapter 3, Maria Rost Rublee contends that "we need to understand the *construction* of threats related to both proliferation and nonproliferation." Jeffrey W. Knopf approaches a security-driven and normative aspect of nonproliferation, asking whether nonproliferation and nuclear disarmament are linked. That is, do states' policies and attitudes toward disarmament affect other states' propensity to proliferate?

In the second part of the book, authors take an empirical approach to questions of dynamics within the regime using regional and country-specific scenarios. Lowell H. Schwartz notes that history seems to indicate U.S. security guarantees have a positive effect in controlling proliferation. He thus examines how U.S. security guarantees affect the willingness of states to make efforts to sustain and strengthen the regime. In chapter 6, Deepti Choubey notes that a "vocal minority" of the 118-member NAM is often characterized as spoilers on matters of nonproliferation. She examines the veracity of this while exploring the role in and stance of the NAM on the regime. In chapter 7, Robert J. Reardon challenges notions that Russia's nonproliferation policies often are driven by a desire to build and maintain a coalition of states hostile to the United States. Closely examining Russian policy regarding the Iranian nuclear situation demonstrates an entirely different set of motivations. To better understand why different Latin American countries have different logics concerning the nonproliferation regime, Arturo C. Sotomayor compares Brazil and Mexico. His chapter identifies the underlying domestic conditions and external influences that explain the differences in their behavior and policies regarding regime. He notes that evolving civil-military relations and U.S. influence have helped shape nonproliferation policy preferences in Latin America. In chapter 9, Jim Walsh grapples with the gap between rhetorical support for the idea of nonproliferation and actions to strengthen regime by examining lag in adoption of an Additional Protocol by some Middle East countries. By understanding lag, Walsh contends we can better understand why some states are slower than others to adopt "nonproliferation measures beyond simple NPT ratification."

Too frequently analysts reduce the nonproliferation regime to the NPT. Some go as far as to refer to NPT regime. Understanding states' orientation to the NPT *is* an important matter. As Scott Sagan notes, "We know very little about why different governments joined the NPT and how their interests and interpretations have shaped the patterns of their compliance behavior . . . [W]e should not expect to find that a state's NPT status is related to its nuclear proliferation behavior in any simple manner."[30] However, the tendency to reduce the regime to the NPT overlooks the insight that can be gained about state nonproliferation behavior if we examine other instruments and take an expansive view of the regime. This has implications both for scholars and practitioners. It is our hope that this examination will lead to further scholarly work in this area. At the same time, we hope that it will move policymakers to think harder about the motivations at work in states' nonproliferation policies.

Notes

1. A small sample of the "regime in crisis" literature includes George Perkovich, "The End of the Nonproliferation Regime?," *Current History* 105, no. 694 (2006): 355–62; Tom Sauer, "The Nuclear Nonproliferation Regime in Crisis," *Peace Review* 18.3 (2006), 334–35;

Joshua Williams and Jon B. Wolfsthal, "The NPT at 35: A Crisis of Compliance or a Crisis of Confidence?," United Nations Association of the United States of America (UNA-USA), 2005; Pierre Goldschmidt, "The Urgent Need to Strengthen the Nuclear Nonproliferation Regime," *Policy Outlook* (Carnegie Endowment for International Peace), no. 25 (January 10, 2006): 1–8,; Pierre Goldschmidt, "Is the Nuclear Non-proliferation Regime in Crisis? If So, Why? Are There Remedies?," paper delivered to the Charlottesville Committee on Foreign Relations (CCFR), Charlottesville, Va., May 11, 2006. For a critique on "regime pessimism" see Jim Walsh, "Learning from Past Success: The NPT and the Future of Non-proliferation," Weapons of Mass Destruction Commission, October 2005, http://www.un.org/disarmament/education/wmdcommission/files/no41.pdf; and Jeffrey Fields and Jason Enia, "The Health of the Nuclear Nonproliferation Regime: Returning to a Multidimensional Evaluation," *Nonproliferation Review* 16, no. 2 (2009): 173–96.

2. Andrew Grotto, "Why Do States That Oppose Nuclear Proliferation Resist New Nonproliferation Obligations? Three Logics of Nonproliferation Decision-Making," *Cardozo Journal of International and Comparative Law* 18, no. 1 (2010): 1–43.

3. Analyst George Perkovich describes the distinctions and refers to efforts to prevent and roll back a state's nuclear capability as "unproliferation." George Perkovich, *India's Nuclear Bomb* (Berkeley: University of California Press, 2001), 7. The antecedent to this comparison is akin to the difference between deterrence and compellence.

4. We are aware of two in progress, one edited by Jeffrey Knopf, who is the author of this volume's chapter 4, and another by Rebecca Gibbons.

5. For example, analysts often refer to the "NPT regime." Fields and Enia discuss this at length. See Fields and Enia, " Health of the Nuclear Nonproliferation Regime."

6. The seminal work on this is Scott D. Sagan, "Why States Build Nuclear Weapons? Three Models in Search of the Bomb," *International Security* 21, no. 3 (1996–1997): 54–86. Other examples include Stephen M. Meyer, *The Dynamics of Nuclear Proliferation* (Chicago: University of Chicago Press, 1984); Jacques E. C. Hymans, *The Psychology of Nuclear Proliferation: Identity, Emotions, and Foreign Policy* (Cambridge: Cambridge University Press, 2006); Dong-Joon Jo and Eric Gartzke, "Determinants of Nuclear Weapons Proliferation," *Journal of Conflict Resolution* 51, no. 1 (2007) 167–94. A burgeoning quantitative literature also explores the acquisition question. See, for example, Sonali Singh and Christopher R. Way, "The Correlates of Nuclear Proliferation: A Quantitative Test," *Journal of Conflict Resolution* 48, no. 6 (2004): 859–85; see also the April 2009 special issue of the *Journal of Conflict Resolution*, which focuses on quantitative approaches to nuclear proliferation.

7. See Scott D. Sagan, "The Causes of Nuclear Weapons Proliferation," *Annual Review of Political Science* 17, no. 14 (2011): 225–44; Mitchell Reiss, *Bridled Ambition: Why Countries Constrain Their Nuclear Capabilities* (Washington, D.C.: Woodrow Wilson Center Press,

1995); Etel Solingen, *Nuclear Logics: Contrasting Paths in East Asia and the Middle East* (Princeton, N.J.: Princeton University Press, 2007); Maria Rost Rublee, *Nonproliferation Norms: Why States Choose Nuclear Restraint* (Athens: University of Georgia Press, 2009).

8. Grotto, "Why Do States."

9. See, for example, Matthew Kroenig, "Exporting the Bomb: Why States Provide Sensitive Nuclear Assistance," *American Political Science Review* 103, no. 1 (2009): 113–33.

10. Brazil publicly states that its position on an Additional Protocol (AP) is based on equity in the regime. However, there are suspicions that Brazil is attempting to obscure the origins of some of its centrifuge technology and inspections under the AP. It might have to account for previously undeclared nuclear activity.

11. Grotto, "Why Do States," 7.

12. Ibid., 8.

13. Ibid., 4.

14. This articulation by a senior State Department official was a main inspiration for this book.

15. Singh and Way, "Correlates of Nuclear Proliferation."

16. Gordon Corera, *Shopping for Bombs: Nuclear Proliferation, Global Insecurity, and the Rise and Fall of the A. Q. Khan Network* (Oxford: Oxford University Press, 2006).

17. Mancur Olson Jr. and Richard J. Zeckhauser, "An Economic Theory of Alliances," *Review of Economics and Statistics* 48, no. 3 (1966): 266–79.

18. Douglas Frantz, "Nuclear Booty: More Smugglers Use Asia Route," *New York Times*, September 11, 2001.

19. Nina Srinivasan Rathbun, "The Role of Legitimacy in Strengthening the Nuclear Nonproliferation Regime," *Nonproliferation Review* 13, no. 2 (2006): 230.

20. Brazil's refusal to sign an Additional Protocol is more complicated than this. Many analysts surmise that Brazil is wary of allowing IAEA inspectors access to enrichment technology whose origins Brazil may be trying obscure.

21. Grotto, "Why Do States," 1–2.

22. Rebecca Johnson, "The 2000 NPT Review Conference: A Delicate, Hard-Won Compromise," *Disarmament Diplomacy*, no. 46 (2000), http://www.acronym.org.uk/46npt.htm.

23. U.S. Department of Defense, *Nuclear Posture Review Report*, April 2010, 15.

24. Richard T. Cupitt, Suzette Grillot, and Yuzo Murayama, "The Determinants of Nonproliferation Export Controls: A Membership-Fee Explanation," *Nonproliferation Review* 8, no 2 (2001): 69–80.

25. Ibid, 70.

26. Joseph Cirincione ed., *Repairing the Regime: Preventing the Spread of Weapons of Mass Destruction* (New York: Routledge, 2000), 20.

27. Lawrence Scheinman, ed., *Implementing Resolution 1540: The Role of Regional Organizations* (New York: United Nations, 2008), 2.

28. Harold Müller, "Europe's Leaky Borders," *Bulletin of the Atomic Scientists* 49, no. 5 (1993): 27.

29. Jayantha Dhanapala, "The State of the Regime," in Cirincione, *Repairing the Regime*, 20.

30. Sagan, "Causes of Nuclear Weapons," 239.

Theoretical Approaches

CHAPTER 1

Explaining Dynamics and Stasis in the Nuclear Nonproliferation Regime

The Challenges of a Multiplicity of Public Goods

Jason Enia

WHY DO STATES that consider themselves party to the nuclear nonproliferation regime—whether as de jure signatories to the Treaty on the Non-Proliferation of Nuclear Weapons (NPT) or as de facto nonproliferators or nonnuclear weapons states (NNWS)—have difficulty signing and implementing measures that would seemingly strengthen the regime? For example, a number of countries that are signatories of the NPT have yet to implement International Atomic Energy Agency (IAEA) safeguards agreements, Additional Protocols, or small quantities protocols required of them in Article III of the NPT.[1] Additionally, since the passage of United Nations Security Council Resolution 1540 (UNSCR 1540) in 2004, there have been a number of concerns about the relative (in)ability to get implementational buy-in from states.[2] And depending on how one interprets Article VI of the NPT, the nuclear weapons states (NWS) have made mixed progress on strengthening the regime through nuclear disarmament.

In a particular light, all of this could be a puzzling phenomenon. One rather superficial line of analysis might lead to the expectation that once the initial accession to the status of a regime "participant" occurs—particularly if it occurs more formally, for example, through a state's signing the NPT and entering into force—states should be willing to proceed with future efforts that contribute to that same goal. And yet, we know this not to be the case. A variety of reasons have been put forward as to the possible causes of this reluctance.[3] Countries may make decisions around nuclear nonproliferation having been influenced by their security environments,[4] their attempts to project power or enhance their bargaining capabilities,[5] their guarantees under the security umbrellas of any nuclear weapons states,[6] their views on discrimination within the regime,[7] their perceptions about the extent to which the "other" is living up to their end of the so-called nuclear bargain,[8] their perceptions of the symbols and norms associated with the regime or weapons themselves,[9] and, finally, their mix of available economic resources coupled with perceptions about the domestic costs and benefits associated with particular decisions.[10]

The theoretical framework employed in this chapter demonstrates that there are fundamental and strategic reasons why building nuclear stakeholders is likely to be extremely difficult, *even* in the hypothetical absence of the challenges listed above. Specifically, the essential mix of qualities of the public goods being provided across the regime leads to a wide variety of collective action challenges. Each of these challenges has associated with it different prospects for failure and thus different prescriptions for success. This chapter makes use of more general theories about collective action and the challenges of international regime formation and maintenance in order to analyze and explain the strategic challenges of regime strengthening.

This chapter begins by asking what types of actions could lead to a strengthening of the nuclear nonproliferation regime. The most common activities are universal implementation of the Comprehensive Safeguard Agreements (CSA). However, this is built on the premise that the full scope of the nonproliferation regime is the NPT. A more comprehensive picture sees the regime as a mix of institutions, processes, and norms around the broad nuclear nonproliferation issue area. With a multiplicity of possible regime-strengthening measures in mind, the second half of the chapter applies a public goods framework to this issue, exploring the collective action challenges associated with these different types of actions.[11] The analysis highlights the notion that a wide range of potential regime-strengthening activities creates a wide array of collective action challenges, each with different implications for the provision of an underlying public good. From a policy perspective, building responsible stakeholders for the broadest public good challenge (nuclear nonproliferation) essentially becomes a problem of alleviating a number of different types of public goods challenges within the regime.

WHAT WOULD "STRENGTHENING THE REGIME" LOOK LIKE?

Any attempt to analyze the state behavior within the nuclear nonproliferation regime must move beyond a focus that simply equates the NPT with the regime.¹² To be clear, the NPT is widely and correctly recognized as the foundational institutional component of the regime, but the regime itself encompasses a number of underlying principles that have their roots in a convergence of expectations,¹³ foundational norms that serve to guide behavior toward the achievement of the goals outlined in the principles,¹⁴ and various sets of rules and behaviors that provide specific means for achieving the goals of the regime.¹⁵

Thus, explaining state decision making within the regime requires that we acknowledge that states have not a singular choice but a number of choices about a number of regime aspects. The introductory chapter to this project, for example, points out a wide variety of institutional choices that nonproliferators have toward regime strengthening, including the aforementioned Additional Protocols and UNSCR 1540, the Comprehensive Nuclear-Test-Ban Treaty (CTBT), the Fissile Material Cutoff Treaty (FMCT), and various amendments to the Convention on the Physical Protection of Nuclear Material (CPPNM). Each of these, and potentially other institutional choices, offers states the opportunity to sign, ratify, and implement its respective components. These processes have the effect of multiplying the possibilities for regime strengthening.

In addition to these oft-considered formal possibilities, it is important to remember that states also have a number of informal possibilities that could theoretically lead to regime strengthening.¹⁶ Often these appear in the form of "initiatives," such as the Nuclear Smuggling Outreach Initiative (NSOI) and the Proliferation Security Initiative (PSI). States can also make choices around the enforcement of these formal and informal treaties. These can include support and implementation of United Nations Security Council (UNSC) sanctions and willingness to take a wide variety of actions with respect to particular cases, activities that the introductory chapter labels "vigilance and cooperative international postures" (6).

The wide variety of choices states continually make regarding their actions within the regime necessitates that analysts consider the possibility that each of these decisions carries a different mix of costs and benefits. If this is the case, there are likely to be different prospects for collective action and reasons for collective action failures. The general insights gained through the careful study of public goods and collective action can serve as helpful guideposts in an effort to formulate meaningful theory.

APPROACHING THE PROBLEM THROUGH THE LENS OF COLLECTIVE ACTION

The publication of Mancur Olson's *The Logic of Collective Action* clarified the public goods problem as a classic failure of collective action.[17] In this conception, the very properties of public goods—specifically the properties associated with their benefits—lead to the expectation that groups of rational actors will have a difficult time providing them. First, the benefits of a public good cannot be restricted based on contribution; these goods are said to be non-excludable. Given this property and the free-riding behavior it is likely to engender, the expectation is that public goods will be underprovided. Group members have little incentive to contribute to a public good beyond the contribution of the first member.[18] Second, an individual's consumption of a public good does nothing to diminish another's ability to consume the same unit of the good; public goods are non-rival.[19] This aspect implies that groups cannot recoup provision costs through usage-based pricing.[20] Again, this essential quality is expected to contribute to the fact that such goods will be underprovided.

The most studied collective action failure around public goods provision is encapsulated in the Prisoner's Dilemma (PD) game.[21] This particular type of collective action failure occurs when decision makers in a strategic interaction face incentives that push them toward a mutually rational decision that is noncooperative in nature, despite the fact that cooperation could have led to a better outcome. The choice to "defect" is driven primarily by a rational fear of becoming the "sucker," a scenario where one party provides the public good in question only to have the other free ride. This type of collective action failure is often (but not always) prevalent with the provision of pure public goods, and it is a direct result of the fact that the preferences of each player are dictated by the essential qualities of publicness inherent in the good itself.

Given a PD scenario, we know quite a bit about the conditions in which this noncooperative outcome is overcome. Axelrod's famous PD tournament, for example, demonstrates that there are cooperative outcomes associated with repeated interaction of the game as players begin to view their strategic options in terms of the way these options might affect them in future periods ("shadow of the future").[22] Within this iterative context there are particular strategies (e.g., "tit for tat") that can ultimately lead to more cooperation relative to others.

However, it is important to remember that the collective action failure represented by the PD story and its representative game-theoretic analyses is only one type of collective action failure that occurs around the provision of public goods.[23] Indeed, the literature on the provision of public goods covers a wide array of collective action failures, and these can be analyzed by considering their variance over three important properties. *First*, Todd Sandler points out that much of Olson's early work on this topic assumes that all members of a group have a similarly linear cost function.[24] However, the reality of comparative advantage is a particularly important consideration as changes in marginal costs may have an effect on the predicted provision of particular types of public goods and on the predicted direction of Olson's exploitation hypothesis.[25]

Second, many types of goods can and do vary in their level of "publicness." Across the two essential qualities of excludability and rivalry, public goods can exhibit complete excludability and lack of rivalry, or they can be "impure," where there is some variance across one or both of these aspects. The mix of properties yields several important subsets of impure public goods, and the specific qualities of each have potentially different implications for its provision.[26]

Club goods, for example, are a class of impure public goods where there is excludability—others can be prevented from enjoying the benefits—but within the group of people that enjoy the benefits, those benefits are at least partly rival.[27] The standard economic theory on clubs demonstrates that clubs can be more effective in internalizing any externalities that may arise from traditional collective action failures. That is, the free ride problems of public goods provision are taken care of, as members are able to exclude others from receiving the benefits; this might be done through membership fees or initiation requirements. The rivalry issues that remain are typically dealt with as the members impose costs on themselves to deal with any congestion issues that may occur. Classic examples of international club goods include the International Telecommunications Satellite Organization (INTELSAT) and international air corridors.[28]

Impure public goods can also take the form where they carry benefits that are excludable (similar to club goods) but they are nonrival. In international affairs, we might point to intelligence as one such good. Actors can be excluded from its benefits, but the consumption of the good by any one actor does not fundamentally diminish another actor's ability to receive the good's benefits. In these types of goods, the exclusion mechanism can mitigate free riding, allowing marginal costs to dictate decisions about provision and consumption.[29]

There are times when a process or exchange produces a joint product, a good that is private along with one that is public.[30] Foreign aid provides an excellent international example. The provision of aid clearly contributes to a global public good as it may result in greater economic stability. However, that provision also provides a private benefit to the particular countries involved in the transaction. Cooperation around these processes tends to reflect the incentives created by the private good. As the excludable benefits are more dominant, markets will tend to dictate the provision of the good. On the other hand, as non-excludable benefits are more dominant, the provision of the good is subject to many of the collective action challenges previously outlined.[31]

The *third* important and variable property of a public good captures the way that individual contributions aggregate to set the overall amount of the good available.[32] Differences in "aggregation technologies" also alter the incentives that different actors have to provide the underlying good, and these different incentives affect the strategic aspects associated with any collective action around the good.

Prior to Jack Hirshleifer's work, the primary way of thinking about the provision of public goods was as having "summation" technologies. With these types of public goods, each contribution is weighted equally and is perfectly substitutable.[33] However, different nonlinear marginal cost structures around provision choices lead to three other types of aggregation technologies. Some public goods may have "weighted sum" aggregation technologies, where particular contributions may matter more than others for the overall amount of the good available. These goods operate similarly to those with summation technologies, but the implied cost differentials mean that individual provisions are no longer perfect substitutes for one another.

Where the amount of the good available is set by the weakest contribution, the aggregation technology is known as "weakest link." Airport security provides an instructive example, as the overall level of the public good is only as good as the weakest effort made. With these goods, individual members have little incentive to contribute more than the weakest link contributes; thus, we will expect to see what Sandler refers to as "matching behavior."[34]

Public goods with "threshold" aggregation technologies are those where the quantity of provision must cross a certain threshold before the public good is available for consumption.[35] International peacekeeping is a good example of a public good with a threshold technology, as peacekeeping forces often have to reach a particular level of resources in order to be effective in a given situation.[36] Finally, public goods may have "best shot" aggregation technologies where the level of the public good is equivalent to the highest contribution. In many of these cases—a cure for a global pandemic, for example—those initially providing the good provide it for everyone.

On a very basic level, the nuclear nonproliferation regime can be thought of as producing the pure public good of global peace. As a vehicle for the production of a pure and public good, it would carry with it all of the expectations for the problems of underprovision due to its essential qualities of non-exclusion and nonrival. It is easy to see how one might be puzzled with the existence of avowed nuclear nonproliferators that seem to be uninterested or unable to take steps to "strengthen" the regime. However, using the framework outlined above, one gains a deeper appreciation for the way that the regime amounts to the production of several types of public goods, each with different aggregation technologies, and thus each with different prospects for strategic behavior and ultimately the provision of each good in question. Inside this analytical framework, building responsible stakeholders for the broadest public good challenge (nuclear nonproliferation) essentially becomes a problem of mitigating a multiplicity of public goods challenges.

AN EXPLANATORY FRAMEWORK WITH OBSERVABLE IMPLICATIONS

As the dynamics associated with the nuclear nonproliferation regime might contain a variety of processes and these processes might each be representative of a different type of collective action challenge around the provision of the specific public good in question, we need to think carefully about the way that these various challenges bump up against one another as a country rationalizes its decisions around issues associated with proliferation and the regime.

Table 1.1 utilizes Todd Sandler and Daniel G. Arce M.'s framework for thinking about the provision of a variety of types of public goods and applies it to the nuclear nonproliferation regime.[37] These different types of goods are organized within the table according to their unique combinations of essential qualities (excludability, rivalry) and aggregation technology. A large number of observable implications emerge from this framework. Here we focus on the two most obvious.

First, it becomes clear that there are a wide variety of public goods that can be associated with the broader nonproliferation regime, and the mix of qualities for each yields potentially different implications for its provision. While many analysts might expect the entire nonproliferation enterprise to be classified as a PD

TABLE 1.1. Selected decisions in the nuclear nonproliferation regime by aggregation technology and qualities of good produce

	Pure Public (non-rival, non-excludable)	Impure Public Good (excludable, non-rival)	Club Good (partly rival, excludable)	Joint Product (partly public, partly private)
Summation	• Participation in CSA (AB, SQP, incl.) • Participation in NPT review conference process • IAEA membership *expectations = difficult provision (PD; chicken)*			
Weighted Sum	• Generalized nuclear disarmament • Coop w/ IAEA inspections • Participation in (ratification of) CTBT • Participation in export control agreements (Wassenaar Arrangement, etc.) • Fissile material cutoff (FMCT) *expectations = undersupply generally; but could have participation if individual benefits are high*	• Export license information exchange (Zangger Committee "Annual Returns") *expectations = undersupply but could have participation if individual benefits are high*	• Potential nuclear fuel bank *expectations = able to mitigate congestion issues through pricing*	• Bilateral nuclear disarmament (e.g., START) • Peaceful nuclear assistance • Ad hoc counter-proliferation • Accession of "outliers" to NPT (e.g., Israel, Pakistan, India) *expectations = provision depends on mix of excludable to total benefits*

Threshold	• Enacting UNSC sanctions expectations = depends on aggregator; most typical game form is assurance, where leadership can make a difference in provision	• Production/revision of Zangger "Trigger List" expectations = depends on aggregator and leadership
Weakest Link	• Curbing nonproliferation to non-state actors (e.g., UNSCR 1540; PSI) • Enforcing test ban (e.g., CTBT) • Enforcing UNSC sanctions • Implementation of CSAs expectations = matching behavior at weakest level; optimal results if preferences & endowments similar	• Strategic trade controls (e.g., NSG, MTCR) • Nuclear-weapons-free zones (NWFZ) • Negative security assurances expectations = provision depends on mix of excludable to total benefits
Best Shot	• Use preemptive/preventative force expectations = efficient provision more likely for discrete than continuous good	• Sharing nuclear intelligence expectations = undersupply with coordination, pooling issues; also overuse

Note: This table draws from Sander, *Global Collective Action*, 58–59, 82, as well as the ideas in Kaul, Grunberg, and Stern, *Global Public Goods*, 3, 13–14.

scenario, this framework pushes back, demonstrating the need for a more nuanced approach to thinking on the types of strategic decisions individual countries make around nuclear nonproliferation.

In this light, we can compare a number of the possible actions within the regime and develop an a priori expectation of whether we should see more or less cooperation. Generally, we would expect that there would be higher levels of cooperation around those goods for which the collective action challenges could at least be partly controlled. For example, those goods that are joint product, threshold, or best shot (where the individual incentives of the provider are high) are more likely to be efficiently provided than those goods that are more excludable and nonrival and that abide by summation technologies.

In addition, a number of choices within the regime clearly result in the production of a joint product. The transfer of peaceful nuclear assistance operates in the same way as foreign aid in this regard. As countries with nuclear technology agree to provide assistance to those that wish to acquire it for peaceful uses, there are a number of public goods created, and critical among them is the peace and security that come as aspects of the NPT are upheld. This, of course, may result in greater global peace and security that is both nonrival and non-excludable. As such, the provision of peaceful nuclear assistance carries with it some of the classic implications for collective action that are dependent on the specific good in question. The particular aggregation technology of the public good portion of the joint product could be considered weighted sum, as different contributions to the provision of nuclear assistance are likely to have differing impacts as to the amount of nuclear assistance available.

But the transfer also produces a private good (fully excludable, fully rival) for both the donor and recipient countries. Given the joint product nature of the good, the prospects for provision will likely depend on the particular mix of publicness and privateness in any one situation. Countries with significant private interests—that is, they are likely to derive significant private benefits—from providing and receiving peaceful nuclear assistance are more likely to provide that good as market forces dictate. However, if the joint product leads toward greater publicness, the good is more likely to face many of the collective action challenges associated with the provision of more pure-public goods that abide by a weighted sum aggregation technology.

Thus, one implication of this framework is that greater participation in any area of regime strengthening over time is negatively related to the level of publicness of the good in question. In any singular regime-strengthening area, we would expect to see greater participation—regime-strengthening activity—in times where the ratio of private to public benefits is relatively high.

> Hypothesis 1. Changes in the overall willingness to participate in any specific regime-strengthening activity are positively related to the ratio of private to public goods produced by that activity.

Second, as countries make these individual choices around the nonproliferation regime, they are likely to be considering multiple issues simultaneously. This reality makes it necessary to consider the multiplicity of strategies involved in these situations. States have to make individual nonproliferation choices considering not only what other states may do on similar issues but also strategically, considering the way that a choice in one aspect of regime strengthening may limit the choices they can make elsewhere. These strategic considerations are likely to be particularly acute when one of the goods in question is a joint product, and a decision in one area may have the effect of reducing the private benefits of another good. However, ceteris paribus we can expect that states will generally make faster cooperative progress in producing those public goods that have better prospects for collective action.

> Hypothesis 2. Individual state willingness to strengthen some regime issue areas and not others is a positive function of the ratio of private to public goods produced by the respective activities.

The public goods framework provides a series of observable implications, expectations about regime behavior that we would have a priori any particular regime realities. In other words, the underlying features of the goods being produced and their respective aggregation technologies demonstrates that their prospects for provision within an international nuclear nonproliferation regime would be varied and challenging in specific ways. The next section offers a preliminary empirical exploration of these expectations.

PRELIMINARY EXPLORATION OF HYPOTHESES
Hypothesis 1

As a preliminary exploration of the hypotheses developed above, we can turn to the general data on the institutional aspects of the nuclear nonproliferation regime. The history of ratification of the regime's institutional cornerstone, the NPT, is revealing when looked at through the lenses supplied by these hypotheses. In 1969 and 1970, as the treaty was being ratified for adoption and then entered into force, a total of fifty-nine states ratified the NPT. As a measure of regime-strengthening activity we focus our attention on the years following entry into force in 1970. Table 1.2 displays the years 1970 through 2006 and the countries that ratified the NPT during each year.

At a glance, the observable pattern of post–entry-into-force ratification of the NPT follows the logic that underpins the first hypothesis. In the twenty-five years following the treaty's entry into force, the years that witnessed the two biggest leaps in ratification were 1975 and 1995. In each of these cases, there are credible stories that we can tell regarding the increase in the ratio of private to public costs and benefits stemming from ratification. For example, India's test of its "peaceful nuclear explosive" in 1974 increased the uncertainty in the global security environment. Countries such as Italy and Germany—which had serious reservations about the NPT that were delaying their ratification—now found themselves recalculating the costs and benefits of such a delay. In this context, the private costs of inaction and the private benefits of action began to grow relative to their incentives to free ride on the public good. Italy, for example, faced increasing pressures from the United States and a "serious chance of an estrangement with the U.S. because of [their] perplexities towards the NPT."[38] Similarly in 1995, several countries were able to take advantage of the private benefits associated with ratification in conjunction with the "big stage" of permanent renewal of the NPT. If the logic of the first hypothesis were not contributing to the pattern we observe with respect to NPT ratification, we would expect to see very little activity post–entry-into-force and certainly not the relative flurries of ratification activity we have observed in response to specific events.

Hypothesis 2

The second hypothesis suggests that we should observe greater willingness, within individual states, to participate in regime strengthening around those goods that have qualities that help to alleviate collective action challenges. For example, within individual good types, we should expect to see individual countries that are more willing to participate in activities that have relatively amenable aggregation technologies. Using Israel as an example, we see a willingness to participate in the PSI and the endorsement of the ratification and entry into force of the CTBT but an unwillingness to allow IAEA inspectors into their nuclear facilities. The logic of the hypothesis holds here as the CTBT and the PSI

TABLE 1.2. Post–Entry-into-Force Ratification of the NPT, 1970–2006

Year	No.	Countries Ratifying
1970	16	Senegal, Morocco, Central African Republic, Madagascar, Guatemala, Uruguay, San Marino, Democratic Republic of the Congo, Lebanon, Kenya, Haiti, Bolivia, Lesotho, Ghana, Maldives, Greece
1971	5	Dominican Republic, Tonga, Burundi, Chad, Holy See
1972	6	Thailand, Benin, Philippines, Fiji, El Salvador, Cambodia
1973	5	Sudan, Honduras, Nicaragua, Cote d'Ivoire, Australia
1974	1	Gabon
1975	13	Venezuela, Grenada, Libyan Arab Jamahiriya, Rwanda, Gambia, Netherlands, Luxembourg, Italy, Germany, Belgium, Republic of Korea, Samoa, Sierra Leone
1976	5	Guinea-Bissau, Bahamas, Suriname, Japan, Singapore
1977	3	Portugal, Switzerland, Panama
1978	2	Congo, Liechtenstein
1979	6	St. Lucia, Cape Verde, Bangladesh, Indonesia, Sri Lanka, Tuvalu
1980	2	Turkey, Barbados
1981	2	Solomon Islands, Egypt
1982	4	Uganda, Vietnam, Nauru, Papua New Guinea
1983	2	Sao Tome & Principe
1984	4	St. Kitts & Nevis, St. Vincent & the Grenadines, Equatorial Guinea, Dominica
1985	8	Democratic People's Republic of Korea, Belize, Antigua & Barbuda, Bhutan, Guinea, Kiribati, Brunei Darussalam, Seychelles
1986	4	Trinidad & Tobago, Yemen, Colombia, Malawi
1987	1	Spain
1988	2	Bahrain, Saudi Arabia
1989	2	Kuwait, Qatar
1990	2	Albania, Mozambique
1991	5	Zimbabwe, Lithuania, South Africa, United Republic of Tanzania, Zambia
1992	11	Myanmar, Niger, Namibia, Azerbaijan, France, Croatia, Uzbekistan, Slovenia, China, Latvia, Estonia
1993	6	Mauritania, Guyana, Armenia, Belarus, Serbia, Slovakia
1994	8	Ukraine, Republic of Moldova, Turkmenistan, Bosnia & Herzegovina, Kyrgyzstan, Georgia, Kazakhstan, Tajikistan
1995	12	Comoros, United Arab Emirates, Vanautu, Chile, Palau, Micronesia, FYR Macedonia, Eritrea, Monaco, Argentina, Marshall Is., Algeria
1996	3	Djibouti, Angola, Andorra
1997	1	Oman
1998	1	Brazil
1999	0	
2000	0	
2001	0	
2002	1	Cuba
2003	1	Timor-Leste
2004	0	
2005	0	
2006	1	Montenegro

Note: Data taken from website of United Nations Office of Disarmament Affairs at http://disarmament.un.org/treaties/t/npt. The countries are coded by the date that the NPT was first deposited to one of the official depository countries. This signifies that both signature of the NPT and domestic ratification processes have been completed. The table includes all ratification after the treaty entered into force on March 5, 1970, through the most recent instance of ratification in June 2006.

ultimately depend on weakest link aggregation technologies where the overall level of the good provided is set by the weakest contribution. In other words, the overall public good provided by an in-force CTBT would be set by the weakest enforcement actions among participants. The prediction for these types of goods is that individual countries will tend to set their individual levels of good provision to match the behavior of the weakest member. Thus, relative to goods with other aggregation technologies, countries' private cost to public benefits ratio is much better. It costs the Israelis (as just one example) relatively little to provide some public good by participating in the PSI compared to the private cost–public benefit ratio it would face with the weighted sum public good of cooperating with IAEA inspections where the level of private cost would be much higher to contribute to the public good.

If we hold the aggregation technology constant and look across good types, we would also expect individual countries to participate in those regime-strengthening activities that have a higher ratio of private to public benefits. The willingness of the United States to participate in bilateral disarmament treaties with Russia (e.g., New START [Strategic Arms Reduction Treaty]) is high relative to another regime-strengthening activity with a similar aggregation technology: ratification and participation in the CTBT. The logic of the second hypothesis appears to hold here as the ratio of private benefits to public benefits is much more favorable to the United States in the production of the joint product good that comes from bilateral disarmament treaties than it is for the CTBT. In the bilateral treaty with Russia, the United States is able to make private gains improving its own security, and this interaction also results in the public good of improvements in global security and regime strengthening. However, with respect to the CTBT much of the hesitation in the United States arises from the perception that it would be providing a public good with very little private benefit and perhaps even significant private cost.[39]

For now, the logic underpinning these hypotheses appears to stand up to the preliminary "sniff test" for these limited examples. Of course, in order to avoid the dangers associated with spurious correlations or post hoc, ergo prompter hoc reasoning, more significant testing is warranted. A series of quasi-experiments that explore a country's regime-strengthening activities across different issue areas or across the same issue area over time would allow for variation across the key independent variables: the aggregation technology and the ratio of private to public benefits.[40] In addition, a careful attempt to falsify the above hypotheses is necessary. Are there cases where individual countries are more willing to participate in certain regime-strengthening activities that have relatively lower private to public benefit ratios than other regime-strengthening activities? Such evidence could help outline the necessary and sufficient conditions under which these hypotheses hold.

POLICY IMPLICATIONS

To the extent that the above hypotheses hold up to more rigorous testing, they have the potential to suggest a number of important policy implications. Both hypotheses point to the notion that we can expect greater regime-strengthening behavior around those issues where the good produced is farther from purely public. While this is a relatively simple insight, it points to the importance of considering the variety of behaviors within the regime as different animals. One cannot merely assume that because a state is a party to the NPT and openly considers itself a member of the nuclear nonproliferation regime, it will be equally willing to participate in all decisions and activities within the regime. These activities need to be considered in light of their separate effects. If the United States, for example, wants to encourage responsible nuclear stakeholders, it should proceed from the premise that certain types of behaviors are going to be *inherently* more difficult for the states involved. It is going to be fundamentally easier to get meaningful cooperation around those sets of behaviors where there is some element that pulls the resulting good away from purely public.

The framework reminds us that private incentives are always going to be important determinants of state decision making regarding regime-strengthening behavior. As such, the regime needs to be continually strengthened through institutions that properly incentivize said behavior. For example, it might be the case that countries facing a regime-strengthening decision that has underlying collective action challenges can be incentivized to contribute to that good through the provision of a public good in some other area, or even the availability of joint product goods that might be part of a related transaction. This suggests that continued progress on disarmament among the NWS—whether through bilateral processes such as START or unilateral or multilateral processes—could theoretically be an important carrot for progress on collective action challenges in other areas such as the execution and full implementation of the CSAs and Additional Protocols.

In addition, this lens provides a cautionary analysis when it comes to dealing with NPT outsiders. To the extent, for example, that the U.S.-India nuclear deal confers private benefits to India outside the scope of the regime, it effectively decreases the ratio of private to public benefits that India might receive from engaging in regime-strengthening behaviors within the regime. If India is able to reap significant private benefits from a bilateral deal for nuclear materials with the United States, its private incentives for becoming a signatory to the NPT effectively decrease. This puts the collective action challenges back into play. Put more succinctly: Why would India become an NPT member if the private benefits from doing so could be had in other agreements?[41] Again, encouraging responsible nuclear stakeholders necessitates an understanding of the way that individual countries, particularly the NPT outsiders, perceive their incentives. These incentives arise out of the particular mix of private and public goods generated by individual actions both within and outside the official nuclear nonproliferation regime.

CONCLUSION

When we apply a more general regime theory/public goods framework to the subject of nuclear nonproliferation, we move away from the view that pitches the nuclear nonproliferation regime as fundamentally different from other regimes in international relations (e.g., the international trade regime). The argument is sometimes made that the existential threats at the heart of decisions about nuclear proliferation make it necessary to think differently about the nonproliferation regime compared with regimes in other issue areas. While it may be true that the consequences of the nonproliferation regime's failure are more serious than others,[42] it does not necessarily follow that the underlying logics associated with that failure are different. In other words, when the consequences of regime decay are uncritically conflated with the causal forces and underlying logic of that decay, the resulting analysis could be incomplete or even faulty.

The public goods lens employed in this chapter differs from the approaches that follow in the other chapters in this volume. Security concerns, domestic politics, and bureaucratic politics (for example) can all alter the way states perceive their costs and benefits around regime compliance, and the end effect can mitigate some collective action concerns. However, it is important to note that these other aspects can also magnify the collective action challenges outlined here. For example, a state with acute security concerns has private costs of participation in nuclear-weapons-free zones that compound the weakest link challenges associated with that good's particular aggregation technology. As the country's costs of compliance increase, the net private good it receives from participation decreases, and the collective action challenges of the weakest link public goods provision begin to play a larger role in structuring incentives.

We need to think more carefully and comparatively about these issues. There have been too few attempts to bring the broader regime theorizing to bear on the subject of nuclear nonproliferation.[43] To the extent that we can learn from general theorizing about the logics associated with international regime formation and dynamics, we may be able to generate some important policy implications for nonproliferation regime participants, as they attempt to incentivize more responsible regime stakeholders. Those countries interested in strengthening the nuclear nonproliferation regime and developing responsible nuclear stakeholders would be wise to consider the incentive structures influencing individual state decision making. While the hypotheses in this chapter need to be tested more rigorously, a collective action approach to the problem provides a promising move in this direction.

Notes

The author thanks the participants in the Defense Threat Reduction Agency/Advanced Systems Concepts Office (DTRA-ASCO) workshop, "Building Responsible Nonproliferation Stakeholders: Exploring State Decision-Making," San Diego, Calif., February 18, 2011, and the International Security Studies Section/International Security and Arms Control Section (ISSS-ISAC) Annual Conference, October 14–15, 2011, Irvine, Calif., for comments on an earlier draft of this chapter. Special thanks go to Patrick Morgan for a detailed set of comments.

1. For an excellent (if now somewhat dated) overview, see the IAEA's report on the issue: Jan Lodding, *Non-proliferation of Nuclear Weapons and Nuclear Security: IAEA Safeguards Agreements and Additional Protocols* (Vienna, Austria: International Atomic Energy Agency, May 2005). By one current (but incomplete) count, there are seventeen "non-nuclear-weapon States that are party to the NPT but have not yet brought into force comprehensive safeguards agreements (CSAs) pursuant to Article III of that Treaty"; IAEA, "Status List: Conclusion of Safeguards Agreements, Additional Protocols and Small Quantities Protocols as of December 20" (International Atomic Energy Agency, December 20, 2010). The list of those states that have not entered into force the Additional Protocols is longer.

2. For example, see Lawrence Scheinman, ed., *Implementing Resolution 1540: The Role of Regional Organizations* (New York: United Nations Institute for Disarmament Research, 2008).

3. Scott D. Sagan, "Why Do States Build Nuclear Weapons? Three Models in Search of a Bomb," *International Security* 21, no. 3 (1996/1997): 54–86, is the most well-known ex-

ploration of nuclear policy determinants; also see Sonali Singh and Christopher R. Way, "The Correlates of Nuclear Proliferation: A Quantitative Test," *Journal of Conflict Resolution* 48, no. 6 (2004): 859–85; Jacques E. C. Hymans, "Theories of Nuclear Proliferation: The State of the Field," *Nonproliferation Review* 13, no. 3 (2006): 455–65; and Andrew Grotto, "Why Do States That Oppose Nuclear Proliferation Resist New Nonproliferation Obligations? Three Logics of Nonproliferation Decision-Making," *Cardozo Journal of International and Comparative Law* 18, no. 1 (2010): 1–43.

4. For example, see T. V. Paul, *Power versus Prudence: Why Nations Forgo Nuclear Weapons* (Montreal: McGill-Queen's University Press, 2000); Singh and Way, "Correlates of Nuclear Proliferation."

5. See Erik Gartzke and Dong-Joon Jo, "Bargaining, Nuclear Proliferation, and Interstate Disputes," *Journal of Conflict Resolution* 53, no. 2 (2009): 209–33; and Matthew Kroenig, "Exporting the Bomb: Why States Provide Sensitive Nuclear Assistance," *American Political Science Review* 103, no. 1 (2009): 113–33.

6. For example, see Anthony DiFilippo, *Japan's Nuclear Disarmament Policy and the U.S. Security Umbrella* (New York: Macmillan, 2006).

7. See Nina Srinivasan Rathbun, "The Role of Legitimacy in Strengthening the Nuclear Nonproliferation Regime," *Nonproliferation Review* 13, no. 2 (2006): 227; Christopher F. Chyba, "Time for a Systematic Analysis: U.S. Nuclear Weapons and Nuclear Proliferation," *Arms Control Today* 38 (December 2008).

8. Chyba, "Time for a Systematic Analysis."

9. Maria Rost Rublee, *Nonproliferation Norms: Why States Choose Nuclear Restraint* (Athens: University of Georgia Press, 2009).

10. Etel Solingen, *Nuclear Logics: Contrasting Paths in East Asia and the Middle East* (Princeton, N.J.: Princeton University Press, 2007); Matthew Kroenig, "Importing the Bomb: Sensitive Nuclear Assistance and Nuclear Proliferation," *Journal of Conflict Resolution* 53, no. 2 (2009): 161–80.

11. Todd Sandler and Daniel G. Arce M., "A Conceptual Framework for Understanding Global and Transnational Public Goods for Health," *Fiscal Studies* 23, no. 2 (2002): 195–222; Todd Sandler, *Global Collective Action* (Cambridge: Cambridge University Press, 2004).

12. Andreas Hasenclever, Peter Mayer, and Volker Rittberger, *Theories of International Regimes* (Cambridge: Cambridge University Press, 1997), 10; Jeffrey Fields and Jason S. Enia, "The Health of the Nuclear Nonproliferation Regime: Returning to a Multidimensional Evaluation," *Nonproliferation Review* 16, no. 2 (2009): 173–96; John Simpson, "The Future of the NPT," in *Combating Weapons of Mass Destruction: The Future of International Nonproliferation Policy*, ed. Nathan E. Busch and Daniel H. Joyner (Athens: University of Georgia Press, 2009), 45–73.

13. Roger K. Smith, "Explaining the Non-proliferation Regime: Anomalies for Contemporary International Relations Theory," *International Organization* 41, no. 2 (1987):

253–81; Harald Müller, "The Internalization of Principles, Norms, and Rules by Governments: The Case of Security Regimes," in *Regime Theory and International Relations*, ed. Volker Rittberger (Oxford: Oxford University Press, 1993), 361–88.

14. Hasenclever, Mayer, and Rittberger, *Theories of International Regimes*, 9; Rublee, *Nonproliferation Norms*.

15. See Müller, "Internalization of Principles," 362; Trevor McMorris Tate, "Regime-Building in the Non-proliferation System," *Journal of Peace Research* 27, no. 4 (1990): 399–414.

16. The distinction here between formal and informal possibilities is meant to reflect the differences between official international agreements and other possible activities. Using the term "informal" is not meant to preclude the possibility that some domestic actions that might increase vigilance and enforcement, for example, might require formal changes to domestic law to enact. In this case, it is only meant to indicate that these actions are not formally part of any international agreements.

17. Mancur Olson, *The Logic of Collective Action: Public Goods and the Theory of Groups* (Cambridge: Harvard University Press, 1965).

18. Ibid., 27–28.

19. Some scholarship refers to nonrivalry as "jointness of supply." See, for example, John G. Head, "Public Goods and Public Policy," *Public Finance* 17, no. 3 (1962): 197–219.

20. Sandler, *Global Collective Action*, 18.

21. See Russell Hardin, "Collective Action as an Agreeable n-Prisoner's Dilemma," *Behavioral Science* 16, no. 5 (1971): 472–81; Steven Brams, *Game Theory and Politics* (New York: Macmillan, 1973); William H. Riker and Peter C. Ordeshook, *An Introduction to Positive Political Theory* (Englewood Cliffs, N.J.: Prentice Hall, 1973).

22. Robert Axelrod, *The Evolution of Cooperation* (New York: Basic Books, 1984); Robert Axelrod and Douglas Dion, "The Further Evolution of Cooperation," *Science*, n.s., 242, no. 4884 (1988): 1385–90.

23. Todd Sandler, *Collective Action: Theory and Applications* (Ann Arbor: University of Michigan Press, 1992); Sandler, *Global Collective Action*, 25.

24. Sandler, *Global Collective Action*, 36–37.

25. Mancur Olson and Richard J. Zeckhauser, "Collective Goods, Comparative Advantage, and Alliance Efficiency," in *Issues in Defense Economics*, ed. Roland McKean (New York: National Bureau of Economic Research, 1967), 25–48; Todd Sandler and Keith Hartley, "Economics of Alliances: The Lessons for Collective Action," *Journal of Economic Literature* 39, no. 3 (2001): 869–96; Sandler, *Global Collective Action*, 36–37.

26. Inge Kaul, Isabelle Grunberg, and Marc Stern, eds., *Global Public Goods: International Cooperation in the 21st Century* (New York: Oxford University Press, 1999); Todd Sandler and Daniel G Arce M., "Pure Public Goods versus Commons: Benefit-Cost Duality," *Land Economics* 79, no. 3 (2003): 355–68; Sandler, *Global Collective Action*, 49–60,

discusses five key types of impure public goods: goods with some rivalry but no exclusion, goods with full exclusion but no rivalry, club goods that have exclusion and are partly rival, joint products, and open-access commons. For the sake of the analysis in this chapter, I have left out open-access commons.

27. James M. Buchanan, "An Economic Theory of Clubs," *Economica*, n.s., 32, no. 125 (1965): 1–14, is foundational on the economic theory of clubs. Todd Sandler and John Tschirhart, "Club Theory: Thirty Years Later," *Public Choice* 93, no. 3/4 (1997): 335–55, provides a literature review thirty years into the field's history.

28. Sandler, *Global Collective Action*, 52–53.

29. Ravi Kanbur, Todd Sandler, and Kevin Morrison, *The Future of Development Assistance: Common Pools and International Public Goods* (Washington, D.C.: Overseas Development Council, 1999).

30. Todd Sandler, "Impurity of Defense: An Application to the Economics of Alliances," *Kyklos* 30, no. 3 (1977): 443–60.

31. Todd Sandler and John F. Forbes, "Burden Sharing, Strategy, and the Design of NATO," *Economic Inquiry* 18, no. 3 (1980): 425–44.

32. Jack Hirshleifer, "From Weakest-Link to Best-Shot: The Voluntary Provision of Public Goods," *Public Choice* 41, no. 3 (1983): 371–86; Richard Cornes and Todd Sandler, "Easy Riders, Joint Production, and Public Goods," *Economic Journal* 94, no. 3 (1984): 580–98.

33. Sandler, *Global Collective Action*, 61.

34. Ibid., 62.

35. Mark Bagnoli and Michael McKee, "Voluntary Contribution Games: Efficient Private Provision of Public Goods," *Economic Inquiry* 29, no. 2 (1991): 351–66.

36. Sandler, *Global Collective Action*, 202–4.

37. Sandler and Arce, "Conceptual Framework"; Sandler, *Global Collective Action*.

38. Leopoldo Nuti, "Italy's Nuclear Choices," UNISCI Discussion Papers, no. 25 (2011), 179, http://revistas.ucm.es/cps/16962206/articulos/UNIS1111130167A.PDF.

39. This perception is, of course, the subject of significant debate. See Chris Schneidmiller, "Senate Decision Key to Future of Test Ban Treaty," *Global Security Newswire*, July 18, 2011, http://gsn.nti.org/gsn/nw_20110714_9351.php, for a helpful overview.

40. See Oran R. Young and Marc A. Levy, "The Effectiveness of International Environmental Regimes," in *The Effectiveness of International Environmental Regimes: Causal Connections and Behavioral Mechanisms*, ed. Oran R. Young (Cambridge, Mass.: MIT Press, 1999), 16–19, for a helpful discussion on approaching these issues.

41. It is worth noting that the ratio of private goods and public goods can change in the interim between the signing of any treaty and its execution. The U.S.-India deal appears to be providing a good example. See Simon Denyer and Rama Lakshmi, "U.S.-India Nuclear Deal Drifts Dangerously," *Washington Post*, July 15, 2011, http://www.washingtonpost.com/

world/asia-pacific/us-india-nuclear-deal-drifts-dangerously/2011/07/07/gIQAJTbeGI _story.html, for recent developments.

42. Even this idea is debated: cf. John Mueller, "The Essential Irrelevance of Nuclear Weapons: Stability in the Postwar World," *International Security* 13, no. 2 (1988): 55–79; John E. Mueller, *Atomic Obsession: Nuclear Alarmism from Hiroshima to Al-Qaeda* (New York: Oxford University Press, 2009); and Graham Allison, *Nuclear Terrorism: The Ultimate Preventable Catastrophe* (New York: Henry Holt, 2005).

43. Johan Bergenäs, "The Slippery Slope of Rational Inaction: UN Security Council Resolution 1540 and the Tragedy of the Commons," *Nonproliferation Review* 15, no. 2 (2008): 373–380, leads a short list of exceptions.

CHAPTER 2

Glass Half Full?
Evaluating the Impact of New U.S. Policy on the Legitimacy of the Nuclear Nonproliferation Regime

Nina Srinivasan Rathbun

THE NUCLEAR NONPROLIFERATION regime and its essential foundation, the Treaty on the Non-Proliferation of Nuclear Weapons (NPT), have been under serious stress for several years. The challenges that have plagued the regime since its inception—universal adherence and the pace of disarmament—persist. But several relatively new threats raise questions about the effectiveness of the treaty in preventing the spread of nuclear weapons. And they interact in worrying ways with the perceived lack of commitment to disarmament and universal adherence. The clandestine pursuit of nuclear weapons by some NPT parties, in violation of their obligations and without the knowledge of the international community and the International Atomic Energy Agency (IAEA), calls into question the effectiveness of safeguards and export controls in preventing proliferation.[1] Several proliferators have received significant assistance with sensitive nuclear technology and materials from a clandestine international network operating out of Pakistan and under the direction of A. Q. Khan.[2] With the recent interest in and new providers for enrichment and reprocessing technology and materials, this long latent threat has increased in significance in recent years.

Efforts to address the proliferation threats have interacted in unhelpful ways with concerns about lack of universal adherence to the NPT and the perceived weakening of commitment to disarmament by the nuclear weapons states (NWS). Critics of the nonproliferation regime have focused on the discrimination inherent in the NPT, whereby some states are permitted to retain nuclear weapons while others are banned from acquiring them. The NPT commitment to nuclear disarmament creates an expectation of the eventual end of this inherent discrimination. Additionally, India, Pakistan, and Israel have never joined the NPT, and all now possess nuclear weapons. The existence of nuclear weapons capable states outside of the treaty reduces the likelihood that NWS will agree to total nuclear disarmament. A failure to persuade states with nuclear weapons to join the treaty as nonnuclear weapons states (NNWS) not only impedes disarmament, but if their actions are legitimized, many may question why they should continue to be bound by the NPT. Any policy that treats non-NPT members with nuclear weapons equally with NPT nonnuclear weapons states also creates a sense of inequality. Any new strategy for addressing proliferation concerns must address the interaction among these factors. The intertwined relationship among new proliferation policies, disarmament, and universality is important because changes may raise strong legitimacy concerns. Indeed, the existing limitations of the nonproliferation regime due to discrimination only serve to enhance the importance of universality and nondiscrimination for the new nonproliferation measures.

The norm of nonproliferation is widely accepted to be in all states' interest. And nearly all states share the taboo against the use of nuclear weapons. Nevertheless, significant numbers of states, including NPT member states, refuse to support strengthening nonproliferation measures in response to newly perceived threats. Andrew Grotto argues that this is due to the symbolism of what new "NPT-plus" measures would mean about the equity of the nonproliferation regime.[3] This, I argue, is due to legitimacy concerns. States clearly have different perceptions of the threat environment and what nonproliferation measures would do to increase or decrease their security and regional stability, as Maria Rost Rublee discusses in the next chapter. States in the Non-Aligned Movement (NAM) are particularly sensitive to any increase in the perceived inequality of the nonproliferation regime as explained in chapter 6. While interests continue to be the main impetus for state support of nonproliferation measures, they are not the only consideration. The perceived legitimacy of the measures continues to be an important factor that can be addressed relatively inexpensively.

The last two administrations in the United States, while embracing the same goals, have taken quite different approaches to the problem of clandestine proliferation. The Bush administration proposed limiting the spread of sensitive nuclear enrichment and reprocessing-related technology to those states that already possess it, created an exception to allow India, a non-NPT party, to participate in the exchange of advanced peaceful nuclear technology without accepting the same nonproliferation obligations as all other nonnuclear weapons states, challenged the "13 practical steps" to disarmament agreed to in the 2000 NPT Final Document, rejected verification measures in arms control agreements, increased the U.S. reliance on nuclear weapons in the 2001 Nuclear Posture Review (NPR), and created a like-minded group of states to interdict illegal shipments of controlled items that can be used for WMD programs through the Proliferation Security Initiative (PSI).[4] The Obama administration embraced the goal of zero in disarmament in a prominent speech in Prague, repudiated restrictions on the supply of peaceful nuclear technology, decreased the U.S. reliance on nuclear weapons in the 2011 NPR, re-created verification measures in new arms control agreements, and allowed for the creation of new rules for supply of sensitive enrichment and reprocessing (ENR)-related technology through the export policies of the major nuclear suppliers, who are formally organized within the Nuclear Suppliers Group (NSG). Do these differences of policy affect the legitimacy of the nonproliferation regime? I argue that they do.

This chapter considers how the two recent American administrations' policies have differed in their impact on the legitimacy of the nonproliferation regime and thereby raised different responses from other states. Legitimacy, in this context, is the acceptance of rules because they are viewed as right and correct, in distinction to acceptance based purely on self-interest or coercion.[5] Legitimate agreements or regimes have numerous advantages. They attract membership of relevant parties; they provide the most cost-efficient and potentially effective mechanism to encourage rule-compliant behavior; and states are more committed to ensuring that these types of regimes are successfully implemented. Legitimacy is no substitute for self-interest. The most stable basis for assuring compliance with the nonproliferation regime is the tangible security benefit it provides. Yet legitimacy can be a relatively inexpensive and important supplement. Legitimacy can be defined in many different ways. I define it as the degree to which regimes ensure sovereign equality. Legitimate regimes are universal and nondiscriminatory. They allow equal participation and decision making for all and do not discriminate among their members in terms of rights and obligations.

The chapter is divided into four sections. The first defines legitimacy and analyzes how a regime can encourage acceptance and internalization of its rules. The second section analyzes the legitimacy of two fundamental institutions in the nuclear nonproliferation regime—the IAEA and the NPT. The third details the various policies and proposals of the Bush and Obama administrations to reinforce this regime and evaluates the degree to which they differ on legitimacy lines. The final section evaluates the responses of other members of the nonproliferation regime to the U.S. policies, to see if those policies that strengthen the legitimacy of the regime receive more support.

MODES OF AUTHORITY AND LEGITIMACY IN INTERNATIONAL REGIMES

International regimes require mechanisms to encourage compliance with their rules.[6] Drawing on Max Weber, Ian Hurd notes that authority in the international realm ultimately rests, as it does in the domestic arena, on three modes of social control: coercion, self-interest, and legitimacy.[7] Every system relies on a varying mixture of all three. Coercion involves enforcement, in the form of actual or potential punishment, to compel actors to obey. This is the mode of authority generally associated with realist approaches to international relations. In the domestic realm, the government generally provides this enforcement power. In the international realm, there is no clear enforcer to play this role. However, within a regime, rules may be enforced by other more powerful parties or by an international organization to which parties have delegated this enforcement authority. In regimes based predominantly on self-interest, actors follow the rules because doing so provides tangible gains.[8] This is the mechanism generally associated with the rationalist approach to international relations. As there is no incentive to violate the agreement, no costly enforcement is needed. States do not enter agreements if they do not expect to comply.

Coercion and self-interest are both powerful mechanisms of ensuring compliance with agreements. However, both have weaknesses that legitimacy can help to address. While often effective in ensuring the desired outcome, coercion is not necessarily efficient because surveillance and punishment to ensure parties comply are costly. Especially in the international system, this mode of control is unlikely to be effective across large areas and for long periods of time. No state or international organization has the ability to watch all actors' behaviors at all times in all places, nor do they have the resources to punish all violations.[9] Enforcement is much more effective when it can be directed specifically at a limited number of situations. In terms of self-interest, the substance of any agreement is not the entire basis of ensuring its acceptance. How decisions are made is often important as well.

Legitimacy helps supplement these other modes of authority. Under legitimate regimes, actors accept and support the rules as "desirable, proper, or appropriate within some socially constructed system of norms, values, beliefs and definitions."[10] This involves internalization of the rules of the regime as desirable in their own right.[11] Legitimacy therefore is a moral or normative concept. There is no such process in the other two mechanisms. Without enforcement, states that can and wish to cheat will do so. If interests change, they will depart from the rules. Legitimacy matters both for compliance and commitment. States will both be less likely to violate the terms of a legitimate agreement and will also be more committed to holding others to their obligations in the case of violation.

Two components of legitimacy are commonly discussed—substantive and procedural. Substantive legitimacy applies to the outcome, content, and product of deliberations, whereas procedural legitimacy pertains to the process by which agreement was reached. Outcomes and process are regarded as legitimate if the states involved believe they are right and correct or just and fair. John G. Ruggie's notion of "qualitative multilateralism" contains both substantive and procedural legitimacy. The multilateral process coordinates national policies of states "on the basis of 'generalized' principles of conduct . . . without regard to the particularistic interests of the parties or the strategic exigencies that may exist in any specific occurrence."[12]

Legitimacy, both substantive and procedural, can be very difficult to distinguish from interests narrowly defined. States might characterize outcomes as legitimate simply when they serve their interests, or when the procedure by which they are reached gives them disproportionate weight. This can be consciously deceptive but just as easily unconscious and natural. Both analysts and negotiators have a difficult time agreeing on what constitutes fair and just outcomes and procedures independent of interests. There are multiple plausible notions of how to define fair and just.[13]

Is there a standard of substantive and procedural legitimacy that can command consensus and serve as a benchmark for evaluating different agreements and the processes used to arrive at them? I argue it is sovereign equality.[14] This principle of conduct provides equal legal rights to states regardless of their material capabilities. Sovereign equality is an attempt to limit the exercise of power in international relations. It has two faces, universality and nondiscrimination. In terms of process, universality means that all, or nearly all, states concerned have a right to participate and a voice in rule creation and management of the regime. Nondiscrimination in procedure means that states have an equal voice in decision making. Nondiscrimination in terms of substance means that rules, once promulgated, apply equally to all.

Regimes that create rules for uniform treatment of all states or members are generally more substantively legitimate than those that do not. However, when equal treatment would affect other important norms detrimentally, then substantive legitimacy may be enhanced by creating a rational basis for distinction among states. For example, equality in outcomes can mean rebalancing benefits in a way that does not simply reflect the power distribution of members. Therefore, regimes can improve their substantive legitimacy by giving less powerful states greater benefits while not requiring as much of them. Discrimination against powerful states can enhance rather than detract from substantive legitimacy. A good example of this is the differential treatment of developing and developed countries in the World Trade Organization.[15] However, any inconsistency must be consistent with the underlying principle of the norm as well as other principles of international society, rather than as a consequence of power differentials.[16]

Agreements and institutions can be procedurally but not substantively legitimate. For example, the negotiations over the United Nations Charter allowed the participation of weaker members, but their concerns about power differentials were ultimately not included in the final agreement, which created a system in which the great powers possessed a veto and a permanent place on the Security Council. Nevertheless, some argue that because smaller states were given a voice in the process, they regarded the outcome as acceptable.[17]

Legitimacy and effectiveness have a difficult relationship.[18] States are more likely to join and comply with regimes they regard as legitimate. Legitimacy has a "compliance-pull," argues Thomas M. Franck.[19] However, expanding participation on an equal basis and requiring equal treatment forecloses the option of exclusion and often leads to lowest common denominator solutions. A proper balance must be struck between legitimacy and effectiveness. The move toward lowest common denominator consensus must be balanced by the ability of the regime to achieve its ultimate goals. By working to improve a regime's legitimacy, it may be possible for actors to create, manage, or reform it in such a way as to ensure a broader degree of compliance, commitment, and participation. This may require more time and compromise than exclusive agreements or coercive ones, since states of all different types and capabilities must be involved from an early stage. The next section analyzes how legitimacy developed historically in the nuclear nonproliferation regime, the IAEA, and the NPT. It provides a benchmark to measure the legitimacy of any new efforts to strengthen the regime.

THE NUCLEAR NONPROLIFERATION REGIME

While some political scientists argue that the very destructiveness of nuclear weapons promotes international stability due to their deterrent effect on rational governments concerned about the risk of escalation during crises, policymakers tend to believe that the proliferation of nuclear weapons leads to increased insecurity in international relations due to the greater likelihood of use, accident, or theft by nonstate actors.[20] The nuclear nonproliferation regime developed in response to this perceived threat. The main goal of the NPT has been and continues to be to reduce the likelihood of a devastating nuclear war by preventing the proliferation of nuclear weapons to countries beyond the five already possessing them in 1967 (the United States, the Soviet Union, Great Britain, France, and China), while permitting all parties to share in the benefits of the peaceful uses of nuclear energy and simultaneously working toward the ultimate elimination of nuclear weapons. Preventing the spread of nuclear weapons required balancing the enormous potential destructive power of nuclear energy with its significant potential to provide energy and technology for development.[21] Nuclear energy was believed for several decades after its discovery to be the solution of all future energy needs. It would be "too cheap to meter." This prospect was not possible without significant international cooperation.

Early efforts failed to forge a verifiable international agreement to prevent the use of nuclear energy for destructive purposes while promoting the use of atomic energy for peaceful and humanitarian ends. Nevertheless, the initial foray into addressing the dilemma provides a baseline for a regime based on procedural legitimacy and embodying universal and nondiscriminatory principles that gained the support of the UN General Assembly.[22] The U.S.-proposed Baruch Plan proposed an International Atomic Energy Development Authority that would control all aspects of the development and use of nuclear energy that could present a danger to international security.[23] All states would participate equally in its decision making, giving it a high degree of universality. Rules would be applied without discrimination. Decisions made by this organization would not fall under the purview of the Security Council, thereby eliminating the possibility that the five permanent members could use their veto powers. The plan would even have eliminated any inequality in nuclear weapons capability. The United States, the only state possessing nuclear weapons at the time, was willing to destroy its own nuclear weapons stockpile, but only after all states renounced the bomb as a weapon and established an adequate system of control, including international punishments for violations. However, the Soviet Union, having not yet acquired nuclear weapons, refused to support the plan, proposing instead a declaration outlawing nuclear weapons with no international control regime to prevent their production.[24] The plan consequently failed as a result of this and the insistence of the United States that the consequences of noncompliance be automatic and not subject to Security Council veto or review.

Subsequently, two less ambitious institutions were able to gain the necessary support of the international community: the International Atomic Energy Agency (IAEA) and the Treaty on the Non-proliferation of Nuclear Weapons, known as the NPT. Established in 1957, in the wake of President Dwight D. Eisenhower's December 1953 "Atoms for Peace" initiative, the IAEA promotes the peaceful use of nuclear energy by offering technology and materials to interested countries while safeguarding those same supplies against diversion to weapons programs and thereby alleviating some of the member states' proliferation fears. As stated in Article II of its statute, "the Agency shall seek to accelerate and enlarge the contribution of atomic energy to peace, health and prosperity throughout the world. It shall insure, so far as it is able, that assistance provided by it or at its request or under its supervision or control is not used in such a way as to further any military purpose."[25] However, the IAEA mandate did not include any obligation on the part of the member states to refrain from developing nuclear weapons through efforts not involving IAEA assistance. Under this safeguards formulation, the IAEA did not seek out clandestine operations but provided assurance of nondiversion by monitoring, auditing, and reporting on the specific nuclear facilities or materials declared by members to the agency.[26]

The IAEA would take on new roles under the NPT, which came into force in 1970. This was the first international agreement that addressed the question of nuclear weapons proliferation.[27] It embodies a "grand bargain" and rests on three pillars: 1) the nonproliferation of nuclear weapons to states not already possessing them by January 1, 1967, 2) the promotion of the development of peaceful uses of nuclear energy, and 3) the ultimate elimination of all nuclear weapons. Cooperation was possible because states agreed to the three pillars, even though different states were interested in different pillars. The NPT embodies most of the principles articulated at the beginning of the atomic age in the UN Atomic Energy Commission (UNAEC) and the Baruch Plan but does not achieve the same degree of legitimacy.

While the NPT places similar obligations on both nuclear weapons and nonnuclear weapons states to prevent the proliferation of these weapons, it discriminates between nuclear weapons states and nonnuclear weapons states. Nuclear weapons states are permitted legally to retain nuclear weapons (while negotiating in good faith toward their elimination) whereas nonnuclear weapons states are prohibited from acquiring them. Nuclear weapons states are bound not to transfer (and nonnuclear weapons states not to receive) nuclear weapons or in any way assist, encourage, or induce any nonnuclear weapons state to acquire nuclear weapons. All NPT parties are bound not to supply nuclear material or equipment without proper safeguards. The export control regime developed to support NPT obligations.[28] In contrast to the earlier IAEA arrangements, nonnuclear weapons states are additionally bound under the NPT to accept full-scope safeguards by the IAEA on all their nuclear facilities and materials. The discrimination between those states that have and those who do not have nuclear weapons is the major factor reducing the legitimacy of the treaty. In fact, the NPT is the only treaty dealing with WMD that discriminates in this way. The Chemical Weapons Convention and the Biological Weapons Convention both require all parties to eliminate all existing stockpiles and pledge not to acquire any new banned weapons.

This discrimination is ameliorated somewhat by the other pillars of the regime. The disarmament pillar dilutes the discriminatory effects of the nonproliferation pillar and strengthens the legitimacy of the regime by creating the expectation that the special rights of the nuclear weapons states will end at some point in the future. All parties pledge to create the conditions that will facilitate the cessation of nuclear weapons manufacture, liquidation of all nuclear stockpiles, and elimination of all nuclear weapons. The parties agree to work toward ending the nuclear arms race and achieving nuclear, general, and complete disarmament. The "peaceful uses" pillar bounds the discrimination to the possession of nuclear weapons only, while reiterating that all states are on an equal legal footing for benefiting from the peaceful uses of nuclear energy and technology. States acknowledge each party's "inalienable right" to develop and use nuclear energy for peaceful purposes and promise to facilitate the fullest possible exchange of equipment, materials, and scientific and technological information, particularly to promote the development of peaceful nuclear applications in developing countries.[29] Joseph S. Nye argued nearly thirty years ago that if states were to try to create a legitimate nuclear nonproliferation regime under the existing political circumstances, they would likely re-create the current one, because it balances the need for effectiveness with the desire for equality.[30] The uneven possession of nuclear weapons is justified in the abstract by compensation from peaceful nuclear assistance and the risk reduction of disarmament. However, any actions to eschew arms control and disarmament efforts or rely more heavily on nuclear weapons would weaken the nonproliferation regime by strengthening the discrimination.[31]

While disarmament and nonproliferation are indirectly linked in the above analysis, they are not the only factors of concern. Jeffrey W. Knopf carefully analyzes different logics on which states might rely to link these two policies, both directly and indirectly, in chapter 4. He concludes that while perceptions of progress will likely on balance enhance nonproliferation efforts, disarmament alone will not address the challenges of the nonproliferation regime. Support for nonproliferation measures must be analyzed in the context of egoistic interest as well as legitimacy concerns with the measures themselves.

Multilateralism is based on "diffuse reciprocity," a general sense that states all benefit and agree on a goal rather than engaging in specific exchanges in a quid pro quo manner, as expected by "specific reciprocity." The expectation is that specific reciprocity precedes diffuse reciprocity.[32] The specific and systematic interests of the states in the nonproliferation regime can over time form the basis for a more general agreement in the overall norms of the regime. In this process, states' interest in the nonproliferation bargain is critical, not only because it creates incentives for interest-based adherence and compliance, but also because it can fundamentally change states' normative evaluation of the importance of the goal and their relationship with one another.[33] Maria Rost Rublee's social psychological discussion of normative linkages, activation, and consistency expand on a possible mechanism for this process in chapter 3. Christopher Way and Karthika Sasikumar argue that nuclear weapons' symbolic meaning has changed due to the normative impact of the nonproliferation regime, though they focus on the self-interests inherent in the grand bargain to explain state timing for NPT signature.[34] T. V. Paul argues that the nonproliferation regime creates norms and principles against proliferation despite its discrimination due both to the systemic and egoistic interests of states as well as the strong norms against nuclear use.[35]

The history of the nuclear nonproliferation regime demonstrates both the benefits and the drawbacks of relying on consensual, multilateral processes to address international security threats. All interested states were involved in the negotiations, fulfilling the universality requirement of procedural legitimacy. In joining, states gain a voice in the decision-making process, leading to healthy debates in both the IAEA and the NPT about the goals of each institution and the nuclear nonproliferation regime generally. While the reliance on consensus in decision making sometimes leads to an inability to act, the gains in procedural legitimacy for both the IAEA and the NPT have now made it very difficult to withdraw and have framed the debate about potential proliferators in a manner that would be impossible in the absence of the regime. The norm against nuclear weapons has developed with the nonproliferation regime and reinforces its legitimacy.[36]

For nearly thirty-six years, the NPT appears to have worked quite well.[37] President Kennedy predicted in the early 1960s that there would soon be twenty to thirty states with nuclear weapons, yet only a handful of states have acquired nuclear weapons, and only one state bound by the NPT may have done so.[38] Indeed, more states have given up nuclear weapons or weapons programs than have acquired them.[39] Before the NPT, several dozen states were openly considering acquiring nuclear weapons. The nuclear nonproliferation regime has a high success rate with relatively low external enforcement costs over the past several decades.[40] Today only a small handful of states are suspected to have nuclear weapons ambitions, and only one state has withdrawn from the treaty.[41] There have been very few violations or suspected violations of IAEA or NPT obligations. Some might argue that the regime merely monitors and ratifies what states' interests would have ensured in any case. The role of the nuclear nonproliferation regime in states' decision whether to develop nuclear weapons is a difficult question and beyond the scope of this essay, but there does appear to be a significant case for the NPT's contribution.

NONPROLIFERATION POLICY EVALUATED

The following section is divided according to the types of initiatives embarked upon by the two U.S. administrations—supply, PSI, and disarmament. I focus on their impact on legitimacy and highlight differences, if any, between the policies of the Bush administration and the Obama administration.

Supply

Mastering the full fuel cycle, including uranium enrichment or reprocessing to separate plutonium, is the most time-consuming and arguably most difficult step in the process of developing nuclear weapons. Building weapons components requires much effort and expertise, but the vast majority of time is spent obtaining fissile material. Centrifuge enrichment has become the method of choice for proliferators. Thus, proliferation concerns are heightened when a state gains this ability because the process of enriching uranium to low levels for civil reactors is the same as for enriching uranium to weapons grade levels. Indeed, the enrichment process is not linear. It takes as much separative work to enrich uranium from 0.7 percent (the natural concentration) to 2 percent as it does to enrich it from 2 percent to 93 percent (weapons grade).[42] Similarly, the technology for reprocessing fuel to separate plutonium for reactors and for weapons is quite similar. Once a country masters the technology necessary to develop fissile material for peaceful purposes through enrichment or reprocessing, it gains the capability to develop the key ingredient for nuclear weapons in a relatively short period of time. While this capability does not include the critical weaponization technology, it shortens the time span considerably. Nevertheless gaining this fuel cycle capability, as opposed to demonstrating an intent to manufacture, does not violate any NPT obligation and, if properly safeguarded, does not violate any IAEA obligations either. Should a country then decide to withdraw from the NPT, it would already possess this critical capability without breaking any legal commitments. This is the scenario that many are trying to render substantially more difficult and costly.

Concern over the nuclear fuel cycle is not new. Following India's 1974 test of a self-described "peaceful nuclear explosive," which major nuclear suppliers perceived as a failure of existing export controls, significant effort went into preventing the further spread of sensitive enrichment and reprocessing technology.[43] The London Group, comprising major nuclear suppliers within and outside the NPT at the time, met in secret to hammer out guidelines to strengthen the existing nuclear export controls.[44] These guidelines called for "restraint" in the transfer of enrichment and reprocessing technology even for peaceful uses, and for suppliers to "encourage recipients to accept, as an alternative to national plants, supplier involvement and/or other appropriate multinational participation in resulting facilities."[45] The London Group's members were further increasing the discriminatory nature of the nonproliferation regime. Not only were nonnuclear weapons states not in the group prohibited from acquiring an actual nuclear weapon, but they were also to be prevented from acquiring enrichment and reprocessing capabilities, which are generally seen as included in the right to "peaceful uses" in Article IV of the NPT.[46]

Because of the discriminatory nature and lack of universality and transparency of these efforts to curtail the transfer of nuclear technology, less developed countries responded unfavorably. Recipient countries were not invited to participate nor informed of the group's deliberations. This led to accusations by those outside the group of cartelism on the part of those possessing the technology.[47] The London Group reemerged as the Nuclear Suppliers Group (NSG) twelve years later when no consensus could be reached for further tightening of the guidelines following the revelations on the Iraqi nuclear program after the first Gulf War. The NSG continues to bear the stigma of its early non-universal and discriminatory foundations.[48]

Supplier Restraint—the Bush Administration's Proposal In his February 2004 speech at National Defense University, President George W. Bush renewed the call for a halt in the transfer of sensitive nuclear technology "to any state that does not already possess full-scale, functioning enrichment and reprocessing plants."[49] At the same time, he proposed to provide assurances of the nuclear fuel supply at a reasonable price. This plan encountered many of the same difficulties gaining legitimacy as the previous NSG effort because supply-side efforts are by their very nature discriminatory. The Bush proposal creates a new layer of discrimination in addition to the existing distinction between those with and those without nuclear weapons and only affects those states not already possessing these technologies. Several countries already possess enrichment and reprocessing capabilities, and not only do they have no plans to give up such capabilities, but they are actively expanding these technologies.[50] Furthermore, implementation would require agreement in the NSG, an exclusive group that does not include technology recipients, bypassing many NPT parties. While the assurances of the sale of nuclear fuel are intended to reduce the proposal's fundamentally discriminatory nature, the proposal would still freeze the current status of nuclear "haves and have-nots" in yet another area.

Like the NSG's original efforts, this proposal goes to the heart of the NPT bargain that states agreeing to forego nuclear weapons would not be limited in any way from pursuing peaceful nuclear programs, as verified by IAEA safeguards. While all recognize that amending the peaceful uses article of the NPT (Article IV) would be impossible, some do not recognize or agree that the Bush proposal would have this de facto result. John Bolton, then the under secretary of state for arms control and international security, stated in the NPT Preparatory Conference in 2004: "The Treaty provides no right to such sensitive nuclear technologies."[51] The NPT's claim to legitimacy, as demonstrated in the previous section, is based on a fine balance of interests and principles that work together to circumscribe and limit the fundamental discrimination inherent in the treaty. Recognition of the inalienable right to the peaceful uses of nuclear energy is essential to this process. All states, regardless of their power or particular situation, retain the right to pursue peaceful nuclear programs that they have as sovereign states and to gain the possibility of assistance with these programs to the degree that such cooperation is feasible. Proposals that undermine this principle weaken the legitimacy of the NPT itself.

Lack of legitimacy will inhibit broader participation and therefore the ultimate ability of this proposal to succeed. It only takes one capable state to share sensitive technology. The suppliers of enrichment and reprocessing technology in the last few decades have not been NSG members. Rather, technology has been transferred by developing countries outside the export control system and by clandestine black market networks, such as A. Q. Khan's.[52] Any effective attempt to address this problem must engage all potential suppliers, which can best be achieved through more universal processes. Criticism based on legitimacy provides a powerful disincentive for states to sign on, even for those that support the goals. Efforts to reinterpret this inalienable right are counterproductive because they unify developing countries (as well as some developed countries) on a principled rather than a purely self-interested basis, which impedes implementation necessary for reaching the goal of preventing the spread of enrichment and processing capabilities. The Bush proposal never gained the support of the NSG.

Rules for Supply While many NSG members rejected the U.S. proposal for a ban on all enrichment and reprocessing transfers, they favored some type of a flexible, criteria-based system for restraining ENR transfers to those states that met some level of nonproliferation standards. The NSG guidelines had stated that suppliers should exercise restraint in supplying sensitive ENR technology but did not specify how and when it would be acceptable. The initial negotiations over criteria in 2004 included NPT membership.[53] Only in 2008 did the United States stop pushing for the ban on all ENR transfers and begin to seriously negotiate criteria for such sensitive transfers.

Initial NSG guidelines for supply of sensitive technology required that IAEA safeguards be applied to any facilities designed, constructed, or operated using transferred technology, and that if any of this technology were reproduced in new facilities in the recipient countries, of the same type or relying on the transferred technology, that IAEA safeguards would apply there as well for a specified number of years.[54] In 1992, NSG guidelines were amended to require IAEA full-scope safeguards as a condition of supply, negating the need for the above requirement.[55] In 2006, the NSG guidelines were amended to include a provision to require the application of IAEA safeguards to facilities using transferred technology even if the recipient states' full-scope safeguards agreement with the IAEA is terminated, and allow for the restitution of the transferred technology and all replications derived from it to the supplier, if the IAEA declares that the application of IAEA safeguards is no longer possible.[56]

In response to the Bush administration proposal, the French proposed that the NSG guidelines should include criteria for sensitive technology transfers that would require the recipient to be an NPT party in compliance with the treaty, have an IAEA comprehensive safeguards agreement and Additional Protocol in effect, be in compliance with one's safeguards agreements, be implementing UNSC Resolution 1540, and have made assurances regarding non-explosive use, effective safeguards in perpetuity, and retransfer, among other safety requirements. In addition, suppliers should "consider" whether the transfer would have a negative impact on the stability and security of the recipient state, and whether it has a credible and coherent rationale for pursuing ENR capabilities in support of a civil nuclear power generation program.[57]

The Bush administration countered with additional factors that suppliers should consider: the transfer must take place under conditions that will not permit or enable the replication of the technology (the "black-box" approach); whether a transfer would stimulate other countries in a region to seek their own sensitive nuclear technology or whether it might lead to instability in the area; and to abide by existing obligations of countries that have agreed to refrain from acquiring such technology.[58] There was significant push back against all of these criteria. In particular, the Netherlands and South Africa argued that all states in good nonproliferation standing are entitled to peaceful benefits of nuclear technology, including ENR. The Dutch and the Canadians argued that all negative criteria on states in good nonproliferation standing were unacceptable, including the French consideration for a "credible rationale."[59]

A "Clean Text" was drafted in the fall of 2008. This included the same objective criteria from the French proposal and added an exemption from the Additional Protocol if another IAEA-approved regional arrangement were in effect (to exempt Brazil and Argentina), and tightened the requirement of being in compliance with IAEA safeguards to prevent the transfer to technology to countries in similar situations as Iran, which "has not been identified by the IAEA as being in serious breach of its safeguards agreement, is not the subject of Board of Governors decisions calling upon it to take additional steps to comply with its safeguards obligations or to build confidence in the peaceful nature of its nuclear program, nor has been reported by the IAEA Secretariat as a state where the IAEA is currently unable to implement its safeguards agreement."[60] It also provided that suppliers would "consider" additional factors, including "whether E&R transfers are intended for peaceful purposes; whether the recipient has a credible and coherent rationale for pursuing an enrichment or reprocessing capability in support of civil nuclear programs; and whether the transfer would have a negative impact on the stability and security of the recipient state and general conditions of stability and security."[61]

The divide within the NSG was between those who wanted to allow for the transfer of sensitive technology to all states that were in good nonproliferation standing (in fact, South Africa continued to argue that adherence to the NPT should be the only requirement), regardless of their reasons or the possible impact on regional security, and those that wanted to add criteria that could weed out potential future proliferators who were currently in good nonproliferation standing. The former base their position on legitimacy—the unbiased application of the same compliance-based criteria to all states regardless of their personalities and potential future actions. Objective criteria based on current compliance with nonproliferation requirements support substantive legitimacy. The latter rely on subjective criteria that put additional barriers up to the transfer of the technology based on the perception of the technology holders.

In June 2011, the NSG finally agreed to the revision of the rules governing the supply of sensitive technology. The 2008 clean text "objective" criteria were approved. The "subjective" criteria were not included. Instead, according to *Arms Control Today*, which obtained a copy of the new guidelines, "it invokes other sections of the guidelines that give suppliers broad authority to ensure that their exports do not contribute to proliferation."[62] Language is also included stating that suppliers should "tak[e] into account at their national discretion, any relevant factors as may be applicable."[63] The U.S. official said the section retains the concept of subjective criteria but "has been written in a much more general manner."[64]

The difference between the two administrations does not appear large, and both desired to restrain the spread of sensitive technology. However, the method was very different. The Bush administration clearly adopted a less legitimate approach that would have created a new discrimination within the nonproliferation regime. As a secondary fall-back strategy, it stressed the character of the state, rather than objective criteria. The Obama administration did not have the same difficulty accepting a criteria-based restraint.

International Fuel Bank The Obama administration criticized the previous administration for its illegitimate attempt to control supply. While it has continued to agree to a criteria-based restriction on the transfer of sensitive nuclear technologies in the NSG, it has repudiated the attempt to freeze the transfer of the technology and focused instead on the guarantee of supply and the creation of an international fuel bank. In Prague in 2009, President Obama stated:

> We should build a new framework for civil nuclear cooperation, including an international fuel bank, so that countries can access peaceful power without increasing the risks of proliferation. That must be the right of every nation that renounces nuclear weapons, especially developing countries embarking on peaceful programs. And no approach will succeed if it's based on the denial of rights to nations that play by the rules.[65]

Under Secretary of State for Arms Control and International Security Ellen Tauscher delivered remarks in 2010 that criticized the Bush administration for its attempt to restrict access to ENR technologies, while indicating that the Obama administration would work toward the same ends through different means—guarantee of supply through an international fuel bank.

> The previous administration proposed to ban these technologies for states that do not already possess them. The problem was that all other countries opposed this approach because they viewed it as an infringement on their sovereignty and on their Non-Proliferation Treaty rights to peaceful nuclear technology. Moreover, the very insistence that others not obtain such capabilities increased demand for them by creating the impression that we are seeking to establish a suppliers' cartel. Instead of reassurance, this had the opposite effect. As President Obama said in Prague, 'no approach will succeed if it's based on the denial of rights to nations that play by the rules.' So the administration is focusing on creating incentives for states considering nuclear energy to choose not to pursue sensitive fuel cycle technologies.[66]

A focus on creating guarantees by strengthening existing national commitments on the part of suppliers through longer-term contracts and government guarantees of commercial agreements and to develop and implement international fuel supply guarantees, possibly through an IAEA-administered international fuel bank, would not encounter the same level of legitimacy concerns as the supply restraint did. These proposals assure a nuclear fuel supply to encourage states voluntarily not to pursue their own indigenous enrichment and reprocessing facilities. Should the supply guarantee or international fuel bank be combined with a supplier-driven embargo or pressure, it would encounter many of the same legitimacy problems as the original Bush proposal. If the supply assurance stands alone as a positive incentive, it would avoid this stumbling block. While it would then likely be viewed as more legitimate by nontechnology holders and thereby more likely gain their general support, it might not be as effective at limiting the spread of enrichment and reprocessing technology, since the incentive might not dissuade countries determined to acquire these technologies.

Involving the IAEA in assuring supply through some type of fuel bank has more legitimacy than a simply bilateral assurance of supply, since parties would negotiate this agreement through multilateral processes and be involved in the management of the bank. Were this to be accompanied by an agreement to give up national rights to develop these technologies indigenously from this point forward, this agreement would lose substantive legitimacy due to discrimination but retain procedural legitimacy. It ultimately would still not necessarily prevent states from proceeding with national development of sensitive technologies since participation would be voluntary. Nevertheless, if states continue to refuse to support a ban on the further spread of sensitive nuclear technology, this alternative provides a more effective solution. While many technical issues appeared to problematize the creation of a fuel bank, the Obama administration and the IAEA have overcome them.[67]

The Obama administration has worked closely with the IAEA to create a fuel bank and to finesse differences between Russia and the IAEA over Russia's creation of a fuel cycle center in Angarsk. After long negotiations, the IAEA Board of Governors approved unanimously the creation of an IAEA fuel bank in December 2010. The Obama administration engaged in extensive lobbying and worked to build as broad of a consensus as possible. A requirement of receiving fuel from the bank is to have a full-scope, comprehensive safeguard agreement with the IAEA in force. While some have tried to frame the fuel bank as requiring states to forgo national ENR, the IAEA background memo was clear in opposing that view:

> The rights of Member States, including establishing or expanding their own production capacity in the nuclear fuel cycle, shall remain intact and shall

not in any way be compromised or diminished by the establishment of international assurance of supply mechanisms. Thus, having the right to receive LEU [low-enriched uranium] from the guaranteed supply mechanism shall not require giving up the right to establish or further develop a national fuel cycle or have any impact on it. The additional options for assurance of supply shall be in addition to the rights that exist at present.[68]

Nevertheless, the Angarsk arrangement for fuel supply seems to have convinced Kazakhstan and Ukraine and possibly Armenia and Mongolia, but not Iran, to refrain from pursuing enrichment.[69] But the bank itself therefore maintains both procedural and substantive legitimacy.

In practice, while the Obama administration assisted the creation of an international fuel bank, it also continues to encourage states to voluntarily renounce their right to ENR technologies in exchange for peaceful nuclear cooperation. This effort, nevertheless, is less illegitimate than a requirement for renunciation as a condition of supply. The voluntary renunciation of a sovereign right to sensitive technologies is tied to bilateral cooperation agreements (though not required), opening the United States to the criticism that it places a restraint on supply of technology. Furthermore, the Obama administration maintains the same position in the NSG on the criteria for supply of sensitive technology as the Bush administration had in its last few months. The emphasis on negotiating with recipient states rather than going through the NSG increases the procedural legitimacy of the strategy, since each state retains its sovereign right to agree or disagree and still retain access to U.S. peaceful assistance. It remains to be seen whether the effort to enshrine this as the model for peaceful cooperation agreements will be successful. While the United Arab Emirates (UAE) agreed to language binding it not to pursue national ENR capabilities, Jordan, Saudi Arabia, and Bahrain agreed that it was their intention to rely on international supply rather than national ENR, but that they were not legally bound to do so.[70]

India-NSG Exception The Bush administration created in 2005 a special exception for India in nuclear cooperation. The U.S.-India civil nuclear agreement allows India to receive technology and materials for its peaceful nuclear program. It requires India to separate its military and civilian programs, agree to IAEA safeguards on its civilian facilities, adhere to a Model Additional Protocol with the IAEA, and be a strong proponent for nuclear nonproliferation, including maintaining its moratorium on testing, supporting the negotiation of a Fissile Materials Cut-off Treaty (FMCT), and securing its nuclear materials and technology through a strong export control regime. In return, the United States promised to work toward full civilian nuclear cooperation.[71] In order for this to be achieved, the United States had to convince the NSG to make an exception for India, a non-NPT party, without full-scope safeguards to allow for peaceful cooperation, and overturn decades-long U.S. nonproliferation policy banning such cooperation. This ban includes India since it would only be allowed to join the NPT as a nonnuclear weapons state.[72]

After three years of U.S. pressure, the NSG agreed to the India exception in 2008, permitting full civilian nuclear cooperation. While several members were reluctant, commercial interests in several nations pushed for the exception.[73] The NSG's guidelines require that all nonnuclear weapons states permit full-scope IAEA safeguards. Indeed, the NSG was originally created in part in response to India's 1974 "peaceful explosive test." The NSG operated under consensus, so all parties had to agree not to block the waiver. Even in the last few days before the September 6 meeting, Austria, Ireland, the Netherlands, Norway, New Zealand, and Switzerland called for strengthening the text to require a termination of cooperation if India were to conduct another nuclear test and prohibit sensitive ENR technology transfer. India sharply responded that it wanted a "clean" waiver. These conditions were dropped after a statement by the Indian foreign minister committing India to continue its moratorium on nuclear testing and a reference in the text of the final decision that it was "based on the commitments and actions" of Indian foreign minister Mukherjee.[74] Several states, including New Zealand, Japan, the Netherlands, and Ireland, made statements during the final agreement maintaining that the NSG exception would terminate if India tests in contradiction to those statements. Nevertheless, the document does not include any automatic termination language but requires that group to meet if circumstances arise.[75]

The final decision met with complete silence according to a diplomat present in the September 6 meeting. Another diplomat described the decision to a Reuters' journalist as "NPT RIP?"[76] Many diplomats felt significant pressure from the United States not to continue to stand in the way of the agreement. The final text includes a repeat of the then current NSG guidelines calling for suppliers to exercise restraint in transferring sensitive technology and states that transfers of sensitive technology exports remain subject to paragraphs 6 and 7.[77] Since the NSG then agreed to new guidelines replacing the "restraints" language of these paragraphs with objective criteria, India does not qualify for transfers of sensitive technology. While this has angered the Indians who claim they received a "clean" waiver, the Obama administration has stated that it fully supports India's clean waiver but reiterates that the text states that sensitive exports remain subject to paragraphs 6 and 7, which were amended to include the new criteria and therefore apply to India.[78]

In this entire case, the Bush and Obama administrations have not held very different positions. They both support closer ties with India and argue that the India exception has no bearing on Pakistan or Israel, who have both lobbied unsuccessfully for a similar waiver. Both administrations see India as a good ally on nonproliferation and wish to use subjective criteria to allow for its inclusion. Supporters of the deal have all focused on the strategic interests of the states involved. India does not pose a security threat to the states involved and has a consistent and strong track record in nonproliferation. Indeed, the goal is to emphasize the differential treatment of a second-tier proliferator like Pakistan and a strong supporter of second-tier nonproliferation actions like India.[79] The assumption is that NPT adherence and compliance is determined by the strategic interests of the state, and therefore the India agreement should have no significant impact on other regions.[80]

Indeed, the Obama administration has proposed that India should be invited to become a member of the NSG and three other export control regimes, even though the NSG and Wassenaar Arrangements both have a requirement of NPT membership.[81] This appears to continue the same logic of differential treatment based on the type of state rather than the application of objective criteria to all states. In order to bring India into the NSG, either the admission criteria would need to be amended "in a manner that would accurately describe India's situation," or the NSG would have to recognize that the objective criteria, known as "Factors to Be Considered," are not "mandatory" criteria enabling a state to join even if it does not necessarily meet all the factors.[82] The first option would create new objective criteria that weaken the NPT as the cornerstone of the nonproliferation regime. The second would weaken the legitimacy of the regime by not holding all states to the same objective and mandatory criteria. The Obama administration states that it does not view this as a unique exception for India, as the 2008 waiver was. Rather, a U.S. state department official argues that it "signals an effort to begin discussions on 'evolving' the membership criteria" of the NSG and other export control regimes so that non-NPT member states can become eligible.[83] This policy weighs the effectiveness of the regime against its legitimacy. If main nuclear states are excluded from the export control regime, proliferation is more likely. However, if they are included even though they do not accept the same obligations of the other members, discrimination is enhanced. Regardless of the option selected, the policy would continue to weaken the legitimacy of the nuclear nonproliferation regime by undermining the principle of universality.

Nondiscrimination should apply *within* the regime for it to enjoy legitimacy. However, this does not imply that parties to the NPT should be treated the same as nonparties. Already under strain because of the special prerogatives of parties with nuclear weapons, the regime is weakened by the creation of a separate category of states outside the regime whose possession of nuclear weapons is recognized and accepted. The joint agreement does just that. While India promises to strengthen its control over nuclear material to prevent its theft or sale as well as meet nuclear safety standards to prevent catastrophes, among other commitments, these positive aspects come at a high cost. The agreement effectively recognizes India, a state that has openly declared its possession of nuclear weapons and refused to adhere to the NPT, as deserving the same treatment as any other nuclear power. India gains the same benefits to peaceful nuclear cooperation as parties to the NPT without the obligations of nonnuclear weapons states. India agrees to separate its civilian from its military nuclear program and allow IAEA inspections in its civilian nuclear program, as all other nuclear weapons states do. Indeed, the India-specific Additional Protocol does not include complementary access or environmental sampling provisions that would permit the IAEA to search for an undisclosed military nuclear program, and India did not agree to disclose to the IAEA any nuclear fuel-cycle-related research and development, nuclear-related imports, and uranium mining.[84]

This recognition seriously weakens the legitimacy of the regime. The agreement does not violate the legal obligation of either India or the United States since the NPT does not ban cooperation on civilian nuclear energy (properly safeguarded) with nonparties. Legality is not the same as legitimacy, however. If states outside the treaty receive the same benefits as those within it without the concomitant obligations, then the incentive to join and remain in the treaty is severely diminished. Combined with the slow progress toward nuclear disarmament, it may encourage some states that only joined the NPT in the 1990s, such as Brazil, to reconsider their support.

It is not possible to pursue special exceptions to general principles on the basis of the political interests of a few states without eroding the legitimacy of the regime itself. Effectiveness may require such a policy. However, in this case, India has no interest in proliferating nuclear weapons to any other actors. Larger strategic interests may support such a policy, but it is important to recognize the trade-off. Perhaps more crucially, the agreement undermines the effort to deny Iran the same civilian capabilities. Nonproliferation cannot only apply to certain "bad" states. Some make the argument that India should be treated differently because it has never legally violated any of its nonproliferation obligations. While a legal distinction between members and nonmembers exists, it is not a firm basis for a political distinction between the two as it lacks legitimacy.

Disarmament

It is on disarmament issues that one can see the sharpest break between the Bush and Obama administrations. While the Bush administration was barely willing to reconfirm the basic disarmament obligation from Article VI, the Obama administration is willing to place zero as a goal and speak of steps by which one can achieve total nuclear disarmament. While the Bush administration refused to include verification measures in the Strategic Offensive Reductions Treaty (SORT) or in any negotiation of a Fissile Material Cut-off Treaty (FMCT), the Obama administration is attempting to strengthen the verified arms control regime by resurrecting the Comprehensive Nuclear-Test-Ban Treaty (CTBT), bringing into effect New START with strong verification measures and pressing for the negotiation of a verifiable FMCT. Finally, while the Bush administration increased the role of nuclear weapons in U.S. defense in the 2001 Nuclear Posture Review, Obama limited their use in the 2010 NPR.

The Bush administration's position on disarmament was based on a fundamental mistrust of arms control and verification. Bush administration policies were based on the usefulness of nuclear weapons for national security. While the Obama administration concurs on the current usefulness of nuclear weapons, it holds a different vision for the future, committing America "to seek the peace and security of a world without nuclear weapons."[85] In order to move concretely toward this future and lead others, Obama promised to reduce the role of nuclear weapons in the security strategy, to reduce warheads and stockpiles, to pursue a global ban on nuclear testing, to cut off the material necessary to build bombs, and to strengthen the nuclear nonproliferation regime.

The Obama administration thereby argues that the goal of preventing proliferation of nuclear weapons and the goal of disarmament are connected. As stated in the 2010 NPR, "By demonstrating that we take seriously our NPT obligation to pursue nuclear disarmament, we strengthen our ability to mobilize broad international support for the measures needed to reinforce the non-proliferation regime and secure nuclear materials worldwide."[86] It believes that if states break the rules, the structure of the nonproliferation regime can help assure that they will face consequences. The Obama administration believes that if it can strengthen all parts of the regime, it will be harder for states to break the rules and get away with it. The Bush administration held that they could strengthen just the nonproliferation aspects of the regime without addressing concerns regarding disarmament or peaceful uses. As Ellen Tauscher, under secretary of state for arms control and international security, said in a speech in Omaha on July 29, 2010:

> We are not so naïve as to believe that problem states will end their proliferation programs if the United States and Russia reduce our nuclear arsenals. But we are confident that progress in this area will reinforce the central role of the NPT and help us build support to sanction or engage states on favorable terms to us. Our collective ability to bring the weight of international pressure against proliferators would be undermined by a lack of effort towards disarmament.

This is an argument based on legitimacy, though not explicitly. The longstanding U.S. policy has been that nonproliferation and disarmament are "two sides of the same coin" and reinforce one another. But the logic why one cannot prevail if the other is neglected is not spelled out. The assumption is that disarmament makes states more willing to engage in nonproliferation efforts because it strengthens the basic bargain. But the reason why this bargain was struck is grounded in legitimacy as stated above. Nonproliferation policies without efforts on disarmament simply re-emphasize and activate states' concerns with the basic discrimination within the NPT.

New START With New START, the Obama administration returned to the reliance on verifiable, legally binding reductions of nuclear weapons. Unlike the SORT, New START re-created the extensive and complex verification regime in 2011 originally created by START I, which lapsed in 2009. While SORT reduced deployed strategic nuclear warheads to between 2,200 and 1,700, New START reduces deployed strategic nuclear warheads to 1,550 and limits deployed strategic delivery vehicles to 700 and deployed and nondeployed launchers to 800.[87]

While the Obama administration claims that this is a reduction of 30 percent below SORT levels, the measure is only valid if one relies on the higher limit from SORT. Exploitable counting rules (i.e., one nuclear warhead will be counted for each deployed nuclear bomber)[88] further limit the "bold" nature of the promise.[89] The treaty covers only deployed strategic warheads and delivery vehicles and all launchers. It does not include warhead stockpiles or nonstrategic nuclear weapons. Now, it is unfair to blame the United States alone for the limited nature of the agreement. The Russians are well known for refusing to consider negotiations over nonstrategic nuclear weapons, since they rely on their larger number to counterbalance NATO's stronger conventional forces. New START includes reductions of nuclear weapons, but the overall impact of these reductions to total disarmament is limited. The arms control endeavor continues to be a game played by the United States and Russia alone, since the numbers do not begin to reach down to Chinese nuclear weapons levels, much less to British and French levels. The Obama administration returned to the language and treaty-reliant behavior of arms control that had been the practice of all American administrations preceding President George W. Bush. While welcomed, this does not change the overall disappointment by many nonnuclear weapons states over the pace of disarmament. Indeed, expectations had been raised by the Prague speech, and many—including American allies—feel disappointed by the lack of transformative changes.

Comprehensive Nuclear-Test-Ban Treaty President Obama's oratory appears to go significantly farther than his actions. In his Prague speech, he set forth the goal for a global ban on nuclear testing and promised that his administration would "immediately and aggressively pursue U.S. ratification of the Comprehensive Test Ban Treaty."[90] This policy overturned the Bush administration position that it would not seek CTBT ratification. Two years after Prague, there have been briefings of senators and their staffs on the CTBT, funding for the Comprehensive Nuclear-Test-Ban Treaty Organization (CTBTO) Preparatory Committee that is tasked with developing the framework to administer the global test ban once the treaty comes into force, support for the International Monitoring System (IMS) stations that assist detecting tests worldwide, participation by Secretary of State Hillary Clinton at the CTBTO annual meeting, and more speeches by administration officials explaining why the CTBT is important and feasible to American national security.[91] But there are no signs that the administration intends to request again for Senate consent for ratification. Indeed, some believe that the administration had to choose between requesting Senate consent for New START and CTBT and chose New START.[92]

The significant effort necessary to prepare for a Senate ratification debate is simply not yet apparent. Under Secretary Tauscher argues that this effort is just about to begin. She argues that the administration did not choose between New START and CTBT, but rather that New START laid the groundwork for making the case for CTBT by educating a new crop of senators on nuclear issues and our stockpile. The argument that the administration will make is based on three points: that we do not need to test to maintain our arsenal; that a CTBT in force will obligate those around the world not to test and create a disincentive; and that we now have a greater ability to detect cheaters.[93] The CTBT will only come into force when China, Egypt, India, Indonesia, Iran, Israel, North Korea, Pakistan, and the United States ratify it. The IMS system is now 75 percent complete and easily detected the North Korean tests in 2006 and 2009. Yet, those who oppose it, including Senator John Kyl (R), doubt that our ratification is likely to encourage others to do the same, doubt the capability of the verification measures, doubt that states would enforce the decision in a timely fashion even if they detected a test, and argue that there may come a time when the United States will want to test to protect its national security.[94] We will see if the administration can move beyond words to convince the reluctant Senate.

Fissile Material Cut-off Treaty The Fissile Material Cut-off Treaty has been blocked from starting negotiations in the Conference on Disarmament (CD) for over a decade. While there were various states that refused to agree to the work plan for the conference for different reasons, the debate over FMCT changed significantly when the Bush administration amended America's stance to pursue negotiations on a FMCT only if it did not include verification measures. The argument is the same that one sees threading throughout the Bush administration's overall logic on disarmament. Treaties cannot be 100 percent verifiable; therefore, if we include verification measures that may fail to detect cheaters, we are making ourselves less safe than if we did not have the treaty in the first place. Enforcement is not likely, so relying on cooperation is not beneficial to our security. We would have a false sense of security that would lead us to act in ways that were detrimental to our national security. This argument against verification and legally binding measures has been made by neoconservatives in the Ford, Reagan, Bush, and Bush II administrations. However, these critics of verification did not convince any Republican president to forgo verification in arms control until

President George H. Bush. The reaction of the international community against the U.S. position was strong and provided a cover to those states that did not want to negotiate an FMCT anyway. When combined with the successful U.S. effort to block a verification regime for the Biological Weapons Convention in 2006, it demonstrated a lack of willingness to create and rely upon multilateral and transparent international organizations.

The Obama administration changed the U.S. position on FMCT to return to the goal of negotiating a verifiable FMCT. The United States has pushed strongly through diplomatic channels to convince holdout states to allow the Conference on Disarmament to begin negotiations. After more than a decade of deadlock in the CD had prevented even an agreement on a work plan for negotiations, it appeared that U.S. efforts had succeeded in 2009 when the CD agreed to begin negotiations on the FMCT, a ban on space-based weapons, and an agreement by NWS not to use nuclear weapons against nonnuclear weapons states and on nuclear disarmament. However, the agreement was short-lived. Pakistan had been the last remaining holdout blocking consensus in the CD to begin negotiations. India promised in the bilateral civilian nuclear agreement with the United States to support negotiations for an FMCT, though not necessarily to agree to join it. Although Pakistan had initially agreed to the work plan, it quickly withdrew its consent. In response, a number of states began informally to discuss the possibility of moving negotiations on the FMCT out of the CD. A group of ten states has urged the UN General Assembly "to consider ways to proceed with the aim of beginning negotiations."[95] France, the United Kingdom, and the United States have joined the others to support exploration of this move.[96] The Obama administration at all levels has emphasized that the U.S. preference is to negotiate the FMCT within the CD, but it is becoming increasingly doubtful that the conference can achieve consensus.[97] UN Secretary General Ban Ki-moon has argued for a specially formed commission or a UN conference, stating that "the CD should not be held perpetually hostage by one or two members. Concerns should be addressed through negotiations."[98] Thus the argument is not between multilateral and unilateral, but among different multilateral bodies in which many governments are represented.

Everyone recognizes that in order to be successful all the permanent members of the UN Security Council (P-5), in addition to other interested parties, must participate. While China had remained outside the discussions in the beginning,[99] the P-5 agreed in July to take steps to renew efforts with other relevant parties to promote FMCT negotiations.[100] This includes the creation of a contact group that would support negotiations for the FMCT in the CD by initiating preliminary technical discussions outside the CD forum.[101] The United States, among others, has considered how the Conference on Disarmament's procedures could be amended to provide continuity on agreed programs of work from year to year. While the Obama administration has not wanted to directly attack the consensus rule, it argues that the rules should prevent its abuse, while taking into consideration national security interests.[102] The Obama administration also seeks to balance the desire for inclusivity in expanding the membership of the CD with considerations of the impact on effectiveness, noting that the CD has failed to function since its expansion to sixty-five members in 1996.[103]

Pakistan is adamantly opposed to any efforts to move the negotiations outside of the CD. Pakistan's UN ambassador Raza Bashir Tarar declares: "The problems faced by the Conference on Disarmament are not of an organizational or procedural nature," adding that world powers are pursuing a fissile material production ban after having built "huge stockpiles of nuclear weapons."[104] Tarar further critiques those who criticize the CD's inactivity by arguing that it "cannot negotiate through cherry-picking issues that some states consider ripe," referring to "a clear pattern of negotiating only those agreements that do not undermine or compromise the security interest of powerful states."[105] The critiques go to the heart of the procedural legitimacy of an institution, in which all states' interests and voices are considered and no states have control over the agenda. The Obama administration has recently halted its attempt to find a new forum for FMCT negotiations, acknowledging that "'forum shopping' is not a good idea for FMCT negotiations."[106] Instead, it aims to focus on amending the CD procedures. The entire effort has indicated the Obama administration's commitment to start FMCT negotiations, while taking into account concerns of perceptions of legitimacy. Although it has been unsuccessful to date in overcoming Pakistani objection to negotiating a FMCT, its policy has remained diametrically opposed to the previous Bush administration that used the CD deadlock to avoid negotiations in a treaty that it did not support.[107]

Nuclear Posture Review The two administrations have also had relatively different foci on the role and importance of nuclear weapons in U.S. national security as demonstrated by the differences between the 2001 and 2010 Nuclear Posture Reviews (NPR). The Bush administration emphasized the potential for nuclear weapons to assist in the global fight against terror and did not consider the impact that the increased potential for the use of nuclear weapons might have on others' behaviors. The Obama administration explicitly took into account the potential effect of a reduced reliance on nuclear weapons on other states' policies. Gary Samore, the White House coordinator for WMD counterterrorism and arms control, proliferation, and terrorism, stated this publicly: "as we crafted the [NPR] document, [we] very consciously intended to influence the perceptions of different foreign audiences. And of course, since different foreign audiences have different interests and perspectives, the document reflects a balance in terms of how we crafted the language and the substance of the review."[108]

The 2001 NPR envisioned nuclear weapons as providing options for deterring a "wide range of threats," including nuclear and large-scale conventional forces. Nuclear weapons were viewed as playing a "unique" role in deterring biological and chemical weapons attacks, and they possessed "unique properties that give the United States options to hold at risk classes of targets."[109] The Bush administration was criticized most vehemently for implying that existing nuclear capabilities were insufficient to attack deeply buried targets and therefore new nuclear weapons should be developed, termed "robust nuclear earth penetrator" weapons.[110] States listed as possible nuclear targets were Iran, Iraq, North Korea, Libya, Syria, and possibly China. The implication was clear that the United States would be willing to consider using nuclear weapons against states that had not necessarily attacked the country with nuclear weapons or indeed even possessed them.

The 2010 NPR departed significantly from that of its predecessor. The main goals are preventing nuclear proliferation and nuclear terrorism, reducing the role of nuclear weapons in U.S. national strategy, maintaining strategic deterrence and stability at reduced nuclear force levels, strengthening regional deterrence and reassuring U.S. allies, and sustaining a safe, secure, and effective nuclear arsenal.[111] The range of possible first use was diminished. While the 2001 NPR allowed the first use of nuclear weapons in response to a biological or chemical weapons attack, the 2010 NPR explicitly disallows first use in those cases (though it reserves the right to change this policy if biological weapons transform the security situation dramatically).[112] The 2010 NPR also provides a stronger negative security assurance than previous U.S. policy, promising not to use or threaten to use nuclear weapons against nonnuclear weapons states party to the NPT and in compliance with their nonproliferation obligations.[113]

For those countries that do not fall under the assurance, the United States envisions a "narrow range of contingencies" in which it would use nuclear weapons to deter a conventional or a chemical and biological weapons (CBW) attack, which does not result in any increase in likelihood of first use against these states.[114] While these unnamed states include some of the ones named in the 2001 NPR, such as Iran, North Korea, Syria, and potentially China (as a NWS), it creates objective criteria for inclusion in the group that aims to encourage states to adhere to the NPT. However, the 2010 NPR does not single out China as a potential adversary but rather treats China in a manner similar to Russia.[115] India, Pakistan, and Israel could also face such deterrence due to their refusal to join the NPT as nonnuclear weapons states. Not only does this increase the benefits for NPT adherence, but it also increases the potential penalties against those who remain outside the regime. Obviously, it does not mean that the United States would either anticipate an attack from such states or respond in the same way. Finally, it is important that the United States reserves the right to determine whether or not a state is in compliance with its NPT nonproliferation obligations for itself.[116] This unilateral determination has led to some criticism, as had the absence of a legally binding negative security assurance, rather than a political policy that could change.[117]

Overall, there is a substantial change, though not a "fundamental rethinking" of the role of nuclear weapons.[118] First use of nuclear weapons remains an option in a reduced set of circumstances, and "no first use" is not an explicit goal. There is no reduction in the operational status of deployed nuclear weapons beyond New START. The triad of nuclear weapons platforms remains.[119] Is this enough, combined with the words and goodwill on CTBT and FMCT and the entry into force of New START?

One cannot deny the overall significant difference between the two U.S. administrations over disarmament. However, the outlier was the Bush administration. In many respects, the Obama administration simply returned to the standard American policies of previous administrations, with incremental improvements. Some argue that incrementalism can never lead to "global zero." Rather, signal events need to punctuate the incremental policies.[120] New START incrementally decreases the levels of nuclear weapons, and the effort to ratify the CTBT and negotiate a FMCT returns to the Clinton administration's policies. The 2010 NPR reduces the U.S. reliance on nuclear weapons and reiterates its former nonlegally binding negative security assurance. This is substantial progress over where the United States was before the Obama administration, but it is not the transformative change that Obama promised in Prague. Indeed, even the embrace of the goal of zero reiterates the "fundamental undertaking" from the 2000 NPT Review Conference's Final Document. Nevertheless, as measured according to the "13 Practical Steps" from the same document, the change in the U.S. position has led to significant progress.[121]

IMPACT OF STRENGTHENING LEGITIMACY IN THE NONPROLIFERATION REGIME

Ultimately, what matters is whether changes of policy that influence the legitimacy of the nonproliferation regime affect other states' positions and actions. While it is too early to tell definitively, there are some suggestive indications that the Obama turnaround has influenced the strength of the nonproliferation regime and the level of support for the regime on the part of other states. One must also disaggregate the impact on changes to the legitimacy of the regime from other potential pathways that might also affect foreign state policies, including the impact on other states' national interests or threat perceptions, enabling domestic actors and changing bargaining structures.[122] It is quite likely that some states that disagree with particular nonproliferation aims due to their own national endeavors are likely to verbally use language of legitimacy to criticize a regime by which they would prefer not to be bound. Thus, if only states that have a fundamental difference of interest respond to changes, we should infer that the legitimacy criticisms are hortatory only. No one expects changes in U.S. policy or rhetoric to change the goals of a state with strong nuclear ambitions.[123] It is harder to disaggregate the path to policy change through enabling domestic actors from the legitimacy pathway. Certain actions that weaken the legitimacy of the regime are also likely to change the influence and persuasive capabilities domestically of the actors who support it and vice versa. Any changes to increase the transparency, qualitative multilateral nature—not only involving more actors but increasing their ability to influence the structure of disarmament and nonproliferation initiatives—and to reduce the perceived discriminatory nature of the regime are likely to bring new authority and influence to domestic actors with an interest in disarmament and nonproliferation. Finally, there may be good old-fashioned bargaining that may lead states to be more willing to support nonproliferation initiatives that the United States desires if they get more of what they want on disarmament. It is very difficult to distinguish this quid pro quo from a policy change due to a change in the legitimacy of the regime. The linkage between disarmament and nonproliferation and peaceful uses and nonproliferation results from both the bargaining of disparate interests and the effort to limit the discrimination within the regime itself. These pathways are also not mutually exclusive. Legitimacy assists institutions that are based on self-interest and vice versa.

Nevertheless, we certainly know that states respond to changes in U.S. policy on nonproliferation. Many states criticized the United States for the increase in reliance on nuclear weapons in the 2001 NPR.[124] Others, including several close allies, expressed concern that the changes and emphasis on unilateralism generally would have potential adverse effects on nonproliferation. Close allies were particularly concerned about the process by which the 2001 NPR had been developed, without close consultation.[125] While it is hard to say for certain that the difficulties that the Bush administration encountered gaining support for its nonproliferation initiatives, including the ban on ENR and PSI, were directly due to its unilateral policies, renewed reliance on nuclear weapons, and reluctance to reiterate U.S. support for disarmament, we know that states spent significant energy criticizing the United States for its policies, and the level of acrimony was heightened in international forums, including the 2005 NPT Review Conference (RevCon) and the Conference on Disarmament.

Similarly, we can see that the change in rhetoric and policy in the Obama administration coincided with a renewed cooperative spirit in the 2010 NPT RevCon. A survey on the impact of the 2010 NPR found convincing evidence that Britain and Russia amended their nuclear strategies to reduce reliance on nuclear weapons in response to U.S. leadership, and at least Indonesia started the process of ratifying the CTBT as a result, though the study found minimal impact on China, France, India, and Pakistan.[126] The same study argues that the new Obama administration's nuclear policy, including the NPR, helped produce a positive outcome at the 2010 NPT RevCon. Indeed, a content analysis of the statements of the parties at the 2010 NPT RevCon demonstrates that of the sixty-nine times the Obama administration's new policies on disarmament and nonproliferation were mentioned, only three instances were negative.[127] Those negative comments were by Iran and Cuba. While Brazil and Egypt, two influential Non-Aligned Movement (NAM) members, continued to be critical of U.S. policies including the 2010 NPR, they played a constructive role at the 2010 NPT RevCon, preventing radical NAM members Iran and Syria from destroying the final document that was agreed to by consensus.[128]

Although states reacted positively at the 2010 NPT RevCon to the Obama administration arms control and disarmament policy changes, they also were aware that the United States had made promises in the past that it had not kept. In particular, the United States promised to bring the CTBT into force as part of the decision for indefinite extension of the NPT at the 1995 NPT Review and Extension Conference, but it failed to follow through.[129] This makes it more difficult to determine at this early period the impact of the Obama administration policies, until there is more follow-through on promises. And in many policies, there is a change in the procedure and rhetoric, but not in the substance of the effort. This applies most particularly to the attempt to restrict the supply of sensitive nuclear ENR technology to new states. While some may be hedging and hoping to hold onto the possibility of pursuing ENR at some future date if need be, some opposition to the restraint on peaceful nuclear cooperation without a doubt derives from "sensitivity about any apparent inequality in the terms of international agreements that divide the world into 'haves' and 'have-nots.'"[130] Brazil was more willing to allow nonbinding language to be included calling for the Additional Protocol and multinational fuel cycle centers than previously, but unwilling to allow any new standards for peaceful cooperation. Harald Müller argues that this was due to the positive environment created by the change in U.S. policies.[131]

The turnaround in U.S. policy was most important for creating a conducive atmosphere that opened the bargaining space for negotiations with the New Agenda Coalition (NAC) and Non-Aligned Movement (NAM). The NAC, headed by Egypt, welcomed the U.S. progress in disarmament, in particular the Prague speech, New START, and the 2010 NPR.[132] The NAM, also headed by Egypt, was not so impressed, describing New START as a "positive, but insufficient development."[133] Müller argues that Egypt would have been unlikely to have been able to "deliver" the NAM to compromise without the positive developments in disarmament and the expectation of more progress. Many of the NAM members mentioned the importance of the "good atmosphere" in allowing work to progress. The change in U.S. policy that strengthened the legitimacy of the NPT undermined support for Iran's attempts to derail the compromise.[134]

Legitimacy is one powerful mechanism for encouraging actors to participate and comply with their promises. In this case, the change did not require a significant change in ultimate goals, merely a change in strategy. While not costless, it is important to consider the potential implication of taking into account legitimacy in addition to interest. If actors, in this case states, believe the rules are legitimate, they internalize the rules and are therefore more likely to follow them and repudiate those who defy them. Any actions that weaken the legitimacy of a regime make it more difficult to achieve universality as states are unlikely to participate in a regime they view as unequal and unfair. While building legitimacy may dilute the ability of a proposal to achieve the ultimate desired goal, without legitimacy, unilateral efforts will likely face difficulties in ensuring the participation and commitment of all the actors necessary for their effective functioning. Efforts to engage in strengthening the legitimacy of the overall regime, while not a panacea, do make states generally more willing to cooperate in the goals of the regime.

Notes

This chapter is in part based on previous work by the author. See Nina Srinivasan Rathbun, "The Role of Legitimacy in Strengthening the Nuclear Nonproliferation Regime," *Nonproliferation Review* 13, no. 2 (2006).

1. The safeguards regime was greatly strengthened following the first Gulf War, with the adoption of the Model Additional Protocol. With the unveiling of long-standing Iranian, Libyan, and Syrian covert nuclear programs, however, new questions have been raised.

2. For a background on the network, see David Albright and Corey Hinderstein, "Unraveling the A. Q. Khan and Future Proliferation Networks," *Washington Quarterly* 28, no. 2 (2005): 111–28; and Esther Pan, "Nonproliferation: The Pakistan Network," Council on Foreign Relations, February 12, 2004, http://www.cfr.org/background/nonpro.php.

3. Andrew Grotto, "Why Do States That Oppose Nuclear Proliferation Resist New Nonproliferation Obligations? Three Logics of Nonproliferation Decision-making," *Cardozo Journal of International Comparative Law* 18, no. 1 (2010): 1–44.

4. For the full text of President Bush's speech, see http://www.whitehouse.gov/the_press_office/Remarks-By-President-Barack-Obama-In-Prague-As-Delivered; see also "Joint Statement between President George W. Bush and Prime Minister Manmohan Singh," July 18, 2005, http://georgewbush-whitehouse.archives.gov/news/releases/2005/07/20050718-6.html.

5. Ian Hurd, "Legitimacy and Authority in International Politics," *International Organization* 53, no. 2 (1999): 379–408.

6. For different perspectives on compliance, see Beth A. Simmons, "Compliance with International Agreements" *Annual Review of Political Science* 1, no. 1 (1998): 75–93; Abram Chayes and Antonia Handler Chayes, "On Compliance," *International Organization* 47, no. 2 (1993): 175–205. Chayes and Chayes emphasize that noncompliance can be due to very different reasons. While some noncompliance may be due to a state's active decision to derogate, other instances of noncompliance may be due to administrative failures of a weak state. Chayes and Chayes argue that the latter is more common.

7. Hurd, "Legitimacy and Authority"; Max Weber, *Economy and Society: An Outline of Interpretive Sociology*, vol. 1 (Berkeley: University of California Press, 1978).

8. Hurd makes an important point that in order for the concept of self-interest to be potentially falsifiable, its boundaries need to be clearly drawn. Self-interest involves self-restraint rather than external enforcement. However, it must also be distinguished from merely "interested" behavior. It is "egoistic," in that the rules or relations with others do not themselves generate any loyalty on behalf of the self-interested actor. In each and every situation, the actor assesses its expected payoff and is ready to abandon any rule should an alternative provide greater benefits. See Hurd, "Legitimacy and Authority," 386–87.

9. See Abram Chayes and Antonia Handler Chayes, *The New Sovereignty: Compliance with International Regulatory Agreements* (Cambridge: Harvard University Press, 1995) for a good explanation of why agreements in which many parties cheat are unsustainable regardless of sanctions.

10. Mark C. Suchman, "Managing Legitimacy: Strategic and Institutional Approaches," *Academy of Management Review* 20, no. 3 (1995), 574.

11. Ernst Haas labels this process of internalization "learning." See Ernst Haas, *When Knowledge Is Power: Three Models of Change in International Organizations* (Berkeley: University of California Press, 1990).

12. John G. Ruggie, "Multilateralism: The Anatomy of an Institution," *International Organization* 46, no. 3 (1992): 571.

13. For an exhaustive account of different notions of justice and fairness, see Cecilia Albin, *Justice and Fairness in International Negotiation* (Cambridge: Cambridge University Press, 2001), ch. 2.

14. The United Nations, as the League of Nations before it, was based on this norm, which was further reinforced through the decolonization process of the 1950s and 1960s. See Robert H. Jackson and Carl G. Rosberg, "Why Africa's Weak States Persist: The Empirical and Juridical in Statehood," *World Politics* 35, no. 1 (1982): 1–24.

15. Albin, *Justice and Fairness*, 45–46, ch. 4, 100–140.

16. Thomas M. Franck, *The Power of Legitimacy among Nations* (New York: Oxford University Press, 1990), ch. 10.

17. Ian Hurd, "Legitimacy and Power in International Relations" (unpublished manuscript, n.d.), ch. 4.

18. Different measures of effectiveness lead to vastly different conclusions on the historical effectiveness of the nonproliferation regime. Critics of the regime tend to overlook the success of the regime in persuading states other than the few "rogue" states not to pursue nuclear weapons, and rather judge the regime solely in terms of its effectiveness in preventing North Korea and Iran from pursuing nuclear weapons. This difference leads to very different conceptions of how to "fix" the regime. For a good analysis of the consequences of these different measures, see Phillip C. Saunders, "New Approaches to Nonproliferation: Supplementing or Supplanting the Regime," *Nonproliferation Review* 8, no. 3 (2001): 123–36.

19. Franck, *Power of Legitimacy*.

20. While Waltz is the most outspoken arguing that the proliferation of nuclear weapons to many states would increase stability in international relations, many view nuclear weapons as making the bilateral relationship between the United States and the Soviet Union during the Cold War more stable. Kenneth N. Waltz, "The Spread of Nuclear Weapons: More May be Better," Adelphi Paper no. 171 (London, International Institute for Strategic Studies, 1981); John J. Weltman, "Nuclear Revolution and World Order," *World Politics* 32 (Spring 1980): 169–93. See national statements to the 2005 NPT Review Conference for a comprehensive overview of parties' positions on nuclear weapons, http://www.un.org/events/npt2005/statements02may.html.

21. Nuclear technology has a wide variety of applications beyond energy, including increasing agricultural yields, treating cancer, and managing water resources, among many others. See the IAEA website for more peaceful applications of nuclear science and technology, www.iaea.org.

22. See the history of the United Nations Atomic Energy Commission (UNAEC): Lawrence Scheinman, *The International Atomic Energy Agency and World Nuclear Order* (Washington, D.C., Resources for the Future, 1987), 49–51. For the original proposal, see "Joint Declaration by the Heads of Government of the United States, the United Kingdom, and Canada, November 15, 1945," in U.S. Department of State, Historical Office, Bureau of Public Affairs, *Documents on Disarmament, 1945–1957*, Pub. No. 7008, 2 vols. (Washington, D.C.: U.S. Government Printing Office, 1960), 1:1–2, as cited in Scheinman, *International Atomic Energy Agency*.

23. The plan was named after U.S. representative to the UNAEC Bernard Baruch, who wrote and presented it. Baruch was originally appointed by President Harry Truman to present what became known as the Acheson-Lilienthal report, after Undersecretary of State Dean Acheson and Atomic Energy Commission chairman David Lilienthal. Instead, Baruch "decided to make significant changes and promote the plan as his own. In particular, Baruch scuttled the notion of international ownership of the means of production of nuclear materials because it was not in keeping with the American free enterprise system." See Leonard Weiss, "Atoms for Peace," *Bulletin of the Atomic Scientists* 59, no. 6 (2003): 31–41, 44, http://thebulletin.org/2003/november/atoms-peace.

24. Scheinman, *International Atomic Energy Agency*, 52–55.

25. See the IAEA website, http://www.iaea.org/About/statute.html.

26. Scheinman, *International Atomic Energy Agency*, 123–24.

27. See "Treaty on the Non-Proliferation of Nuclear Weapons," http://www.un.org/disarmament/WMD/Nuclear/NPTtext.shtml for the text of the NPT.

28. The Zangger Committee (http://www.zanggercommittee.org/Seiten/default.aspx) was established in the early 1970s to define the materials and equipment that required controls. The Nuclear Suppliers Group (originally the London Group, see below),

founded in 1975, also formed to ensure that materials and equipment would not be misused for prohibited purposes.

29. NPT Article IV.

30. Joseph S. Nye, "NPT: The Logic of Inequality," *Foreign Policy*, no. 59 (1985): 123–31.

31. Ibid., 128.

32. Stephen D. Krasner, ed. *International Regimes* (Ithaca, N.Y.: Cornell University Press, 1983).

33. Roger K. Smith, "Explaining the Non-proliferation Regime: Anomalies for Contemporary International Relations Theory," *International Organization* 41, no. 2 (1987): 253–81.

34. Christopher Way and Karthika Sasikumar, "Leaders and Laggards: When and Why do Countries Sign the NPT?," REGIS Working Paper no. 16, November 2004, 33–34.

35. T.V. Paul, "Systemic Conditions and Security Cooperation: Explaining the Persistence of the Nuclear Non-proliferation Regime," *Cambridge Review of International Affairs* 16, no. 1 (2003): 135–54.

36. Tannenwald writes about a norm against the use of nuclear weapons, rather than the acquisition. Nina Tannenwald, *The Nuclear Taboo: The United States and the Non-use of Nuclear Weapons since 1945* (Cambridge: Cambridge University Press, 2005).

37. See Joseph S. Nye, "Maintaining a Nonproliferation Regime," *International Organization* 35, no. 1 (1981): 15–38. Some, however, argue that the decision to pursue nuclear weapons is a national decision that is unrelated to the nonproliferation regime. For different perspectives on why states pursue nuclear weapons, see Mitchell Reiss, *Bridled Ambition: Why Countries Constrain Their Nuclear Capabilities* (Washington, D.C.: Woodrow Wilson Center Press, 1995); Scott D. Sagan, "Why Do States Build Nuclear Weapons? Three Models in Search of a Bomb," *International Security* 21, no. 3 (1996/1997): 54–86; and Jacques E. C. Hymans, *The Psychology of Nuclear Proliferation: Identity, Emotions, and Foreign Policy* (Cambridge: Cambridge University Press, 2006).

38. India, Pakistan, and Israel never joined the NPT and therefore are not bound by its legal obligation not to acquire nuclear weapons or assist others in doing so. North Korea is the only NPT party believed to have possibly acquired nuclear weapons. See Joseph Cirincione, Jon B. Wolfsthal, and Miriam Rajkumar, *Deadly Arsenals: Nuclear, Biological and Chemical Threats*, 2nd ed. (Washington, D.C.: Carnegie Endowment for International Peace, 2005) ch. 14, 279–94, for a more detailed analysis of the North Korean program.

39. South Africa, Kazakhstan, Ukraine, and Belarus all gave up nuclear weapons, while Libya, Argentina, and Brazil, among others, gave up weapons programs. Many others including Japan, West Germany, Sweden, Italy, South Korea, and Switzerland gave up nuclear weapons ambitions. See Cirincione, Wolfsthal, and Rajkumar, *Deadly Arsenalsu*, part 5, 315–418, for a detailed factual account of these success stories. See Francis J. Gavin,

"Blasts for the Past: Proliferation Lessons from the 1960s," *International Security* 29, no. 3 (2004): 100–135 for a full account of the countries considering nuclear weapons and the possible proliferation waves the Johnson administration faced before negotiating the NPT.

40. The IAEA provides the predominant enforcement cost through its safeguards budget, which in 2004 was a little over $100 million, a very small cost relative to the amounts countries invest in their military budgets. For the 2004 IAEA budget, see http://www.iaea.org/About/budget.html. Other costs would include the cost of maintaining export controls.

41. North Korea announced its withdrawal from the NPT on January 10, 2003. See Jean du Preez and William Potter, "North Korea's Withdrawal from the NPT: A Reality Check," James Martin Center for Nonproliferation Studies, research report (April 8, 2003), http://cns.miis.edu/stories/030409.htm.

42. See International Atomic Energy Agency, *Multilateral Approaches to the Nuclear Fuel Cycle: Expert Group Report to the Director General of the IAEA*, (Vienna: International Atomic Energy Agency, 2005), 56–60, for an analysis of the different techniques for enriching uranium.

43. Although India was and is not a member of the NPT, its actions would have been permitted under the NPT Article V. This article is now effectively defunct following agreement on the Comprehensive Nuclear-Test-Ban Treaty. For an analysis of the India case and Western, particularly U.S., response, see Scheinman, *International Atomic Energy Agency*, 174–78.

44. The group included Belgium, Canada, Czechoslovakia, the Federal Republic of Germany, France, the German Democratic Republic, Italy, Japan, the Netherlands, Poland, Sweden, Switzerland, the Union of Soviet Socialist Republics, the United Kingdom, and the United States of America. For a history of the Nuclear Suppliers Group, see Tadeusz Stulak, "The Nuclear Suppliers Group," *Nonproliferation Review* 1, no. 1 (1993): 2–10; and Scheinman, *International Atomic Energy Agency*, 190–92. For a review of the internal dynamics of the NSG, see M. J. Wilmshurst, "The Development of Current Nonproliferation Policies," in *The International Nuclear Non-proliferation System: Challenges and Choices*, ed. John Simpson and Anthony G. McGrew (New York: St. Martin's Press, 1984), 28–38.

45. For the original guidelines agreed to by all fifteen members in 1977 and transmitted to the IAEA in 1978, see "Communication Received from Certain Member States Regarding Guidelines for the Export of Nuclear Material, Equipment or Technology," http://www.iaea.org/Publications/Documents/Infcircs/Others/infcirc254.shtml.

46. The broad interpretation of this right is clear from the historical record, even on the U.S. side. William Foster, then director of the Arms Control and Disarmament Agency, stated in his testimony before the Senate during the NPT ratification debates in 1968, "Neither uranium enrichment nor the stockpiling of fissionable material in connection with

a peaceful program would violate Article II so long as these activities were safeguarded under Article III. Also clearly permitted would be the development, under safeguards, of plutonium-fueled power reactors, including research on the properties of metallic plutonium." U.S. Arms Control and Disarmament, *Documents on Disarmament* (Washington, D.C.: U.S. ACDA, 1969), 504, as cited by Scheinman, *International Atomic Energy Agency*, 28–29. Germany also went to great lengths when signing the NPT to emphasize that "no nuclear activities ... for peaceful purposes are prohibited nor can the transfer of information, materials and equipment be denied to non-nuclear weapon states merely on the basis of allegations that such activities or transfers could be used for the manufacture of nuclear weapons or other nuclear explosive devices." *Documents on Disarmament*, 609–10, as quoted in Scheinman, *International Atomic Energy Agency*, 182. Non-Aligned Movement (NAM) members, including most developing countries, interpret this right in the same way.

47. Stulak, "Nuclear Suppliers Group, 5–6. These charges are also frequently made during NPT Review Conferences and its Preparatory Committee meeting. For records of recent NPT Review Conferences, see http://www.un.org/disarmament/WMD/Nuclear/NPT_Review_Conferences.shtml.

48. While the NSG has provoked significant opposition by some NPT parties, the Zangger Committee in contrast has remained relatively uncontroversial as a consequence of its acceptance of universal and nondiscriminatory rules in clarifying NPT obligations. The Zangger Committee developed to interpret Article III of the NPT, obligating parties not to provide "source or special fissionable material" or "equipment or material especially designed or prepared for processing, use, or production" of this material without the application of safeguards. Rather than preventing the acquisition of sensitive technology, the committee defines the types of activities requiring safeguards, and these definitions apply equally to all states. Unlike the NSG, it does not aim to prevent access to nuclear technology and equipment so it treats all states similarly. It involves all interested NPT parties in its deliberations to determine which materials and equipment require safeguards. This list of material and equipment forms the Zangger Committee's "trigger list" and has been continually updated by the committee as needed. See http://www.iaea.org/Publications/Documents/Infcircs/2000/infcirc209r2.pdf for more information.

49. For the full text of President Bush's speech, see http://georgewbush-whitehouse.archives.gov/news/releases/2007/10/20071023-3.html.

50. For an overview of various suppliers' plans, see International Atomic Energy Agency, *Multilateral Approaches*, 62–66.

51. Fred McGoldrick, *Limiting Transfers of Enrichment and Reprocessing Technology: Issues, Constraints, Options*, Project on Managing the Atom (Cambridge, Mass.: Belfer Center for Science and International Affairs, May 2011), 24.

52. Chaim Braun and Christopher F. Chyba, "Proliferation Rings: New Challenges to the Nuclear Nonproliferation Regime," *International Security* 29, no. 2 (2004): 5–49, and Saunders, "New Approaches to Nonproliferation," both recognize this change in supply mechanisms.

53. Daniel Horner, "NSG Revises Rules on Sensitive Exports," *Arms Control Today*, July/August 2011.

54. IAEA Information Circular, INFCIRC/254/Part 1.

55. INFCIRC/254/Rev. 1/Part 1. See McGoldrick, p. 7–8.

56. INFCIRC/Rev. 8/Part 1.

57. McGoldrick, *Limiting Transfers*, 13.

58. Ibid., 14.

59. Ibid., 15.

60. Ibid.

61. Ibid., 16.

62. Horner, "NSG Revises Rules."

63. As cited in ibid.

64. Ibid.

65. See Prague speech (2009), http://www.whitehouse.gov/the_press_office/Remarks-By-President-Barack-Obama-In-Prague-As-Delivered.

66. Ellen Tauscher, "Addressing the Nuclear Fuel Cycle," January 19, 201), speech delivered at the Hoover Institution, Stanford University, Stanford, Calif. See text from the speech at http://www.state.gov/t/us/136426.htm.

67. These issues include the question of whether it would be an actual bank or a virtual bank, addressing the different types of fuel used by reactors around the world, the financing of the bank, the pricing mechanism, the location, the location of the decision to stop supply on nonproliferation grounds, and the arbitration process for appealing decisions to stop supply, among many others.

68. Daniel Horner, "IAEA Board Approves Fuel Bank Plan," *Arms Control Today*, January/February 2011, http://www.armscontrol.org/act/2011_01-02/Fuel%20Bank.

69. McGoldrick, *Limiting Transfers*, 3–4.

70. Ibid., 29.

71. See U.S. White House, Office of the Press Secretary, "Joint Statement between President George W. Bush and Prime Minister Manmohan Singh," http://georgewbush-whitehouse.archives.gov/news/releases/2005/07/20050718-6.html, and U.S. Department of State, "Fact Sheet: United States and India: Strategic Partnership," http://georgewbush-whitehouse.archives.gov/news/releases/2006/03/20060302-13.html. For a good analysis of the issues, see Fred McGoldrick, Harold Bengelsdorf, and Lawrence Scheinman, "The U.S.-India Nuclear Deal: Taking Stock," *Arms Control Today* 35, no. 8 (2005): 6–12, http://www.armscontrol.org/act/2005_10/OCT-Cover.

72. Under the NPT, India is legally defined as a nonnuclear weapons state, regardless of its refusal to sign the treaty. The NPT defines a nuclear weapons state as "one which has manufactured and exploded a nuclear weapon or other nuclear explosive devise prior to 1 January 1967." NPT Article IX, para 3, "Treaty on the Non-Proliferation of Nuclear Weapons (NPT)," http://www.un.org/disarmament/WMD/Nuclear/NPTtext.shtml.

73. These include the United Kingdom, France, and Russia. Switzerland, Austria, and Sweden have conversely indicated significant reservations to the proposal. See Boese (November 2005).

74. Wade Boese, «NSG, Congress Approve Nuclear Trade with India,» *Arms Control Today* 38:8 (Oct 2008), p. 27–8.

75. Ibid.), 28.

76. Ibid., 27.

77. Horner, "NSG Revises Rules," 30.

78. Daryl G. Kimball, "New Nuclear Supplier Rules a Net Plus," *Arms Control Today* 41, no. 6 (2011): 4; Horner, "NSG Revises Rules," 30.

79. T.V. Paul, "The U.S.-India Nuclear Accord: Implications for the Nonproliferation Regime," *International Journal* 62, no. 4 (2007): 845–61.

80. Sumit Ganguly and Dinshaw Mistry, "The Case for the U.S.-India Nuclear Agreement," *World Policy Journal* 23, no. 2 (2006): 11–19.

81. Eric Auner, "Obama Easing Export Controls on India," *Arms Control Today* 40, no. 10 (2010): 39.

82. The two options are delineated in a confidential May 23rd U.S. "Food for Thought" paper circulated to NSG members. Horner, "NSG Revises Rules," 29.

83. Auner, "Obama Easing Export Controls," 41.

84. Peter Crail, "IAEA Approves India Additional Protocol," *Arms Control Today* 39, no. 3 (2009).

85. Barack Obama, "Remarks by President Barack Obama," Hradcany Square, Prague, Czech Republic, April 5, 2009, http://www.whitehouse.gov/the_press_office/Remarks-By-President-Barack-Obama-In-Prague-As-Delivered.

86. U.S. Department of Defense, *Nuclear Posture Review Report*, April 6, 2010, 12, http://www.defense.gov/npr/docs/2010%20nuclear%20posture%20review%20report.pdf.

87. Treaty Between the United States of America and the Russian Federation on Measures for the Further Reduction and Limitation of Strategic Offensive Arms (New START), April 8, 2010, entered into force Feb 5, 2011. See http://www.state.gov/documents/organization/140035.pdf.

88. New START, Art. III(2b), 4.

89. Paul Meyer, "Looking Back: Prague One Year Later: From Words to Deeds?," *Arms Control Today* 40, no. 4 (2010): 66.

90. See Obama, "Remarks," Prague speech.

91. Ellen Tauscher, "Comprehensive Nuclear Test Ban Treaty Organization Enhances Our National Security," DipNote: U.S. Department of State Official Blog, March 2, 201), http://blogs.state.gov/index.php/site/entry/nuclear_test_ban_treaty.

92. Ellen Tauscher, "The Case for the Comprehensive Test Ban Treaty," speech, Arms Control Association Annual Meeting at the Carnegie Endowment for International Peace, Washington, D.C., May 10, 2011, http://www.state.gov/t/us/162963.htm.

93. Ibid.

94. Martin Matishak, "Top Republican Remains Opposed to Nuclear Test Ban," *Global Security Newswire*, March 29, 2011, http://gsn.nti.org/gsn/nw_20110329_7806.php.

95. The ten states include Australia, Canada, Chile, Japan, Germany, Mexico, the Netherlands, Poland, Turkey and the UAE. "10 States Call for More Action on Nonproliferation," *Global Security Newswire*, May 2, 2011, http://gsn.nti.org/gsn/nw_20110502_7345.php.

96. "Nations Weigh Taking Fissile Material Talks outside Disarmament Forum," *Global Security Newswire*, May 17, 2011, http://gsn.nti.org/gsn/nw_20110516_7823.php.

97. Ellen Tauscher, "The Nonproliferation and Disarmament Nexus," speech, Foundation for Strategic Research Conference, Paris, France, June 29, 2011, http://www.state.gov/t/us/167987.htm; Elaine Grossman, "U.S. Opposes Moving Nuclear Material Talks out of Geneva: Senior Official," *Global Security Newswire*, August 4, 2011, http://www.nti.org/gsn/article/us-opposes-moving-nuclear-material-talks-out-of-geneva-senior-official/.

98. "U.N. Chief Floats Measures to Break Conference on Disarmament Stalemate," *Global Security Newswire*, July 28, 2011, http://gsn.nti.org/gsn/nw_20110728_7841.php.

99. "Nations Weigh Taking Fissile Material."

100. Rose Gottemoeller, assistant secretary of state for arms control verification and compliance, "Remarks by Rose Gottemoeller at a High Level Meeting on Revitalizing the Work of the Conference on Disarmament," New York, July 27, 2011, http://usun.state.gov/briefing/statements/2011/169152.htm.

101. Grossman, "U.S. Opposes Moving Nuclear Material."

102. Gottemoeller, "Remarks by Rose Gottemoeller."

103. Ibid.

104. "Pakistan Warns against Fissile Material Talks outside Disarmament Forum," *Global Security Newswire*, August 1, 2011, http://gsn.nti.org/gsn/nw_20110801_3303.php.

105. Ibid.

106. Grossman, "U.S. Opposes Moving Nuclear Material."

107. The Bush administration withdrew support from negotiating a FMCT early in its term of office as it conducted a review of U.S. policy and only came to support negotiations without verification measures.

108. Gary Samore, remarks at "International Perspectives on the Nuclear Posture Review," Carnegie Endowment for International Peace, Washington, D.C., April 22, 2010, http://www.carnegieendowment.org/files/0422carnegie-samore.pdf, as cited in Scott D.

Sagan and Jane Vaynman, "Introduction: Reviewing the Nuclear Posture Review," in "Arms, Disarmament, and Influence: International Reactions to the 2010 Nuclear Posture Review," special issue, *Nonproliferation Review* 18, no. 1 (2011): 17.

109. Sagan and Vaynman, "Introduction," 23.

110. Ibid., 19–20.

111. U.S. Department of Defense, *Nuclear Posture Review Report, 2010*, April 2010, http://www.defense.gov/npr/docs/2010%20nuclear%20posture%20review%20report.pdf.

112. Ibid., vii-viii.

113. Ibid., viii.

114. Ibid.

115. Sagan and Vaynman, "Introduction," 22–23.

116. Paul Meyer, "Prague One Year Later: From Words to Deeds?" *Arms Control Today* 40, no. 4 (2010): 64–68.

117. Nabil Fahmy, "Mindful of the Middle East: Egypt's Reaction to the New U.S. Nuclear Posture Review," *Nonproliferation Review* 18, no. 1 (2011): 172.

118. Meyer, "Prague One Year Later," 64.

119. Ibid., 65.

120. Jacqueline C. Reich, "Achieving the Vision of the NPT," *Nonproliferation Review* 18, no. 2 (2011): 369–87.

121. Sharon Squassoni, "Grading Progress on 13 Steps toward Disarmament," Carnegie Endowment for International Peace, *Policy Outlook*, April 5, 2009, http://www.carnegieendowment.org/files/13_steps.pdf.

122. Sagan and Vaynman, "Introduction," 27–33.

123. Scott D. Sagan and Jane Vaynman, "Conclusion: Lessons Learned from the 2010 Nuclear Posture Review," in "Arms, Disarmament, and Influence: International Reactions to the 2010 Nuclear Posture Review," special issue, *Nonproliferation Review* 18, no. 1 (2011): 240, citing Christopher F. Chyba and J. D. Crouch, "Understanding the U.S. Nuclear Weapons Debate," *Washington Quarterly* 32 (2009): 29; and Christopher F. Chyba, "Time for a Systematic Analysis: U.S. Nuclear Weapons and Nuclear Proliferation," *Arms Control Today* 38 (2008), www.armscontrol.org/act/2008_12/Chyba.

124. Lewis A. Dunn, Gregory Giles, Jeffrey Larsen, and Thomas Skypek, *Foreign Perspectives on the U.S. Nuclear Policy and Posture: Insights, Issues and Implications*, SAIC for the Defense Threat Reduction Agency, December 12, 2006, www.fas.org/irp/agency/dod/dtra/foreign-pers.pdf.

125. Ibid.

126. Sagan and Vaynman, "Conclusion," 238.

127. Harald Müller, "A Nuclear Nonproliferation Test: Obama's Nuclear Policy and the 2010 NPT Review Conference," *Nonproliferation Review* 18, no. 1 (2011): 230.

128. Ibid. Brazil has observer status in the NAM.

129. Sagan and Vaynman, "Conclusion," 254.
130. Ibid., 255.
131. Müller, "Nuclear Nonproliferation Test," 226–27. This study is based on a content analysis of all statements of NPT parties at the 2010 NPT RevCon.
132. Ibid., 225.
133. Ibid.
134. Ibid.

CHAPTER 3

Construction of Threat and Nuclear Nonproliferation Measures
Considerations on Theory and Policy

Maria Rost Rublee

WHY DO STATES RESIST the creation or strengthening of measures that inhibit nuclear proliferation? While in the past one could surmise that some states felt that nuclear proliferation was in their interest (e.g., China and Pakistan), today almost all countries are opposed to other states' proliferation. Why, then, have we seen multiple states either fail to support or actively seek to undermine efforts to stop proliferation? From Washington's point of view, nuclear proliferation is a clear and present danger. American analysts assume that most states agree with this assessment, and certainly it seems reasonable that states that have given up nuclear weapons programs or that are active in disarmament diplomacy would feel the same way. Yet this is not the case: states that have given up nuclear weapons (South Africa) or active nuclear weapons programs (Brazil), as well as states that lead in disarmament (Egypt), have opposed measures that seem clearly linked to stopping proliferation, such as making the Additional Protocol (AP) standard and establishing fissile material banks.[1] What explains such behavior?

As Andrew Grotto has noted, this question remains virtually unexplored in the political science literature.[2] While many studies examine the sources of proliferation, and a smaller subset examines the sources of nonproliferation, almost none systematically address why states choose to support—or not—nonproliferation measures. Grotto argues for three different logics for nonproliferation support: regime symbolism (norms), relative power (security), and opportunity costs (economics). However, as Grotto notes, these logics can be interpreted by different states in different ways; for example, some countries will feel normative pressure to strengthen nonproliferation (Japan), while others will feel normative pressure to weaken it (Brazil). For this reason, while Grotto's logics provide explanatory power, I argue that it may make more sense to think about support for nonproliferation through the lens of threat construction.

CONSTRUCTION OF THREAT:
PROLIFERATION AND NONPROLIFERATION

To understand why states may resist nonproliferation measures, we need to understand the construction of threats related to both proliferation and nonproliferation. What seem to be mere differences of opinion regarding nonproliferation are actually much more: policy differences flow out of different social constructions of reality. When it comes to nuclear politics, symbols, rules, concepts, categories, and meaning differ—sometimes dramatically—among states. The U.S. experience with the Treaty on the Non-Proliferation of Nuclear Weapons (NPT)—as the first state to develop nuclear weapons, the only state to use nuclear weapons, the global military hegemon with far-reaching diplomatic power, a major player in the international nuclear industry—is radically different than the South Africa, Brazilian, or Egyptian experience. As a result, reality when it comes to nonproliferation measures will seem quite different to different states. Moreover, each state will understand its perception of reality as reality in fact, leading to the potential for confusion, misunderstanding, and refusal to compromise. As Michael Barnett notes,

> The possibility that this constructed reality presents itself as an objective reality relates to the concept of social facts. There are those things whose existence is dependent on human agreement and those things whose existence is not. Brute facts such as rocks, flowers, gravity and oceans exist independently of human agreement and will to continue to exist even if humans disappear or deny their existence. Social facts are dependent on human agreement and are taken for granted. Money, refugees, terrorism, human rights, and sovereignty are social facts. Even though they are wholly dependent on human agreement and will exist only so long as that agreement exists, we treat them as objective facts and thus as constraints on action.[3]

Social facts are constructed, existing only because of the meaning and value attributed to them by people, informed by experience and culture.[4] This distinction is critical if we are to understand why countries have such varying ideas on nonproliferation measures. Resistance to nonproliferation measures is not just about those measures, but also a resistance to largely Western-defined social constructs about the meaning of proliferation, nonproliferation, and disarmament. The fight over nonproliferation measures is about the meaning of these concepts, their relations to each other, and how states should act in response to them. The frustration implicit in Grotto's question—"Why do states that oppose nuclear proliferation resist new nonproliferation obligations?"—is grounded in a Western perception of reality in nuclear politics. This observation is not a criticism of Grotto, and the following analysis is not a criticism of the Western reality. Rather, I argue that if we want to influence the states in question, we must understand their social construction of nuclear proliferation, nonproliferation, and disarmament.

To do so, we must break down the assumptions that underpin Grotto's question. For state elites, how is "proliferation" constructed as a threat? Just as important, how is nonproliferation policy constructed: as a remedy to proliferation, as a well-meaning but ineffective tool to stop proliferation, as a threat in its right? These questions highlight the fact that for a state to support measures to stop nuclear proliferation, its decision makers must agree with the following premises[5]:

1. Nuclear proliferation is a serious threat.
2. Nuclear proliferation can be stopped or at least slowed.
3. Specific nonproliferation measures will be effective. (One can agree with 1 and 2 above while disagreeing that a specific nonproliferation measure will work.)
4. Support for specific nonproliferation measures will enhance, or at least not undermine, a country's status, security, or economic potential.
5. Support for specific nonproliferation measures will enhance, or at least not undermine, the individual elite's or political party's political prospects.

Premises 4 and 5 highlight the fact that nonproliferation measures can actually be constructed as threats in their own right by a state with "clean hands" (that is, it does not intend to acquire nuclear weapons nor help spread nuclear weapons technology). Indeed, if elites reject any of the above premises, they may choose to refuse to support, or even choose to undermine, nonproliferation measures. In addition, even if elites accept all five premises above, they may still resist nonproliferation measures if they accept any of the following premises that frame nonproliferation as a threat:

1. Lack of progress on disarmament is a greater impetus for proliferation than any current loopholes in the nonproliferation regime.
2. Perceived U.S. bullying is a greater impetus for proliferation than any current loopholes in the nonproliferation regime.
3. Standing up for the right to full access to the nuclear fuel cycle will provide more benefits (internationally or domestically) than supporting nonproliferation measures.

The most important aspect of both sets of premises is that all are based at least in part on socially constructed ideas, as the examination below demonstrates. Indeed, while the analysis shows that material factors are not unimportant, in each case those material factors are filtered through different understandings of social reality. The point is not that material factors are unimportant, but rather that the social understanding of those material factors must be recognized if we are to forge partnerships for strong nonproliferation measures.

First, however, we should explore whether typical objections to additional nonproliferation measures are simply smokescreens for elites who have material interests in opposing them. For example, Christopher Ford argues that the typical argument about how the lack of disarmament for nuclear weapons states (NWS) undermines nonproliferation is not credible.[6] Much of his argument rests on the unexamined and somewhat problematic assumption that arms reductions equals or "counts as" disarmament, which raises the question of how nuclear disarmament as a concept is constructed. But beyond this, three points give credence to the proposition that it is differing social facts, rather than pure material self-interest, that leads to resistance to new nonproliferation measures. First, the arguments are not created out of thin air but make logical sense when considering the vastly differing experiences of countries and elites. Second, in some cases rejecting new nonproliferation measures may allow elites to accrue certain material benefits, such as increased domestic popularity. However, in many of these cases, this material benefit accrues because of the social construction of nonproliferation and disarmament within the larger populace.[7] A good example of this can be found in Iran's eventual rejection of the IAEA/Western proposal for a fuel swap. Iranian president Mahmoud Ahmadinejad initially offered a tentative acceptance of the deal, but he was severely criticized at home for the decision, including from progressive reformers. Because access to the full nuclear fuel cycle had been politically constructed as a "sovereign right" within Iran, Ahmadinejad had no freedom of movement. Finally, one might turn the question on its head and ask why we would expect all countries to perceive the world as we do. In anthropology, sociology, and some segments of politics, such an assumption would be immediately suspect. The best evidence that resistant countries are talking and acting in good faith, rather than with subterfuge, would be changes that occur in response to nuclear weapons states' disarmament progress. We have seen some evidence along these lines; for instance, the Indonesian government declared it would seek ratification of the Comprehensive Nuclear-Test-Ban Treaty (CTBT) in response to Obama's disarmament initiatives. However, further evidence is needed but cannot be expected until more progress is made on disarmament.

How do social constructs influence elite perceptions of nuclear proliferation, nonproliferation, and disarmament? The following discussion examines this question.

Nuclear proliferation is a serious threat. First, what does "nuclear proliferation" mean? Does it only include a state's attempted acquisition of nuclear weapons, or is nuclear hedging included?[8] How does one distinguish between hedging and the acquisition of the complete fuel cycle for nuclear energy?[9] Is nuclear proliferation dangerous only when enemies are concerned, and not friends? (Recall how during the 2003 nuclear crisis with North Korea, U.S. senator John McCain said the United States should allow Japan to develop its own nuclear weapons, and U.S. vice president Dick Cheney implied that Tokyo may be interested in their own military nuclear capability.[10]) Is nuclear proliferation acceptable when it leads to a balance of power in the region (i.e., Pakistan in response to India, or Iran in response to Israel)? Second, in particular charges of nuclear proliferation, can the evidence be trusted? Is the state in question actually trying to acquire nuclear weapons? Who is making the charge, and what motives might they have for it? Third, what does "serious threat" mean? Who should feel threatened by proliferation? From the perspective of a global hegemon, proliferation could be perceived as threatening because it has the potential to disturb the status quo. However, other states may not feel the same sense of threat. Often, if an aggressive rival develops nuclear weapons, a state will respond with a nuclear weapons program of its own. So then why should we expect the perception of a serious threat to lead to greater support for nonproliferation? But if a state does not feel immediately threatened by a likely proliferator, it may not perceive the possible proliferation as a serious hazard and thus may see the need for additional nonproliferation measures. Both "nuclear proliferation" and "serious threat" are socially constructed, rather than clear-cut descriptions on which all can agree.

Nuclear proliferation can be stopped or slowed. States that resist nonproliferation measures probably do not do so because they believe that nuclear proliferation is inevitable. However, the current construction—that proliferation is avoidable—is a 180-degree turn from the thinking after the end of World War II. After the United States used atomic weapons against Japan in 1945, advanced militaries around the world began to plan to acquire their own atomic bombs. Atomic "wonder weapons" were seen as a logical acquisition for technologically sophisticated countries. However, the growth of international antinuclear sentiment, combined with a great power desire to maintain a monopoly, led to a reconstruction of what "nuclear weapons" meant to states—from military tool to immoral device. Many argue that the negotiation of the NPT helped cement this about-face in perceptions of military nuclear capability. Before the NPT, acquiring nuclear weapons was an act of national pride; after the treaty, it became an "act of international outlawry," as noted by U.S. ambassador Thomas Graham.[11] The current dominant belief—that proliferation is avoidable—is clearly a social construction.

Today, not all analysts agree. Using basic realist assumptions, it seems clear that if one can acquire the ultimate deterrent—one that may reduce the risk of conventional war as well as provide immunity against a nuclear attack—it would be prudent to do so.[12] However, this type of argumentation comes mostly from conservative quarters within the United States, rather than from countries that resist nonproliferation measures. Nevertheless, should the belief spread that proliferation is inevitable—a belief that could be strengthened if Iran acquires nuclear weapons—then this will be another challenge in encouraging states to support nonproliferation measures.

Specific nonproliferation measures will be effective. The influence of social constructions on this premise depends greatly on the specific nonproliferation measures in question. Some measures are quite technical and likely are not influenced greatly by unstated social facts. For example, whether one thinks universal adoption of the Additional Protocol will be effective at reducing proliferation is based mostly on technical assessment on how greater access to nuclear facilities will uncover discrepancies. However, if one describes bombing nuclear facilities as a nonproliferation measure, then clearly social constructions shape assessment of likely effectiveness. A stickier measure is economic sanctions, a Western-favored nonproliferation measure used against states seen in violation of their NPT commitments. However, not only does the academic literature question the utility of sanctions, but some policymakers outside the United States argue that sanctions isolate states in question, making it more difficult to solve the political and security issues that drive illicit behavior in the first place. For example, former Brazilian president Luiz Inacio Lula da Silva argued strenuously against sanctions on Iran, saying, "It is not prudent to push Iran against a wall. The prudent thing is to establish negotiations."[13] Lula's claim has some support: in the case of Libya, Målfrid Braut-Hegghammer argues that sanctions increased its isolation, which made it difficult for Tripoli to chart a more cooperative path, as well as radicalized its nuclear decision making.[14]

Support for specific nonproliferation measures will enhance, or at least not undermine, a country's status, security, or economic potential. This premise is the focus of Grotto's work, in which he analyzes alternative logics regarding state nonproliferation decision making. Many of the factors he discusses can be framed as social constructs. For example, support for nonproliferation measures is a virtual certainty in Japan, where antinuclear peace groups publicize bureaucratic efforts (or lack thereof) toward nonproliferation and disarmament. In Japan, it's a "no brainer" to support nonproliferation measures, even though they come at a cost for the country (Japan hosts more IAEA inspections than any other country in the world). In Brazil, where compliance with global nonproliferation norms came slowly, through regional efforts, and deep concerns about IAEA inspections have been voiced, it's a "no brainer" to resist additional nonproliferation measures. This is not just a difference of opinion; the two countries have different worldviews on the matter. This is illustrated through comments in the 2010 NPT Review Conference. A member of the Japanese delegation opined that it was a shame that some countries hated the AP. Another country, which refused to support universalization of the AP, argued that their state came to the NPT Review Conference in full compliance with their NPT obligations, and they had no intention of leaving the conference in violation of them.[15]

Support for specific nonproliferation measures will enhance, or at least not undermine, the individual elite's or political party's political prospects. In most countries, burnishing one's nonproliferation credentials is not likely to increase the likelihood of gaining or staying in office. However, in countries where this is the case, it is likely due in part to social construction, perhaps an elite or even national conscience on nuclear nonproliferation and disarmament. The country most likely to fit into this category is Australia, where refusing to sell uranium to India was a matter of political pride.[16] On the other hand, in some countries, supporting additional nonproliferation measures can be hazardous to one's political health, as is discussed below.

Lack of progress on disarmament is a greater impetus for proliferation than any current loopholes in the nonproliferation regime. If fear of a rival's nuclear weapons programs drives further proliferation, then patching holes in the nonproliferation regime will not stop the dam from bursting. If envy over the status that nuclear weapons seem to accord other countries may lead to further proliferation, then the solution is to devalue nuclear weapons, rather than make them harder to acquire (which may increase their desirability even more). If concerns about discrimination and inequity keep states from supporting nonproliferation measures that they otherwise would promote, then meeting those concerns may provide a better solution than trying to outfox them diplomatically. Fear, envy, and inequality may seem misplaced from an American point of view, but they are part of the socially constructed reality for other states around the world.

Perceived U.S. bullying is a greater impetus for proliferation than any current loopholes in the nonproliferation regime. According to this line of reasoning, nuclear-armed states are deluded into thinking that strengthening the nonproliferation regime will stop proliferation, not realizing that their own aggressive behavior is more likely to instigate proliferation. Even if nonproliferation measures are seen as worthwhile, in this case it may make sense to refuse to support them until nuclear-armed states agree to greater security for nonnuclear weapons states. Again, this type of belief rests on social constructs. Washington decision makers support additional nonproliferation measures out of a genuine desire to enhance both U.S. and global security. But some countries may think that from its perch at the top of the world, the United States may not realize how threatening some of its behavior may seem (from refusal to offer a blanket no-first-use guarantee to threats of preemptive strikes against Iran).

Standing up for the right to full access to the nuclear fuel cycle will provide more benefits (internationally or domestically) than supporting nonproliferation measures. Although some Americans may see anticolonialist language as just rhetoric, in some parts of the world people perceive continued colonial experiences in economics and diplomacy. Given the already discriminatory nature of the NPT, nonproliferation measures that require nonnuclear weapons states (NNWS) to give up rights will surely engage the anticolonialist sentiments already alive. In 2006, Gamal Mubarak announced Egypt's renewed nuclear energy plans in the language of anticolonialism to great effect. The same language can be used to gain international prestige. Brazilian president Lula's nuclear diplomacy with Iran, emphatic in the right of states to peaceful nuclear energy, was a part of Lula's strategy to strengthen Brazil's standing on the world stage. In Iran, perceived capitulation on the sovereign right to enrich uranium brought tremendous criticism down on Iranian president Mahmoud Ahmadinejad in late 2009, leading to a reversal on his tentative acceptance of the Western-sponsored uranium swap deal. This means that leadership in Iran has fewer negotiating choices because of the domestic construction of the right to enrich uranium as a nonnegotiable entitlement. Asking developing countries to give up perceived rights is bound to create trouble, not simply because of rhetoric or politics, but because of the social construction of anticolonialism in many of these states.

POLICY IMPLICATIONS OF NONPROLIFERATION SOCIAL CONSTRUCTIONS

The above discussion may make the prospect of increasing support for nonproliferation measures seem daunting. State elites must not only agree with one or more of the premises undergirding the halting of proliferation, but they also cannot agree with any of the three premises that frame nonproliferation as a threat. However, one of the important policy implications of recognizing social constructs is that while they seem to be objective facts, they are not, and constructs can be reshaped through both material and nonmaterial methods.

Elsewhere, I have argued that a social psychology framework allows us to specify the mechanisms through which attitude change can take place.[17] In this essay, I argue that these same psychological mechanisms can be used to shape threat construction. While my previous work focused on using norms to change attitudes, the same processes are useful in describing how to change social facts—beliefs and perceptions fuelled by culture and experience.[18] First, I review the relevant social psychological processes and then discuss how they could be used to influence the social constructions that inform other states' nonproliferation decision making.[19]

Norm Transmission

The first relevant set of social psychological mechanisms relate to how norms are transmitted: in particular, through explicit communication (injunctive norms) and behavior (descriptive norms). The concept of *descriptive norms* is simply an elaborate way of saying people notice what you do at least as much as what you say. Observing others helps people understand what is "correct" or "normal" in a novel, ambiguous, or uncertain situation. The greater number of actors behaving in a certain way, the more we believe that behavior is correct. The concept of descriptive norms tells us that watching what others do does more than just give us information—it shapes our perception of social reality and our understanding of the proper response. In addition, descriptive norm transmission can be "received" without the recipient being consciously aware of it: "the behavior of others in our social environment shapes our own interpretation and response to a situation, even without overt indoctrination."[20] For instance, when large numbers of actors behave in a certain way, this behavior can become automatic or unquestioned. "It's just what a civilized state does," whether referring to constructing science bureaucracies, signing the UN declaration on human rights, or signing the NPT.

Injunctive Norms are the norms with which most of us are familiar: "Clean your plate," "Don't lie or cheat," "Don't seek weapons of mass destruction." Injunctive norms can prescribe proper behavior or proscribe improper behavior. These types of norms usually bring social rewards for those who comply, or social sanctions for those who do not, whether stated or not. While the reframing effect of descriptive norms is subtle, injunctive norms clearly set out to change perspectives and interpretations.[21]

Norm transmission sounds sterile and not particularly earth shattering. And yet it encompasses some of the messiest and most contentious activities internationally, and it is at the heart of how actors try to persuade others. A great number of actors transmit norms—from states to politicians, from international organizations to nongovernmental organizations to norm entrepreneurs. The NPT's opening for signature in 1968, and entry into force in 1970, served and still serves as the main source of formal normative transmissions regarding nuclear nonproliferation. Before the negotiations leading to the creation of the NPT, there were no formally agreed-upon behavioral expectations regarding the acquisition of nuclear weapons. After the NPT, there were clear formal normative transmittals that designated nuclear weapons acquisition as unacceptable. The NPT's injunctive normative content was quickly reinforced by descriptive norms—that is, the very large number of states that signed and ratified the NPT. Within ten years of its entering into force, the NPT had 111 member states.[22] After the dissolution of the Soviet Union, states saw that new countries gave up the nuclear weapons on their territory and joined the NPT. However, since the mid-1990s, descriptive norm transmissions regarding nuclear nonproliferation have been murkier. India and Pakistan both detonated nuclear weapons, with muted reaction from the international community. While the official

U.S. justification for its invasion of Iraq was to keep it from acquiring nuclear weapons, North Korea is basically permitted to flaunt a nuclear weapons program. Under the Bush administration, the United States began a new drive to modernize its nuclear forces, as well as beginning new nuclear weapons research into bunker-busters and miniaturized nuclear weapons, for example. While the large majority of states have adhered to their NPT commitments, the anomalies seem to dominate world news. At this point, it would be fair to say that with regards to nuclear nonproliferation, injunctive and descriptive norms are in contention.

Understanding norm transmission can aid us in devising policy prescriptions to help shift constructions of threat with regard to nonproliferation measures. Perhaps the most important lesson is descriptive and injunctive norms must be in concert. For example, if Washington wishes to stop countries from developing indigenous fuel cycle capabilities, then it needs to discourage them across the board, rather than focusing on a handful of states. Energetic effort on multilateral fuel banks and a fissile material cutoff treaty should be accompanied by UAE-style nuclear agreements (in which domestic enrichment is expressly rejected). This will send the message that not only does Washington preach "no new enrichment facilities," but it also practices it through a number of methods. This consistency between what we say and what we do is important for at least two reasons. First, gaps between the descriptive and injunctive norms give wiggle room for states such as Iran, whose diplomats are perfectly capable of pointing out that it seems the United States wishes to deny Muslim or Middle Eastern countries the sovereign right to the fuel cycle while permitting it for others, such as Vietnam (whose nuclear agreement with the United States does not forbid enrichment). Second, this double standard reinforces, rather than diminishes, anticolonial social constructions. It also reinforces the social fact accepted by some that the NPT is not a neutral treaty agreement applied equally to all members, but rather it is a political tool used by the United States and its allies to reward friends and punish enemies.

Another lesson for encouraging states to accept new nonproliferation measures is to invest serious diplomatic resources into gaining as much acceptance for the measures among as many states as possible. Grotto's description of how Indonesia and thirteen other holdout states became isolated at the 1995 NPT Review Conference on that matter of indefinite extension is a good example. Washington is trying to sell the social construction that responsible states support nonproliferation measures (injunctive norm); it needs to back that up with a long list of states that do so (creating a supportive descriptive norm). This will also help undermine the social construct that nonproliferation measures advantage nuclear weapons states and disadvantage nonnuclear weapons states.

Norms Processing

International actors are bombarded with large numbers of normative messages, many of them conflicting, from both external and domestic sources. It may seem that using norms as an explanatory variable is impossible, since the number of norms "out there" support just about any course of action. How do actors process and sort through normative transmissions, and how do we understand what norms matter and why? Based on social psychology research, three main mechanisms are proposed through which norms are processed, helping us begin to understand why some norms win out over others. In addition, norm transmitters may experience greater success in persuasion if they are able to frame their messages in ways amenable to these mechanisms.

Linking A classic example of linking is an ad by People for the Ethical Treatment of Animals, aimed toward environmentalists; it reads, "If you give a damn about the earth, become a vegetarian." Linking connects a norm to well-established values. In evaluating how to respond to a norm, actors often consider how it fits in with their current value system. For the nuclear nonproliferation regime, adherence to the norm has often been linked to international legitimacy. With near-universal membership, states face pariah status in remaining outside the NPT. South Africa's president acknowledged such, saying that his decision to take apart his state's nuclear weapons program was fueled in part by his desire for South Africa "to take its rightful place in the international community."[23]

Activation Even within social psychology, the use of norms as an explanatory tool has been criticized on the basis that a variety of norms apply to any given situation, some of which may be incompatible (for example, the norm of nuclear nonproliferation versus the norm of national pride). Further research uncovered that situational cues can activate one norm over another. "In fact, there may be multiple, and even incompatible norms vying for attention in many situations, and our actions may depend to a large extent on the type of norm that is triggered by the context."[24] In short, activation means "being made focal" or "having been highlighted." In some cases, injunctive norms and descriptive norms, or subjective norms and descriptive norms, were in direct competition with each other—the norm that had been emphasized tended to win out. Robert Cialdini and Melanie Trost reported, "This series of studies indicated that, at any given time, an individual's behavior is likely to flow with the norm that is currently focal, even when other types of norms might be relevant and even contrary in the situation" (161). For example, in one study, subjects who were given paper trash and saw another person litter were far more likely to litter than subjects who were also given paper trash and saw another person throw their trash in a trash receptacle. In the real world, norm activation is much more complex, since decisions have far more import than littering and a host of norms are activated by a number of different actors at any one time. However, it is important to note that people are more likely to adhere to a norm that has been emphasized, which means that the activity of emphasizing norms is not a useless one.[25]

What specifically does "activation" look like? Activities that highlight or make a norm a focal point qualify as activation. Holding a dramatic public relations event to convey a message would count. For example, when Greenpeace members chained themselves to the front door of the U.S. Environmental Protection Agency Headquarters to protest what they consider to be a weak ruling on clean air issues, they received press coverage, and Greenpeace members were able to state their views on the issue. Agency officials had to respond to the criticisms. In effect, the norm of environmental protection was activated, with Greenpeace able to explain why its view of the norm was superior, and agency officials were forced to defend their interpretation as well as to engage a group they would otherwise ignore. Another example of activation would be submitting a UN resolution to call attention to an issue. Egypt has made an art of activation of the nuclear nonproliferation norm through this manner. In 1974, Egypt sponsored an Iranian resolution calling for a nuclear-weapons-free zone (NWFZ) in the Middle East. Each year since then, Egypt has crafted and sponsored the resolution itself. By 1980, Israel no longer abstained, and the resolution has been adopted by consensus in the UN General Assembly. Other forms of activation could include devoting a speech to an issue, taking out a full-page advertisement in the *New York Times* to show a proposal's very long list of important signatories, or coordinating a series of events around a specific topic to promote a particular interpretation of a norm.

Consistency Social psychology has found that the best predictor of future behavior is past behavior. The need to both appear and be consistent is a powerful motivator. This need is often engaged through making commitments; once commitments have been made, people tend to behave in ways that are consistent with them. In particular, commitments that are active, effortful, public, and viewed as internally motivated are most likely to generate consistent future behavior.[26] In fact, small commitments, once met, make actors much more likely to commit to larger actions. Social psychologists theorize this is the case "because performance of the initially requested action causes a self-perception change; that is, individuals come to see themselves as possessing certain behavior-related traits." Indeed, Cialdini describes this phenomenon as commitments "growing their own legs," so that once an initial request is completed, commitments lead to inner change.[27] People often generate additional reasons to justify their commitments—new reasons that have nothing to do with the initial request. Then external requests are no longer necessary to gain compliance, since it has become internally motivated.[28]

The international social environment fostered by the NPT has encouraged states to process and accept the norm of nuclear nonproliferation. The preamble of the NPT is a series of "links" that connect universally held values and previously made commitments to its own establishment, with the implication that just as states hold these values and honor these commitments, so should they commit to the NPT. In terms of activation, the negotiations leading up to, and the actual creation of the NPT, gave interested parties something to "activate." Before this, nonnuclear activists could not point to a formal document in which states agreed to refrain from nuclear acquisition. With the emergence, establishment, and strengthening of the NPT, an actor (whether a state or NGO or individual) that is interested in influencing potential proliferators can activate—that is, bring to the forefront—the norm of nonproliferation. Suddenly, the potential proliferator must face this norm and risk defying it. The mere activation of a norm does not mean it will prevail; in complex policymaking decisions, certainly a number of norms are being activated at the same time. But without the NPT, the nuclear nonproliferation norm had no official platform from which to be activated and less credibility with which to activate it. The realm of competing norms was enlarged by the NPT, and with its continued success, the nuclear nonproliferation norm is not easily dismissed. Now that the nuclear nonproliferation norm has been established and maintained by the NPT framework, some states are activating the norm outside of that framework. For example, the Big Three (Britain, France, and Germany) sought to engage Iran on its troublesome nuclear program, offering a mix of social and material inducements, so that the IAEA would not have to declare Iran in violation of its NPT agreements.[29]

Consistency is potentially a powerful force in keeping states in adherence to the nuclear nonproliferation norm for two reasons: public commitments and past behavior. First, once a state commits publicly to the treaty, even if policymakers do not intend to abide by it, any violations of the treaty may cause cognitive dissonance among state elites, potentially making such behavior less likely. Because individual elites commit a state to a treaty, however, this may make consistency less powerful. If a new set of elites comes to power, it may feel less commitment to a treaty ratified by their political opponents. However, the value of public commitment to forgoing nuclear weapons can be seen in the establishment of nuclear-weapons-free zones, in which policymakers from states agreed to keep nuclear weapons out of the region. "Nuclear-weapon-free zones have sought to establish norms against the acquisition of nuclear weapons without even attempting to establish supporting sanctions or rewards."[30] Second, for the large group of states that have not only ratified the NPT but have also abided by it, their previous adherence creates momentum to continued adherence. Violating the NPT means not only violating a public commitment but also reversing decades of compliance and support to a widely held international norm.

Policy Implications Understanding norm processing can aid us in devising policy prescriptions to help shift constructions of threat with regard to nonproliferation measures. Finding ways to link support for nonproliferation measures with social constructs already held by resistant states is important. In this case, Washington will want to skirt the negative social constructs that these states have on nonproliferation obligations and instead engage with more promising ones related to promotion of international cooperation, the potential for southern countries to contribute meaningfully to nuclear global governance, and the links between nonproliferation and disarmament. Obama attempted to do this in his encouragement of Brazil's negotiations with Iran on the uranium fuel swap, but unfortunately the devil was in the details, and the proposed Brazil-Turkey plan was not one that the United States could support. However, one failure does not mean that the United States should abandon this strategy. Giving resistant states such as Brazil and South Africa places at the table—and allowing them to help shape negotiations—will link nonproliferation measures with positive social constructs, while also undermining the negative social construct that Washington allows only friends to play in nuclear diplomacy. Linkages between disarmament and nonproliferation are also very important; Scott Sagan's suggestion that nonproliferation measures are part of NNWS' disarmament obligations is a promising line of thought.

Norm Potency

Norm transmission takes place under a wide variety of conditions, some favorable to norm acceptance and some less favorable. Political science has something to say on this topic; for example, a rule of thumb in comparative politics is that cultural changes come more easily in times of crisis. Social psychology offers a broad perspective on the topic, helping us to see how different conditions affect the influence of norms. By understanding these, norm entrepreneurs and others interested in winning adherents can attempt to create or avoid these conditions. The following three conditions may influence the potency of normative transmissions:

Uncertainty Without a doubt, uncertainty exerts the largest and most wide-ranging effect on influence outcomes. Decades of research have consistently shown that actors are more likely to accept group influence when dealing with a subjective task as opposed to an objective task—because the subjectivity creates uncertainty. In addition, uncertainty also increases the likelihood of an actor internalizing group influence (persuasion) as opposed to simply conforming. Whether a task itself is unclear, or the results of a decision are hard to predict, actors are more open to outside influence. A cost-benefit equation in flux—when costs and benefits seem to be rising or falling—would meet this definition. Ambiguous costs and benefits, or those open to debate, also would: For example, do nuclear weapons really provide the benefit of security, or do they undermine it by making a state a target? A clear but difficult task or decision also evokes uncertainty. People are more like to accept outside input under these conditions, due in part because of the perception of increased room for error.[31]

Similarity When a norm transmitter is similar to us, or someone with whom we desire a good relationship, we are more open to their normative influence.[32] A number of studies confirm, "a similar source can trigger normative behavior more easily than a dissimilar source."[33] Why? Identification. When actors want to establish or maintain a relationship, they are more likely to defer to their requests and to accept their influence. When members of a group believe they are valued by the group, or value the group, conformity increases.[34]

Conflict

Of the three main conditions that affect normative influence, conflict is the only one that decreases its potency. Any explicit intergroup division creates group polarization, but it is possible to overcome in-group/out-group divisions through contact. However, intergroup conflict immediately quashes efforts at cooperation and influence. During conflict, members automatically side with their own group, and close themselves off to outside sources of influence, thus shutting down a potential transmission mechanism.

The international social environment (created by the nuclear nonproliferation framework) has influenced the potency of the nuclear nonproliferation norm in a number of ways. First, the NPT and associated frameworks undermined to some extent the traditional notion that nuclear weapons enhance a state's security and thus created uncertainty for policymakers, making them more likely to accept group norms. How did this happen? The NPT created social and material incentives for forgoing nuclear weapons, as well as making it technically and practically difficult to develop a nuclear weapons program. In other words, the NPT dramatically changed the cost-benefit equation for nuclear weapons acquisition. The certainty of the value of nuclear weapons was replaced by uncertainty over whether nuclear weapons were worth the new economic and social costs, as well as uncertainty about whether they were needed given the commitment of nuclear weapons states not to use nuclear weapons against nonnuclear weapons states. The continued strengthening of IAEA protocols (strengthened after the Gulf War and currently being strengthened through the creation of the Additional Protocol) lets policymakers know that the cost-benefit equation continues to shift, as inspections become more intrusive and the costs of hiding noncompliance increase. The likely effect of such uncertainty is to convince many policymakers to accept the group norm.

Understanding that actors are more likely to accept the influence of similar others gives us a more refined view of how persuasion occurs in the nuclear nonproliferation arena. Given that the strong normative message has been for nuclear forbearance, why do some states continue to violate the NPT? One potential explanation is that those outside of the NPT are also outside of the international community. Iraq, Iran, Libya, and North Korea could all be described as dissatisfied with the international status quo. When their political elite "receive" normative transmissions regarding nuclear nonproliferation, it may actually backfire, given that they actively oppose the status quo that created the NPT. As John M. Levine and E. Tory Higgins argue, "majorities produce public compliance but not private acceptance in minorities.... Social influence only occurs if the source and targets are members of the same group and the source's position represents (is prototypical of) the group norm."[35] Their group of "similar others" may actually be working on nuclear programs as well (for example, recent news of Pakistani scientist A. Q. Khan's unauthorized assistance for the secret Iranian nuclear program). The major outlier to this explanation is Israel, which could be considered a supporter of the international community. However, one could argue that Israel receives support for its nuclear program by the refusal of the United States to take action against Israel because of it.

Policy implications Understanding norm potency can aid us in devising policy prescriptions to help shift constructions of threat with regard to nonproliferation measures. For example, linking nonproliferation to disarmament (discussed above) can help generate uncertainty in resistant states about the impact of their refusal to support nonproliferation obligations. If Washington or other allies—or intellectuals within the resistant states—can raise questions about whether refusal to support nonproliferation measures is damaging prospects for disarmament, then this will disturb current threat constructions related to nonproliferation. Supporting serious academic work on the issue, preferably with scholars from the states in question, has real potential. Similarity is also a useful and under-utilized tool. Rather than all the messages about nonproliferation obligations coming from Washington and its allies, we need to enlist supportive states that are seen as more independent and more credible. Libya would be an excellent example, although current conditions in Libya's leadership (with growing rivalry between Gadhafi's sons over succession) and other issues make this an unlikely prospect. Norway, with its very active disarmament promotion agenda, would be an excellent ally on the issue; New Zealand would also be a promising partner, because of its interest in both nonproliferation and disarmament, as well as its reputation for standing up to the United States on nuclear issues. Finally, conflict needs to be avoided with resistant states as much as possible; it only makes sense that diplomatic or economic conflict with Washington will reinforce negative social constructs regarding U.S. bullying.

Notes

1. See, for example, Frank Braun, "Analysis: Brazil and Additional Protocol," *UPI International Intelligence*, July 1, 2005, and Leonard S. Spector and Benjamin Radford, "Algeria, Emirates Plan Nonproliferation-Friendly Nuclear Programs; Egypt Keeps Fuel Cycle Options Open, Rejects Expanded IAEA Monitoring," *WMD Insights*, June 2008, http://www.wmdinsights.com/I25/I25_ME1_AlgeriaEmirates.htm.

2. Andrew Grotto, "Why Do States That Opposed Nuclear Proliferation Resist New Nonproliferation Obligations? Three Logics of Nonproliferation Decision-Making," *Cardozo Journal of International and Comparative Law* 18, no. 1 (2010): 1–43.

3. Michael Barnett, "Social Constructivism," in *The Globalization of World Politics*, ed. John Baylis and Steve Smith, 3rd ed. (Oxford: Oxford University Press, 2005), 259.

4. For a discussion of social facts, see John R. Searle, *The Construction of Social Reality* (New York, Free Press, 1995).

5. Note that elites need not support all of these premises. Elites could be uninterested in stopping nuclear proliferation but interested in the political benefits (either domestically or internationally) that could be gained by doing so. However, in most cases, one would expect that elites would agree with the first three premises and likely the last two as well.

6. Christopher A. Ford, "Nuclear Disarmament, Nonproliferation, and the 'Credibility Thesis,'" Hudson Institute Briefing Paper, September 2009, http://www.hudson.org/files/publications/Nuclear%20DisarmamentCF909.pdf.

7. An example of resistance to new nonproliferation measures that could be construed as purely based on material benefits is Brazil's rejection of the Additional Protocol. Signing the Additional Protocol could make it impossible for the country to continue its partial shielding of its centrifuges at Resende, which some claim are based on a stolen design. However, even here, social constructs come into play. The Brazilians see themselves as world-class experts in safeguarding and believe the insinuation that they need more thorough outside inspections is an insult to their competence. On these points, see Maria Rost Rublee, "The Nuclear Threshold States: Challenges and Opportunities Posed by Brazil and Japan," *Nonproliferation Review* 17, no. 1 (2010): 49–70.

8. On nuclear hedging, see Ariel Levite, "Never Say Never Again: Nuclear Reversal Revisited," *International Security* 27, no. 3 (2002/2003): 59–88.

9. For excellent analysis of the question of intent versus capability, see Rebecca Hersman and Robert Peters, "Nuclear U-Turns," *Nonproliferation Review* 13, no. 3 (2006): 539–53.

10. "Japan's Long Fuse," *Christian Science Monitor*, May 9, 2003. For discussion of the Japanese interpretation of these statements, see Mitsuru Kurosawa, "East Asian Regional Security and Arguments for a Nuclear Japan," paper prepared for a workshop on "Prospects for East Asian Nuclear Disarmament," March 11–12, 2004, 2–3.

11. Thomas Graham Jr. *Disarmament Sketches: Three Decades of Arms Control and International Law* (Seattle: Institute for Global and Regional Security Studies and University of Washington Press, 2002).

12. For a clear statement of this position, see Kenneth Waltz's contributions in Scott D. Sagan and Kenneth N. Waltz, *The Spread of Nuclear Weapons: A Debate Renewed*, 2nd ed. (New York: W. W. Norton, 2002).

13. "Brazil Rebuffs U.S. Pressure for Iran Sanctions," *BBC News*, March 3, 2010. President Lula did agree that his country would enforce sanctions against Iran once they passed the United Nations Security Council. See "Brazil Will Back Iran Sanctions," *Al Jazeera*, August 11, 2010.

14. Målfrid Braut-Hegghammer, "Libya's Nuclear Turnaround: Perspectives from Tripoli," *Middle East Journal* 62, no. 1 (2008): 68–69. See also Michael Collins Dunn, "MEJ Author Målfrid Braut-Hegghammer on Libya's Nuclear Rollback," *MEI Bulletin* 59, no. 1 (2008): 8–9.

15. William Potter, Patricia Lewis, Gaukhar Mukhatzhanova, and Miles Pomper, "The 2010 NPT Review Conference: Deconstructing Consensus," James Martin Center for Nonproliferation Studies, Monterey, Calif., June 17, 2010, 14.

16. Katharine Murphy, "No to Indian Uranium Sales," *Age* (Melbourne), February 11, 2011.

17. Maria Rost Rublee, *Nonproliferation Norms: Why States Choose Nuclear Restraint* (Athens: University of Georgia Press, 2009).

18. The term "social fact" originated with Emile Durkheim, who explained the concept in this way in his *Rules of Sociological Method*: "Here, then, is a category of facts with very distinctive characteristics: it consists of ways of acting, thinking, and feeling, external to the individual, and endowed with a power of coercion, by reason of which they control him." Within sociology, norms are often characterized as a subset of social facts. In contrast, in political science, the term "social fact" is usually limited to refer to subjective concepts that have become accepted as objective reality, such as sovereignty, money, and the state. This is distinct from the commonly accepted definition of norms (shared standards of acceptable behavior), which is defined by its "ought" component. Emile Durkheim, *Rules of Sociological Method*, ed. Steven Lukes; trans. W. D. Hall (New York: Free Press, 1982).

19. The discussion of social psychological processes is drawn from my book *Nonproliferation Norms*, ch. 2.

20. Robert B. Cialdini and Melanie R. Trost, "Social Influence: Social Norms. Conformity and Compliance," in *The Handbook of Social Psychology*, vol. 2, 4th ed., ed. Daniel T. Gilbert, Susan T. Fiske, and Gardner Lindzey (Boston: McGraw-Hill, 1998), 155. On descriptive norms, see Robert B. Cialdini, Carl A. Kallgren, and Raymond R. Reno, "A Focus Theory of Normative Conduct: A Theoretical Refinement and Reevaluation of the Role of Norms in Human Behavior," *Advances in Experimental Social Psychology* 24 (1991): 201–34; James B.

Stiff, *Persuasive Communication* (New York: Guilford Press, 1994); Leon Festinger, "A Theory of Social Comparison Processes," *Human Relations* 7, no. 2 (1954): 117–40; John W. Thibaut and Harold H. Kelley, *The Social Psychology of Groups* (New York: Wiley, 1959).

21. Cialdini and Trost, "Social Influence," 157.

22. Rodney W. Jones and Mark G. McDonough, with Toby F. Dalton and Gregory D. Koblentz, *Tracking Nuclear Proliferation: A Guide in Maps and Charts, 1998* (Washington, D.C.: Carnegie Endowment for International Peace, 1998), 19–22.

23. David B. Ottaway, "South Africa Agrees to Treaty Curbing Nuclear Weapons; Important Gain in U.S.-Led Campaign," *Washington Post*, June 28, 1991.

24. Cialdini and Trost, "Social Influence," 161. Cialdini and Trost describe a number of different experiments and studies in which descriptive norms activated everything from littering to extradyadic sexual relations to tipping.

25. No clear hierarchy of norms can be stated; for example, we cannot say that descriptive norms will always trump injunctive norms. The matter of norm activation has rich potential for study in terms of the types of activation available, what happens when different descriptive norms compete, and more. Norm entrepreneurs are undoubtedly in the business of not only norm creation, but also norm activation.

26. J. M. Goldgeier and P. E. Tetlock, "Psychology and International Relations Theory," *Annual Review of Political Science* 4 (2001), 93.

27. Robert Cialdini, *Influence: Science and Practice*, 4th ed. (Boston: Allyn and Bacon, 2001), 178, 84.

28. Goldgeier and Tetlock argue: "Most psychologists would probably agree that most political actors (psychopaths excluded) will gradually internalize the norms of fair play implicit in international institutions. These norms can become functionally autonomous from the interests that may once have inspired them" ("Psychology and International Relations Theory," 67).

29. Paul Taylor and Louis Charbonneau, "EU Big Three Offered Iran Carrot for Nuclear Deal," Reuters News Service, September 19, 2003.

30. Ronald B. Mitchell, "International Control of Nuclear Proliferation: Beyond Carrots and Sticks," *Nonproliferation Review* 5, no. 1 (1997): 40.

31. John M. Levine and E. Tory Higgins, "Shared Reality and Social Influence in Groups and Organizations," in *Social Influence in Social Reality: Promoting Individual and Social Change*, ed. Fabrizio Butera and Gabriel Mugny (Toronto: Hogrefe & Huber, 2001). Levine and Higgins argue, "Evidence indicates that conformity is higher when group members are responding to difficult or ambiguous questions and have low confidence in their position. Moreover, conformity is greater on difficult tasks when the desire to be accurate is high rather than low" (39).

32. As Petty and Wegener note, "A great deal of work suggests that people like other people with whom they share similar attitudes (e.g., Byrne & Griffitt, 1966) or ideology

(Newcomb, 1956) and dislike those with whom they disagree (e.g., Rosenbaum, 1986). This source-receiver similarity has also been shown to increase persuasion (e.g., Brock, 1965)" (348). Richard E. Petty and Duane T. Wegener, "Attitude Change: Multiple Roles for Persuasion Variables," in *The Handbook of Social Psychology*, vol. 2, 4th ed., ed. Daniel T. Gilbert, Susan T. Fiske, and Gardner Lindzey (New York: McGraw Hill, 1998), 323–90.

33. Cialdini and Trost, "Social Influence," 158. See also Richard M. Perloff, *The Dynamics of Persuasion* (Hillsdale, N.J.: Lawrence Erlbaum, 1993), 146.

34. Cialidini and Trost, "Social Influence," 166.

35. Levine and Higgins, "Shared Reality," 40.

CHAPTER 4

Nuclear Disarmament and Nonproliferation

Examining the Linkage Argument

Jeffrey W. Knopf

IS THERE A CONNECTION between nuclear weapons states' policies on nuclear disarmament and the likelihood of nuclear proliferation? Article VI of the Treaty on the Non-Proliferation of Nuclear Weapons (NPT) calls for good-faith negotiations to eliminate nuclear weapons. This has led some commentators to suggest that unless the NPT-recognized nuclear weapons states are perceived to be seriously committed to and making progress toward disarmament, the nonproliferation regime will unravel. Other observers, in contrast, contend that nuclear weapons state actions on disarmament have no bearing on the factors that might lead to the further spread of nuclear weapons.

Policy experts have strongly asserted both positions. On one side, for example, former U.S. officials George Shultz, William Perry, Henry Kissinger, and Sam Nunn see the connection between disarmament efforts and nonproliferation as obvious. This so-called gang of four has endorsed nuclear abolition owing in large part to concern about the dangers of proliferation, such as an increased risk of nuclear terrorism. To halt proliferation, they argue, will require a "realization that continued reliance on nuclear weapons as the principal element for deterrence is encouraging, or at least excusing, the spread of these weapons, and will inevitably erode the essential cooperation necessary to avoid proliferation."[1]

In an essay published around the same time as the Shultz et al. op-ed, Josef Joffe and James W. Davis put forward an equally confident version of the anti-linkage position: "[T]he premise that the have-nots will arm because the haves have not disarmed does not hold. It reflects neither history nor present-day realities. The truth is that the decisionmaking of aspiring nuclear powers is only remotely related, if it is related at all, to the strategic choices of the existing nuclear powers."[2]

This issue became a point of contention in the debate in 2010 over whether to ratify the New Strategic Arms Reduction Treaty (START) between the United States and Russia. In testimony before the Senate Armed Services Committee, Rose Gottemoeller, the lead U.S. negotiator for the treaty, argued that treaty ratification would contribute to nonproliferation: "By demonstrating that we are living up to our obligations under Article VI of the Nuclear Non-Proliferation Treaty (NPT), we enhance our credibility to convince other governments to help strengthen the international nonproliferation regime and confront proliferators."[3] In Senate floor debate, however, the treaty's leading critic challenged these claims. According to Jon Kyl, "[O]ne can argue that the dramatic reduction in the arsenals of Russia and United States of strategic weapons has been a good thing.... But it has had no discernible effect on nuclear proliferation. We have had more proliferation since, after the Cold War, we began to reduce these weapons."[4]

If both sides of the argument can be advanced with equal conviction, then a more systematic analysis is required.[5] Too often, participants in the debate state claims about the relationship between nuclear disarmament and nonproliferation as if they are self-evident, with only a brief or even no discussion of the supporting logic and evidence. This chapter aims to elaborate and assess the theoretical underpinnings of the debate. Specifically, it seeks to identify all of the different theoretical logics that might support conclusions either in favor of or against what the chapter calls "the linkage hypothesis." By identifying different mechanisms that might lead to predictions of either a correlation or a lack of correlation between disarmament and nonproliferation, the following discussion aims to facilitate future empirical testing of the linkage premise. Once there is greater clarity about the different logics that might create or prevent a linkage, it will be easier to determine the types of empirical evidence most pertinent to evaluating the linkage hypothesis.

The following analysis distinguishes between direct and indirect forms of potential linkage. In direct linkages, something about the existence or behavior of nuclear weapons states will lead to proliferation by others. In indirect linkages, something about nuclear weapons state behavior will affect some other variable, which will in turn affect proliferation. As is shown below, most recent comments on the possible link between disarmament and nonproliferation place greater emphasis on indirect linkages, especially the proposition that nonnuclear weapons states will not cooperate to enforce nonproliferation if nuclear weapons states do not fulfill what nonnuclear states perceive to be the latter's disarmament obligations.

The chapter proceeds as follows. First, it summarizes the different elements of what is often called the NPT "bargain" to show where the supposed link between nonproliferation and disarmament fits in the larger NPT context. Second, it discusses a handful of recent studies that have attempted to examine whether such a link really exists. The third section summarizes relevant theoretical perspectives and the hypotheses associated with them regarding whether nuclear weapons state disarmament efforts might affect proliferation. The fourth section outlines some empirical tests that would potentially be relevant for testing the various hypotheses and draws out the policy implications of the preceding analysis. The chapter concludes that signs of a commitment to nuclear disarmament by the nuclear weapons states will tend on balance to enhance support for nonproliferation. Because of the multitude of other factors that affect state decision making, however, progress on disarmament will not by itself address all of the challenges to making the nonproliferation regime effective.

THE NPT AS A SET OF BARGAINS: PLACING DISARMAMENT IN CONTEXT

The NPT, which opened for signature in 1968 and entered into force in 1970, reflected three sets of bargains: one among nuclear weapons states, one among nonnuclear weapons states, and one between nuclear haves and have-nots. In the first bargain, contained in Article I, existing nuclear weapons states agreed not to help any other countries, including their own allies, to join the nuclear club.[6] A second bargain involved a series of "I won't if you won't" agreements among nonnuclear states. For states that preferred not to acquire nuclear weapons, but only as long as their neighbors and rivals remained nonnuclear as well, the NPT offered a convenient multilateral mechanism for establishing such mutual non-acquisition pacts.

Discussions of the NPT, however, typically give most attention to the third bargain. The NPT is unusual in international law in that it enshrines inequality by recognizing two categories of states: nuclear and nonnuclear. Only the five countries that had demonstrated nuclear weapons possession by testing devices before the treaty opened for signature were permitted to join as nuclear weapons states (since the breakup of the Soviet Union, the five acknowledged nuclear weapon states have been China, France, Russia, the United Kingdom, and the United States). All other countries were required to forswear nuclear weapons and join as nonnuclear weapons states. To persuade nonnuclear states to accept their unequal status required three concessions from nuclear weapons states. First, Article IV of the NPT promised that nonnuclear weapons states would retain the right to develop peaceful uses of nuclear technology and pledged assistance to help them do so. Second, states that committed themselves not to seek the bomb requested security assurances to prevent the threat or use of nuclear weapons against them. No agreement could be reached on legally binding text, meaning that security assurances are not contained in the NPT itself. Instead, assurances have been offered in a variety of side arrangements.[7]

Nonnuclear weapons states viewed security assurances as a bridging mechanism to provide security against nuclear threats in the short to medium term. In the long term, these states sought to ensure that the inequality of the NPT would not last forever. Their ultimate security against nuclear threats, contained in Article VI, would be disarmament by the nuclear weapons states. This represented the third concession required to close the NPT bargain. In its entirety, Article VI states: "Each of the Parties to the Treaty undertakes to pursue negotiations in good faith on effective measures relating to cessation of the nuclear arms race at an early date and to nuclear disarmament, and on a Treaty on general and complete disarmament under strict and effective international control."[8]

Some commentators have argued that Article VI does not constitute a legally binding commitment to nuclear disarmament. Christopher A. Ford, a former nonproliferation negotiator in the George W. Bush administration, interprets Article VI as suggesting that nuclear disarmament was only meant to be achieved at the same time as or after general and complete disarmament.[9] On the face of it, moreover, the carefully negotiated wording calls only for a "good faith" effort, not necessarily actual achievement of nuclear disarmament. Other legal experts dispute this interpretation. Daniel H. Joyner contends that the negotiating history of the NPT, language about disarmament in its preamble, and standard methods for interpreting international law show that the NPT really does entail a nuclear disarmament obligation, one that enjoys equal weight with the treaty's nonproliferation and peaceful use pillars.[10] The International Court of Justice shares this view, as it ruled in 1996 that the NPT requires negotiations eventually "to achieve" the actual result of nuclear disarmament.[11] More important, a strictly legal interpretation is not sufficient. As noted by Thomas Graham Jr., who had arms control responsibilities in several administrations, Article VI has to be viewed as a political bargain.[12] Nonnuclear weapons states believe the nuclear weapons states promised to pursue nuclear disarmament. Rather than legal arguments about the correct interpretation of the treaty text, these political expectations—and nonnuclear states' perceptions of whether they are being met—account for the behavior predicted by the linkage hypothesis.

Recognizing the different sets of bargains involved in the NPT leads to two conclusions. First, Article VI creates a clear basis for linking nuclear nonproliferation and disarmament. It reflects a perceived bargain in which nonnuclear weapons states expect to see progress toward nuclear disarmament by the nuclear weapons states as part of the price to keep the nonnuclear states inside the treaty regime. Second, however, Article VI is only one part of the larger NPT agreement. To the extent that states emphasize other elements of the bargain, the practical importance of the disarmament-nonproliferation linkage might not be great. If nonnuclear states care more about security assurances or access to peaceful uses of nuclear technology or sustaining the "I won't if you won't" bargain to prevent further proliferation, then progress toward disarmament might not loom large in their strategic calculations. In short, one cannot predict on the basis of the NPT text itself how important the link between disarmament and nonproliferation will be in practice. Because the strength of the linkage cannot be inferred directly from the NPT text, evaluating the hypothesis requires analysts to consider the theoretical logics that might connect or delink disarmament and nonproliferation and to examine empirical evidence on the strength of this linkage in practice.

RECENT RESEARCH

Although commentators have long expressed strong—and contradictory—views on whether or not activity related to nuclear disarmament affects nonproliferation, there has not been much research to assess the merits of either view. In recent years, however, several scholars have begun exploring how nonproliferation and disarmament might—or might not—be linked. As with the public debate, their conclusions remain divided, although supporters of the linkage hypothesis far outnumber those who reject it.

To my knowledge, a 2007 book chapter by Steven E. Miller represents the earliest academic publication to focus explicitly on the linkage hypothesis. Miller put forward seven arguments for why nuclear weapons state behavior on disarmament affects nonproliferation.[13] In a subsequent analysis with similar conclusions, Harald Müller identified five causal pathways that might link nonfulfillment of Article VI pledges and nuclear proliferation.[14] The analyses by Miller and Müller did not delve deeply into empirical evidence, but a report by Deepti Choubey made this its focus. Choubey interviewed officials from sixteen nonnuclear weapons states. Many of them predicted that nonnuclear states would be reluctant to take new steps to strengthen nonproliferation given a perception that nuclear weapons states have not lived up to the disarmament part of the NPT bargain.[15] Soon after the release of Choubey's report, Christopher F. Chyba proposed that future empirical analysis disaggregate countries into different types. He hypothesized, for example, that disarmament progress is unlikely to affect determined proliferators but might influence some of the more activist nonnuclear NPT states such as members of the New Agenda Coalition.[16]

Christopher Ford has offered the most detailed critique of the linkage hypothesis. He makes two arguments.[17] First, he disputes claims that the nuclear weapons states, and the United States in particular, have failed to take significant action on their Article VI commitments. He points out that there have been deep cuts in U.S. and Russian arsenals since the peak of the Cold War, and he notes that the United States has taken some military missions away from nuclear weapons and reassigned them to various conventional options.[18] Second, Ford contends that there is no empirical correlation between progress on disarmament and cooperation to enforce nonproliferation. He observes that more states joined the NPT when superpower nuclear arsenals were larger than have joined since they have reached lower numbers.[19]

The import of this observation remains a subject of dispute. Nonnuclear states tend not to view nuclear arms reductions as the best indicator of nuclear weapons state compliance with Article VI; they attach greater weight to what they see as indicators in weapons state policies of a future intent to keep nuclear weapons indefinitely.[20] As a result, even if there is no correlation between previous stockpile reductions and nonproliferation, this is not the only relevant empirical evidence for assessing the linkage hypothesis. The way nonnuclear states have responded, or failed to respond, to significant stockpile reductions remains relevant but must be supplemented by other empirical tests. The analysis in the rest of this chapter clarifies what these other tests might look like.

The foregoing studies emphasized either theoretical arguments or empirical evidence but did not do much to combine the two. Three recent studies have moved further toward considering both logic and evidence. The best existing study, by Andrew Grotto, asks why some states that support the NPT nevertheless resist measures to strengthen the treaty.[21] These measures, which he calls "NPT-plus" policies, include the Additional Protocol, limits on nuclear fuel cycle activities, and sanctions against new proliferators. Grotto follows Scott D. Sagan's well-known depiction of three models of proliferation, which emphasize security, norms, and domestic politics, respectively,[22] to identify possible causes of support or nonsupport for NPT-plus measures.

The norms model provides the main argument for why states that support the NPT might still refrain from cooperating to enforce it. A belief that nuclear weapons states have failed to live up to Article VI obligations lies at the heart of this argument. Grotto does not devote much attention to potential direct links between nuclear weapons state policies and proliferation. Instead, he advances an interesting twist on the indirect linkage argument. Grotto observes that states might vary in the degree to which their policies are influenced by the disarmament norm contained in the NPT bargain. States that feel dissatisfied with other aspects of the international order and thereby consider themselves "have-nots" in general, he hypothesizes, will be more likely to withhold cooperation on NPT enforcement if they perceive a lack of commitment to disarmament on the part of nuclear weapons states.[23]

Grotto also recognizes that disarmament considerations might not prove decisive. State decisions about nonproliferation policy might have other causes, which Grotto locates in the security and domestic politics models. For example, states facing threats from potential new nuclear nations will likely cooperate to enforce nonproliferation even if they think that nuclear weapons states have not made sufficient progress on Article VI, whereas states with domestic economic interests in developing nuclear technology or exporting nuclear materials will be wary of NPT-plus measures even if they are satisfied with nuclear weapons state efforts on disarmament.[24]

Although Grotto devotes most of his analysis to explicating alternative theoretical lenses, he also explores relevant empirical evidence. In support of the norms hypothesis, Grotto points out that nearly all of the countries with developed economies have accepted the Additional Protocol. In contrast, at the time he wrote, fewer than one-third of the members of the nonaligned movement had adopted the Additional Protocol.[25] Because these states express more dissatisfaction with the global order in general, their reluctance to embrace the Additional Protocol fits the predictions of the norms model. As his main empirical example, however, Grotto considers the 1995 NPT Review Conference. Because the NPT had an initial duration of twenty-five years, this conference had to determine the treaty's future; it decided to extend the NPT indefinitely. Grotto finds all three models helpful for explaining some of the decision making that led even skeptical countries to ultimately support making the treaty permanent. Because all three models have some explanatory power, Grotto concludes that greater progress toward nuclear disarmament would not by itself bring about full support for NPT-plus measures. If not sufficient, though, such progress would nevertheless be beneficial.

In a recent book, Sverre Lodgaard makes a distinction similar to the differentiation between direct and indirect linkages introduced above. He suggests that disarmament (or its absence) could affect either state decision making (the direct linkage) or management of the nonproliferation regime (the indirect linkage). Like Chyba, Lodgaard sees value in disaggregating states, but he differentiates within those that have undergone nuclear reversal. Among these, he predicts that lack of progress on disarmament would be most likely to affect the calculations of states that are still hedging; states that have internalized an antinuclear norm are unlikely to change course.[26] This analysis seems to apply only to the direct linkage argument, however, as one can imagine that states firmly committed to nuclear renunciation might nevertheless withhold cooperation on new nonproliferation measures if they believe nuclear-armed states are not living up to their obligations.

With a more empirical orientation, a special issue of the *Nonproliferation Review* edited by Scott D. Sagan and Jane Vaynman examines international reactions to the Obama administration's 2010 Nuclear Posture Review and President Barack Obama's initiatives on arms control and disarmament. The editors' stated goals include exploring whether U.S. behavior on nuclear disarmament influences the policies of other states.[27] Sagan and Vaynman identify four causal pathways that might produce such a linkage, but unfortunately most of the case studies in the volume do not attempt to assess these pathways. The empirical findings offer mixed support: some states have been unimpressed by the latest Nuclear Posture Review whereas others have reacted positively. The clearest positive finding comes from an analysis of the 2010 NPT Review Conference by Harald Müller. He shows that Obama administration policies facilitated a relatively successful review conference, especially compared to the utter collapse of the previous 2005 conference.[28] Although narrowly focused, this volume contains the most in-depth empirical research so far. Ultimately, Sagan and Vaynman reach a similar conclusion to Grotto's: that progress on nuclear disarmament is a necessary but not sufficient condition for sustaining nonproliferation.[29]

The studies discussed here represent significant improvement over the nearly pure assertion that has characterized most commentary on the possible disarmament-nonproliferation link. Viewed collectively, they point in three directions in which further research would be useful. None of the studies by itself catalogues all of the potential causal pathways that could affect the relationship between disarmament and nonproliferation. In addition, none of them attempts the systematic assessment of empirical evidence favored by social scientists. Finally, the studies do not always describe the microfoundations of the causal or empirical arguments they make. That is, they do not explain why, to give an example, a perceived violation of norms might lead states to withhold cooperation on enforcing the NPT and thereby jeopardize the whole regime. The next section of this chapter attempts to identify and describe all of the potentially relevant causal pathways, including the different microlevel foundations that might provide a causal mechanism for the various arguments. In doing so, it consolidates all of the causal pathways identified in the various studies discussed above plus introduces some additional possibilities.

POSSIBLE CAUSAL MECHANISMS FOR THE LINKAGE AND NONLINKAGE HYPOTHESES

Scholars who do research on nuclear proliferation have developed a number of theories to explain patterns of nuclear proliferation and restraint.[30] Traditional analyses emphasize access to technology and security considerations as key drivers. As adherence to the NPT has grown, others have come to see the nonproliferation regime itself as an important factor. More recently, some studies have emphasized norms and ideas or internal factors such as domestic coalitions and leader psychology. These explanations, in turn, can be linked to more general theoretical approaches in international relations. Security explanations fit well with realist theory. Institutional aspects of the nonproliferation regime are a logical focus for neoliberal institutionalism. Norms and ideas represent central concerns in social constructivism. Finally, domestic politics and psychological factors serve as key variables in theories based at levels of analysis below the international system. Given that prevailing explanations have affinities with realism, institutionalism, constructivism, and two lower levels of analysis, the following analysis groups possible arguments relating to the linkage hypothesis into five broad categories: security perspectives, institutional and bargaining perspectives, norms arguments, domestic factors, and psychological considerations.

The security, norms, and domestic politics perspectives have been the source of almost all the existing arguments on both sides of the linkage debate. Institutional and psychological perspectives, in contrast, have received little attention. As a result, the hypotheses identified below in association with those two perspectives are mostly new. Where possible, each section differentiates hypotheses in terms of whether they predict direct linkages between disarmament and nonproliferation, indirect linkages, or no linkage, although not necessarily in that order. In general, arguments for and against the linkage hypothesis tend to illustrate limitations on the other perspective, suggesting that neither is universally applicable. This means some degree of linkage likely exists, but of varying strength depending on circumstances.

Security Considerations

Security motivations lie at the heart of the leading theoretical argument against the linkage hypothesis. The primary critique of the linkage hypothesis holds that proliferation results mainly from causes other than the actions of the NPT nuclear weapons states.[31] The most common variant of this claim invokes security concerns. It relies on a traditional security explanation for proliferation but locates the relevant security threats in states' regional environments.[32] In this view, local rivals, rather than the global superpowers, drive proliferation decisions. If regional rivalries or aggressive neighbors loom largest in proliferation decisions, then the arsenals of the NPT nuclear states will not factor in the calculations of the states most likely to pursue a new nuclear program. The case of Israel supports this perspective. Israel did not fear a superpower nuclear threat. Instead, it perceived an existential threat from its conventionally armed neighbors and sought nuclear weapons as an ultimate deterrent against being overrun.[33]

Two possible exceptions, however, could still make NPT nuclear weapons states relevant: the local rival could also be a nuclear weapons state, or a nuclear weapons state could pose a long-distance threat that creates security concerns.[34] In either of these scenarios, security considerations could produce a direct link between the continued maintenance of nuclear arsenals by one or more of the five nuclear states and new proliferation cases. India provides a possible example of the first situation. India shares a disputed border with China, and the two fought a border war in 1962. Many Indian elites point to a potential threat from China, including from China's nuclear weapons, as a major motivation for India's efforts to develop a nuclear arsenal.[35] This suggests that security concerns could in some cases directly motivate states involved in a regional rivalry with a nuclear weapons state to seek their own deterrent.

A second scenario in which security concerns could lead to a link between nuclear weapons state behavior and proliferation involves relatively weak pariah or renegade regimes that find themselves on the receiving end of threats by NPT nuclear states. The direction of causality can be tricky here. Efforts by rogue states to explore a nuclear option may be one reason why they draw the ire of nuclear weapons states, in which case proliferation would be the cause rather than the result of a new security threat to the state. Yet even states without an active intent to develop nuclear weapons might find themselves being threatened by a nuclear weapons state. Such a state might fear that the United States in particular will seek to impose regime change as a result of that state's involvement in some combination of chemical and biological weapons efforts, support for terrorism, conventional threats against its neighbors, and unsavory human rights practices. The most likely form of U.S. military action would be a coercive bombing campaign or conventional invasion, but in some circumstances a rogue regime might fear being the subject of nuclear coercion or attack. The U.S. Nuclear Posture Review in the George W. Bush administration, for example, contemplated possible preemptive use of nuclear weapons against chemical and biological weapons sites.[36] The possibility of such threats could motivate a rogue state without an active nuclear program to decide it needs a nuclear deterrent. This would be a second scenario in which security concerns might produce a direct link between continued nuclear possession by NPT weapons states and further proliferation. The two linkage pathways identified here, moreover, seem unlikely to have been greatly affected by U.S. and Russian nuclear arms reductions since the Cold War. As long as nuclear weapons states retain usable nuclear arsenals, their capacity to pose a nuclear threat could lead certain nonnuclear states to seek the capacity to respond in kind.

If security threats posed by nuclear weapons states can directly motivate proliferation in response, then an indirect linkage scenario also becomes possible. States that are not threatened by an NPT nuclear weapons state might nevertheless be threatened by a neighbor that seeks nuclear weapons in response to such a threat. Pakistan is the obvious example. Pakistan's nuclear weapons program clearly emerged in response to India's effort. To the extent India decided to seek the bomb because of a perceived threat from China, then Pakistan's nuclear program represents an indirect consequence of the impact of nuclear weapons state behavior on India's choice. Should a threat posed by an existing nuclear weapons state become a direct motivation for proliferation in another case, that case could potentially trigger similar spillover effects leading to further proliferation.

This danger should not be overstated. Recent research suggests that there is nothing inevitable about proliferation chain reactions.[37] Proliferation does not always beget further proliferation. Yet, even if indirect effects of security threats posed by nuclear weapons states will not always lead to secondary proliferation, the risk remains that they will do so in some cases. Hence, security concerns could be one possible source of indirect linkages between a lack of disarmament and new cases of proliferation.

Critics of the linkage hypothesis also have a second security-based counterargument to the linkage proposition. This one represents an especially important challenge because it suggests that disarmament would actually have the opposite effect. Many analysts believe that security guarantees provided by nuclear weapons states, in the form of extended nuclear deterrence, serve to inhibit proliferation. According to this logic, states protected by a "nuclear umbrella" do not need their own deterrent and hence will not seek nuclear weapons. If the nuclear weapons states really started to disarm, however, they might eventually reach numbers of nuclear weapons so low that their allies would begin to doubt the continued credibility of extended deterrent commitments. At this point, progress toward nuclear disarmament could suddenly lead to increased proliferation. As Keith B. Payne, a long-time defense analyst and former official in the George W. Bush administration, puts the point: "The presumption that United States movement toward nuclear disarmament will deliver nonproliferation success is a fantasy. On the contrary, the United States nuclear arsenal has itself been the single most important tool for nonproliferation in history, and dismantling it would be a huge setback."[38]

The security guarantees offered by nuclear weapon states are a form of positive security assurance. A recently published study that I directed, which includes several case studies, finds that positive security assurances have played a role in preventing proliferation.[39] This provides empirical support for the claim that disarmament might be counterproductive for nonproliferation. This support comes with important caveats, however. The case findings also show that the impact of security assurances is conditional on other factors, including the perceived legitimacy of nonproliferation norms.[40] Some states accept reliance on a nuclear umbrella rather than seek a deterrent of their own because they are already moving toward rejecting the legitimacy of nuclear weapons. Were the legitimacy of the nonproliferation regime and its norm against nuclear weapons possession to crumble, it is not clear if nuclear security guarantees would continue to be an effective inhibitor to proliferation. If nonproliferation norms become too weakened, even allies protected by a nuclear umbrella might be tempted to reconsider their choice.

Apart from the equivocal empirical evidence, the prediction that disarmament would trigger greater proliferation as a result of the removal of security guarantees also rests on an assumption that nonnuclear states will continue to need protection via extended deterrence, but with progress toward nuclear abolition the need for extended deterrence might go away. The nuclear weapon states are unlikely to eliminate their nuclear capabilities unless they have high confidence that no other actor is able to suddenly break out with a covertly developed nuclear arsenal. Complete nuclear disarmament, if it is ever reached, will occur only when international political relationships have improved and strong verification measures have been put in place. In such circumstances, nonnuclear states would be unlikely to perceive nuclear threats that would motivate them to develop their own nuclear weapon program.

In addition, positive security assurances are not universal. Many states do not have a nuclear-armed ally. For these states, the actions of nuclear weapons states could potentially motivate decisions to proliferate or to refrain from cooperating on nonproliferation efforts. This means a lack of progress on nuclear disarmament could have contradictory effects, providing proliferation-inhibiting assurances to some while creating proliferation-facilitating motivations for others. Because some countries do value nuclear security guarantees, any serious movement toward abolition will require careful management of alliance relations and associated security assurances.

One final security-related argument comes from those who endorse the linkage hypothesis. In addition to the possibility that a nuclear weapons state arsenal poses a security threat, another potential direct link involves a demonstration effect of nuclear weapons state activities. Through the development of new weapons, shifts in doctrine, or strong statements about the continued value of nuclear weapons possession, a nuclear weapons state might demonstrate that it sees unique military utility in having a nuclear capability.[41] This could encourage other states, especially those that look to the military superpowers for lessons about the elements of a strong defense, to see military utility in acquiring the bomb for themselves.

In sum, security considerations provide two reasons for expecting no linkage or even a negative correlation between disarmament and nonproliferation, but they also suggest two possible sources of direct linkage and one indirect linkage. Although skeptics of the linkage hypothesis often cite security explanations for proliferation as a reason why nuclear disarmament will not change patterns of proliferation, this is true only if weapons possessed by the NPT nuclear states are never perceived as a potential threat by any other state or as an object lesson in the military value of the bomb. Many states will have more powerful motivations for their actions than whether or not the nuclear weapons states are committed to disarmament, but one cannot logically conclude from this that every state will lack meaningful concerns about what the nuclear weapons states do.

Institutional and Bargaining Perspectives

Research on proliferation has often reflected realist thinking about security, and, to some degree, it has also drawn on social constructivism and the domestic and individual levels of analysis. Proliferation research does not cite the literatures on bargaining and institutions nearly as much, yet these literatures offer potential insights relevant to the linkage hypothesis. These research programs focus on situations in which states have a mixture of common and conflicting interests, and they explore the conditions under which such states will reach agreements or will develop and sustain international regimes.[42] Like realism, they assume that states will act as rational, self-interested actors, but they suggest some additional pathways beyond traditional security arguments that could either produce linkage or account for its absence. In particular, they point to some possible indirect connections that have not received much attention.

Although this chapter discusses several mechanisms that might directly link continued nuclear weapons possession by the nuclear weapons states and proliferation, most people who believe in a disarmament-nonproliferation linkage emphasize indirect connections between the two. The most frequently hypothesized indirect linkage predicts that nonnuclear weapons state perceptions that NPT nuclear states are not serious about disarmament will lead them to withhold cooperation on measures to strengthen the NPT. With less cooperation on nonproliferation, presumably the likelihood of future proliferation will increase. Yet commentators do not always make clear what underlying causal process would lead to reduced cooperation. This chapter identifies several different microfoundations that could produce this behavior.

Existing discussions generally imply a normative or psychological foundation for the indirect linkage. Drawing on institutionalist theory, though, makes it possible to also give an account based on rational self-interest. Nonnuclear weapon states may withhold cooperation as a way to pressure nuclear weapons states to do more to comply with Article VI, and, consistent with institutionalist theory, they might do so out of self-interest, specifically an interest in nuclear abolition. Nonnuclear states might believe that they have an interest in nuclear disarmament even if they do not perceive themselves to be in imminent danger of attack by a nuclear weapons state. Realist folk wisdom holds that today's friend might still turn out to be tomorrow's enemy. Hence, prudent states will not want to leave themselves permanently vulnerable to possible nuclear coercion or attack, just in case a benign security situation turns less benign in the future. This gives them an interest in pushing for eventual nuclear disarmament.

In addition, one should not forget the Cold War context in which states negotiated the NPT. Had there been a U.S.-Soviet nuclear war, no state would have escaped unscathed. Many of the allies and friends of the superpowers would also have been targeted with nuclear weapons. Even states not directly targeted would have been exposed to radioactive fallout and suffered great economic harm from the destruction of the world's leading economies. Nonnuclear weapons states sought measures to halt the arms race and achieve disarmament in part because they wanted to avoid becoming collateral damage in the event of a superpower nuclear war. Indeed, the NPT's preamble lists "the devastation that would be visited upon all mankind by a nuclear war" first among the motivations for concluding the treaty.[43] In short, although security explanations have emphasized threats from hostile or nuclear-armed neighbors, many states also have a generic security interest in reducing and if possible eliminating the danger of nuclear war. As South Africa's foreign minister, Nkosazana Dlamini Zuma, put the point at a Nuclear Suppliers Group meeting in 2007: "Whilst South Africa is committed to the continuous review and strengthening of measures aimed at preventing the proliferation of weapons of mass destruction, we believe that real progress in securing our world from the threat of nuclear weapons can only be achieved through concomitant progress in the area of nuclear disarmament."[44]

What can states with a general interest in nuclear abolition do if the nuclear weapons states seem disinclined to move in that direction? Neoliberal theories of cooperation suggest a possible answer. Neoliberalism focuses on mixed-motive situations in which states will benefit from mutual cooperation but also have incentives to defect. When defection occurs, because there is no central authority that can enforce agreements, states must rely on their own efforts to bring about compliance. Cooperation research points to the potential value in this context of using a strategy of tit for tat.[45] Under this strategy, if the other side defects, one responds by defecting in turn but then resumes cooperation if the other does too. When the other side sees that it will not get away with exploitation and will fare worse under mutual defection than it did under mutual cooperation, its rational self-interest will lead it to return to cooperation.

How might this tit-for-tat strategy operate in the nonproliferation regime? The nonproliferation regime suffers from the problem that strict tit for tat, meaning defection in kind, is undesirable. If a new state, such as North Korea, defects from the regime by developing nuclear weapons, states in its region, such as South Korea or Japan, could respond in kind. These states, however, do not actually want to "go nuclear" or to experience a nuclear arms race in their region. Indeed, the whole point of the regime is to prevent proliferation, not add to it. This makes threats to retaliate in kind counterproductive to the regime's goals and less than fully credible as a deterrent to the initiation of new nuclear weapons programs. In practice, therefore, the international community relies instead on imposing sanctions and enhancing denial measures, such as export controls, rather than on answering proliferation with proliferation.

If ensuring that some new country will not join the nuclear club ranks as the greatest interest for a nonnuclear weapons state, then its self-interest should lead it to cooperate in imposing these enforcement measures. In some cases, however, a state may calculate that it has an equal or greater interest in promoting progress toward nuclear disarmament. Such a calculation may be especially likely for middle powers in regions without an immediate proliferation threat— states such as Brazil, Indonesia, or South Africa. What should states with an interest in enforcing disarmament commitments do if they perceive noncompliance by the NPT nuclear states? Again, the option of strict tit for tat is not desirable. A state could respond to a perceived lack of seriousness about disarmament by initiating its own nuclear weapons program. But if its goal is to foster a nuclear-weapons-free world, this represents movement in the wrong direction. Because the initial term of the NPT ran for twenty-five years, nonnuclear weapons states could exert leverage before 1995 by threatening not to support renewal of the treaty if the nuclear weapons states did not do more on disarmament. Since the decision to make the treaty permanent, this option is no longer available. Today, if a state wants to practice tit for tat by defecting in some other way that is still linked to the nonproliferation regime, the logical option would be to withhold its cooperation from the various NPT-plus measures to strengthen the regime. If nuclear weapons states get the message, they may conclude that their own interest in preventing proliferation requires them to commit more strongly to nuclear disarmament.

Viewing the nonproliferation regime as an ongoing bargaining process, Sagan and Vaynman identify a less coercive way than use of tit for tat in which disarmament and nonproliferation might become indirectly linked. In their special issue on international reactions to the Obama Nuclear Posture Review, Sagan and Vaynman highlight how signs of renewed commitment to disarmament can change bargaining dynamics.[46] When nonnuclear weapon states do not expect nuclear weapon states to be receptive to new disarmament measures, they have no incentive to offer new compromise proposals. But when nuclear states appear serious about making progress on Article VI, this creates a more favorable environment for negotiations. It can encourage nonnuclear states to come forward with new bargaining offers in the hope they will be reciprocated via concrete steps on disarmament. Along these lines, Tanya Ogilvie-White and David Santoro have proposed several specific "mini-bargains" that would trade modest moves toward disarmament for specific nonproliferation actions, such as more states signing the Additional Protocol.[47]

One further potential source of indirect linkage between disarmament and nonproliferation also reflects institutional logic. It concerns perceptions of credibility. Failure by nuclear weapons states to follow through on one aspect of the NPT bargain might raise doubts about the strength of their commitment to other parts of the bargain.[48] Nonnuclear states might fear that if nuclear states do not fulfill their pledges on Article VI, they might also not uphold their Article I commitments not to help new states acquire nuclear weapons or their Article IV commitments to assist with the development of peaceful uses of nuclear technology. In short, there might be spillover effects from Article VI to the perceived credibility of the whole treaty regime, thereby lessening the incentives for nonnuclear weapon states to accept new nonproliferation measures or to help enforce compliance.

Reaction to the U.S.-India nuclear deal suggests how this process might work. The U.S. deal to assist India's civilian nuclear sector did not directly contradict Article VI. It was, however, widely perceived as a violation of Article IV.[49] Most NPT parties believe that technical assistance in the development of peaceful uses of nuclear energy promised under Article IV should be reserved for nonnuclear weapons state parties to the NPT to create an incentive for nonsignatories to join. When the United States offered similar benefits to India despite the latter's nonmembership in the NPT, it led observers to question the U.S. commitment to the

NPT as a whole. This could make nonnuclear state members less willing to invest in the treaty. Complaints about the nuclear weapons states' commitment to Article VI could have similar corrosive effects on how others perceive the credibility of the whole NPT bargain and its likely future survival. States that come to believe that the nuclear weapons states do not care greatly if the NPT survives will be unlikely to cooperate in efforts to sustain the regime.

Although institutionalist logic can be invoked to provide foundations for an indirect linkage argument, its emphasis on self-interest as the reason for cooperation also suggests several possible arguments against the linkage hypothesis. One possible counterargument directly disputes the prediction that lack of progress on disarmament will lead nonnuclear states to withhold cooperation. Most nonnuclear NPT members, one could argue, will continue to cooperate to strengthen the nonproliferation regime because it is in their interest to do so. The vast majority of NPT parties do not want to see new states obtain nuclear weapons. If states follow their national interests and it is in the interest of most states to stem further proliferation, then most states will likely continue to cooperate on measures to stop proliferation.

The decision of the 1995 Review Conference to make the NPT permanent reflected this kind of interest calculation. In the lead-up to the extension decision, many of the nonnuclear weapons states expressed unhappiness with nuclear weapons states' efforts to date on Article VI. In the years immediately preceding the conference, however, revelations about the nuclear weapons programs of Iraq and North Korea made many states realize that nuclear proliferation remained a real danger. In these circumstances, many states concluded that their interests in strengthening the regime by extending the treaty permanently outweighed their desire to retain leverage over nuclear weapons states by agreeing to only a temporary extension. This is not the whole story, because the conference outcome also depended on compromises offered by the nuclear weapons states with regard to disarmament—most notably commitments to conclude a comprehensive test-ban treaty and create a strengthened review process. Yet the argument that most states concluded that they had a national interest in upholding the nonproliferation regime captures an important core truth.[50]

Similar to the security-based counterarguments to the linkage hypothesis discussed above, however, this argument for expecting no linkage also may not hold universally. For some states, stopping further proliferation may not be the most important interest. Rising middle powers located in regions where proliferation is unlikely may believe that they have a greater national interest in eliminating some of the remaining gaps between them and the great powers. Countries such as Brazil or South Africa will not be greatly threatened by a North Korean bomb, but they may be highly motivated to reduce some of the remaining inequality between themselves and the five official nuclear powers. The counterargument based on interests is hence best interpreted as leading to a differentiated prediction: the greater a state's interest is in preventing proliferation, the more likely it is to cooperate with nuclear weapons states on enforcement. The less clear it is that a state has such an interest, or the stronger a potentially countervailing interest, the less likely it is to cooperate.

This latter proposition could also serve as a different rejoinder to the indirect linkage hypothesis. It accepts the argument that nonnuclear weapons states might decline to cooperate with NPT-plus measures. It suggests, however, an alternative explanation that does not link that decision to a lack of progress on disarmament. Some states will not join in multilateral efforts to strengthen nonproliferation because they have no national interest in doing so, or they have an active interest against doing so—for instance, if they have an economic interest in developing or exporting nuclear materials or technology.[51] States that perceive no likely threat to themselves from nuclear proliferation will be reluctant to pay the costs of participating in enforcement measures, because there will be no benefits adequate to outweigh the costs. States, in short, may not cooperate for the simple reason that it is not in their interests, rather than because they feel discriminated against by the nuclear weapons states.

As with other rejoinders to the linkage hypothesis, the argument that states may lack an interest in cooperating to enforce nonproliferation has limitations. It might not be their top priority, but many states still have some interest in preventing proliferation. Even if currently suspected NPT violators are geographically distant, states have reasons to see unchecked nuclear proliferation as contrary to their interests. If current violators are allowed to develop nuclear weapons with impunity, this will reduce the disincentives for other states to follow suit. If the nonproliferation regime unravels, states that face no proliferation threat today could in the future find that some of their regional rivals have started to explore a nuclear option. Uncertainty about the future creates an incentive to uphold nonproliferation norms even against suspected NPT violators that pose no threat to one's own state.

The danger of nuclear terrorism creates an additional reason to limit as much as possible the number of states with nuclear weapons programs. New nuclear states might not be able to adequately safeguard their nuclear materials, leading to increased risk that such materials could fall into the hands of violent non-state actors. In a globally interconnected world, many countries could contain sites that are attractive targets for violent extremist groups. The 1998 attacks on U.S. embassies in Kenya and Tanzania show that no country can count on being immune from terrorist violence. This means that all states have an interest in limiting as much as possible the number of places where terrorists might find an opportunity to acquire nuclear weapons or materials. This same consideration also creates another reason for an interest in nuclear disarmament, as even established nuclear weapons states could find it difficult to completely secure their nuclear materials forever against potential diversion to terrorists.

One additional argument for expecting no linkage can be derived from a bargaining perspective. Complaints about Article VI compliance by nonnuclear states could simply be an attempt to gain a tactical edge in bargaining, but not something such states truly believe. This charge becomes especially plausible if compliance with Article VI has actually been good. Some critics of the linkage hypothesis make precisely this claim, pointing to evidence that nuclear weapon states have made both firm commitments to and substantial progress toward nuclear abolition. The United States, for example, has reduced its nuclear forces from a Cold War peak of more than 30,000 warheads to about 5,000 warheads, and it is committed by the New START agreement to limit its deployed strategic warheads to 1,550.[52] At the 2000 NPT Review Conference, moreover, the final document included an "unequivocal undertaking by the nuclear-weapon states to accomplish the total elimination of their nuclear arsenals."[53] President Obama, in a speech in Prague in 2009, reiterated the U.S. commitment to eventual nuclear abolition. Some observers say that these facts refute the premise of a lack of progress on disarmament. If one believes that the NPT nuclear states have made a good-faith effort to comply with Article VI, and posits that this should be obvious to the nonnuclear weapons states, then the latter's complaints about the disarmament pillar of the nonproliferation regime will appear insincere. In this view, the rhetoric about disarmament serves as a smokescreen that enables some nonnuclear weapons states to hide the real reasons why they have resisted doing more to uphold their end of the NPT bargain. This leads to a prediction that virtually no actions the nuclear-armed states might take on disarmament (other than perhaps actually going to zero) would produce meaningful new action on nonproliferation.[54]

A certain amount of state rhetoric in international politics is clearly insincere, but this does not justify dismissing out of hand all state complaints about a lack of progress on disarmament. Perceptions, by definition, are in the eye of the perceiver. However much government officials in nuclear weapons states may believe that their countries have made good-faith efforts to implement Article VI, these efforts might not be interpreted the same way in other countries. More than forty years after the NPT entered into force, the United States and Russia each continue to possess thousands of warheads. As part of the price of obtaining Senate ratification of New START, moreover, the Obama administration pledged to spend $85 billion over ten years to modernize the U.S. nuclear weapons complex.[55] A situation in which the leading nuclear weapons states will retain thousands of weapons and plan to spend heavily on nuclear modernization could reasonably be interpreted as reflecting something less than an unequivocal commitment to disarmament.

The United States can legitimately argue that it has made great strides away from the nuclear arms race that characterized the Cold War and has not been given sufficient credit for this. NPT nonnuclear states, however, are also looking for signs that the inequality between nuclear haves and have-nots will not last indefinitely. They see the failure of some countries to ratify the Comprehensive Test-Ban Treaty, the lack of negotiations on a Fissile Material Cut-off Treaty, and the continued importance of nuclear deterrence in military doctrines as discouraging signs.[56] For these reasons, substantial nuclear arms reductions from Cold War levels are, in their eyes, not enough to demonstrate a nuclear weapons state commitment to actually achieve nuclear disarmament. A statement to the 2008 NPT PrepCom by the New Agenda Coalition (Brazil, Egypt, Ireland, Mexico, New Zealand, South Africa, and Sweden) directly addressed this point: "The New Agenda Coalition welcomes indications from some nuclear-weapon States that further cuts in nuclear arsenals are being advanced. However, the Coalition remains seriously concerned that intentions to modernize other nuclear forces seem to persist. The Coalition reiterates that States should not develop new nuclear weapons or nuclear weapons with new military capabilities or for new missions, nor replace nor modernize their nuclear weapon systems, as any such action would contradict the spirit of the disarmament and non-proliferation obligations of the treaty."[57]

If true (and the claims at this point are impressionistic rather than corroborated by systematic data analysis), an absence of nonnuclear state responsiveness to deep cuts by Russia and the United States should be considered evidence against the linkage hypothesis. If nuclear have-nots had responded positively by embracing new nonproliferation measures, this would certainly have been cited as evidence in favor of the linkage hypothesis. The failure of such evidence to materialize thus legitimately counts against the hypothesis. This empirical observation is not by itself decisive, however. Nonnuclear states have long identified other steps beyond nuclear arms reductions as important indicators for how they evaluate nuclear weapon state compliance with Article VI. Because of this, additional empirical tests, discussed below, are necessary to fully evaluate the linkage hypothesis.

As with security considerations, institutionalist perspectives yield mixed expectations. Some states see nuclear disarmament as an important interest and might as a result withhold cooperation on nonproliferation if they perceive a failure by nuclear weapon states to fulfill Article VI obligations. In other cases, states will make different self-interest calculations that would lead one to expect no linkage between disarmament and nonproliferation.

Norms

Critics of the linkage hypothesis tend to base their case on arguments about interests. To them, states that proliferate or refuse to cooperate with new nonproliferation measures have other reasons for doing so unrelated to disarmament. And if states do have a strong interest in nonproliferation, critics expect this to override any unhappiness these states feel about a lack of greater progress on disarmament. As has been shown, security and institutionalist arguments about state interests can also be invoked in support of the linkage hypothesis. Those who see a connection between disarmament and nonproliferation, however, tend to rest their case more heavily on the impact of norms.

Norms can be a source of both direct and indirect linkages. The most commonly invoked direct linkage that involves norms points to a perception that nuclear weapons possession confers status. The fact that the five NPT nuclear weapons states are also the five permanent UN Security Council members (P-5), and hence the only Security Council members with veto power, sends an unfortunate signal that nuclear weapons have "political utility" and not just military utility.[58] The longer the P-5 maintain policies indicating a desire to retain nuclear weapons indefinitely, the more this creates a direct motivation for other states seeking great power status to imitate them. India presents a potential example. Many observers of the Indian program discount official claims that the Indian bomb was a response to security threats from China. They see it more as an expression of India's striving for great power status.[59]

Norms also provide a possible basis for two indirect linkage pathways. Norms could be a reason why nonnuclear states withhold cooperation when they believe that nuclear states are not fulfilling Article VI obligations. As noted above, Grotto identifies the norms model as the central explanation for why states refrain from embracing NPT-plus measures. Yet Grotto and others who emphasize norms do not always give a full account of the causal mechanism that would produce the linkage effect. This chapter proposes three alternative microfoundations that could give force to a norms argument. First, institutionalist logic could complement a norms argument. As discussed above, states with self-interest reasons for favoring a norm have incentives to punish defection. According to this logic, states that see an interest in nuclear abolition will have rational reasons to sanction noncompliance with Article VI and its associated disarmament norm as a way to encourage future compliance.

A second possibility involves the logic of norms themselves. If state leaders believe in the value of norms and are committed to upholding them, this logically entails a secondary norm of enforcing norms by reacting against norm violations. Rather than an instrumental logic of consequences in which states try to elicit cooperation with disarmament norms by using tit for tat to show the consequences of not complying with Article VI, states may follow a normative logic of appropriateness in which it is seen as proper to sanction others who defy agreed-upon norms.[60] This normative logic is not entirely satisfying, however, because it does not explain why states would want to invest energy in the secondary norm of norm enforcement. A third possible microfoundation, drawn from psychology, is described below. It could complement a norms argument by explaining why an actor might react strongly against perceived norms violations.

Norms could also create an indirect connection between disarmament and nonproliferation through perceptions of double standards. Norms should gain in legitimacy when there is consistency in upholding them. If powerful actors claim that norms apply to others but then these actors exempt themselves, the charge of hypocrisy could undermine support for the norms in question. There have been accusations that the nuclear weapons states, especially the United States, follow a double standard: they get to judge whether others are in compliance with nonproliferation obligations, but they do not allow others to judge whether they are in compliance with disarmament obligations. This makes it harder to enlist support for holding nonnuclear state parties accountable for NPT violations.[61] The corrosive effect of perceived double standards can be seen in the question posed by a former UN ambassador from Singapore: "How can the violators of UN principles also be their enforcers?"[62]

Those who believe there is no linkage between disarmament and nonproliferation generally devote little attention to norms. As a result, all existing norms-based arguments suggest either a direct or indirect linkage.

Domestic Politics

The security, institutional, and norms perspectives all emphasize features of the international system. Sources of state decisions to proliferate or to reject new nonproliferation measures might also be found in internal politics. With respect to the linkage hypothesis, especially in its direct form, internal factors provide another basis for predicting no linkage. Critics of the linkage hypothesis often claim that decisions to acquire nuclear weapons are not driven by nuclear weapons state behavior, but by other factors. One version of this critique, described above, highlights regional security concerns. A second variant of this argument focuses instead on internal causes of proliferation. Much of the recent proliferation literature has discounted the adequacy of security explanations. It has instead located much of the impetus for nuclear weapons development in internal factors, including domestic political coalition dynamics and the psychology of individual leaders.[63] If state decisions about nuclear acquisition arise purely from such domestic-level factors, then they are unlikely to be affected by nuclear weapons state policies. Some critics of the linkage hypothesis cite Iran and North Korea as examples of states whose nuclear programs have internally driven motivations (including leaders or regimes that seek to project power or achieve regional dominance independently of the external security environment). This leads them to argue that additional steps to fulfill Article VI requirements will not reduce proliferation.[64]

Proliferation, however, can have multiple causes. Domestic coalitions and the worldviews of political leaders probably account for part of the explanation in many cases, but usually not the whole story. Given their long-standing frictions with regional neighbors and the United States, Iran and North Korea plausibly have security concerns alongside their domestic motivations for wanting the bomb. To the extent internal factors have a role in explaining proliferation, a greater commitment to disarmament by nuclear weapons states will not alone be sufficient to prevent any future possibility of proliferation. Where multiple causes operate, however, acknowledging the impact of internal factors does not logically preclude nuclear weapons state actions from also having some impact on proliferation. Explanations based on an individual leader's psychology, for example, still have to account for the content of the leader's beliefs. A power-hungry, norm-defying leader might be attracted to nuclear weapons acquisition because he or she views the bomb as providing power and status to the nuclear weapons states and wants to obtain what they have. The causal factors of an individual leader's psychology and nuclear weapons state behavior could thus be interactive rather than mutually exclusive.

It is also possible for states to be internally divided. There can be differences of opinion within ruling circles, or between rulers and other influential domestic actors, about whether a state should seek nuclear weapons or should embrace new nonproliferation measures. Such internal divisions can create a pathway for either direct or indirect linkages. When there are internal debates, the statements, policies, and actions of nuclear weapons states can become ammunition in those debates. A strong embrace by nuclear weapons states of the value of nuclear weapons will strengthen the position of those in nonnuclear states who favor a nuclear program or a more reserved stance on nonproliferation. Signs of greater commitment to disarmament, in contrast, should help those who support stronger nonproliferation policies.[65] In these scenarios, domestic politics function as an intervening variable rather than a separate causal factor; internal divisions open a pathway that can connect causal mechanisms with nonproliferation outcomes. Overall, as with security and institutional perspectives, domestic-level considerations have mixed implications, suggesting that they may foster linkage in some cases but not others.

Psychological Considerations

Although they have not received much attention in previous discussions of the linkage hypothesis, findings from research on psychology suggest additional mechanisms that could create a linkage. In particular, psychological factors offer the most persuasive microfoundations for why nonnuclear states might attach great importance to disarmament norms. In this sense, psychological mechanisms can function as a complement to norms arguments.

Several lines of research suggest that people—and even other species—have an innate concern with fairness and justice.[66] Outcomes that strike people as inequitable can provoke strong, emotional reactions. Sometimes these reactions lead people to do things that economic rationality deems contrary to their self-interest. Studies of the ultimatum game provide supporting evidence. In this game, one player offers a division of, say, $10 provided by the researcher. The second player then either accepts or rejects the offer. The game ends there. By economic logic, the first player could propose to keep $9 and offer the other player just $1, and the second player should agree because he or she will still achieve a net gain. In practice, however, the more uneven the proposed split, the more likely the second player is to reject it. When people feel their sense of fair play offended, they react more to the perceived injustice than to a strictly economic cost-benefit calculation.[67]

Concerns over fairness might be the most powerful basis for predicting an indirect linkage. Some states might simply become angry at what they see as continued foot-dragging by the nuclear powers. If so, they may lash out against states that they think have reneged on their end of the bargain. The problem will be that much worse in the case of the nonproliferation regime because the original bargain encoded an inequality. It let some states keep nuclear arms even though all others had to forgo them. This inequality was made tolerable to some states only by the promise it would be temporary.[68] Because nonnuclear states view the original NPT terms as already favoring nuclear weapons states, this makes perceived noncompliance with Article VI all the more likely to cause nonnuclear states to react angrily to new demands on them.[69] Why, they will ask, should they agree to do more when the nuclear states have not yet fulfilled their original promises?

Several researchers have presented evidence that fairness concerns play a role in decisions not to participate in measures to strengthen nonproliferation. They have found that some leading nonaligned states reject the idea that they should accept additional restrictions on peaceful nuclear technology, restrictions that were not part of the original NPT agreement, when in their view the nuclear weapons states have not made sufficient progress on implementing Article VI.[70] For example, shortly before the 2010 NPT Review Conference, Egypt's UN ambassador stated in a speech to the General Assembly, "We are not as nonnuclear weapon states going to accept that each time there is progress on disarmament that we have to take more obligations on our side."[71] Similarly, Brazil's ambassador to the 2010 NPT Review Conference called it "simply not fair" to impose new verification measures on nonnuclear states when nuclear states had put forward no timeline for eliminating nuclear weapons.[72]

If indirect linkages arise from a psychological mechanism such as this, then nuclear weapons states are unlikely to gain much by pointing to deep cuts in their nuclear arsenals. Even though the United States and Russia have agreed to substantial reductions over the last twenty-five years, leaders of nonnuclear states do not seem to credit this as conveying sufficient commitment to Article VI. Psychological factors might explain why. According to this perspective, the difference that matters most is the one between haves and have-nots. If some states get to have nuclear weapons and others do not, this inequality will rankle and cause resentment, and this resentment may lead nonnuclear weapons states to withhold cooperation with NPT-plus measures. This might still be the case even if there are further cuts, if it also appears that the NPT nuclear states have no intention of going lower.

Although they are most likely to lead to indirect linkages, psychological dynamics associated with perceptions of fairness might also produce a direct link from a perceived lack of progress on disarmament to proliferation. As noted, states that feel discriminated against might react with feelings of anger or wounded pride. In some cases, these feelings can produce a defiant response toward the international community, especially among countries that already define their national identity in oppositional terms. Jacques E. C. Hymans has argued that psychological factors associated with ideas about national identity can be a potent motivation for some state leaders to favor nuclear weapons acquisition. Proliferation efforts are especially likely, according to Hymans, when leaders with high levels of national pride also perceive high levels of opposition to their state among outside powers.[73] Continued efforts by nuclear weapons states to enforce nonproliferation while holding onto their own nuclear arsenals could produce exactly the psychological feelings that Hymans believes lead states to initiate nuclear weapons programs.

Suggestive evidence for this direct linkage pathway can be found in the rhetoric that potential proliferators have sometimes employed. Argentine diplomats, for example, used to refer to the NPT as "disarmament of the disarmed." They interpreted the nonproliferation regime as an attempt to prevent developing countries from acquiring indigenous technological capabilities that would enable them to reduce dependence on and to compete with developed countries. Argentina's efforts to master the nuclear fuel cycle were, on this view, more a response to perceived inequality and discrimination than part of a conscious effort to develop a nuclear deterrent.[74] India's diplomatic rhetoric has been even more pointed, characterizing the NPT as "nuclear apartheid."[75] A detailed history of India's nuclear program by George Perkovich supports this hypothesized linkage. Perkovich highlights how keenly Indian elites felt the sting of their country's former colonial status.[76] They saw the nuclear program, in part, as a way to prove that India was capable of accomplishing anything its former colonial overlords could do. To the extent that continued nuclear weapons possession becomes associated with legacies of colonialism or new forms of imperialism, elites in developing nations, especially those that are former colonies, may be motivated to pursue a nuclear option as a reaction against the slights of ongoing discrimination. As was the case with the literature on norms, proponents of the no-linkage position have not drawn on the psychology literature, so existing propositions from this perspective all favor the linkage hypothesis.

Summary

This section has sought to identify all the potentially significant arguments both for and against the linkage hypothesis. It has grouped them according to five theoretical perspectives, involving security, institutions and bargaining, norms, domestic politics, and psychology, respectively. Most previously developed arguments in the debate have been framed in terms of security, norms, or internal politics. By adding institutional and psychological perspectives, this chapter has pointed out additional causal pathways relevant to the hypothesis, including some that provide alternative microfoundations for how norms might exercise an effect.

Some of the hypotheses identified predict a direct linkage in which nuclear weapons state behavior directly motivates proliferation; others suggest an indirect linkage in which perceived shortcomings on disarmament have effects that indirectly increase the chances of proliferation; finally, other hypotheses predict no linkage at all. In addition to sorting hypotheses by theoretical approach, it would be useful to group them by prediction. Hence, this is how they are summarized here. Table 4.1 also lists all the hypotheses, sorted by the nature of the linkage predicted and the causal mechanism involved.

Four hypotheses envision a potential direct link between nuclear weapons state behavior and new cases of proliferation. A perceived lack of commitment to nuclear disarmament could stimulate new nuclear weapons programs due to a security threat posed by a nuclear weapons state, a demonstration effect that suggests nuclear weapons have military utility, a demonstration that nuclear weapons confer status, or a reaction against ongoing discrimination and inequality.

Seven pathways might indirectly link disarmament and nonproliferation. First, a nuclear program started by one state as a direct response to a threat from a nuclear weapons state could trigger secondary proliferation in that state's neigh-

TABLE 4.1. Hypotheses about the Connection between Nuclear Disarmament and Proliferation

HYPOTHESIZED	SOURCE OF CAUSAL MECHANISM			
Linkage	Security	Institutions/Bargaining	Norms	Domestic Politics	Psychology

Linkage	Security	Institutions/Bargaining	Norms	Domestic Politics	Psychology
None	• Regional threats cause proliferation, so NWS are irrelevant • Nuclear security guarantees inhibit proliferation, so disarmament will increase proliferation	• States with interest in NP will cooperate regardless of DA concerns • States with no interest in NP will not cooperate regardless of DA issue • States claim to care about DA as bargaining tactic but do not mean it	N/A	• Internal motivations drive proliferation, so NWS are irrelevant	N/A
Direct	• NWS can pose threat that motivates proliferation • NWS demonstrate military utility of weapons to others	N/A	• Association of nuclear weapons with great power status encourages others to imitate	• (Where internal debates exist, other mechanisms in this row will tilt debate in favor of NW acquisition)	• Anger at unfair, discriminatory regime will prompt creation of a nuclear program out of defiance

Indirect	• States that get nuclear weapons in response to threat from NWS encourage secondary proliferation in their neighbors	• States with interest in DA will withhold cooperation on NP to get NWS to do more on DA • NWS actions on DA will increase bargaining space for NNWS to offer new initiatives on NP • NWS noncompliance with Article 6 undermines credibility of regime, so NNWS will not invest in it	• States that care about norms will seek to enforce norms by withholding cooperation on NP to punish noncompliance on DA • NWS hypocrisy undermines norms, so NNWS do not feel need to enforce NP norm	• (Where internal debates exist, other mechanisms in this row will tilt debate against cooperation with NP)	• Anger at unfair, discriminatory treatment will prompt noncooperation with NP

Notes: NWS = nuclear weapon state; NNWS = nonnuclear weapon state; NP = nonproliferation; DA = disarmament; ( ) = intervening variable, not separate causal mechanism bors. Rather than focus on the possibility that a state could launch a new nuclear program, the other six indirect pathways involve state decisions to refrain from participating in new nonproliferation measures. Nonnuclear states might choose to withhold cooperation on nonproliferation strengthening measures for three distinct reasons: as a rational incentive to elicit greater nuclear weapons state compliance with Article VI, out of a belief in a norm of enforcing other norms, or as an emotional response to the perceived failure of nuclear weapons states to uphold their end of the NPT bargain. Lack of progress on disarmament could also call into question the credibility of nuclear weapons state commitments to other parts of the NPT bargain, making nonnuclear states think that they are less likely to benefit from investing in the regime. Lack of progress could also lead to charges of hypocrisy, undermining the nonproliferation norm associated with the regime. Conversely, in the seventh indirect pathway, movement on disarmament could change bargaining dynamics and increase the space for reciprocal concessions on nonproliferation. In addition, most of the direct and indirect pathways could be affected by the intervening variable of domestic politics. Where internal debates exist, the pathways summarized above could help tilt the balance in the direction of policies that are unfavorable for nonproliferation.

The chapter has also identified six reasons why there might be no link or even an inverse correlation between nuclear disarmament and nonproliferation. Three respond mainly to the direct linkage hypothesis. The first two involve other possible explanations for proliferation: it may be driven by threats arising from sources other than the NPT nuclear states or alternatively by internal factors. If these factors predominate, behavior by the nuclear haves would not be the main factor triggering proliferation, and linkage would not exist. A third critique of the direct linkage hypothesis suggests that disarmament might even be counterproductive. Certain states might be restrained by the existence of nuclear security guarantees and would reconsider their nonnuclear path were disarmament measures to call these security guarantees into question.

Three further counterarguments address indirect linkages. If states have a strong interest in nonproliferation, one can predict that they will cooperate with NPT-plus measures out of self-interest even if they are dissatisfied with the degree of progress on disarmament. Conversely, an alternative explanation for a lack of cooperation might be that some nonnuclear states simply lack an interest in implementing new nonproliferation measures and would not act on them regardless of what happens on the disarmament front. Finally, complaints about compliance with Article VI could be insincere and a way of deflecting attention from the real reasons certain nonnuclear weapon states do not want to go along with measures to strengthen nonproliferation.

These counterarguments provide a strong basis for caution before predicting that new disarmament efforts by the nuclear weapon states would have a decisive effect in strengthening the nonproliferation regime. There are too many other factors at play to expect that further action on Article VI would dissuade all future efforts at proliferation or elicit robust cooperation across the board in upholding nonproliferation commitments. At the same time, analysis of the counterarguments has revealed that they do not preclude some possibility of linkage between disarmament and nonproliferation. Possible exceptions exist to each of the arguments for expecting no linkage. The counterarguments are best interpreted as suggesting limiting factors on the linkage hypothesis, but they do not rule it out and certainly do not disprove it. Even when all the possible counterarguments are taken into account, some possibility of a linkage effect remains. Estimating the actual strength of this linkage will require supplementing theoretical analysis with empirical research.

IMPLICATIONS FOR RESEARCH AND POLICY

This chapter has identified many different possible hypotheses about the relationship between nuclear weapons state efforts on disarmament and the commitment of other states to nonproliferation. This theoretical exercise has implications for empirical analysis. It means no one test or piece of evidence may be sufficient to evaluate whether there is a linkage. The different hypotheses discussed above lead to several different predictions. Evidence that supports or disconfirms one will not necessarily rule in or rule out the others. To fully assess the strength of the linkage between nuclear disarmament and nonproliferation, several different empirical tests will be necessary.

In particular, the foregoing analysis shows that one common empirical argument against the linkage hypothesis does not provide an adequate basis for rejecting it. Critics of the linkage proposition argue that more states moved to join or support the NPT when superpower nuclear arsenals were much larger than they are now, and that adherence with NPT norms has actually declined, or at least not increased, since the United States and Russia made deep cuts.[77] None of the theoretical arguments for expecting a linkage, however, would lead one to predict a linear correlation between the extent of reductions in U.S. and Russian arsenals and the level of support for the NPT. The lack of a more favorable response to stockpile cuts among nonnuclear states does make it important, though, to determine other forms of empirical evidence that are relevant for evaluating the linkage hypothesis. The theoretical arguments for predicting either direct or indirect linkages do not suggest that support for the NPT will be pegged to the extent of cuts in nuclear weapons state arsenals relative to Cold War peaks. They suggest instead that symbolic indicators of a nuclear weapons state commitment to Article VI will be key.

The importance of symbolic indicators has implications for the types of empirical evidence that would permit a more compelling assessment of the linkage hypothesis. Such an assessment must start by ascertaining the types of actions by nuclear weapons states that convey seriousness about Article VI to nonnuclear weapons states. One obvious yardstick exists. The 2000 NPT Review Conference agreed to thirteen "practical steps ... to implement Article 6."[78] The steps included entry into force of the Comprehensive Test-Ban Treaty and negotiations on a Fissile Material Cut-off Treaty, new nuclear arms reduction treaties and preservation of the Antiballistic Missile Treaty, greater transparency about and a reduced role for nuclear weapons in security policies, and work to improve verification capabilities for a potential future abolition agreement.[79] The thirteen steps and other NPT Review Conference outcomes suggest several indicators on which nonnuclear weapons states seem to rely to assess the weapons state commitment to disarmament. These indicators provide different ways of measuring nuclear weapons state compliance with Article VI that could be incorporated into future attempts to assess the linkage hypothesis. Instead of focusing solely on the size of nuclear arsenals, research should also consider whether or not nonnuclear states respond positively when nuclear weapons states do any of the following: sign new nuclear arms control treaties, halt nuclear testing, ratify the test ban treaty, halt nuclear modernization efforts, reduce the role of nuclear weapons in military doctrine, or accept strong language regarding disarmament obligations as part of the final document at an NPT Review Conference. The most probative tests of the linkage hypothesis would assess the extent of correlation between movement toward or away from these types of steps and greater nonproliferation commitments by nonnuclear weapon states.

It would also be interesting to compare alternative mechanisms that support the linkage hypothesis to see if some might be stronger than others. This could be done by looking for patterns of regional variation or even variation across individual states. For example, if state behavior is driven by national interests, especially security interests, cooperation on enforcement should be greatest in regions where states confront serious threats from proliferation. This suggests that the greatest rates of cooperation will be found in the Middle East and East Asia, with Europe somewhere in the middle, and Africa and Latin America least motivated to join in enforcement efforts. If, in contrast, perceptions of fairness dominate decision making, the regional patterns will be different. States in Asia and the Middle East will be among the least likely to cooperate in multilateral enforcement measures. With their legacies of colonialism and perceptions of double standards in the treatment of non-NPT members Israel and India, these states will be likely to withhold cooperation. States in Europe, which have little reason to view themselves as having been treated unfairly, will now be the most likely to cooperate.

In sum, it is possible to identify types of evidence that in principle would be helpful for evaluating the linkage hypothesis, in both its direct and indirect forms. A full empirical assessment of the linkage hypothesis will require careful collection of evidence concerning both different types of nuclear weapons state behavior and multiple ways in which nonnuclear states might respond. Until appropriate data can be collected and analyzed, any claim that the historical record either confirms or refutes the linkage hypothesis will be premature.

Despite the absence of strong empirical tests, some conclusions can be reached on the basis of the survey of potentially relevant theoretical hypotheses. When all of the plausible arguments for and against the linkage proposition are considered, it becomes apparent that the counterarguments to the linkage hypothesis do not logically preclude the possibility of linkage. They suggest, rather, that in some cases other considerations will matter more and hence override the factors that might produce linkage. This is unlikely to be true in every case, however. As a result, signs of a commitment to and progress toward nuclear disarmament among the P-5 would likely have the net effect of strengthening support for nonproliferation measures. At the same time, the same analysis applies to the arguments in support of the linkage hypothesis. Neither individually nor taken all together do the mechanisms that could produce either direct or indirect linkage appear likely to be decisive in every case. They will apply to some states in some circumstances, but in other cases their influence will not be significant. This means that greater progress on Article VI obligations will not, by itself, restore full health to the nonproliferation regime. Some of the challenges confronting the NPT arise from other causes and will have to be addressed with other solutions. Even with this caveat, the analysis in this chapter strongly suggests that increased evidence of nuclear weapons state commitment to eventual nuclear disarmament would, on balance, be likely to increase cooperation with the nonproliferation regime.

Four policy recommendations follow. First, nuclear weapons states, especially the United States, have not always made wise choices with respect to their diplomatic rhetoric. If they want their messages about nonproliferation and disarmament to have weight, they need to listen to and actually hear what nonnuclear weapons states have to say. Legalistic arguments that Article VI does not require nuclear disarmament will only increase frictions with states whose cooperation the United States hopes to secure. Pointing to nuclear arms reductions as evidence of compliance with Article VI will likewise not suffice. To convince nonnuclear states that they are serious about eventual disarmament, nuclear weapons states need to embrace and show progress on an array of measures, such as those adumbrated in the thirteen steps.

Second, significant movement toward nuclear disarmament could have undesirable nonproliferation consequences given the importance some states attach to the protection offered by extended nuclear deterrence. If nuclear weapons states do move onto a clear path toward global zero, they will need to communicate and coordinate with their allies who enjoy nuclear security guarantees. Ensuring the adequacy of verification and enforcement measures in support of global zero will be critical for convincing allies that value a nuclear umbrella that nuclear abolition will not jeopardize their security.

Third, because nuclear disarmament will not by itself be decisive in shoring up the nonproliferation regime, it may not be wise to base advocacy for nuclear abolition on the purported necessity of disarmament as a nonproliferation tool. One need not dismiss the linkage hypothesis, as Christopher Ford does, to see merit in his conclusion that the assessment of disarmament should be based on the feasibility and desirability of nuclear abolition in its own right, apart from its possible connection to the nonproliferation agenda.[80]

Fourth, as Scott Sagan has argued, the link between disarmament and nonproliferation is a two-way street, with implications for nonnuclear weapons state policies. According to Sagan, all parts of the NPT, including Article VI, involve "shared responsibilities."[81] In this regard, if nonnuclear weapons states want to make it realistically possible for the P-5 to eliminate their nuclear stockpiles, they need to help ensure that nuclear disarmament can be accomplished safely. In particular, they need to help keep the nonproliferation regime as strong as possible, to minimize the possibility that a new state could suddenly break out with a covertly developed nuclear weapon. If nonnuclear states really care about nuclear disarmament, one of the best ways they can show this is by demonstrating their own commitment to uphold and enforce nonproliferation norms. Helping to create conditions that make abolition appear feasible will strengthen the ability of nonnuclear weapons states to advocate for further nuclear weapons state action to fulfill Article VI.

CONCLUSION

There has been much speculation about whether the continued maintenance of nuclear arsenals by the NPT nuclear weapons states increases the risk of future proliferation. Possible linkages could be either direct or indirect. Some states may be directly motivated to proliferate in reaction to the postures or behaviors of one or more of the nuclear weapons states. Others will not themselves seek nuclear weapons but may feel less reason to cooperate to uphold the NPT, indirectly lowering the barriers to proliferation. This chapter has identified several mechanisms that could lie behind both the direct and the indirect linkage scenarios. It has also identified a number of hypotheses for why there might not be any connection between disarmament and nonproliferation, or even an inverse correlation.

The analysis in this chapter shows that no individual hypothesis is likely to apply to all cases. The counterarguments offer persuasive reasons to think that not all states will react to the disarmament issue in the way assumed by those who expect a linkage. At the same time, the counterarguments do not logically rule out any realistic possibility of linkage. Analysis of the arguments in toto leads to prediction that in some, but not all, cases either a direct or an indirect linkage will be a factor in a nonnuclear state's decision making. This means that efforts to fulfill Article VI commitments should help to strengthen the nonproliferation regime even though they will not be a cure-all for every ailment confronting the regime.

To say anything more definitive requires additional empirical research. By clarifying the logical structure of the relevant hypotheses, this chapter has helped to identify the types of evidence and analysis that are necessary. The empirical evidence cited in the debates to date has not been highly diagnostic, and more fine-grained analyses are needed.

Notes

This chapter is reprinted by permission from *International Security*, Winter 2012/13, vol. 37, no. 3, pp. 92–132, © 2012 by the Presidents and Fellows of Harvard College and the Massachusetts Institute of Technology.

1. George P. Shultz, William J. Perry, Henry A. Kissinger, and Sam Nunn, "Deterrence in the Age of Nuclear Proliferation," *Wall Street Journal*, March 7, 2011.

2. Josef Joffe and James W. Davis, "Less Than Zero: Bursting the New Disarmament Bubble," *Foreign Affairs* 90, no. 1 (2011): 8.

3. Assistant Secretary of State Rose Gottemoeller, "The New START Treaty," testimony before the Senate Armed Services Committee, Washington, D.C., July 29, 2010.

4. U.S. Senate, *Treaty with Russia on Measures for Further Reduction and Limitation of Strategic Offensive Arms*, 111th Cong., 2d sess., 2010, treaty doc. 111–15.

5. This point has been made previously in Christopher F. Chyba, "Time for a Systematic Analysis: U.S. Nuclear Weapons and Nuclear Proliferation," *Arms Control Today* 38, no. 10 (2008): 24–29.

6. On the importance the superpowers attached to this bargain, see George Bunn, *Arms Control by Committee: Managing Negotiations with the Russians* (Stanford, Calif.: Stanford University Press, 1992), ch. 4.

7. For a history of security assurances in relation to the NPT, see John Simpson, "The Role of Security Assurances in the Nuclear Nonproliferation Regime," in *Security Assurances and Nuclear Nonproliferation*, ed. Jeffrey W. Knopf (Stanford, Calif.: Stanford University Press, 2012), 57–85.

8. "Treaty on the Non-Proliferation of Nuclear Weapons (NPT)," *IAEA Bulletin*, July 1, 1968, http://www.iaea.org/Publications/Magazines/Bulletin/Bull104/10403501117.pdf.

9. Christopher A. Ford, "Debating Disarmament: Interpreting Article VI of the Treaty on the Non-Proliferation of Nuclear Weapons," *Nonproliferation Review* 14, no. 3 (2007): 401–28.

10. Daniel H. Joyner, *Interpreting the Nuclear Non-Proliferation Treaty* (Oxford: Oxford University Press, 2011).

11. International Court of Justice, "Legality of the Threat or Use of Nuclear Weapons: Advisory Opinion," The Hague, July 8, 1996, *ICJ Reports 1996*, 263–64.

12. Thomas Graham Jr., "The Origin and Interpretation of Article VI," statement presented at the *Nonproliferation Review* Luncheon Briefing, James Martin Center for Nonproliferation Studies, Washington, D.C., November 29, 2007, http://cns.miis.edu/activities/071129_nprbriefing.

13. Steven E. Miller, "Proliferation, Disarmament, and the Future of the Nonproliferation Treaty," in *Nuclear Proliferation and International Security*, ed. Morten Bremer Maerli and Sverre Lodgaard (New York: Routledge, 2007), 50–70.

14. Harald Müller, "The Future of Nuclear Weapons in an Interdependent World," *Washington Quarterly* 31, no. 2 (2008): 71–72; Harald Müller, "Nuclear Disarmament and the Nonproliferation Treaty," *WMD Insights*, no. 29 (2008/2009).

15. Deepti Choubey, "Are New Nuclear Bargains Attainable?" (Washington, D.C.: Carnegie Endowment for International Peace, 2008).

16. Chyba, "Time for a Systematic Analysis."

17. Christopher A. Ford, "Nuclear Disarmament, Nonproliferation, and the 'Credibility Thesis,'" Hudson Institute Briefing Paper (Washington, D.C.: Hudson Institute, September 2009).

18. Needless to say, there is disagreement about this question as well. Critics point out that the United States continues to invest in nuclear modernization, that the 1,500 nuclear weapons that will remain after New START is implemented will still appear to be overkill to states with no nuclear weapons, and that the United States has proposed adding new missions to its nuclear forces, especially in the Bush years. See Graham, "Origin and Interpretation of Article VI"; Russ Wellen, "Are Nonproliferation and Disarmament, Once Joined at the Hip, Headed for Divorce?," *Huffington Post*, December 11, 2010, www.huffingtonpost.com/russ-wellen-/are-nonproliferation-and-_b_795306.html.

19. How to interpret this data is not obvious. There were more nonmembers available to join in the early years of the NPT and a dwindling pool of potential new members once most states had joined. Thus, the rate of joining would likely have gone down regardless of whether there has been progress on disarmament.

20. Choubey, "Are New Nuclear Bargains Attainable?," 7; Tanya Ogilvie-White and David Santoro, "Disarmament and Non-proliferation: Towards More Realistic Bargains," *Survival* 53, no. 3 (2011): 106.

21. Andrew Grotto, "Why Do States That Oppose Nuclear Proliferation Resist New Nonproliferation Obligations? Three Logics of Nonproliferation Decision-Making," *Cardozo Journal of International and Comparative Law* 18, no. 1 (2010): 1–44.

22. Scott D. Sagan, "Why Do States Build Nuclear Weapons? Three Models in Search of a Bomb," *International Security* 21, no. 3 (1996/1997): 54–86.

23. Grotto, "Why Do States," 8–17.

24. Ibid., 22–32.

25. Ibid., 16.

26. Sverre Lodgaard, *Nuclear Disarmament and Non-proliferation: Towards a Nuclear-Weapon-Free World?* (Milton Park, Abingdon, Eng.: Routledge, 2011), ch. 9, esp. 172–73, 176.

27. Scott D. Sagan and Jane Vaynman, "Introduction: Reviewing the Nuclear Posture Review," in "Arms, Disarmament and Influence: International Responses to the 2010 Nuclear Posture Review, special issue, *Nonproliferation Review* 18, no. 1 (2011): 26.

28. Harald Müller, "A Nuclear Nonproliferation Test: Obama's Nuclear Policy and the 2010 NPT Review Conference," *Nonproliferation Review* 18, no. 1 (2011). Some observers question the significance of this outcome, arguing that reaching agreement at a review conference is not meaningful unless it leads to concrete actions that bolster nonproliferation. Christopher Ford, "Disarmament versus Nonproliferation?" New Paradigms Forum, October 29, 2010, http://www.newparadigmsforum.com/NPFtestsite/?p=531.

29. Scott D. Sagan and Jane Vaynman, "Conclusion: Lessons Learned from the 2010 Nuclear Posture Review," in "Arms, Disarmament, and Influence: International

Responses to the 2010 Nuclear Posture Review," special issue, *Nonproliferation Review* 18, no. 1 (2011): 240.

30. This chapter does not reference all the major studies that propound each theory. For a two-volume set that cites and discusses all of the key studies, see William C. Potter and Gaukhar Mukhatzhanova, eds., *Forecasting Nuclear Proliferation in the 21st Century* (Stanford, Calif.: Stanford University Press, 2010).

31. Pierre Hassner, "Who Killed Nuclear Enlightenment?" *International Affairs* 83, no. 3 (2007): 462–63; Joffe and Davis, "Less Than Zero," 8.

32. T.V. Paul, *Power versus Prudence: Why Nations Forgo Nuclear Weapons* (Montreal: McGill-Queen's University Press, 2000). Paul's book does not evaluate the linkage hypothesis; it is cited here as the best academic study to make a case for the primacy of the regional security environment in explaining proliferation.

33. Avner Cohen, *Israel and the Bomb* (New York: Columbia University Press, 1998), 148–50.

34. Müller, "Nuclear Disarmament."

35. T. V. Paul, "The Systemic Bases of India's Challenge to the Global Nuclear Order," *Nonproliferation Review* 6, no. 1 (1998): 1–11; Šumit Ganguly, "India's Pathway to Pokhran II: The Prospects and Sources of New Delhi's Nuclear Weapons Program," *International Security* 23, no. 4 (1999): 148–77.

36. George Bunn and Jean du Preez, "More Than Words: The Value of U.S. Non-Nuclear-Use Promises" *Arms Control Today* 37, no. 6 (2007): 18.

37. William C. Potter and Gaukhar Mukhatzhanova, "Divining Nuclear Intentions: A Review Essay," *International Security* 33, no.1 (2008): 139–69.

38. Keith B. Payne, "A Vision Shall Guide Them? The Strategic Risks of President Obama's Call for Nuclear Disarmament," *National Review*, November 2, 2009, 20–21.

39. Knopf, *Security Assurances*.

40. On this point, see also Maria Rost Rublee, *Nonproliferation Norms: Why States Choose Nuclear Restraint* (Athens: University of Georgia Press, 2009).

41. Miller, "Proliferation, Disarmament," 65; Müller, "Nuclear Disarmament."

42. Robert O. Keohane, *After Hegemony: Cooperation and Discord in the World Political Economy* (Princeton, N.J.: Princeton University Press, 1984).

43. "Treaty on the Non-Proliferation of Nuclear Weapons (NPT)," *IAEA Bulletin*, July 1, 1968, http://www.iaea.org/Publications/Magazines/Bulletin/Bull104/10403501117.pdf.

44. Quoted in Noel Stott, "Motivations and Capabilities to Acquire Nuclear, Biological, or Chemical Weapons and Missiles: South Africa," in *Over the Horizon Proliferation Threats*, ed. James J. Wirtz and Peter R. Lavoy (Stanford, Calif.: Stanford University Press, 2012), 76.

45. Robert Axelrod, *The Evolution of Cooperation* (New York: Basic Books, 1984).

46. Sagan and Vaynman, "Introduction," 32; Sagan and Vaynman, "Conclusion," 240.

47. Ogilvie-White and Santoro, "Disarmament and Non-proliferation."

48. For research suggesting that a reputation for keeping (or breaking) promises affects credibility, see Anne E. Sartori, *Deterrence by Diplomacy* (Princeton, N.J.: Princeton University Press, 2005).

49. Oliver Bloom, "Is a Key Element of the NPT Dead?," Center for Strategic and International Studies, July 13, 2010, http://csis.org/blog/key-element-npt-dead.

50. Lewis A. Dunn, "High Noon for the NPT," *Arms Control Today* 25, no. 6 (1995): 3–9.

51. Grotto, "Why Do States," 28–32.

52. Arshad Mohammed and Phil Stewart, "U.S. Says Nuclear Arsenal Includes 5,113 warheads," Reuters, May 3, 2010, http://www.reuters.com/article/idUSTRE64251X20100503.

53. Rebecca Johnson, "The 2000 NPT Review Conference: A Delicate, Hard-Won Compromise," *Disarmament Diplomacy*, no. 46 (2000), http://www.acronym.org.uk/dd/dd46/46npt.htm.

54. Ford, "Disarmament versus Nonproliferation?"

55. U.S. White House, Office of the Press Secretary, "Fact Sheet: An Enduring Commitment to the U.S. Nuclear Deterrent," November 17, 2010, http://www.whitehouse.gov/the-press-office/2010/11/17/fact-sheet-enduring-commitment-us-nuclear-deterrent.

56. Miller, "Proliferation, Disarmament," 54; Nabil Fahmy, "Mindful of the Middle East: Egypt's Reaction to the New U.S. Nuclear Posture Review," *Nonproliferation Review* 18, no. 1 (2011): 169–71; Irma Argüello, "The Position of an Emerging Global Power: Brazilian Responses to the 2010 U.S. Nuclear Posture Review," *Nonproliferation Review* 18, no. 1 (2011): 188–91.

57. Quoted in Joyner, *Interpreting the Nuclear Non-Proliferation Treaty*, 73.

58. Müller, "Nuclear Disarmament."

59. Paul, "Systemic Bases."

60. On the logic of appropriateness versus the logic of consequences, see James G. March and Johan P. Olsen, *Rediscovering Institutions: The Organizational Basis of Politics* (New York: Free Press, 1989); Kjell Goldmann, "Appropriateness and Consequences: The Logic of Neo-Institutionalism," *Governance* 18, no. 1 (2005): 35–52.

61. Miller, "Proliferation, Disarmament," 66.

62. Quoted in Choubey, "Are New Nuclear Bargains Attainable?," 8.

63. Etel Solingen, *Nuclear Logics: Contrasting Paths in East Asia and the Middle East* (Princeton, N.J.: Princeton University Press, 2007); Jacques E. C. Hymans, *The Psychology of Nuclear Proliferation: Identity, Emotions, and Foreign Policy* (Cambridge: Cambridge University Press, 2006).

64. Stephen Rademaker, "Blame America First," *Wall Street Journal*, May 7, 2007.

65. Miller, "Proliferation, Disarmament," 65–66; Sagan and Vaynman, "Introduction," 18, 31.

66. Kristen Renwick Monroe, Adam Martin, and Priyanka Ghosh, "Politics and an Innate Moral Sense: Scientific Evidence for an Old Theory?" *Political Research Quarterly* 62,

no. 3 (2009): 614–34; Marc Bekoff and Jessica Pierce, *Wild Justice: The Moral Lives of Animals* (Chicago: University of Chicago Press, 2009).

67. David A. Welch, *Justice and the Genesis of War* (Cambridge: Cambridge University Press, 1993); Jonathan Mercer, "Emotional Beliefs," *International Organization* 64, no. 1 (2010): 10–11; Janice Gross Stein, "The Psychology of Assurance: An Emotional Tale," in Knopf, *Security Assurances*, 35–56.

68. This is the clear conclusion of the most detailed study of the NPT negotiations ever written. See Mohamed Ibrahim Shaker, *The Nuclear Non-Proliferation Treaty: Origin and Implementation, 1959–1979* (London: Oceania, 1980), 2:564, http://cns.miis.edu/activities/100525_shaker_egypt_un/index.htm.

69. Cecilia Albin, *Justice and Fairness in International Negotiation* (Cambridge: Cambridge University Press, 2001), 203.

70. Choubey, "Are New Nuclear Bargains Attainable?," 1, 3, 11; Maria Rost Rublee, "The Nuclear Threshold States: Challenges and Opportunities Posed by Brazil and Japan," *Nonproliferation Review* 17, no. 1 (2010): 54; Lodgaard, *Nuclear Disarmament*, 84–85.

71. Fahmy, "Mindful of the Middle East," 171.

72. Ogilvie-White and Santoro, "Disarmament and Non-proliferation," 116n19.

73. Hymans, *Psychology of Nuclear Proliferation*.

74. Julio C. Carasales, "The So-Called Proliferator That Wasn't: The Story of Argentina's Nuclear Policy," *Nonproliferation Review* 6, no. 4 (1999): 51–64.

75. Jaswant Singh, "Against Nuclear Apartheid: The Case for India's Tests," *Foreign Affairs* 77, no. 5 (1998): 41–52.

76. George Perkovich, *India's Nuclear Bomb: The Impact on Global Proliferation* (Berkeley: University of California Press, 1999).

77. On this argument, see also Robert Kagan, "Why Is the GOP Fighting This Treaty?," *Washington Post*, July 30, 2010.

78. "2000 Review Conference of the Parties to the Treaty on the Non-Proliferation of Nuclear Weapons," final document, vol. 1, pt. 1, New York, 2000, 14–15.

79. For a slightly dated scorecard of how much progress has been made on the thirteen steps, see Sharon Squassoni, "Grading Progress on 13 Steps toward Nuclear Disarmament," Carnegie Endowment for International Peace, *Policy Outlook*, April 5, 2009.

80. Ford, "Nuclear Disarmament," 13.

81. Scott D. Sagan, "Shared Responsibilities for Nuclear Disarmament," *Daedalus* 138, no. 4 (2009): 157–68.

Country and Regional Explorations

CHAPTER 5

How Supportive of the Nonproliferation Regime Are the United States and Its Allies?

U.S. Security Guarantees and the Free Rider Problem

Lowell H. Schwartz

HISTORICAL EVIDENCE INDICATES that the protection offered by a U.S. security guarantee often formalized in a bilateral or multilateral treaty is one of the most effective measures in controlling nuclear proliferation.[1] In numerous cases once states were offered U.S. security guarantees, they ratified the Treaty on the Non-Proliferation of Nuclear Weapons (NPT) and adherents to the precepts of the nuclear nonproliferation regime. Even an implicit understanding of protection such as the relationship between Sweden, a formally neutral country during the Cold War, and the United States was enough to convince them not to acquire nuclear weapons.[2] In some cases the United States placed a great deal of pressure on states to shelve their nuclear ambitions, such as South Korea and Taiwan, while in other cases, such as Australia, a relatively benign security environment and U.S. security guarantees were enough to close off the nuclear option.[3]

The question this essay explores is how U.S. security guarantees impact states' willingness to support, sustain, and strengthen the nonproliferation regime. Does the confidence of U.S. protection provide them with a justification for inaction or lacked enforcement of the measures necessary to prevent the spread of nuclear weapons? Or is the opposite true—once a state makes the decision not to acquire nuclear weapons, does it actively and strictly enforce the nonproliferation regime in order to ensure neighboring states remain nonnuclear as well?

DEFINING KEY TERMS

Academic literature and government policy documents discuss several types of security assurances. This chapter focuses on *positive security assurances*, which are promises by a nuclear state to come to the aid of a nonnuclear state if it is threatened or attacked by nuclear weapons. During the Cold War both superpowers offered these types of security guarantees to their allies. For example, North Korea in 1961 signed a treaty with the Soviet Union that included a mutual defense clause that committed one party to aid the other if it was attacked. The Soviet Union entered into similar agreements with members of the Warsaw Pact.

Negative security assurances are promises not to use or threaten the use of nuclear weapons against nonnuclear states. The Non-Aligned Movement (NAM) has consistently sought political commitments from nuclear weapons states never to use or threaten to use nuclear weapons against nonnuclear weapons states. Despite NAM states' demands, negative security assurances were not contained in the NPT, and this has consistently been an issue at subsequent review conferences.[4]

U.S. government reports have occasionally referred to "30 plus countries being covered by the American nuclear commitments."[5] The most famous of these is the Article V commitment of the NATO founding treaty, which states that an armed attack against any member state will be considered an attack against all other NATO states. This is generally interpreted as implying the possible use of nuclear weapons in case of an attack upon NATO states. The United States also has defense treaties with Japan, South Korea, Australia, and Taiwan.

One of the complicating factors is determining whether there is a difference between a *nuclear* and a *nonnuclear* security guarantee. During the Cold War when the main threat was a nuclear-armed Soviet Union, extending the umbrella of nuclear deterrence over U.S. allies was viewed as an essential component of U.S. policy. It played an integral role in building alliances, keeping them together in the face of serious military threats, and encouraging allies to forego developing their own nuclear arsenals. Because the United States and its European allies at least initially were conventionally inferior to Soviet forces in Europe, the United States sought to tightly link nuclear and nonnuclear security guarantees. The United States wanted the Soviet Union to believe that a conventional attack on Europe or Asia might lead to a nuclear response.

The United States took many steps to assure its NATO allies of its commitment to their security in the face of Soviet attack, including a wide range of diplomatic measures and consultations, forward-based and dedicated nuclear forces, and joint planning and exercises. In Asia, efforts to assure allies about the U.S. nuclear commitment were not as fully developed as they were in Europe. But the United States took those commitments seriously enough that it based conventional forces and even tactical nuclear weapons in South Korea and Japan. Deployments of conventional forces continue today, but tactical weapons were removed in the 1990s.

The demise of the Soviet Union has significantly diminished the conventional and nuclear threat to Europe from Russia. As a result, the prominence of the U.S. nuclear deterrent has receded as a component of European security. This has led to questions about the continuing relevance of the relatively small number of nuclear forces still stationed in Europe. However, the emerging nuclear threat from Iran and the Russian-Georgia conflict may cause the U.S. extended deterrent to become a feature once again in the European security planning. In Asia, the Soviet threat has also receded, but new threats have emerged that are concerning to U.S. allies. China's massive conventional modernization, particularly of its conventional ballistic missile forces, has raised concerns in Taiwan and Japan. North Korea's recent nuclear tests and missile deployments also have raised red flags in Japan and South Korea. These concerns have prompted both Japan and South Korea to raise pointed questions about U.S. policies and deployments, questions that they would not have asked even a few years ago.

PRELIMINARY HYPOTHESES

One of the greatest difficulties in analyzing the impact of the U.S. security guarantee is disentangling it from other explanatory factors. The states to which the United States offers security guarantees have many common characteristics. Almost all of them are industrialized nations with high levels of economic development. Their government structures tend to be democratic rather than authoritarian. Finally, they tend to be status quo powers that are supportive of the current international architecture set up in 1945.[6] All of these factors apart from whether the United States has offered these states security guarantees are likely to impact states' willingness to support, sustain, and strengthen the nonproliferation regime.

This essay does not attempt to untangle these factors. Instead it assesses the degree of support for the nonproliferation regime among states with a security guarantee from the United States and what factors might lie behind this support or lack thereof. Given the expectation that states similar to the United States will support the nonproliferation regime, this essay spends more time on the negative side of the equation. Namely, why have U.S. allies occasionally undermined global nonproliferation efforts?

This perspective produces several hypotheses derived from the introductory chapter, which are posed in question format and are explored throughout this chapter.

> Hypothesis 1. *Threat Perception*: Does a state's perception of the direct threat of proliferation influence its willingness to implement or vigorously support nonproliferation measures?
>
> Hypothesis 2. *The Free Rider/Security Guarantee Problem*: Do states offered a security guarantee shirk their nonproliferation regime responsibilities because of a feeling of relative security?
>
> Hypothesis 3. *Discrimination*: Does the discriminatory nature of the treaty, which at its core provides international legitimacy for some powers to possess nuclear weapons and outlaws it for others, contribute to states' willingness to adhere to the nonproliferation regime? More broadly, is adherence connected to the general support or opposition to the international political order?
>
> Hypothesis 4. *Political or Economic Interests*: Are there circumstances when the economic and political benefits of exporting nuclear technological materials outweigh the proliferation security concerns?

FRAMEWORK FOR ASSESSING STATES' LEVEL OF SUPPORT FOR SUSTAINING AND STRENGTHENING THE NONPROLIFERATION REGIME

An important initial analytical step is determining what actively supporting or impeding the nuclear nonproliferation regime means. In their essay "The Health of the Nuclear Nonproliferation Regime," Jeffrey Fields and Jason Enia provide a helpful framework to analyze the nonproliferation regime.[7] They see two guiding principles behind the regime: the spread of nuclear weapons harms prospects for peace and security; and nuclear-armed states should not assist nonnuclear weapons states in the development of nuclear weapons.[8] The health of the regime according to Fields and Enia should be judged on whether these principles remain in the interest of states and the regime evolves to deal with new challenges to the core principles. To provide a comprehensive and accurate assessment of the regime, Fields and Enia utilized a multidimensional framework. This framework can be applied to individual states to judge how supportive they are of the nuclear nonproliferation regime.

The first element of the regime is normative. Does a state through its behavior and policies reinforce or undermine the normative values of the nonproliferation regime: that the spread of nuclear weapons is harmful to international security and that nuclear-armed and nuclear-capable states should not assist nonnuclear states in developing nuclear weapons. Some states might add an additional normative element that the nuclear weapons states move toward disarmament as articulated in Article VI of the NPT. However, the notion that this underlies the nonproliferation regime is hotly disputed.[9]

The second element is scope. Does a state seek to increase membership in the regime? Does a state encourage states outside the regime to join the regime and to ratify the NPT? How willing is a state to expand the scope of the issues covered by the regime when new factors threaten the health of the regime? For example, since the attacks of September 11 concerns about nuclear terrorism have grown. A state's willingness to expand the scope of the regime to confront this new challenge would indicate a supportive position.

The third element is strength. Does a state support measures to ensure compliance with the rules and expectations of the regime? Or is it willing to sacrifice compliance if it clashes with other national priorities? This would include support for antismuggling efforts and multilateral sanctions against actors violating the rules of the regime.

The final element is organization. Does a state actively participate in and support the organizational underpinning of the nonproliferation regime? This would include providing staff and inspectors for the International Atomic Energy Agency (IAEA) and participating in the NPT Review Conferences.

ASSESSING THE UNITED STATES

Before assessing states that have an explicit or implicit U.S. security guarantee, it is worth considering how well the United States performs against the standard laid out in the section above. Is the United States a full-fledged supporter of the nuclear nonproliferation regime, or has it been willing to sacrifice the principles of the regime when they conflicted with higher national security priorities?

On the first element of the nonproliferation regime, the normative, for the most part the United States has a good record. The United States was the driving force behind the establishment of the NPT, seeking to move its nonproliferation activities from a bilateral to a multilateral process. The nation diplomatically reached across the Iron Curtain, convincing the Soviet Union that curtailing the proliferation was in the interests of both superpowers. The United States sees the spread of nuclear proliferation as harmful, and since the end of the Cold War nonproliferation has been a central pillar of U.S. foreign and security policy. In his April 2009 speech in Prague, President Obama indicated that dealing with the threat of further nuclear weapons proliferation would be the utmost security priority for the United States.[10]

The Nuclear Posture Review (NPR) lays out the official U.S. nuclear policies. In the 2010 NPR the Obama administration indicated that it is strongly in the U.S. national interest to move toward a world without nuclear weapons.[11] With the conclusion of the New Strategic Arms Reduction Treaty (START) with Russia, the United States has continued to reduce its nuclear forces in line with its obligations in Article VI of the NPT to move toward disarmament. In the near term, the NPR outlined a series of objectives for U.S. nuclear policy to reduce nuclear dangers. Among the most important objectives were preventing nuclear proliferation and nuclear terrorism, reducing the role of U.S. nuclear weapons in U.S. national security and U.S. strategy, and maintaining strategic deterrence and stability at reduced-force levels.

The United States also is supportive of elements two and four of the Fields/Enia framework of the nonproliferation regime (expanding the scope and organization support). The United States has been in the forefront of expanding the nonproliferation regime to address smuggling and other potential nuclear terrorism issues that have been raised since the attacks of September 11. It has also sought to shift the rules of the regime to make it more difficult and punishing to withdraw from the NPT. Finally, the United States has strongly encouraged and put pressure on states to join and ratify the NPT. U.S. determination to expand the scope of the NPT has made it one of the most universally adhered-to treaties, with 189 signatories.

Despite these positive features, some recent actions call into question the U.S. commitment to element three (strength) and the normative aspect of not assisting nonnuclear states in developing nuclear weapons. Many analysts point to the Bush and Obama administrative initiatives to exempt India from global nonproliferation rules that prevent the United States and other states from commercial nuclear activities with India as a serious blow to the nonproliferation regime.[12] The United States signed an agreement with India to allow joint U.S.-Indian nuclear efforts and pressured the Nuclear Suppliers Group and the International Atomic Energy Agency to make an exception to NSG guidelines. The nuclear deal provided significant benefits to India by privileging it as a nonsignatory of the NPT (despite possessing nuclear weapons) to all of the rights without the obligations of the treaty. The deal imposed few obligations on India, as it was not obligated to sign the Comprehensive Nuclear-Test-Ban Treaty nor to place a moratorium on additional production of fissile material. The deal will allow India to continue to build up its nuclear forces unencumbered by many international restrictions. The U.S. initiative is clearly an attempt to establish a stronger strategic relationship with India. Critics argued that at the same time the deal allows India to expand its nuclear weapons capability to balance that of China.

The U.S. willingness to "normalize" India's nuclear program at the same time as it leads the charge against North Korea's and Iran's nuclear programs plays into a viewpoint of U.S. hypocrisy on nonproliferation. The United States seems unconcerned with or is willing to overlook proliferation to its allies and friends but will utilize all means of power at its disposal to prevent proliferation to powers hostile to it. The United States obviously is not alone in its selective concerns about proliferation. China has long supported Pakistan's nuclear program. It would not be surprising if China increased its cooperation with Pakistan with or without NSG approval in light of U.S. nuclear arrangements with India. In addition, China has consistently sought to weaken sanctions against North Korea despite its record of proliferation.

U.S. ALLIES ARE GENERALLY SUPPORTIVE OF THE NONPROLIFERATION REGIME

In general, support for the nonproliferation regime is high among industrialized democratic states allied with the United States. This is true across all four elements of the regime. Statistical analysis indicates strong support by nations allied with the United States for the nonproliferation regime. Quantitative analysis by Matthew Kroenig has shown that states that are dependent on a superpower patron for their security are less likely to provide sensitive nuclear assistance.[13] The statistical evidence is particularly strong when a nonnuclear state has a defense pact with a superpower and relies on it for security.[14]

In regard to the second element, scope, U.S. allies have been among the most eager to expand participation in the regime and to have it confront new challenges. With minimal exceptions all the member states in NATO and in the Organisation for Economic Co-operation and Development (OECD) have signed an IAEA Additional Protocol.[15] By comparison, only about a third of the Non-Aligned Movement states have an Additional Protocol in force.

In terms of ensuring compliance with the rules and expectations of the regime, U.S. allies lead the way in placing pressure on North Korea and Iran to dismantle their nuclear programs. There have now been four rounds of sanctions against Iran because of its violations of UN resolutions on its nuclear program. The latest round of sanctions against Iran was co-sponsored by France, Germany, the United Kingdom, and the United States. Leadership on rolling back North Korea's nuclear program has also come from U.S. allies in Asia. South Korea and Japan have been part of the six-party talks, which are aimed at ending North Korea's nuclear program through a negotiating process. Japan and increasingly South Korea have placed their own tough economic sanctions against North Korea because of its nuclear weapons program.

It is particularly interesting to review the level of support for the nonproliferation regime in states such as South Korea and Taiwan, which abandoned nuclear weapons ambitions under U.S. pressure. Taiwan in many ways is a natural candidate to become a nuclear weapons state. It is a small isolated power facing a hostile nuclear-armed foe, which also has considerable conventional military capabilities arrayed against Taiwan. Yet, despite its circumstances Taiwan has chosen not to become a nuclear state even though it possesses the technical expertise to do so. It is hard not to conclude that Taiwan's dependence upon the United States was the pivotal factor in restraining Taiwan's nuclear program. On two occasions, one in the mid-1970s and the other in the late 1980s, the United States through the IAEA forced Taiwan to dismantle suspect faculties.[16]

Taiwan is a member of the NPT and has implemented additional safeguards suggested by the IAEA. In addition, Taiwanese officials played a vital role in the first publicized interdiction executed under the Proliferation Security Initiative (PSI). On August 8, 2003, a North Korean cargo vessel, *Be Gaehung*, was detained in the Kaosung Harbor in Taiwan after American intelligence indicated that the ship contained chemicals used in the manufacture of rocket fuel. During the interdiction, the vessel was boarded and inspected by Taiwanese naval forces, and 158 barrels of phosphorus pentasulfide were unloaded and confiscated by government officials.

Taiwan has not assisted nonnuclear states in developing nuclear weapons. Taiwan meets most of the requirements expected of regime members. It has repeatedly revised its export control legislation and coordinates frequently with its counterparts in the United States and Japan. Its export control system is regarded as one of the strongest in the region.[17]

There are many similarities between South Korea's and Taiwan's international positions. Like Taiwan, South Korea is a small state that faces a hostile neighboring state with considerable military capabilities directed against it, including nuclear weapons. Again like Taiwan, South Korea has chosen not to become a nuclear state even though it has one of the most active and successful civilian nuclear energy programs in the world. Being a prosperous state and a highly advanced science power with a great deal of knowledge about nuclear technology, South Korea could easily have built a small nuclear capability. However for domestic political reasons and because of its reliance on the United States to enhance its security, South Korea has not developed nuclear weapons, and since the 1970s it has been mostly in compliance with IAEA safeguards.[18]

South Korea's main focus in the area of nonproliferation has been in East Asia, particularly North Korea. Its diplomatic efforts to bring North Korea back into compliance with the NPT have occupied most of its attention. It has been less active in the nonproliferation regime overall and a generally quiet presence at the various NPT review conferences.

In 2004, the Korean government overhauled and strengthened its nonproliferation institutions and practices. The adoption of UN Security Council Resolution 1540 spurred this review, which called on nations to update their weapons of mass destruction (WMD) nonproliferation and export control policies and laws. In May 2009, South Korea agreed to participate in the PSI, joining ninety-four other countries that had joined by the spring of 2009. Although it is not directly connected, it is worth noting that on June 16, 2009, the United States and South Korea issued a joint statement about the future of their alliance.[19] The statement specifically said the "continuing commitment of extended deterrence, including the U.S. nuclear umbrella," assures and reinforces the robust defense alliance of the two nations. This was one of the most explicit endorsements of U.S. nuclear security guarantees ever issued.

The main area of contention between the United States and South Korea (ROK) over nonproliferation policy has been the need to renew the ROK-U.S. nuclear energy agreement initially signed in 1972 and revised in 1974. It officially expires in March 2014. The current ROK-U.S. nuclear agreement gives the United

States the right to veto the reprocessing of U.S.-origin fuel or any other alteration in form of content. To date, the United States has not consented to any reprocessing of U.S.-supplied nuclear fuel in South Korea. South Korean nuclear authorities complain that they are running out of storage space for spent reactor fuel, and this is limiting the development of their nuclear industry. They would like the new agreement to allow them to reprocess spent fuel so they can close the fuel cycle. The United States is concerned that the method of reprocessing suggested by South Korean officials could provide the fissile material necessary for nuclear weapons.

This problem is compounded by South Korea's desire to become a large-scale international exporter of nuclear plants. In 2008, South Korea won a $20 billion contract to develop nuclear power plants for the United Arab Emirates (UAE), and it is also building a research reactor in Jordan. Some South Korean officials complain that the United States is seeking to limit South Korea's export potential and that it has an outdated view of the country, which contributes to U.S. fears that South Korea is still desirous of nuclear weapons.[20]

The U.S. view is that sensitive technology should not be transferred to those countries that do not possess nuclear weapons. While South Korea does not have nuclear weapons, it has withheld information on some scientific work it has done. This was illustrated in 2004 when the IAEA revealed that South Korea failed to report in a timely manner on a variety of nuclear tests including uranium enrichment and plutonium separation. The United States is also concerned that any South Korean reprocessing program would undermine the 1992 North and South Korean Joint Declaration on the Denuclearization of the Korean Peninsula. At a time when the United States and South Korea are focused on dismantling North Korea's nuclear program, there are fears a reprocessing agreement would jeopardize ongoing negotiations. In the fall of 2010, South Korea and the United States began discussion on the form and structure of a new civil nuclear cooperation agreement between the two countries.

WHY DO U.S. ALLIES OCCASIONALLY UNDERMINE GLOBAL NONPROLIFERATION EFFORTS?

Despite the generally high level of support U.S. allies provide to the nonproliferation regime, it is notable how often U.S. allies have supplied sensitive nuclear assistance to nonnuclear states. Why has this occurred if in general the states with U.S. security guarantees are supportive of the nonproliferation regime?

France and Germany are two interesting case studies for why U.S. allies sometimes undermine and oppose global proliferation. In the dataset constructed by Matthew Kroenig detailing sensitive nuclear assistance, transfers by France and Germany comprised six of fourteen cases, or about 40 percent of them. It is fair to say up until 1990 France and Germany along with China were key actors in global proliferation. By the 1990s all of these powers were eclipsed by Pakistan, which through the A. Q. Khan network was responsible for sensitive transfers to Iran, Libya, North Korea, and perhaps others.[21]

Both defeated Axis powers Germany and Japan made the decision early on not to acquire independent nuclear weapons capabilities. However, they also choose to develop large civilian nuclear industries, which they sought to bolster through exports. The tension between these two policy decisions was apparent in West Germany throughout the Cold War.

West Germany in 1954 made the unilateral declaration that it would not manufacture nuclear, chemical, or biological weapons on its territory. This aspect of the Paris Accords was an important component of West Germany's reintegration into Europe. The Paris Accords restored German sovereignty and allowed it to join the European Economic Community and NATO. Despite West Germany's nonnuclear status, its security heavily depended on nuclear forces, which were under U.S. control. For a time during the 1960s West Germany and the United States considered creating a multilateral force (MLF) of intermediate range nuclear forces under the joint control of the United States and NATO members, including Germany. Ultimately Soviet objections derailed this proposal, and the United States moved toward a different strategy, the Non-Proliferation Treaty (NPT).[22]

The difficult negotiations over the NPT indicated West Germany's reluctance at the time to completely give up the nuclear option and its concerns about the treaty's impact on nuclear industry. In 1965 and 1966, West German finance minister Franz Joseph Strauss argued that the NPT would allow the Soviet Union to interfere with Germany's nuclear industry and technological development. He and others also feared it would impinge on Germany's nuclear sharing arrangements with NATO.[23] These concerns for the most part were dealt with during the NPT negotiations. The language of the treaty reassured Germany that its vital security and economic interests would not be negatively affected.[24] In addition, Germany's deference to U.S. leadership and reliance on security guarantees from Washington contributed to its reluctance to stand in the way of the strong U.S. desire to slow the pace of nuclear proliferation. However, the slow pace of formal ratification of the treaty demonstrated that Germany had less than wholehearted support in the late 1960s and 1970s for an unbalanced nuclear proliferation regime.

One of the underlying strengths of West Germany's economy after World War II was its ability to export high-quality products. Germany's prowess in this area was nurtured and fostered by the German government through generous export promotion polices. One element of these policies was that until the early 1990s export control laws were based on a liberal view of trade restrictions. The underlying view of German law was that the state's foreign trade in principle is unrestricted, with export controls being the exception. In contrast, U.S. exports are subject to control unless explicitly permitted.[25] This view was bolstered through an export control apparatus that was tightly linked to the business community, with the Ministry of Defense having only marginal influence over the export approval process.[26]

The nuclear power industry was not an exception to this point of view. During the 1960s and 1970s it become a centerpiece of industrial renewal and was viewed as a solution to the energy shortage predicted by environmental advocates.[27] Germany's desire to foster civilian nuclear power and technology led it toward a willingness to conclude nuclear agreements with many powers inside and outside the NPT system. The three most criticized agreements were nuclear deals with Argentina, Brazil, and Iran. The Brazilian nuclear agreement was the largest and most extensive. West Germany in 1975 signed an $8 billion agreement to provide Brazil with complete fuel-cycle technology and two power reactors. While the deal was within the letter of Germany's NPT obligation, it certainly was a questionable transfer to a state that had not signed the NPT and that some viewed as a proliferation risk. In fact, it was later discovered that Brazil did have a parallel secret nuclear weapons program at the time.

Germany also sought to limit the scope of various components of the nonproliferation regime. It was one of the key forces in limiting the NPT system to fissile material flow control and restricting the IAEA safeguards system to verifying nonnuclear weapons states' reports of civilian nuclear material flow.[28] This proved to be an important hindrance to the IAEA attempts to uncover Iraq's covert nuclear weapons program in the 1990s. Germany did join the Nuclear Suppliers Group (NSG) in 1974. Once again, however, it sought to limit and weaken the degree of constraints imposed. It agreed to a formula that restrained the transfer of sensitive nuclear technology but not a straight prohibition.[29]

A number of explanations have been offered by scholars for Germany's resistance to strengthening nonproliferation efforts until the early 1990s. The most straightforward reason is purely economic interests. Germany sought to promote and strengthen a profitable industry through allowing it to benefit from foreign sales. Germany as a nonnuclear weapons power was keen on ensuring that its civilian nuclear industry was not placed at a disadvantage in comparison to nuclear powers like the United States and France. Another suggested explanation is West Germany's strategy during the Cold War. One element of West German policy was to encourage trade between the West and the East. This was viewed as a way to decrease the isolation of East Germany and other parts of communist Europe, which from a German strategic point of view would ease tensions and reduce the chances of war. The United States, on the other hand, sought strict export rules to weaken and hinder the economic and technological development of the communist world as much as possible.

A final explanation is West Germany's role in the international system. The United States was the primary architect of the international system and saw proliferation anywhere as a threat to the international order. West Germany, on the other hand, had a more regional perspective. It had less to fear, at least during the Cold War, from potential proliferation in South America or the Middle East. These were not areas of primary concern for West German security.

Germany's changing perceptions of both its threat environment and its role in the international system offer two potential explanations for the sudden reverse of German export control policies in the early 1990s. Over the five-year period between 1989 and 1994 Germany's export control system underwent a dramatic shift, moving from taking a liberal view of export control to having laws among the strictest and most comprehensive in the world.[30] Post-unification Germany became Europe's largest economic and political power. It now had a leadership role in Europe and sought to impose an export control regime across Europe that matched its own strict standards. In addition, the end of the Cold War moved nuclear proliferation to the top of international security concerns. These fears caused a renewed emphasis on preventing rogue powers and terrorists from obtaining nuclear weapons. This likely shifted the economic versus security interest balance in Germany more toward the security side.

French policies and views on nonproliferation have many similarities to West Germany's, with one important difference: France became a nuclear-armed state in 1960. President Charles de Gaulle could not accept French exclusion from the nuclear club, which already included the United States, Britain, and the Soviet Union. He and his advisers viewed nuclear weapons and nuclear power as symbols of technological achievement and military progress in the modern world and felt it was inconceivable that France would not possess them.[31] De Gaulle was also determined to demonstrate his independence from the United States and to avoid France's security being completely dependent on the United States. This was despite France's defense pact with the United States through NATO.

As was the case with West Germany, France pursued nuclear cooperation agreements to bolster and expand the reaches of its nuclear industry. The French nuclear power industry, like Germany's, is closely associated with the government, and the nuclear industry is heavily promoted abroad by the government. Therefore there is strong economic pressure for France to export its nuclear technology.

Another reason France has been an active exporter of nuclear technology is its desire to increase its geopolitical influence in various regions of the world, especially the Middle East.[32] In 2008, France signed a nuclear cooperation agreement with the United Arab Emirates and on the same day concluded another deal setting up a military base in the UAE. In the last two years France has also signed nuclear cooperation agreements with Algeria, Libya, Morocco, Qatar, and Tunisia.

France's efforts to bolster the French nuclear industry and to improve its influence through the sale of nuclear technology have occasionally been controversial. The most notorious case of French nuclear assistance was to Iraq. In 1974 French premier and future president Jacques Chirac agreed to supply Iraq with a nuclear reactor in exchange for oil concessions. Iraqi leader Saddam Hussein even went to Paris to sign the deal in order to ensure that only reactors with proliferation potential were supplied.[33] The French government should have been aware that the reactors it was selling could easily be used to produce weapons-usable materials. In 1981 Israel bombed and destroyed the reactor, setting back the Iraqi nuclear weapons programs.

France also signed several nuclear cooperation agreements with Pakistan. In 1976 it signed a highly controversial agreement to construct a hundred-megaton facility that could separate a hundred kilograms of plutonium per year. This project was terminated in 1978 because of heavy U.S. pressure. Another French nuclear transfer that ultimately was canceled due to U.S. pressure was a transfer to Taiwan. France in 1975 agreed to provide Taiwan with a plutonium reprocessing facility. The United States had previously warned Taiwan against acquiring such a reprocessing plant. Under intense U.S. pressure Taiwan canceled the transaction and in September 1976 expressed an explicit commitment not to develop nuclear weapons. As a sign of good faith Taiwan dismantled the facilities related to reprocessing, and the United States took possession of the key component parts.

France, on the other hand, has been a strong supporter of the NPT and many of the surrounding policy tools to prevent proliferation. Although France did not sign the treaty in 1968, it agreed to respect the provisions of the treaty. In 1992 it acceded to the NPT as the Cold War came to an end. Even though it was not a member of the NPT, it became a member of the Nuclear Suppliers Group (NSG), which set standards for nuclear exports control. As a member of this group France has actively sought to ensure that NSG activities do not impede the peaceful development of nuclear energy.

PRELIMINARY HYPOTHESIS TESTING

The evidence presented in this chapter provides some support and contradicts a number of the hypotheses drawn here from the introductory chapter. At its core the nonproliferation regime is based upon a treaty that is inherently discriminatory. In accordance with the basic power structure of the international order, some states are given the right to possess nuclear weapons while others are not. A state's view of the nonproliferation regime may be linked to its general views about the current distribution of power and wealth in the international system. At the most extreme are states that seek to overturn the current system, while at the other extreme are states that favor no change to the status quo. Hypothesis 3 states that adherence to the nonproliferation regime will follow a state's general acceptance of the current international order.

As discussed throughout this chapter, U.S. allies with security guarantees are generally status quo powers. They seek to strengthen the existing set of global institutions and to maintain the current balance of international power, which is favorable to them. The evidence presented in this chapter supports the view that U.S. allies see nuclear proliferation as threat to the current balance and therefore seek to curtail it as much as possible. States with U.S. security guarantees are major beneficiaries of the discriminator nonproliferation regime. States such as Japan, South Korea, and Germany receive the protection of a nuclear umbrella without having to incur the costs of developing nuclear weapons, and at the same time the nonproliferation regime puts international pressure on other nonnuclear states not to develop nuclear weapons themselves.

In general it is NAM states that focus on the discriminator nonproliferation regime, arguing that the nuclear weapons states are taking seriously their commitment to move toward general nuclear disarmament. Egypt, for example, has said that further progress on disarmament should be the determining factor in whether the scope of the NPT is expanded into new areas. Among the nuclear-armed states, China, which is often viewed as conflicted about the current international order, has been accused of proliferating to improve its position in relation to the United States.[34] A less severe case is Indonesia, which has historically opposed portions of the NPT as institutionalizing inequities in international relations.[35] We therefore find some evidence to support Hypothesis 1.

This chapter also finds evidence to support Hypothesis 4 (political and economic interests versus the danger of proliferation). The French and German cases provide compelling evidence for the economic versus security trade-off present in nonproliferation policy. All nuclear-capable suppliers including U.S. allies undertake a delicate dance in their attempts to balance their economic and security interests. It is a dance that weighs the economic benefits of exporting nuclear enrichment, fuel production, and plutonium separation technology for nuclear power versus the danger of increasing the risk of nuclear proliferation. In addition, nuclear cooperation agreements are often used to achieve political benefits by increasing geopolitical influence in various regions. In some situations these economic and political benefits are judged to be more important than strict adherence to the nonproliferation regime. Examples of this include the U.S. nuclear deal with India, German nuclear commercial contracts with Brazil in the 1970s and 1980s, and French cooperation with Pakistan in the 1970s.

When considering U.S. allies there is some support for Hypothesis 1: that states' perception of the threat of proliferation influences their level of implementation of aspects of the nonproliferation regime. France and Germany are good examples as both, at least during the years of the Cold War, were willing to sell nuclear technology to states that were not a direct threat to them. States such as Brazil and Argentina in Latin America presented very little threat to them, and in these cases they were more lax in enforcing nonproliferation standards. The United States as a global power in general has seen the threat of proliferation anywhere as a danger to the existing international order, while U.S. partners and allies often worry less about the proliferation risk if it occurs in a region of secondary or tertiary concern.

Finally, there does not seem to be a great deal of evidence for the free rider problem with U.S. allies, as stated in Hypothesis 2. U.S. allies are among the most active international supporters of the nonproliferation regime: they are supportive across all four areas of the elements of the regime and, along with the United

States, are the critical international actors upholding the regime. It even could be argued that in comparison to the United States, where support for the regime has often swung from administration to administration, U.S. allies have been more steadfast and consistent in their support for the principles of the nonproliferation regime.[36]

CONCLUSION

It is not altogether surprising that states involved in security alliances with the United States are among the strongest supporters of the nonproliferation regime. These mostly developed and democratic states tend to see the international security environment in a similar manner to the United States and thus see further nuclear proliferation as a threat. In the most pressing proliferation cases, North Korea and Iran, U.S. allies in Asia and Europe are the strongest supporters for tough coordinated international actions. They also have supported actions to expand the scope of the regime to new issues and to encourage as many states as possible to join the NPT.

However, even states highly dependent on the United States for their security have their own economic and political interests. This has occasionally put them at odds, particularly before 1990, with U.S. nonproliferation goals. The nuclear power industry in many countries is a large employer and a sizable energy producer. As is the case with many industries, economic opportunities abroad present themselves, and the financial gain that might accrue has to be weighed against the security risk. There are many cases where the economic gain of allowing the nuclear industry to export sensitive technology was judged to be more important than the security risk posed by proliferation.

These judgments of economic gain versus security risks are often influenced by a desire to grow national economies through increasing states' level of exports. Government policies to promote exports often trump tighter security controls. This can lead to resistance when the United States and others suggest new antiproliferation measures that might disadvantage export-producing industries. Political interests also sometimes overcome proliferation concerns. The willingness of the United States to normalize India's nuclear program shows that even a superpower can favor political interests. U.S. allies, because of their role in the international system and their desire to expand their influence, have occasionally come to different conclusions than the United States about whether certain actions threaten the nonproliferation regime. European states, for example, have been willing to export sensitive technology to regions of secondary security concerns to them, such as Latin America. The United States, on the other hand, often views the threat of proliferation anywhere as a threat to the nonproliferation regime. This has caused the United States to place pressure to cancel transactions between its exporting allies and states receiving technology.

Finally, it is worth asking whether the end of the Cold War has increased the alignment of U.S. views and those of allied states on the proliferation regime. It is notable that most of the serious disagreements between the United States and its allies occurred before 1990, with Turkey's position on Iran's nuclear program being an important exception. The end of the Cold War has decreased global focus on conflicts between the great powers and has increased concerns about the dangers posed by regional powers and terrorism. With nuclear proliferation to regional powers and terrorism groups high on the international agenda, all actions connected with the nonproliferation regime have gained greater importance. This may have caused a shift at least in the minds of U.S. allies toward the U.S. position that nuclear proliferation anywhere is a threat to the international system, thus making them more willing to support, sustain, and strengthen the nonproliferation regime.

Notes

1. Sara Z. Kutchesfahani, "The Relevance of Historical Experience to Current Nuclear Proliferation Challenges," 2009 PONI Conference Series (Washington, D.C.: CSIS, 2009), 5–22; Bruno Tertrais, "Security Guarantees and Nuclear Non-Proliferation," *FRS Notes* 2011 no. 14 (Paris: Fondation pour la Recherche Stratégie, 2011).

2. Paul M. Cole, *Sweden without the Bomb: The Conduct of a Nuclear-Capable Nation without Nuclear Weapons* (Santa Monica, Calif.: RAND, 1994); Thomas Jonter, "The United States and Swedish Plans to Build the Bomb," in Knopf, *Security Assurances*, 219–45.

3. T. V. Paul, *Power versus Prudence: Why Nations Forgo Nuclear Weapons* (Montreal: McGill-Queen's University Press, 2000).

4. John Simpson, "The Role of Security Assurances in the Nuclear Nonproliferation Regime," in Knopf, *Security Assurances*, 57–85.

5. "Report of the Secretary of Defense Task Force on DoD Nuclear Weapons Management, Phase II: Review of the DoD Nuclear Mission," Arlington, Va., December 2008, 6.

6. Andrew Grotto, "Why Do States That Oppose Nuclear Proliferation Resist New Nonproliferation Obligations? Three Logics Of Nonproliferation Decision-Making," *Cardozo Journal of International and Comparative Law* 18, no. 1 (2010): 17.

7. Jeffrey Fields and Jason Enia, "The Health of the Nuclear Nonproliferation Regime: Returning to a Multidimensional Evaluation," *Nonproliferation Review* 16, no. 2 (2009): 173–96.

8. Ibid., 176.

9. See Joachim Krause, "Enlightenment and Nuclear Order," *International Affairs* 83, no. 3 (2007): 483–99.

10. Barack Obama, "Remarks by President Barack Obama," Hradcany Square, Prague, Czech Republic, April 5, 2009.

11. U.S. Department of Defense (DoD), *Nuclear Posture Review Report*, April 2010, Washington, D.C., http://www.defense.gov/npr/docs/2010%20nuclear%20posture%20review%20report.pdf.

12. See, for example, George Perkovich, "Toward Realistic U.S.-Indian Relations," Carnegie Endowment for International Peace, October 2010, http://carnegieendowment.org/publications/?fa=41797.

13. Matthew Kroenig, "Exporting the Bomb: Why States Provide Sensitive Nuclear Assistance," *American Political Science Review* 103, no. 1 (2009): 113–33.

14. Ibid.

15. Grotto, "Why Do States."

16. David Albright and Corey Gay, "Taiwan: Nuclear Nightmare Averted," *Bulletin of the Atomic Scientists* 54, no. 1 (1998): 54–60.

17. Mark Wuebbels, "Is Taiwan Getting Serious about Export Controls?," *Nonproliferation Review* 12, no. 2 (2005): 391–404.

18. See Paul, *Power versus Prudence*, 122–24, and Etel Solingen, *Nuclear Logics: Contrasting Paths in East Asia and the Middle East* (Princeton, N.J.: Princeton University Press, 2007), 82–99, on why South Korea decided not to become a nuclear-armed state.

19. U.S. White House, Office of the Press Secretary, "Joint Vision for the Alliance of the United States of America and the Republic of Korea," June 16, 2009, http://www.whitehouse.gov/the_press_office/Joint-vision-for-the-alliance-of-the-United-States-of-America-and-the-Republic-of-Korea.

20. Bong-Geun Jun, "U.S.-ROK Nuclear Energy Cooperation from Tutelage to Partnership: Nonproliferation Factor," U.S.-ROK Workshop on Nuclear Energy and Nonproliferation, Washington, D.C., January 20, 2010.

21. Gordon Corera, *Shopping for Bombs: Nuclear Proliferation, Global Insecurity, and the Rise and Fall of the A.Q. Khan Network* (Oxford: Oxford University Press, 2006).

22. Paul, *Power versus Prudence*, 40.

23. Ibid.

24. Krause, "Enlightenment and Nuclear Order," 489.

25. Beverly Crawford, "A Teutonic Shift: The Revolution in German Policy on Nonproliferation and Dual Use Export Controls," paper presented at 47th Annual ISA Convention, San Diego, Calif., March 22–25, 2006.

26. Ibid.

27. Ernst Urich von Weizsacker, chairman, Bundestag Committee on Environment, Nature Protection, and Nuclear Safety, paper prepared for Aspen Institute, March 2005.

28. Harald Müller, "German National Identity and WMD Proliferation," *Nonproliferation Review* 10, no. 2 (2003): 1–20.

29. Ibid.

30. Crawford, "Teutonic Shift," 1.

31. Philip H. Gordon, "Charles de Gaulle and the Nuclear Revolution," in *Cold War Statesmen Confront the Bomb: Nuclear Diplomacy since 1945*, ed. John Lewis Gaddis, Philip H. Gordon, Ernest R. May, and Jonathan Rosenberg, 216–35 (Oxford: Oxford University Press, 1999).

32. Mycle Schneider, "Nuclear France Abroad: History, Status, and Prospects of French Nuclear Activities in Foreign Countries" (Paris: Mycle Schneider Consulting, May 2009). http://www.nirs.org/nukerelapse/background/090502mschneidernukefrance.pdf.

33. Solingen, *Nuclear Logics*, 143.

34. Thomas C. Reed and Danny B. Stillman, *The Nuclear Express: A Political History of the Bomb and Its Proliferation* (Minneapolis: Zenith Press, 2009), 249–50; on Chinese views on the international system see Evan S. Medeiros, *China's International Behavior: Activism, Opportunism, and Diversification* (Santa Monica, Calif.: RAND Corporation, 2009). http://www.rand.org/pubs/monographs/MG850.

35. Grotto, *Why Do States*, 19–21.

36. On the erosion of U.S. support during the Bush administrations for the underlying principles of the nonproliferation regime, see William Walker, "Nuclear Enlightenment and Counter-enlightenment," *International Affairs* 83, no. 3 (2007): 431–53.

CHAPTER 6

The Nonproliferation Motivations of the Non-Aligned Movement

Deepti Choubey

ONE OF THE BEST WAYS to measure the health of the nonproliferation regime is to observe the Treaty on the Non-Proliferation of Nuclear Weapons (NPT) Review Conference. The May 2010 Review Conference can be, at best, characterized as an incremental success with the adoption of a final document. Scratching beneath the surface of the final document reveals a host of unresolved issues among the acknowledged nuclear weapons states, between nuclear and nonnuclear weapons states, and also between primarily developed countries and the members of the Non-Aligned Movement (NAM). Officials in the capitals of developed countries are usually quick to blame the NAM for the lack of progress in shoring up the nonproliferation regime, particularly when it comes to nonproliferation-specific measures.[1] This impulse, posing as an explanation, is far too facile as it treats the NAM monolithically, a dangerous approach that frequently leads to strategies that marginalize rather than engage this grouping of states. Because the NAM includes 118 members across four continents and is the largest organized group of states within the NPT context, a deeper investigation is required to illuminate how the NAM overall and various member states approach nonproliferation. Defaulting to simple characterizations of the NAM states as "radical" or "spoilers" misses the bigger picture and opportunities to work with potential partners to strengthen nonproliferation efforts. Indeed, like the NPT Review Conference, where outcomes are based on consensus, new solutions to pressing problems in the regime are unlikely to gain traction without the support of the NAM. Therefore, discerning how the NAM conceptualizes nonproliferation and attendant activities should be central to efforts to advance the nonproliferation agenda particularly as it evolves necessarily over time.

The objective of nonproliferation is to prevent the transfer of nuclear weapons and weapons-usable nuclear materials (e.g., highly enriched uranium and separated plutonium), as well as related technology and information, to other states. A more precise definition of what activities are included in the concept of nonproliferation is necessary. Traditionally, nonproliferation has meant states foregoing nuclear weapons (usually by ratifying the NPT), adopting full-scope safeguards, implementing export controls, and supporting nuclear-weapon-free zones.[2] As thinking about the dual-use nature of nuclear technology and the weaknesses of the regime evolved, so did the need for additional measures such as adopting the Additional Protocol (AP) and ratifying the Comprehensive Nuclear-Test-Ban Treaty (CTBT).[3] Sparking perhaps the greatest change to the concept of nonproliferation is the advent of nonstate actors, the rise of rogue states, and the specter of nuclear terrorism, which further catalyzed efforts on the security of nuclear materials. With these new risks, counterproliferation efforts emerged such as participating in the Proliferation Security Initiative (PSI), combating nuclear smuggling, and implementing United Nations Security Council Resolution 1540 (UNSCR 1540). These initiatives were supplemented by expanding the legal foundation for the security of nuclear materials through negotiating the 2005 Amendment to the Convention on the Physical Protection of Nuclear Materials and the International Convention for the Suppression of Acts of Terrorism. For the primarily developed states that hold nonproliferation as an urgent priority, the definition of what activities contribute to the goal of nonproliferation has broadened not only in terms of the numbers and types of initiatives but also how the goal relates to the security of the nation-state. Specifically, the more traditional definition of nonproliferation includes activities that govern a state's own behavior whereas the broadened definition includes a conceptual shift where states also must contribute to global norms and efforts to stymie the aspirations of other malicious actors. This shift has revealed a conceptual gap in need of bridging with the NAM, the vast majority of which are developing countries. Specifically, only 7 of the 118 members possess more than a kilogram of weapons-usable nuclear materials, whereas the rest struggle to understand what their responsibilities are, considering their limited resources and other pressing challenges and priorities.[4] This is an example of how some of the disparities between developed and developing countries on nonproliferation measures may be due to a different understanding of what the nonproliferation obligation requires. Differing perceptions of the threat and its urgency may also account for the lag in NAM states adopting the broader dictates of the nonproliferation agenda in the twenty-first century.

Another explanatory factor is credibility. Characterized now as a moderate NAM state, even Indonesia connects the lack of disarmament progress to nonproliferation. Indonesia's opening statement at the 2010 NPT Review Conference asserts: "Pending the total elimination of nuclear weapons, it is incumbent that nuclear weapon states provide negative security assurances to the nonnuclear weapon states. Only then would their often expressed concern about the threat of nuclear proliferation carry greater resonance."[5] Indonesia's view is different from the explanation that nonnuclear weapons states hold back on advancing nonproliferation objectives to gain leverage for further disarmament measures. Instead, Indonesia's statement reveals that some nonnuclear weapons states see the primary source of the threat to be the nuclear weapons held by nuclear weapons states. Therefore, their view is that until that threat is neutralized through negative security assurances for nonnuclear weapons states, it will be hard for states like Indonesia to fully embrace or prioritize other sources of the threat and how to address them. These kinds of concerns from the NAM should not be discounted.

Instead, they should be addressed using the broader conception of the nonproliferation agenda. As an example, if the NAM, particularly those states without nuclear weapons, could imagine the process involved in achieving a world without nuclear weapons (e.g., the dismantlement of warheads and measures to ensure the nuclear materials in them are secure and not used to secretly reconstitute a nuclear weapons capability), they would see how nuclear materials security measures are congruent, supportive, and ultimately necessary for their ultimate goal of nuclear disarmament.

Furthermore, another reason not to ignore the concerns of the NAM is that as a diverse collection of states, they have demonstrated their ability to influence the terms of various aspects of nuclear debates. On negative security assurances, which were initially offered voluntarily by nuclear weapons states, the NAM has converted that offer into a demand for a legally binding agreement. Similarly, the NAM has also played a norm entrepreneur role in the creation of the nuclear taboo against the further spread and use of nuclear weapons, arguably an effort core to the nonproliferation vision and goal.[6]

When assessing the members of the NAM across the traditional nonproliferation measures listed above, the NAM can be characterized as generally doing better than is commonly understood considering the constraints imposed by NAM principles and the lack of resources to support nonproliferation. NAM principles about legitimacy, sovereignty, and non-interference shape the views of some states regarding issues such as export controls and enforcement. However, resource constraints, in the form of economic and human capital (e.g., skilled technocrats, diplomats), are another factor inhibiting the full implementation of some nonproliferation obligations. There are a handful of states that raise concerns about their commitment to nonproliferation (e.g., Iran, Syria, Myanmar), but their behavior may have little to do with their NAM association. Therefore, their suspected lack of commitment should not as strongly color characterizations of the NAM as they do today.

This analysis addresses the relevance of the NAM's origin, highlights the nonproliferation motivations of several key nonnuclear weapons states that demonstrate the diversity of views within the NAM, and provides policy implications derived from a better understanding of NAM motivations. This chapter does not address nuclear-armed states that are members of the NAM, namely, India, Pakistan, and North Korea.[7]

NON-ALIGNED MOVEMENT ORIGIN AND EVOLUTION

The origin of the Non-Aligned Movement elucidates why its members have varying levels of enthusiasm for nonproliferation responsibilities and activities. The NAM was founded in response to the collapse of colonialism during the Cold War and the creation of a bipolar world dominated by two military alliances (NATO and the Warsaw Pact). It sought to ensure that new states could exercise their inalienable right to self-determination and independence. This meant offering an alternative to being subsumed by the blocs fashioned by the Soviet Union and United States. The 1955 Bandung Asian-African Conference convened twenty-nine heads of states and developed the Ten Principles of Bandung that would govern the founding principles of the NAM. Several of these principles, such as the emphasis on sovereignty, non-intervention into the internal affairs of other countries, and abjuring the use of force, provide insight into the hesitancy some NAM states may show when asked to more fully participate in the nonproliferation regime. Based on the Ten Principles, the primary objectives of non-aligned countries included the following list:

> The support of self-determination, national independence and the sovereignty and territorial integrity of States; opposition to apartheid; non-adherence to multilateral military pacts and the independence of non-aligned countries from great power or block influences and rivalries; the struggle against imperialism in all its forms and manifestations; the struggle against colonialism, neocolonialism, racism, foreign occupation and domination; disarmament;

non-interference into the internal affairs of States and peaceful coexistence among all nations; rejection of the use or threat of use of force in international relations; the strengthening of the United Nations; the democratization of international relations; socioeconomic development and the restructuring of the international economic system; as well as international cooperation on an equal footing.[8]

Since the 1990s, the conception of the challenges the NAM faces has further expanded to include "the necessity of protecting the principles of International law, eliminating weapons of mass destruction, combating terrorism, defending human rights, working toward making the United Nations more effective in meeting the needs of all its member states in order to preserve International Peace, Security and Stability, as well as realizing justice in the international economic system."[9] The NAM's issue agenda is extremely diverse and ranges from economic development to disarmament. The end of the Cold War and the failure of socialism forced the NAM to debate its relevance. In the post–Cold War era, the nuclear issue, more so than the other items on the crowded NAM agenda, is one of the greatest challenges to the NAM identity as three NAM members (India, Pakistan, and North Korea) have developed nuclear weapons or nuclear weapons capabilities. At the 14th Summit of the Non-Aligned Movement in Cuba in 2006, the member countries reaffirmed their commitment to the "ideals, principles and purposes upon which the movement was founded and with the principles and purposes enshrined in the United Nations Charter."[10]

That summit also resulted in one of the more recent articulations of the NAM's purpose, which include:

> Promoting multilateralism and the central role for the United Nations; serving as a forum for developing countries to promote and defend their common interests; settling all international disputes by peaceful means; encouraging sustainable development through international cooperation; condemning unilateralism and hegemonic domination in international relations; confronting threats of the use of force and acts of aggression; promoting comprehensive reform of the United Nations Security Council; pursuing universal and non-discriminatory nuclear disarmament; prohibiting the development, production, acquisition, testing, stockpiling, transfer, use or threat of use of nuclear weapons; promoting the establishment of nuclear-weapon-free-zones (NWFZ) where they do not already exist; and promoting international cooperation in the peaceful uses of nuclear energy and to facilitate access to nu-

clear technology, equipment and material for peaceful purposes required by developing countries.[11]

One of the key differences in the articulation of the NAM's purpose over time is the increasing attention paid to nuclear-related issues. The principles and purpose of the NAM combine to reveal its ethos as a movement on nuclear issues. That ethos manifests as a basic commitment to nonproliferation as traditionally defined, but it balks against the inherently discriminatory nature of the regime and views disarmament as the only solution to address inequities. Further exacerbating that sense of unfairness are perceptions that more and more obstacles are being created to NAM states realizing the potential contribution peaceful uses of nuclear energy could make to their economic development. Moreover, this is a movement that views with deep skepticism efforts outside of the UN, international law, and the text of the NPT to prevent proliferation. These efforts may range from export controls, the threat of sanctions, the imposition of unilateral sanctions, the threat of the use of force, and the use of force. That said, the NAM has made significant contributions to the traditional measures of nonproliferation and is also making progress on the additional activities that have come to be defined as contributing to the goal of nonproliferation.

EVALUATING THE NON-ALIGNED MOVEMENT NONPROLIFERATION RECORD

The attention paid to the positions of a few vocal non-aligned states sometimes obscures the broader nonproliferation record of the NAM. For instance, every member of the NAM (except for India, Pakistan, and North Korea) is party to the NPT. Many of them even acceded to the treaty before some of the acknowledged nuclear weapons states. As evidence of their commitment to nonproliferation, NAM states overwhelmingly are part of nuclear-weapon-free zones. When such zones were originally conceptualized in the 1950s, they were thought of as a regional approach to nonproliferation.[12] These zones have also represented nonproliferation innovations. For instance, the Central Asian Nuclear-Weapon-Free Zone (CANFWZ), to which Turkmenistan and Uzbekistan are party, is the first zone that requires participating parties to adopt the Additional Protocol and meet international standards regarding the security of nuclear facilities. Another innovation has come from Mongolia, which declared itself in 1992 to be a one-state nuclear-weapon-free zone.[13] Some NAM states have a right to confidently assert their nonproliferation and even their disarmament credentials. For instance, Belarus voluntarily surrendered the nuclear weapons it inherited after the dissolution of the Soviet Union, and South Africa is the only state to have indigenously produced nuclear weapons and then verifiably dismantled them.

Another multilateral legal instrument that holds strong nonproliferation meaning for the Non-Aligned Movement is the Comprehensive Nuclear-Test-Ban Treaty. Even the final document from the 2010 NPT Review Conference emphasizes the nonproliferation value of the test ban when it states:

> The Conference reaffirms the essential role of the Comprehensive Nuclear-Test-Ban Treaty within the nuclear disarmament and non-proliferation regime and that by achieving the cessation of all nuclear weapon test explosions and all other nuclear explosions, by constraining the development and qualitative improvement of nuclear weapons and ending the development of advanced new types of nuclear weapons, the treaty combats both horizontal and vertical proliferation.[14]

The Non-Aligned Movement's opening statement delivered by Indonesia focused on the importance of the CTBT.[15] Indonesia, as one of the nine Annex II countries whose ratification is necessary for the treaty to enter into force, also announced that it was seeking CTBT ratification in the hopes of inspiring the others to do the same and followed through with ratification in 2012. Beyond coverage of this issue in the NAM statement, twenty-one other NAM countries chose to specifically address it in their own speeches.[16] As a gauge of NAM commitment to nonproliferation, the CTBT reveals some important fissures within the NAM. Aside from China, the United States, and Israel, the currently remaining Annex II states are all members of the NAM (Egypt, India, Iran, North Korea, and Pakistan).[17] India, Pakistan, and North Korea's positions are not likely to be influenced by the NAM. However, Indonesia is one of the few states that has a workable relationship with North Korea and could be an effective intermediary for convincing North Korea when the time is right. Egypt and Iran have both signed but not ratified the CTBT. To the extent Iran's domestic dynamics and perception of its security environment has shaped its position on nuclear issues, the NAM position on the CTBT is unlikely to influence Iran to convert its signature to ratification. Egypt is a country that refrains from adopting certain measures in the hopes it creates leverage for other disarmament activities. Egyptian officials have stated privately that the NPT is the last treaty Egypt will ratify until Israel accedes to the NPT as a nonnuclear weapons state. The current state of CTBT ratification demonstrates that the vast majority of states that are members of the NAM eventually fulfill their obligations, but for the few that remain, other principles or concerns influence their choice not to strengthen the nonproliferation regime.

In terms of safeguards, the four NAM nonnuclear weapons states with more than a kilogram of weapons-usable material, along with twenty-seven other NAM states with less than that amount or no materials at all, have concluded a Comprehensive Safeguards Agreement (CSA) with the International Atomic Energy Agency (IAEA); an additional twenty-four states have a modified Small Quantities Protocol (SQP) that better addresses concerns about states that have a kilogram or less of weapons-usable nuclear materials and tightens the criteria for eligible states[18]; and thirty-five states have at least an SQP in place.[19] That leaves, however, eleven states with nothing in place, and for the most part they are among the poorest in the world. The eleven that have neither a CSA nor an SQP in place include Benin, Cape Verde, Djibouti, Equatorial Guinea, Eritrea, Guinea, Guinea-Bissau, Liberia, Sao Tome and Principe, Somalia, and Timor-Leste. Also in the arena of safeguards and required nonproliferation innovations is the effort to have as many states as possible adopt voluntarily the Additional Protocol that complements CSAs. As of March 2014, there are 122 Additional Protocols in force, and an additional twenty-one states have signed but not yet completed ratification (excluding India from those who have signed but not ratified for the sake of this analysis). Those two numbers combined represent the progress and future potential of this important element to shore up the nonproliferation regime. With the forty-seven NAM states having adopted it and the sixteen that have signed it, the NAM countries represent 43 percent of that progress and potential.[20] One of the more vocal critics of the AP is Egypt. Egypt's position is directly related to Israel and supports the "discrimination" hypothesis for why states do not support certain nonproliferation measures. Egypt insists that it will not adopt the AP until Israel institutes comprehensive safeguards on its nuclear facilities. There are also objections to converting what is supposed to be a voluntary measure to an obligation (e.g., making the Additional Protocol a condition of supply). Many NAM states see that as changing the rules in the middle of the game. What worries them is that these changes to the rules are further disadvantaging their access to nuclear energy for economic development purposes. Egypt's approach to the AP, borne out of its concerns about discrimination in the regime, is similar to its approach on other initiatives. Egypt will not adopt the CTBT, AP, or even various nuclear materials or terrorism conventions until Israel accedes to the NPT as a nonnuclear weapon state. This is the perfect example of a state holding back on other commitments in the hopes it creates leverage for greater disarmament progress by nuclear weapons states. However, finding other states explicitly enacting this same strategy is hard. Egypt gains attention for its position because it views itself as a leader within the Arab world and within the Non-Aligned Movement. Recognizing that Egypt is a "big" state in comparison to most other members of the NAM, Egypt feels the obligation to be a voice to hold nuclear weapons states accountable to their obligations. Implementing the 1995 Resolution on the Middle East, which calls for the creation of a zone free of weapons of mass destruction, is an example of an issue on which Egypt has been a tireless advocate and hard negotiator.

Beyond what safeguards implementation and Additional Protocol adoption reveal about the diversion of nuclear materials for military purposes, the production capabilities and holdings of nuclear materials should also bear on the NAM's nonproliferation record. Iran is the only NAM nonnuclear weapons state with an enrichment facility, and no NAM nonnuclear weapons state operates reprocessing facilities.[21] None of the NAM nonnuclear weapons states are producing weapons-usable highly enriched uranium (HEU) or separated plutonium (Pu), although the fate of the Iranian Arak reactor that would produce plutonium would change that. In terms of civilian HEU holdings within NAM states, Belarus has at least 87–127 kilograms; South Africa has 610–760 kilograms; Iran has 7 kilograms; Uzbekistan has 5–20 kilograms.[22] Ghana, Jamaica, Nigeria, and Syria have a little less than 1 kilogram.[23] According to the International Panel on Fissile Material, China and Canada have projects in place to convert Miniature Neutron Source Reactors to low-enriched uranium (LEU) in Ghana, Jamaica, Nigeria, and Syria[24]; Vietnam in 2013 removed all weapons-usable nuclear material from its territory; the fate of Iran's spent HEU fuel from the Tehran Research Reactor is likely tied to any deal for refueling the reactor and the broader negotiations aimed at seeking a comprehensive agreement; Uzbekistan is on track to be cleaned out in the next few years; Belarus had made a commitment to remove or convert its HEU, but that effort has hit roadblocks; and South Africa has converted its research reactor to LEU and has been minimizing some of its material holdings. There are, of course, a few cases where questions have been raised about a state's activities and intentions (e.g., Iran, Syria, and Myanmar). These states are the exception and not the norm within the Non-Aligned Movement. This picture about nuclear materials production capabilities of the NAM helps explain why so few NAM members have deep technical expertise on nuclear issues. This lack of expertise as it relates to human resource constraints is important when it comes to issues of determining noncompliance and taking measures to enforce compliance. This connection is discussed in more depth in the "Enforcement of Nonproliferation Compliance" section below.

ADDRESSING NONSTATE THREATS

To address the different threat perceptions among states, in April 2010 President Obama convened forty-seven countries for a Nuclear Security Summit in Washington, D.C. As reiterated at the follow-up 2012 Summit in Seoul, the objective of the summits is to develop a common understanding of the "threat posed by nuclear terrorism, to agree to effective measures to secure nuclear material, and to prevent nuclear smuggling and terrorism."[25] Out of the forty-seven countries represented, thirteen (not including India and Pakistan) were NAM states, many of which do not possess large quantities of HEU or Pu. Their inclusion indicates the attempt to fashion a broader conception of the nuclear threat and its global consequences even to states that do not possess nuclear materials or may not be targets of a nuclear terrorism attack. States that prioritize nuclear terrorism as a threat must address the perception from developing states that a nuclear terrorist attack is far more likely to occur in Washington or London than it is in Kigali. The first summit resulted in a Summit Communiqué and a Work Plan along with voluntary commitments ranging from promises to ratify international conventions addressing nuclear terrorism and the physical protection of nuclear materials to financial contributions to the IAEA to efforts to improve nuclear security measures at home. The second summit demonstrated implementation of some of these commitments. As much as these steps reflect necessary progress, in total they are insufficient for addressing the threat of nuclear terrorism and its global consequences. In some ways, even this unique forum for convening leaders at the highest level and from a diverse group of states underscores the work remaining in forging a stronger consensus about the threat as urgent, persistent, and real, as well as the priority actions needed to organize internationally to effectively tackle that threat.

To date, there are ninety-two parties to the International Convention for the Suppression of Acts of Nuclear Terrorism, and thirty-eight NAM states (not including India) have ratified it (or taken action having the same legal effect); a further thirty-one have also signed but still need to ratify.[26] Seventy-two NAM states (not including India) have adopted the Convention on the Physical Protection of Nuclear Materials, but only twenty-two have adopted the 2005 amendment that makes it legally binding for a state "to protect nuclear facilities and material in peaceful domestic use, storage as well as transport while also providing for greater cooperation among states to respond to instances of stolen or smuggled nuclear material, to mitigate any radiological consequences of sabotage, and to prevent and combat related offences."[27] Two-thirds of states must ratify the amendment for it to take effect. Capacity constraints inhibit some states from taking the steps to adopt these agreements. There are thirteen terrorism-related conventions, and each requires capacity within foreign ministries and other branches of government to formalize commitment to them. Because the NAM states as a principle the "rejection of and opposition to terrorism in all its forms and manifestations,"[28] bureaucratic capacity to implement these international legal obligations domestically and competition from other issues are likely the reasons for lags in adoption among most members. Syria and Iran, as suspected state sponsors of terrorism, may have other reasons for their ambivalence toward these agreements. To help with the bureaucratic capacity issues and to ensure that nuclear security measures are implemented more fully and with greater effectiveness, Indonesia has developed through the Nuclear Security Summit process a National Legislation Implementation Kit on Nuclear Security. This kind of leadership from a NAM state can be meaningful as many of the NAM states in need of such assistance may be more willing to take it when developed by a peer rather than engaging with another Western or developed country initiative.

Beyond international legal agreements, counterproliferation has arisen as another way to combat the spread of nuclear weapons and materials from so-called rogue states and nonstate actors. Counterproliferation spans many kinds of activities, but NAM views and participation in efforts such as the Proliferation Security Initiative reveal other explanations for why NAM states may forego active participation. Interdiction is at the heart of the Proliferation Security Initiative, which is an ad hoc effort that "aims to stop the trafficking of weapons of mass destruction (WMD), their delivery systems, and related materials to and from states and nonstate actors of proliferation concern."[29] The PSI is one of the best examples of the broadened definition of nonproliferation as one that applies to both state and nonstate actors, does not require formalization through the UN system, and is based on voluntary actions by states consistent with their domestic and international obligations. The PSI is seen as an innovation by many analysts, but its nature runs counter to the principles of the NAM. Although one-third of the states listed as Proliferation Security Initiative participants are from the NAM, one notable absence is Indonesia.[30]

As the largest archipelagic country, Indonesia holds a crucial strategic position for interdiction activities; however, for that very reason the Indonesian government has concerns about how the interdiction principles of the PSI can be applied without undermining the UN Convention on the Law of the Seas. Beyond that, Indonesia has other political, legal, and technical difficulties with the PSI. It has urged PSI proponents, particularly the United States, to bring the PSI within the UN context as that would help ease some of Indonesia's concerns. The Indonesian example demonstrates the discomfort of many NAM countries with ad hoc measures. Moreover, many NAM states may not be as geographically relevant for PSI activities and may not have the national resources to effectively contribute (e.g., naval capabilities). For those who lament the uneven participation of states in newer nonproliferation measures, they should be cautioned against thinking all measures can be equally applied across states.

Aside from interdiction efforts, there are also counter-smuggling and second line of defense initiatives that require the cooperation of other states. Evaluating these programs is beyond the scope of this analysis, but the lack of participation in these programs may have more to do with the effectiveness of these efforts vis-à-vis the nature of the problem. Many analysts argue that these initiatives are likely to be highly porous and expensive and as such should not be overly relied on. If this is the case, asking poorer NAM states to participate in such activities seems like a waste of political capital and other resources. One missing hypothesis about why states may not be enthusiastic about certain nonproliferation measures is that those states think that the nonproliferation measures are ineffective. In an era of expanded nonproliferation activities, policymakers and analysts should be careful not to assume all activities are equally good or necessary for all states.

ENFORCEMENT OF NONPROLIFERATION COMPLIANCE

Enforcement measures highlight the tension between the traditional definition of nonproliferation held by the NAM and the evolved context in which states that prioritize nonproliferation operate. The conceptual paper for the project catalyzing this publication posits support for sanctions as part of the broader definition of nonproliferation. There is, however, a crucial distinction between nonproliferation as a goal and the steps taken to enforce compliance (e.g., sanctions). This distinction has meaning for the NAM as it militates against their support for sanctions. Again, NAM principles are instructive for why some states have an allergy to sanctions, particularly those that are imposed outside of the UN context.

NAM principles that may weigh heavily on how member states view sanctions include "non-interference in the internal affairs of states; rejection of attempts at regime change; refraining from exerting pressure or coercion on other countries, including resorting to aggression or other acts involving the use of direct or indirect force, and the application and/or promotion of any coercive unilateral measure that goes against international law or is in any way incompatible with it, for the purpose of coercing any other State to subordinate its sovereign rights, or to gain any benefit whatsoever."[31] In the context of the confrontation with Iran, there have been U.S.-EU imposed sanctions, additional sanctions from other countries, and sanctions imposed by the UN Security Council. From the principles listed above, non-UN sanctions carry less water with NAM states as they are seen as lacking legitimacy. Not all measures approved in the UN context, however, have the full support of the NAM. UNSCR 1540, which imposes a binding obligation on all states, is also deemed illegitimate by some NAM states. The core of their argument is that a legal instrument that imposes an obligation on all states should have been discussed among all states and not just within the smaller confines of the UN Security Council. In addition to the legitimacy issue, some NAM states may not support sanctions because they think sanctions are ineffective and a vestige of imperialism, and because of capacity issues in implementing sanctions.

Aside from how much states support sanctions regimes, another compliance issue illustrates the limitations of the NAM as fully participating in nonproliferation activities. In September 2009 at the IAEA General Conference, Iran attempted to gain the consensus support of the NAM for a resolution prohibiting military attacks on all nuclear facilities. Iran failed to gain that support when Chile and Singapore blocked the consensus in favor of Iran's resolution.[32] In the following weeks, the secret enrichment facility near Qom was revealed and two months later, the IAEA Board of Governors called Iran to task again. Considering the role states like Chile and Singapore played in obstructing that latest maneuver from Iran, it may seem possible for them to also play a stronger role in noncompliance determinations. Unfortunately, human resource capacity constraints are an inhibiting factor. Many non-aligned states, even those like Singapore that are more economically developed, simply do not have enough people with the technical skills or experience to wade too deeply into compliance debates at the IAEA or elsewhere. As noted above, except for Iran, no NAM nonnuclear weapons state has advanced fuel cycle facilities (e.g., reprocessing or enrichment facilities). Because NAM officials lack a robust technical background, they tend to be skeptical of allegations against other NAM members (certainly the case before the Qom revelation in Iran), or they default to repeating principled positions (e.g., all states have an inalienable right to the peaceful uses of nuclear energy).

NUCLEAR ENERGY AND NONPROLIFERATION

Nuclear energy interests are another strong motivator for NAM states as they assess additional nonproliferation obligations or activities. Steps that Belarus, the United Arab Emirates (UAE), and Mongolia have taken best exemplify this hypothesis. For instance, Belarus, the only NAM state bordering Europe, was not invited to the 2010 Nuclear Security Summit. At the end of 2010, Belarus pledged to eliminate all of its stocks of HEU by the 2012 Nuclear Security Summit in South Korea.[33] Aside from seeking an invitation to the 2012 Summit, Belarus was likely motivated by efforts to develop its first civilian nuclear power plant. It expected that the pledge to eliminate its HEU would smooth the way for the United States to approve nuclear cooperation between Belarus and either South Korea or Japan. U.S. approval is required because nuclear cooperation with South Korean and Japanese vendors entails the transfer of U.S.-origin nuclear technology. Broader challenges in the U.S.-Belarus relationship have stalled this effort.

The UAE, meanwhile, has concluded what is touted as a gold-standard nuclear cooperation agreement with the United States. The terms of it include the UAE voluntarily foregoing indigenous enrichment and reprocessing. This is noteworthy as the UAE intends to build ten nuclear reactors, which would make it the first Middle Eastern country to operate so many nuclear power reactors.[34] To further burnish its nonproliferation credentials, the UAE also adopted the Additional Protocol, participates in the Proliferation Security Initiative, is a partner in the Global Initiative to Combat Nuclear Terrorism, and is working with the U.S. Department of Energy to implement the Megaports Initiative. The UAE has worked to be transparent and assure the international community of its peaceful purpose in addressing its growing energy demands. The UAE is another example of how energy needs can drive more robust nonproliferation engagement.

Mongolia's nonproliferation motivations are derived from both geopolitical and commercial considerations. After the collapse of the Soviet Union, Mongolia seized the opportunity to define and secure its national security interests. Mongolia declared itself to be a one-state nuclear-weapons-free zone and since then has worked to ensure that Mongolia is internationally respected and has a strong nonproliferation record. Mongolian officials prize this nonproliferation record as they explore civilian uses of nuclear energy. The country possesses substantial uranium reserves and is eager to bring nuclear energy to its people. In November 2010, Mongolia signed a memorandum of understanding (MOU) with the Toshiba Corporation in Japan. Under this MOU, Mongolia and Toshiba would explore possible cooperation in developing Mongolia's mineral resources including uranium and providing strategic advice on nuclear systems, transmission, and distribution networks.[35] Using its own uranium resources as the asset, Mongolia could be preparing the groundwork to play a role in international fuel services and providing value-added services such as fuel fabrication and even possibly storage of spent fuel of Mongolian uranium that is first exported abroad. Mongolia's experience and future with nuclear energy is another example of how commercial interests can support nonproliferation goals. Mongolia's uranium reserves are partially an impetus for its civilian nuclear energy endeavors. There are many African countries such as Gambia and Namibia that also cite their uranium reserves in connection to bringing nuclear energy to their people for economic development purposes. In some cases, these countries are more open to multilateral fuel arrangements and less rigid about the principles governing the peaceful uses of nuclear energy than other NAM states.

POLICY IMPLICATIONS

With states like Iran, Syria, Egypt, and even Myanmar dominating nuclear-related headlines, it is easy to transfer questions about their commitment to nonproliferation to the other states within the Non-Aligned Movement. A closer look at the nonproliferation record of the larger group on both traditional and newer measures of nonproliferation reveals that most states are fulfilling their obligations consistent with their views of the nonproliferation threat and within the constraints defined by principles and resources. Moving away from monolithic characterizations of the NAM, pursuing opportunities to build human capital resources, and recognizing the limits to finding common ground on perceptions of the threat of proliferation could lead to more effective policy approaches and the identification of potential partners from countries that treat nonproliferation as an urgent priority.

To the extent NPT Review Conferences matter in shoring up commitment to nonproliferation norms, countries that want to bolster the regime should start now to develop relationships with an assortment of countries within the NAM. Iran is the chair of the NAM for the 2015 NPT Review Conference, and it is unclear how the separate negotiations track with Iran will apply to the dynamics of the Review Conference and how the United States as a main player in the negotiations will (as needed with Egypt at the 2010 Review Conference) find a modus vivendi with Iran. Indonesia is continuing to play its role as the nonproliferation and disarmament coordinator within the NAM. This is good news as states like Indonesia can be an important counterbalance to extreme ideological inclinations from other NAM states. For instance, it was Indonesia that pushed to have the NAM coordinated statement at the 2009 Preparatory Committee meeting acknowledge President Obama's Prague speech. Such a mention may seem like a small thing, but it contributes to atmospherics that can matter for negotiations. One way to search for potential partners is to review previous statements made at Review Conference proceedings. States that acknowledge the Prague speech, welcome even small steps toward nuclear reductions, support efforts for securing nuclear materials, and seem open to multilateral fuel arrangements are countries to be cultivated to ensure the NAM consensus position remains a workable one within the multilateral negotiating context.

Another way to identify potential states with which to work is to analyze the NAM membership for states that have resources relevant to the nuclear fuel cycle. Many of these states may not be interested in capital-intensive civilian nuclear energy programs, but they are interested in developing their uranium resources. Helping NAM members exploit other aspects of the nuclear fuel cycle could be another way to reframe the "inalienable right to peaceful uses of nuclear energy" and to diminish current resentment.

Some officials in Washington and other capitals have been known to dismiss NAM positions as just the views of a few career diplomats in Geneva. Certainly, there are some NAM diplomats who have worked nuclear issues for a long time and have earned reputations for themselves. But with further scrutiny, their views hew closely to non-aligned principles. This handful of diplomats comes from the few NAM states that either have the resources or the philosophical commitment to be active on such a technical issue. That there are only a few of these personalities speaks to a larger problem that inhibits more robust nonproliferation participation from NAM states. This is the problem of how resource constraints undercut the development of technical expertise within foreign ministries. This challenge may also be an opportunity for developed countries to cooperate with developing countries in an effort to train diplomats or other relevant officials. Such education efforts might also help build bridges to countries that otherwise would not receive attention on this agenda.

The IAEA provides "nuclear security missions, evaluations and technical visits ... for helping states to assess their nuclear security needs, and provide a basis for formulating plans."[36] The International Nuclear Security Advisory Service helps states identify their nuclear security requirements and can lead to cooperative steps between the state and the IAEA as well as a bilateral partner. Another program that could be very helpful to NAM states is the Integrated Nuclear Security Support Plan in which the IAEA provides states with an integrated plan for nuclear security improvements and assistance. The completed plan typically addresses six components of work related to nuclear security: legal and regulatory framework, prevention, detection, response, human resource development, and follow-up.[37] The Integrated Nuclear Security Support Plan identifies the responsible entities and organizations within the state as well as the timeframe for the implementation. This process takes into account both technical and financial matters and includes donors that may be able to support the implementation of parts of the plan.

Beyond what states can do to make better use of the IAEA programs, there are also opportunities for certain nuclear and nonnuclear weapons states to collaborate to help NAM states build the technical proficiency of their human capital (e.g., diplomats, technical advisers). For instance, the United Kingdom partnered with Norway on verification and disarmament-related projects. The United Kingdom, as a nuclear weapons state, could partner with a nonnuclear weapons state that has strong disarmament credentials such as New Zealand to conduct workshops further educating NAM officials on some of the complexities of compliance and other technical issues. Having a nuclear weapons state as one of the sponsors would lend credibility to the exercise and might also ensure use of the right lexicon. A state like New Zealand that is a vocal proponent of disarmament provides the bridge between the nuclear weapons state and the NAM states. One of the key principles of the NAM is that the "most effective way of preventing terrorists from acquiring weapons of mass destruction is through the total elimination of such weapons."[38] For much of the NAM, disarmament is the ultimate strategy for achieving nonproliferation. Unfortunately, this is a view that misses the reality of what measures will still be needed to achieve and maintain a world without nuclear weapons.

Finally, efforts to find common ground on what constitutes the threat, such as the 2012 Nuclear Security Summit, should continue. There will be limits, however, to how much common ground can be identified due to philosophical positions and geopolitical interests. Identifying the interests and motivations of other states, beyond those states that are most vocal or most obviously problematic, can create the groundwork for eventually moving beyond bloc politics. The recommendations laid out above also can improve understanding between countries that prioritize nonproliferation and NAM states. Such understanding is required for changing the discourse among these states and for ensuring they are constructively working with, and not just talking past, each other.

Notes

1. This is in contrast to measures that promote disarmament or peaceful uses of nuclear energy and that could also contribute to strengthening the nonproliferation regime overall.

2. Nuclear-weapon-free zones were first thought of as a regional approach to nonproliferation in the 1950s. Only later was this grouping also thought to be helpful as a disarmament measure. Scott Parrish and Jean du Preez, "Nuclear-Weapon-Free Zones: Still a Useful Disarmament and Nonproliferation Tool?," Weapons of Mass Destruction Commission, 2005 http://www.wmdcommission.org/files/No6-ParrishDuPreez%20Final.pdf (accessed January 15, 2011).

3. The final document from the 2010 NPT Review Conference reaffirmed that "by achieving the cessation of all nuclear weapon test explosions and all other nuclear explosions, by constraining the development and qualitative improvement of nuclear weapons and ending the development of advanced new types of nuclear weapons, the treaty combats both horizontal and vertical proliferation." United Nations, "Final Documents of the 2010 NPT Review Conference," May 28, 2010, http://www.un.org/en/conf/npt/2010/ (accessed July 10, 2013).

4. See 2014 Nuclear Threat Initiative (NTI) Nuclear Materials Security Index (data model), http://www.ntiindex.org (accessed March 13, 2004).

5. H. E. Dr. R. M. Marty M. Natalegawa, "Statement of the Republic of Indonesia at the General Debate at the 2010 NPT Review Conference," New York, May 3, 2010, http://www.reachingcriticalwill.org/images/documents/Disarmament-fora/npt/revcon2010/statements/3May_Indonesia.pdf (accessed July 10, 2013).

6. For more on the NAM as a norm entrepreneur see Nina Tannenwald, *The Nuclear Taboo: The United States and the Non-use of Nuclear Weapons since 1945* (Cambridge: Cambridge University Press, 2008) and T. V. Paul, *The Tradition of Non-use of Nuclear Weapons* (Stanford, Calif.: Stanford Security Studies, 2009).

7. However, these excluded states, particularly India, do play a role in NAM deliberations. Their ability to obstruct consensus positions using proxies and to serve as an irri-

tant to NAM deliberations should not be underestimated. To avoid confusion, the numerical analysis in this chapter does not include these three states either.

8. Non-Aligned Movement, XV Summit of the Non-Aligned Movement, "History and Evolution of the NAM," July 11–16, 2009, http://www.namegypt.org/en/AboutName/History AndEvolution/Pages/default.aspx (accessed January 14, 2011, but no longer accessible).

9. Ibid.

10. Ibid.

11. Ibid.

12. Parrish and du Preez, "Nuclear-Weapon-Free Zones."

13. Agency for the Prohibition of Nuclear Weapons in Latin America and the Caribbean (OPANAL), "Mongolia's Nuclear-Weapon-Free Status," http://www.opanal.org/NWFZ/Mongolia/mongolia_en.htm (accessed January 14, 2011).

14. United Nations, "2010 Review Conference of the Parties to the Treaty on the Non-Proliferation of Nuclear Weapons Final Document," May 28, 2010, http://www.un.org/en/conf/npt/2010/ (accessed July 10, 2013).

15. Indonesia created the NAM working group on disarmament when it chaired the NAM in 1992–1995. Since then, it has played a crucial role as the trusted coordinator, spokesperson, and negotiator for that group.

16. Meri Lugo, "CTBT at the RevCon," Project for the Comprehensive Nuclear Test Ban Treaty, May 21, 2010, http://www.projectforthectbt.org/RevConStatements (accessed January 14, 2011).

17. Comprehensive Nuclear-Test-Ban Treaty Organization, Preparatory Commission for the Comprehensive Nuclear-Test-Ban Treaty Organization, "Status of Signature and Ratification," January 31, 2011, http://www.ctbto.org/the-treaty/status-of-signature-and-ratification/?print=1&states=4&region=63&no_cache=1&submit.x=8&submit.y=5 (accessed January 31, 2011).

18. International Atomic Energy Agency, "Safeguards Statement for 2009 and Background to the Safeguards Statement," December 31, 2009, http://www.iaea.org/safeguards/documents/es2009.pdf (accessed February 14, 2014).

19. For more information about the importance of the modified Small Quantities Protocol, see Paul Kerr, "IAEA Board Closes Safeguards Loophole," *Arms Control Today* 35, no. 9 (2005), http://www.armscontrol.org/act/2005_11/NOV-IAEALoophole (accessed March 15, 2011); 2014 NTI Nuclear Materials Security Index.

20. The assessment makes use of the IAEA report on the status of the Additional Protocol as of March 12, 2014, http://www.iaea.org/safeguards/documents/AP_status_list.pdf (accessed March 14, 2014), and the NAM members with Additional Protocols in force (absent the nuclear-armed states excluded from this analysis) according to the data models supporting the 2014 NTI Nuclear Materials Security Index, http://www.ntiindex.org (accessed March 13, 2014).

21. International Panel on Fissile Materials, "Global Fissile Material Report 2010: Balancing the Books: Production and Stocks," December 2010, http://www.fissilematerials.org/ipfm/site_down/gfmr10.pdf (accessed January 14, 2011).

22. For estimates of civilian HEU holdings for all countries except Uzbekistan, see James Martin Center for Nonproliferation Studies, "Civilian Highly Enriched Uranium: Who Has What?," Nuclear Threat Initiative, Washington, D.C., July 2013, http://www.nti.org/heu-map/. For estimates about Uzbekistan's civilian HEU holdings, see 2014 NTI Nuclear Materials Security Index (data model), http://www.ntiindex.org (accessed March 13, 2014).

23. "Civilian Highly Enriched Uranium"; 2014 NTI Nuclear Materials Security Index.

24. International Panel on Fissile Materials, "Global Fissile Material Report 2010."

25. U.S. Department of State, "Nuclear Security Summit, Seoul 2012," Bureau of International Security and Nonproliferation, March 5, 2012, http://www.state.gov/t/isn/nuclearsecuritysummit/2012/index.htm.

26. United Nations, Treaty Collection, "International Convention for the Suppression of Acts of Nuclear Terrorism," April 13, 2005, http://treaties.un.org/Pages/ViewDetailsIII.aspx?&src=IND&mtdsg_no=XVIII-15&chapter=18&Temp=mtdsg3&lang=en (accessed March 14, 2014).

27. International Atomic Energy Agency, "International Conventions and Legal Agreements: Convention on the Physical Protection of Nuclear Material," http://www.iaea.org/Publications/Documents/Conventions/cppnm.html (accessed March 14, 2014).

28. Non-Aligned Movement, XV Summit of the Non-Aligned Movement, "History and Evolution."

29. U.S. Department of State, "Proliferation Security Initiative," Bureau of International Security and Nonproliferation, http://www.state.gov/t/isn/c10390.htm (accessed January 14, 2011).

30. U.S. Department of State, "Proliferation Security Initiative Participants," September 10, 2010, http://www.state.gov/t/isn/c27732.htm (accessed January 14, 2011).

31. Non-Aligned Movement, XV Summit of the Non-Aligned Movement, "History and Evolution."

32. Mark Heinrich, "IAEA's Poor Nations Split on Iran's Attack Ban Bid," Reuters, September 16, 2009, http://www.reuters.com/article/2009/09/16/us-nuclear-iran-ban-idUSTRE58F41220090916 (accessed December 14, 2010).

33. U.S. Department of State, "U.S.-Belarus Bilateral Meeting," December 1, 2010, http://www.state.gov/r/pa/prs/ps/2010/12/152168.htm (accessed February 14, 2014).

34. Miles A. Pomper, "U.S., UAE Sign Nuclear Cooperation Pact," *Arms Control Today*, March 2009, http://www.armscontrol.org/print/3555 (accessed February 14, 2014).

35. Toshiba Corporation, "Toshiba Signs Memorandum of Understanding on Cooperation in Development of Mineral Resources and Social Infrastructure with Mongo-

lia's MNFCC," press release, November 26, 2010, http://www.toshiba.co.jp/about/press/2010_11/pr2601.htm (accessed January 26, 2011).

36. International Atomic Energy Agency, "Nuclear Security Advisory Services," November 6, 2010, http://www-ns.iaea.org/security/advisory.asp?s=7&l=48 (accessed March 15, 2011).

37. Ibid.

38. XV Summit of the Non-Aligned Movement, *Relevant Documents, Final Document*, July 2009, http://www.namegypt.org/en/RelevantDocuments/Pages/default.aspx (accessed January 14, 2011, but no longer accessible).

CHAPTER 7

Russia, Iran, and the Nuclear Nonproliferation Regime

Robert J. Reardon

THE CENTRAL QUESTION of this book—why states often fail to act in support of the international nonproliferation regime, or even appear to actively work against it—is one that is frequently asked of Russia. Many Western observers have been critical of Russia's approach to nuclear nonproliferation and have cast Moscow as a spoiler in international nonproliferation efforts. Russia, along with China, is a perennial holdout in UN Security Council deliberations on sanctions against suspected proliferators and a vocal opponent of resolutions authorizing military force.

This chapter seeks to shed greater light on Russia's nonproliferation policies by examining in detail Moscow's policies toward the Iranian nuclear issue. In doing so, it challenges the common assertion that Russia often sacrifices its own interests in preventing the spread of nuclear weapons in a misguided effort to maintain an outsized influence in world affairs and build a network of support among states hostile to the United States. According to this view, President Vladimir Putin and other key decision makers in Moscow harbor near-delusional pretensions to superpower status left over from the Cold War, misperceive Russia's relationship with the United States as a zero-sum game, and callously disregard or fail to appreciate the global threat posed by the spread of nuclear weapons.[1] This view conforms to a broader narrative that portrays Russia as an outlier state whose domestic and foreign policies differ sharply from those of its peers.[2]

A careful reading of the evidence suggests that this is inaccurate. Russia's policies on the Iran nuclear question are best viewed as rational policy choices based on a complex calculus of competing short- and long-term interests. These include national and subnational economic interests, as well as both global and regional strategic ones. Russia has an interest in preventing the spread of nuclear weapons and specifically in preventing Iran from developing a nuclear arsenal.

However, like all states, Moscow must weigh this goal in light of the means it has at its disposal to achieve it, the costs of such actions, and the effects such measures would have on other interests of the state. In many circumstances, Russia is willing to compromise its nonproliferation objectives in the interest of other goals that it considers more pressing.

At least in this regard, Russia is not an outlier. The United States has also been willing to compromise its nonproliferation policies in cases such as Israel and Pakistan, where other interests were judged to be sufficiently important to discourage taking strong measures like economic sanctions, which the United States has preferred in other proliferation cases. Similarly, economic interests played an important role in the U.S. decision to sign a nuclear cooperation pact with India, despite the country's development of nuclear weapons—in contrast to Iran, which has not yet done so—and its refusal to sign the Treaty on the Non-Proliferation of Nuclear Weapons (NPT). These policies may well have been wisely chosen. However, regardless of their wisdom, they were not set according to the U.S. interest in upholding the international nonproliferation regime, but rather in spite of it. Russia's policies toward Iran should be considered in a similar light.

At the same time, Moscow's reluctance to support economic sanctions and the threat of military force should not always be interpreted as a cynical justification for self-interested behavior. There are genuine differences between the United States' and Russia's estimates of the magnitude of the Iranian threat and the efficacy and appropriateness of particular policies. The Russians have tended to view the Iranian nuclear program as less of an imminent threat than the Americans have. Russian leaders have been more sanguine about Iran's ability to develop nuclear weapons, the time it would require for them to do so, and the risk that Iran could use Russian civilian nuclear cooperation to further its weapons aims.[3] This view has, however, been greatly challenged by Iran's undeniable technical progress over the years, a fact that accounts for shifts in Moscow's threat assessment.

RUSSIA'S IRAN POLICIES SINCE THE SOVIET ERA
Yeltsin Era: Subnational Actors and the Weakness of the Central State

Russian involvement in the development of Iran's nuclear and missile programs was greatest during the presidency of Boris Yeltsin in the 1990s. This cooperation took place largely in spite of Kremlin policies, as the weakness of the central Russian state in the years immediately after the disintegration of the Soviet

Union allowed for private actors and even state bureaucracies to act in their own particular interests, either out of profit motives, ideological convictions, or both. The Russians agreed to provide Iran with light-water nuclear reactors (LWRs) in 1992, and in January 1995 they signed a contract to build a single 900-megawatt reactor at the unfinished Bushehr nuclear power station.[4] The $1 billion Bushehr contract fueled existing U.S. anxieties over Iran's nuclear ambitions and was met with strong opposition from the Clinton administration, as well as from Congress, which threatened to sever U.S. aid to Russia.[5]

Moscow, however, resisted U.S. diplomatic pressure and argued that its nuclear cooperation with Iran was of a purely civilian nature. Russia's minister of atomic energy Viktor Mikhailov framed the issue in terms of a global competition for civilian nuclear markets: "If Russia refuses to build reactors in Iran, it may follow the same way as North Korea ... [a]nd then not Russia but the United States will come along, together with its partners, to build the same nuclear industry in Iran." Mikhailov pointed out that Bushehr was of a similar design to the reactors the United States had agreed to provide to North Korea under the 1994 Agreed Framework.[6]

Tensions between the United States and Russia increased with the revelation that secret side agreements to the Bushehr contract promised the transfer of sensitive nuclear fuel cycle technology to Iran, a much more troubling arrangement than the reactor itself.[7] Most alarming was an agreement to negotiate the sale of a gas-centrifuge uranium enrichment facility, which could be used to produce highly enriched uranium (HEU) fuel for a nuclear weapon.[8]

The deal appears to have been brokered by the Ministry for Atomic Energy (Minatom) without the direction—or even the knowledge—of the Kremlin.[9]

After being confronted by the United States, Yeltsin quickly retreated on fuel-cycle technology transfers to Iran but stood firm on the sale of reactors. Yeltsin also agreed to high-level diplomatic coordination with the United States on the issue through a joint commission headed by Vice President Al Gore and Prime Minister Viktor Chernomyrdin to assure the Americans that Iran would not be provided with sensitive technology.[10] Additionally, Moscow required Tehran to agree to return all spent fuel from Bushehr to Russia. In December 1995, Chernomyrdin sent a letter to Gore affirming that Russia would limit its nuclear cooperation with Iran to the one reactor at Bushehr, the training of Iranian engineers, and provision of fuel for the reactor, for as long as the reactor was under construction (at the time believed to be five years).[11] Yet while the Yeltsin government was willing to limit its sales to Iran to civilian reactors and conventional arms, Russian firms—and even government bureaucracies, including Minatom—continued to pursue transfers of sensitive nuclear and ballistic missile technologies. In the mid-1990s, reports began to publicly emerge that Russian defense firms had been transferring sensitive missile technologies to Iran.[12]

Yeltsin's inability to enforce his own policies was compounded by the fact that many in Moscow, particularly influential hardliners and nationalists, viewed the transfers to Iran sympathetically out of ideological convictions. Russian hardliners were suspicious of Yeltsin's policies toward the West and saw closer ties with Iran as a useful way to offset American influence. Mikhailov and others who stood to profit from such transfers were more than willing to pay lip service to these claims in order to win support in Moscow.[13]

Despite making the issue a priority, the Clinton administration's efforts to pressure Moscow on this issue, often through the establishment of regular high-level diplomatic channels, met with only limited success. Moscow did, however, make several important concessions. Russian export controls were tightened. In several well-publicized cases, Russian firms were forced to cancel contracts, and in November 1997 the Federal Security Service (FSB), Russia's domestic security agency, arrested an Iranian diplomat for trying to buy missile designs.[14] A major concession came in January 1998, when, under enormous pressure from the United States—whose Congress was threatening to impose sanctions on Russian firms—Moscow announced a "catch-all" decree on missile exports, which would require all Russian firms to cooperate with Moscow in all cases of technology transfer that could lead to the proliferation of nuclear weapons or ballistic missiles.[15] Later that year, U.S. national security adviser Sandy Berger and Russian national security adviser Andrei Kokoshin orchestrated a crackdown on recalcitrant Russian companies and scientific institutes by having Moscow publish a list of entities that were under investigation, which were in turn subjected to "trade restrictions" (i.e., sanctions) by Washington.[16]

Moscow failed to rein in private firms and state bureaucracies seeking to profit from illicit sales to Iran for the remainder of Yeltsin's presidency. Leadership changes at Minatom in 1998 made matters worse by bringing in Yevgeniy Adamov as its new chief. Adamov proved to be just as willing to pursue freewheeling civilian nuclear deals—including those that involved the transfer of technologies that could be used to produce nuclear weapons—as Mikhailov had, yet he was more capable of wielding political sway in Moscow.[17] In late 1998, it was revealed that Adamov's former research institution, NIKIET, was involved in negotiations to sell a heavy-water research reactor to Iran, as well as a uranium conversion facility. The U.S. imposed sanctions on NIKIET in 1999 and succeeded in pressuring Moscow to stop the NIKIET deals only by using a multibillion-dollar Cooperative Threat Reduction plan to purchase Russian HEU as leverage.[18]

Russian nuclear and missile cooperation with Iran was restricted to relatively minor transfers of technology and expertise, and there is little evidence that Iran benefited significantly from Russian assistance during this period. Much of this has to do with the fact that the assistance that was provided came from firms and state institutions pursuing short-term profits rather than boosting Iranian capabilities or developing a long-term relationship. Also, because these actors were operating without the official approval of the state, they had an interest in minimizing their transactions with Iran to those that would not attract scrutiny. In the end, these deals proved to be of less significance than Washington had feared, and likely contributed little, if anything, to Iran's later progress in its missile program.[19] At the same time, the Clinton administration's efforts to win Moscow's cooperation were not entirely unrewarded, and they did succeed in preventing the transfer of technologies such as centrifuges or heavy-water reactors that would have provided a significant boost to Iran's nuclear efforts. Although the Bushehr reactor deal would go forward, no other contracts were successfully concluded.

Russia's Iran Policies during the Putin Era

Russia's Iran policies changed dramatically after Vladimir Putin assumed the presidency in 2000. Through a combination of improved economic performance and domestic reform, Putin was able to successfully strengthen the authority of the central Russian state and rein in rogue bureaucracies.[20] In 2001, as part of a major reshuffling within the government, Putin replaced Evgeniy Adamov, who had been running Minatom as a private fiefdom, with Alexander Rumyantsev, a well-respected engineer who headed the prestigious Kurchatov Institute. Rumyantsev proved to be a more controllable minister and also more sensitive to Western interests than his predecessors.

Russia's improved economic fortunes in the 2000s, built largely on oil revenues, also allowed the Kremlin to pursue a more independent foreign policy course than Yeltsin had. In particular, Putin was more willing than his predecessor to forge stronger relationships with regional powers like Iran that lay outside the U.S. orbit as a means to establish an independent power base in critical regions. Over U.S. objections, Putin allowed a ban on conventional arms sales to Iran to lapse and began to actively pursue arms deals and civilian nuclear cooperation with Tehran. In March 2001, Iranian president Mohammed Khatami was invited to Moscow, where the two countries signed a cooperation pact—their first since the Iranian Revolution—and discussed an expansion in arms sales worth as much as $300 million a year.[21] Yet Putin continued to emphasize Moscow's commitment to nuclear nonproliferation and limited discussions with Iran to less sensitive nuclear technologies.

At the same time, the Russian economy's—and Putin's political fortunes'—dependence on oil exports made it imperative that the Kremlin maintain good relations with Western buyers and investors. Putin was the first head of state to contact President Bush after the September 11 attacks, and in October 2001 he announced that Russia would close its listening posts in Cuba and Vietnam. However, Putin felt his overtures toward Washington were not reciprocated, and he was particularly disturbed by the U.S. invasion of Iraq, the administration's decision to abrogate the Anti-Ballistic Missile (ABM) Treaty and develop ballistic missile defenses in Poland and the Czech Republic, and U.S. support for NATO enlargement into the Baltics.[22] These sources of tension between the United States and Russia created both strategic and domestic political disincentives for the Kremlin to back U.S. policy preferences on issues like Iran and an incentive to use its influence on those issues to signal its displeasure with U.S. policies. The result was a foreign policy that accommodated U.S. strategic policies on key issues such as NATO expansion and missile defense, while frequently coming into conflict with the United States on regional issues, particularly in the Middle East and in South and East Asia.[23]

As Iran's relationship with the West has become increasingly hostile, Russia's policies have been pushed further into alignment with the United States and Europe, and its relationship with Iran has worsened. Revelations in 2002 and 2003 about the Iranian nuclear program, and especially about the country's uranium enrichment facility at Natanz, raised significant complications for Russian policy. While in the wake of these discoveries Moscow continued to maintain that Iran lacked the capability to build nuclear weapons—still a commonly held view among Russian elites—they sparked a change in this view.[24] By the middle of 2003, Russia had begun to lend stronger support, at least rhetorically, to IAEA efforts to discover Iran's intentions and uncover the extent of its past nuclear activities. Moscow both publicly and privately pushed Tehran to sign the Additional Protocol to allow surprise IAEA inspections and to freeze their uranium enrichment program.[25]

At the same time, Russia sought to prevent a repeat of the run-up to the Iraq invasion, when, in the Kremlin's view, the United States used evidence of an Iraqi nuclear program as a pretext to expand U.S. influence in the region, reducing Russia's in the process. Russia therefore refused to back any strongly worded IAEA resolution that could trigger a referral of the matter to the UN Security Council—a move that the Bush administration preferred.[26] Russia's position, however, differed more greatly from the U.S. stance than it did from European powers, which also largely preferred a more measured approach.

Russia sought to draw a distinction between Iran's enrichment program and the Bushehr reactor, and it staunchly maintained the position that there was "no link" between the current nuclear crisis and Moscow's civilian nuclear commitments with Iran.[27] Putin reflected what many hardliners in Moscow believed by publicly portraying U.S. efforts to pressure an end to Bushehr as a market grab, stating that the U.S. was seeking to "use the nuclear card in unfair competition in the Iran market."[28] Yet Moscow was also willing to use its contract for Bushehr as a source of leverage to push Iran toward making concessions with its enrichment program, and it repeatedly delayed progress on the reactor even after Iran signed an agreement to return spent fuel to Russia in 2005.[29]

Russia's relationship with Iran became more problematic with the election of Mahmoud Ahmadinejad in 2005. Negotiations broke down between Iran and the EU-3 (United Kingdom, France, and Germany), and Iran ended its two-year suspension of the enrichment program, making Russia's opposition to a stronger approach less sustainable. Seeking to maintain a central role in managing the crisis, as well as forestall any American or Israeli resort to preventive military force, Moscow pushed Iran to accept a compromise plan under which Iran would send its uranium to Russia for enrichment and conversion to fuel rods that would then be shipped back to Iran. The deal would allow the Iranians to continue to assert their right to enrich, while removing any need for doing so.[30] Yet Moscow also sought to deter a military attack by providing Iran with thirty Tor-M1 surface-to-air missiles and the more sophisticated S-300 air defense system.[31]

In early 2006, Russia agreed to abstain in an IAEA vote to "report" Iran to the Security Council but insisted on additional negotiations before it would consider sanctions, even as Iran rejected Moscow's enrichment proposal.[32] After a negotiating initiative by the United States (which for the first time took direct part in the negotiations), the United Kingdom, France, Russia, China, and Germany (the "P5+1") failed, Iran escalated the crisis by rapidly pushing forward with its enrichment program and vocally challenging the authority of the UN.[33] Iran's continued intransigence forced Russia to support UN Security Council Resolution 1737, which passed unanimously in December 2006 and for the first time imposed UN sanctions on Iran. The resolution called for the freezing of financial assets of Iranian groups and individuals associated with the nuclear program, but Russia successfully fought to include language that exempted the Bushehr project, conventional arms sales, and Russia's oil and gas investments in Iran.[34] In early 2007, Russia delivered the first shipments of Tor-M1 anti-aircraft missiles to Iran.[35]

Despite Moscow's efforts to maintain its relationship with Iran, as tensions rose between Iran and the West, Russia's policies tacked further toward the West's position. In early 2007, Russia announced that it would again delay fuel delivery for Bushehr, citing Iran's failure to meet payments.[36] Iran claimed that they had met their financial obligations and argued that Russia was delaying the project as a means of applying political pressure on Tehran to freeze uranium enrichment. Statements by Russian officials suggest that both motives were at play, and that Iran's financial woes—in particular, its increasing difficulty in making its hard currency payments in dollars—provided an excuse for Russia to apply pressure for political reasons.[37] In March 2007, work on the nearly completed reactor was delayed indefinitely, and most of the Russian engineers working on the project were withdrawn.[38] Russia also continued to support sanctions in the Security Council. A second sanctions resolution (1747) passed with surprising speed in March 2007. The new sanctions raised the number of Iranian companies and officials subjected to financial sanctions and introduced a ban on arms exports from Iran. Still, most arms sales *to* Iran were not banned, and Russia's nuclear cooperation with Iran was unaffected.

U.S.-Russian relations deteriorated during the last years of the Bush administration. In 2007, the Bush administration announced its intention to deploy missile defense systems in Poland and the Czech Republic, which inflamed tensions with Moscow.[39] In response, Russia tested a new RS-24 ICBM (intercontinental ballistic missile) that it claimed could defeat U.S. missile defense systems and threatened to retarget its weapons at Europe, while American and Russian rhetoric grew heated.[40] This in turn led to Russian posturing on the issue of Iran. In October 2007, Putin became the first Russian leader to visit Iran since World War II and met privately in Tehran with Ahmadinejad. Putin used the occasion to affirm Russia's commitment to civilian nuclear cooperation with "Iran's peaceful nuclear program" and to strongly reaffirm Moscow's opposition to the use of military force against Iran's nuclear facilities.[41] Also, after repeated delays, in late 2007 Moscow announced that it would send its first shipment of low-enriched uranium (LEU) fuel for the Bushehr reactor to Iran. The move came just as talks were breaking down with the West over Kosovo independence.[42] In December 2007, the Iranians claimed that the Russians had even agreed to sell them the sophisticated s-300 antimissile system—a claim that was quickly denied by the Kremlin.[43]

Yet despite the symbolism of these moves, on more substantive matters Russia continued to drift toward the West's position, as Iranian defiance of the IAEA and the UN, and rapid technical progress on the nuclear program, continued to limit Moscow's choices. During Putin's visit to Tehran in 2007, American officials suggested that despite a public show of support, the Russian president took a stronger line in private meetings with Ahmadinejad and Ayatollah Khamenei.[44] Likewise, Russia supported a third set of sanctions in early 2008 but again fought to water down its terms. In return for Russian support of sanctions, the Bush administration signed a 123 Agreement for civilian nuclear cooperation—long sought by Moscow—that opened the door for a windfall from importing spent fuel to Russia.[45]

The remainder of 2008, however, saw little progress. As elections approached in the United States, Russia—now under a new president, Dmitri Medvedev—had little incentive to engage with the lame-duck Bush administration. Even as Washington offered increasing concessions to Tehran and agreed to send a high-ranking U.S. diplomat to talks—with Iran pushing forward with its nuclear efforts all the while—Moscow continued to resist strong measures against Tehran, maintained its commitment to nuclear cooperation, and opposed the setting of hard deadlines by the UN Security Council. The August 2008 Russian invasion of Georgia, coming in the final months of the Bush administration and as the presidential election cycle entered its final stretch, brought U.S.-Russian relations to a post–Cold War low. Further progress on Iran would have to wait until a new president took office in Washington.

OBAMA AND THE "RESET"

By the time the Obama administration took office, U.S.-Russian relations had declined to its nadir as a result of the August 2008 Russian use of military force in Georgia. Also, progress had not been made in 2008 on the Iran issue, as Russia opposed the setting of any hard deadlines for Iranian compliance in the Security

Council. The new administration's "reset" policy sought to jump-start Washington's relationship with Moscow and make U.S.-Russian relations a higher priority. Soon after taking office, the Obama administration signaled to Moscow that it would be willing to compromise on its plans to put antimissile defenses in Eastern Europe in return for greater Russian cooperation on Iran.[46] The administration also put U.S. sanctions efforts on hold while it pursued an engagement strategy with Iran, hoping to solidify international support for tougher measures should diplomacy fail.

Improved relations with Washington, unrest in Iran after the 2009 election, and the revelation of the Fordo enrichment facility all helped to lead Moscow to further align its policies with those of the West and introduced greater discord into the Russia-Iran relationship.[47] In September 2009, Russia agreed to further UN sanctions against Iran should upcoming negotiations with Iran over the confidence-building "fuel swap" proposal fail to produce positive results.[48] The proposal, which resembled an earlier Russian proposal, would provide for Iran's enriched uranium to be shipped to Russia for further enrichment and conversion to fuel for Iran's Tehran Research Reactor. Yet after months of optimistic negotiations, the plan failed. Additionally, Iran announced in December 2009 its plans to construct ten new enrichment facilities, and in February 2010 began to enrich uranium to the 20 percent level, which the fuel-swap plan had aimed to prevent. This outcome made another round of sanctions inevitable. In June 2010, Russia voted in favor of Resolution 1929, which imposed sanctions on arms sales to Iran. Russia also agreed to kill plans to sell Iran the S-300. Russia's investments in Iran, however, and its commitment to complete the Bushehr reactor would remain untouched.[49]

In spite of the initial success of the reset, U.S.-Russian relations began to sour once again in 2011 as political change swept the Middle East with the Arab Spring, as political changes in Libya, and especially Syria, threatened to weaken Russia's influence in the region. Although Russia did not veto a UN Security Council resolution authorizing force in Libya, Russian leaders quickly criticized the NATO bombing campaign.[50] Russia's Iran policy is more likely to be directly affected by the civil conflict in Syria, as Russia and Iran are both key supporters of the Bashar al-Assad regime, which is opposed by the United States and its Western allies. Russia and China have both used their veto power in the UN Security Council to block Western-sponsored measures against Assad. Syria's geopolitical significance to both Russia and Iran creates a linkage between the Syrian conflict and the Iran nuclear issue by creating an incentive for Russia to use the Iranian issue as leverage, and for the West—as well as Sunni Arab states—to use the Syrian conflict to reduce Iran's regional influence. This connection between the two issues reportedly weighs heavily in the Obama administration's decision making.[51]

Russia's tolerance for increasing sanctions against Iran also appears to have reached its limit. A November 2011 IAEA report that presented evidence of military-related nuclear activities in Iran prompted the United States and its allies to adopt new sanctions against Iran's financial and energy sectors. Moscow, however, called the report "politicized" and announced it would not consider new UN sanctions against Iran and would limit itself only to implementing sanctions specifically required by Security Council resolutions.[52] Instead of new sanctions, Russia instead proposed a "step-by-step" plan that would exchange sanctions relief for improved transparency measures in Iran's nuclear program in incremental stages.[53] Moscow's anxieties about the use of military force against Iran have heightened in the wake of both NATO's military campaign in Libya and Western support for Syrian rebels. Russia has vociferously criticized the threat of air strikes and claims an attack would lead to "disaster."[54]

RUSSIA'S INTERESTS IN IRAN:
ECONOMIC AND STRATEGIC, GLOBAL AND REGIONAL

Russia faces a set of competing interests in the Iranian nuclear issue that are both regional and global, both economic and strategic. While there exists a vigorous debate in Russia on how priorities ought to be assigned to these issues, and which policy courses will most effectively address them, there is a general consensus among Russia's most important decision makers that the country's most pressing goals are to maintain good relations with the West and access to its markets, capital, and technology, while simultaneously setting an independent policy orientation. As a result, Russia is willing to break from the Western policy consensus on issues such as Iran, but not at the expense of bringing about a radical change in relations with the West.

Global Strategic Interests

As one of the two dominant nuclear powers, Russia has an interest in preventing nuclear proliferation, as it naturally seeks to maintain a status quo in which it is one of only a handful of states with a nuclear weapons capability. Moscow has no interest in diluting the advantage this confers. Also, Russia must necessarily be concerned that Iran's acquisition of nuclear weapons would destabilize the Middle East, the Caucasus, and Central Asia, all key border regions.

Russia views the Iran nuclear standoff as a way to maintain global influence, particularly in the sense of playing the role of an essential broker in major world affairs, and one that is independent of the United States. Thus the Iran nuclear issue is not simply a security concern for Russia; it also impacts the country's international status as an indispensible power entitled to a seat at the table in major international debates. Moreover, by staking out positions independent of the West that champion regional actors like Iran, Russia can enhance its appeal within the Non-Aligned Movement.

Russia also has a strong interest in maintaining its leverage in global affairs through its position as a permanent member of the UN Security Council. Russia's interests here have been complex. On the one hand, Russia has an interest in preventing the United States from using the authority of the Security Council to sanction the use of military force or to expand its own influence, as—in Moscow's view—it has done in Iraq and Libya and seeks to do in Syria. On the other hand, Iran's refusal to recognize the Security Council's authority on the nuclear issue challenges this source of Russian influence and has pushed Russia toward a firmer stand on Iran's nuclear activities.

Moscow has used its position as deal broker to put forward its own negotiating proposals, as it has with the step-by-step proposal, and its prestige would be enhanced if it were to play a major role in any breakthrough with Iran. Similarly, Moscow has sought to play a direct role in any settlement, such as enriching uranium for Iran's reactors. Yet Russia can benefit in this way only if the standoff is resolved on its own terms, and a continued stalemate in which Russia remains a central figure on the world stage may be preferable to a resolution that is reached through bilateral negotiations between the United States and Iran that exclude Russia.

Finally, Russia has proved willing to use the Iran issue as a source of bargaining leverage in its relationship with the United States by extracting concessions from Washington in other areas valuable to Moscow in return for improved support for the United States' Iran policies. Most notably, Russia has successfully sought to link its support for Iran sanctions to the deployment of U.S. missile defenses in Europe.[55] However, Iran's utility as a bargaining chip is only a minor consideration for Moscow, which has a set of genuine strategic interests. As a result, U.S. efforts to exchange concessions in other issue areas in return for Russian support for U.S. policies on Iran can only achieve so much without also addressing these interests.

Most important for Moscow, however, is its need to maintain good relations with the West, especially the United States. Although Russia has sought to both establish itself as a more independent international actor and develop stronger ties to the increasingly important countries in the East, it still depends on a stable and cooperative relationship with the United States and its European allies for its security and economic well-being. Even as Moscow's relationship with the West has soured in recent years, Russia nonetheless enjoys what are perhaps the most benign strategic conditions on its western border in its history. This is no small matter considering that the country's most serious security threats have traditionally come from the West, and that Russia is greatly outmatched by Western—especially American—economic and military power. Russia benefits from its cooperative arrangements with NATO and its strategic arms control treaties, intelligence sharing, and combined antiterrorism efforts with the United States. Russian economic growth, at least in the near future, depends on good relations with the West and access to Western capital and markets. As a result, there are limits to Moscow's willingness to adopt policies on the Iran question that diverge from those of the United States and its allies.

There are, however, important limits to Russia's dependence on the West. Russian and Western interests frequently diverge, not least on issues related to competition for influence in the regions on Russia's western and southern borders. Also, Russia's size and power grant it a significant degree of independence in its foreign policy. In many ways, Russia's influence makes it at least as indispensable to the West as the West is to Russia. Stability in Europe and the Middle East are both dependent on Russian cooperation. Russia also controls a substantial share of the energy resources on which Europe depends. Russia's position in international forums such as the Security Council also requires the West to take Moscow's interests into account in multilateral efforts, and failure to do so in cases such as intervention in the Balkans or in Iraq have carried a price.

Regional Strategic Interests

Russia's relationship with Iran also reflects Iran's position as a major player in a critical Russian border region. As one of the Middle Eastern states with which Russia has the closest relationship, Iran serves as a central conduit of Moscow's regional influence. Iran is additionally important to Russia because of its influence in other regions critical to Russia's security: the Caucasus, Central Asia, and the Caspian region. Iran has religious and cultural ties with many of the populations in this area and has historically exercised substantial political power in the region. Russia views cooperation with Iran as an essential component of maintaining stability along its southern frontier. This concern became particularly acute after the breakup of the Soviet Union created several new independent Central Asian states with Muslim-majority populations and during Russian military operations in Chechnya. Iran has been a useful partner in this regard, either remaining aloof or actively cooperating in security issues in both the Caucasus and Central Asia.

Russian-Iranian cooperation in Central Asia and the Caucasus reflects a set of concurrent interests shared by the two countries rather than a quid pro quo arrangement. Both Russia and Iran have important strategic motives for their mutual caution and restraint, and both share a strong interest in maintaining stability in the region and excluding American and Turkish influence.[56] Much has been made of Iran's reluctance to become engaged in the two Russian wars in Chechnya and the dispute between Azerbaijan and Armenia over Nagorno-Karabakh. Viewing these conflicts through the lens of Islamic solidarity, it would be expected that Iran would more assertively support its Muslim co-religionists. Iran's cautious and aloof stance, however, reflects a pragmatism in Iranian foreign policy that Tehran has repeatedly demonstrated in its dealings with other states.[57] Iran is a multiethnic state that has minority ethnic groups such as Azeris and Tajiks within its borders that are shared with bordering states in Central Asia and the Caucasus. As a result, Tehran is concerned that ethnic disputes in those regions could spill over into Iran itself, giving Iran a strong interest in resolving such disputes rather than fueling them by supporting one side. This was a particular concern in the conflict over Nagorno-Karabakh, which could have drawn Iranian Azeris into the fight.[58] Russia and Iran also recognize that instability in these regions risks providing the Americans or Turks—who both have demonstrated an interest in expanding their influence there—an opening. This has given both sides a reason to moderate their policies in the region, and indeed the Russians have also shown restraint in Central Asia (even as they have been far more willing to assert themselves in the Caucasus, where Moscow sees itself as having a vital interest).

To a large extent, Iran's restraint in the region is also dictated by its limited power. While the former Soviet states in Central Asia share religious and historical ties with Iran, they are also culturally and linguistically distinct and share stronger ties with Turkey than Iran. Also, after many years under Soviet rule, these states have little in common with Iran's brand of conservative Islam: these are secular states in which cultural norms of clothing, diet, drinking, and the public role of religious devotion are much more similar to Russia's than to Iran's. The gulf between Iran and Chechnya is even greater. It is unlikely that Iran would be able to seriously challenge Russian dominance in the region even if it were to try, and an attempt to do so could carry large costs and risks.

Russia and Iran also both have important interests in the Caspian Sea, a critical region for natural gas. As two of the five littoral Caspian Sea states, Russia and Iran share mutual interests in the energy politics in the region. Most importantly, the two states have collaborated to prevent the United States and its European allies from building pipelines for Caspian natural gas that would bypass Russian and Iranian territory.[59] The three Central Asian former Soviet states that border the Caspian—Turkmenistan, Azerbaijan, and Kazakhstan—all have impressive gas reserves and currently depend on pipelines through either Iran or Russia to export natural gas. Iran and Russia would both stand to lose should a trans-Caspian pipeline be constructed that bypassed their territories. This cooperation is not always smooth, however. Moscow and Tehran are in a prisoner's dilemma on the Caspian issue: while the first-choice outcome for both would be to cooperate against U.S. encroachment in the region, both states also have to fear that the other will defect from an agreement and cut a deal with the United States and with the Central Asian states.

In other ways, Iran and Russia are competitors in the Caspian. Both have been party to long-standing disputes over how the seabed and water rights ought to be divided among the littoral states. Both Russia and Iran compete to win the support of the other three states in order to expand their footprint in the region—a competition that Russia has consistently been winning. These dynamics have demonstrated the limits of Russian-Iranian cooperation and the degree to which it has been a marriage of convenience rather than a stable strategic partnership. Particularly with respect to the European market, in fact, Moscow has demonstrated a more adversarial stance toward Iran and proved itself willing to aggressively close Iran out of that lucrative export market.[60]

Relations between Russia and Iran are also complicated by Russia's desire to maintain ties with both Israel and Sunni Arab states and to play the role of peace broker in the Arab-Israeli conflict. Despite good relations between Israel and Iran under the shah, and the lack of any obvious security incentive for Iran to adopt a hostile position toward Israel, Iran has nonetheless identified Israel as one of its principal antagonists. The relationship between the two countries is openly hostile: Iran provides material and rhetorical support to Hezbollah and Hamas, while Israel has identified Iran's nuclear program as an existential threat and has considered the use of preventive force to forestall Iran's development of a bomb. Russia's relationship with Israel, while complicated, is very different from Iran's. Israel is an increasingly important strategic and economic ally of Russia and is home to a large population of Russian emigrants. Trade ties between the two countries are thick and growing.[61] Also, the two countries have entered into joint production agreements for sophisticated weapons systems such as AWACS and UAVs.[62] Russia's ties with Israel have become a sticking point in the country's relationship with Iran, and vice versa. Similarly, Russia has sought to improve its ties with Sunni Arab states such as Saudi Arabia, which have long-standing grievances toward Iran. Russia's delicate diplomacy in the Middle East and its attempt to maintain influence with competing and frequently mutually hostile actors in the region make for fragile relationships with each, including Iran.

Economic Interests

In the 1990s and early 2000s, Moscow viewed Iran as an important market for its nuclear and defense trade, with substantial growth potential; however, such hopes have dwindled over the past decade. International tensions over the Iranian nuclear program and increasingly tough economic sanctions, as well as Iran's deteriorating economic situation and its failure to demonstrate an ability to make timely hard-currency payments, have soured Moscow's hopes for trade expansion in the country.[63] Other markets such as China and India have proven to be far more lucrative and important markets for Russian nuclear and arms exports. The heady days when Russia and Iran planned large increases in civilian nuclear sales are gone. Russia's involvement in Iran's nuclear program will almost certainly be limited to Bushehr for the foreseeable future. Even with Bushehr, Russia's interest in completing the reactor had, by the late 2000s, became more a question of reputation than of profit. If Russia were to have backed out of its contract, it would have signaled to other potential clients that Moscow was an unreliable supplier that could not be counted on should Western competitors put diplomatic pressure on it.

More important to Moscow is Iran's role in the global energy market.[64] For Russia, Iran plays the dual role of a potential market for Russian investment and a competitor for export markets. While Russia's nuclear and arms sales to Iran declined, Russian investment in the country's oil and gas industry grew. Russian gas giant Gazprom first entered the Iranian market in 1997 when it signed an agreement for development of the Southern Pars gas field. Over the following decade, Russian investments expanded to include billions of dollars in the development of oil and gas deposits, and the two countries entered into several formal economic cooperation agreements.[65]

However, even as trade between the two countries has grown, expansion of trade with Iran has become less of a priority for the Kremlin, as worsening relations between them and the uncertainty and risk presented by the economic sanctions have led the Russians to seek to limit their vulnerability. The volume of trade between Iran and Russia has always been small, both in absolute terms and as a share of Russia's overall foreign trade. Despite occasional government pronouncements—particularly from Tehran—about new initiatives to expand the volume of trade, Moscow has not taken any significant concrete steps in recent years to suggest this is a priority for the Kremlin. On the contrary, over the past several years Russia has proved reluctant to fully capitalize on the opportunity that has opened up for expansion in the Iranian energy market by the exodus of Western and other firms.[66]

Russia and Iran are also competitors in the energy export market, and Moscow has thus benefited from Iran's pariah status and from sanctions against Iran, which have given Moscow an advantage in pipeline disputes in the Caspian and have strengthened Russia's dominant position in the European energy market.[67] Also, Russia's economy depends on oil prices being high, which is more likely so long as the Iranian nuclear crisis continues and Iran remains under sanctions.

Russia's economic interests in Iran pale in comparison to its economic ties to the West. The country's economic fortunes over the past decade, and to a large degree the political fortunes of Vladimir Putin and his domestic allies, have depended on the country's energy exports, with Europe its largest market by far. More than two-thirds of Russia's oil and gas exports go to Europe, with the remainder largely destined for the former Soviet republics. Despite Russia's attempts to use its position as the dominant energy supplier to its political advantage, such as by restricting the flow of gas, such attempts have instead revealed that influence generally runs in the other direction: Europe's role as a near-monopsony buyer, and its large share of Russia's overall trade and foreign investment, has put Moscow in a position of relative dependence.[68]

Russia's nuclear sector also has more to gain from good relations with Europe and the United States than it does from exports to Iran. The United States represents an enormous potential market for Russia's nuclear industry, and Russia is ambitious to import spent fuel originally supplied by the United States. The recently signed U.S. 123 Agreement with Russia offers a potential boost to Russia's nuclear industry but increases its reliance on the United States.[69] The United States also commands considerable influence with many of Russia's most lucrative potential nuclear clients.

Domestic Political Factors

The weakness of the central state during Boris Yeltsin's presidency, and the existence of a large defense-industrial complex that was left without its traditional sources of funding after the Soviet breakup, allowed subnational actors to pursue private deals with Iran independent of the Kremlin. State weakness also provided the bureaucratic leaders of these institutions with disproportionate political power in Moscow and gave them a strong hand in shaping Russian policy. However, the Russian central state was greatly strengthened under Putin, and opportunities for independent behavior by subnational institutions were reduced, leading to noticeable changes in Russia's Iran policies.

Under Boris Yeltsin, nuclear and defense-related cooperation with Iran—mostly in the form of technology transfers—was strongly pursued by elements of the country's enormous defense-industrial complex, which enjoyed both substantial autonomy to pursue their own narrow economic interests independent of state policy and political cover in Moscow that complicated Kremlin efforts to bring these bureaucracies under central control.[70] The lack of state funding for these industries, and the absence of a domestic market for their products, pushed them to look abroad for sources of financing. Unable to compete with Western suppliers, they turned to states with which many Western firms were either unable or unwilling to do business, including Iran, Syria, Cuba, India, and China. The weakness of the central state during these years meant that these bureaucracies were often free to pursue nuclear or arms deals independently—in effect setting their own foreign policies. Moscow's efforts to impose its will on these actors was further complicated by the powerful networks of supporters these institutions could put to work. Nationalists in Moscow were willing to provide political cover for nuclear or arms sales to countries such as Iran because such deals suited their foreign policy preferences. The FSB and other state agencies charged with enforcing export controls were often willing to look the other way—or even to actively facilitate foreign contacts—if they stood to profit themselves.

However, it has been the oil and gas industry that has been the engine of Russia's economic growth in the past decade. Russia's ability to extract these resources (which to a large extent depends upon foreign investment) and find markets for them abroad, and the extent to which these resources can command high prices on the world market, will—at least in the near to medium term—determine the country's future economic trajectory.[71] Over the past decade, Vladimir Putin has successfully brought the nuclear and defense bureaucracies under central control by strengthening the state, reorganizing the bureaucracy, going after the country's powerful oligarchs, and replacing ministers and bureaucrats with allies.[72] At the same time, Putin has brought the country's powerful oil and gas firms under Kremlin control. These efforts have given Russia's giant oil and gas sector much greater influence than the defense-industrial complex over state policies, making Russia's foreign policy far more sensitive to the country's oil and gas interests than the nuclear and defense establishments.[73]

The Kremlin has also had to contend with powerful nationalist factions in Moscow that prefer a more oppositional stance toward the United States. These factions have seen states such as Iran as useful allies in a global balancing strategy against the United States and have pressed for greater cooperation with them.[74] Particularly during times when the United States adopted policies that challenged Russian regional hegemony—such as NATO expansion or the conflict in Georgia—the Kremlin has been forced to take a more confrontational stance than it would otherwise prefer in order to maintain domestic legitimacy and meet political challenges from nationalist hardliners. This has been particularly relevant over the past decade, as such nationalist sentiments have resonated more strongly with Vladimir Putin and his political confidants than was the case with the Yeltsin administration.

Nonetheless, Putin and former president Medvedev have both proved to be fundamentally pragmatic decision makers who have judged smooth relations with the West a core interest, if not of Russia as a whole then for their own personal economic interests and those of their political allies.[75] Overall, Russia has adopted a consistent policy course over the past two decades, and Russia's policy has shifted more in response to Iran's own behavior and the strategic context than domestic political changes within Russia.

CONCLUSION

Rather than a reflection of Russian irrationality, neo-Soviet revanchism, or delusions of grandeur, Russia's policies on the Iranian nuclear issue have largely been rational responses to its complex strategic and economic interests. Although Russia has an interest in stemming nuclear proliferation in general, and in preventing Iran from acquiring nuclear weapons in particular, Moscow's interests in the Iranian nuclear issue cannot be reduced to a single dimension and must be viewed in terms of a broader set of often contradictory pressures. It is not clear that this is substantially different from the approach the United States has adopted in other proliferation cases such as India, Pakistan, or Israel, where U.S. policies were informed by a number of different considerations, many of which led the United States to forgo more coercive strategies in order to protect other interests that it considered to be more valuable.

Russia's interests in Iran have not been static. While nuclear, missile, and arms sales have offered Russia short-term economic gains in the past, this is no longer the case. Nor have such profits ever driven Moscow's overall policy orientation. In the wake of the Soviet collapse, while the Russian central state was still considerably weakened, independent actors—both state bureaucracies such as Minatom and small firms or even individuals in the case of missile-technology sales—engaged in technology transfers with Iran, often without even the knowledge of the Kremlin. During the 1990s, Russia was a fertile shopping ground for Iranian agents looking to purchase Russian weapons and technology. This came to an end after Putin assumed the presidency and strengthened the Kremlin's authority.

Moscow's economic interests in Iran have changed as well, largely as a result of Iran's oppositional policies toward the West under Ahmadinejad and the sanctions imposed by the United States and its European allies. Russian enterprises that were once eager to expand their investments in Iran's energy sector are now more reluctant to do so and have instead focused on expanding their operations in more lucrative markets. At the same time, Russia's own status as a major energy exporter allows it to benefit in many ways from sanctions against what could otherwise be a key competitor for market share.

Moscow's strategic interests in Iran have grown as the nuclear standoff has taken a more prominent position on the world stage, and particularly as the main protagonists in the standoff have become increasingly embroiled in civil conflicts elsewhere in the region, especially in Syria. Russia's policy choices must be considered within this broader context, adding to its already significant longer-term interests in maintaining a relationship with Iran. Iran is likely to remain a strategically important regional power on Russia's southern frontier over the long term and is likely to have a major impact on a number of issues important to Russia, including regional stability, Islamist terrorism, and the disposition of Caspian energy resources. These issues will remain important long after the current nuclear crisis ends, whether that happens with Iranian compliance with UN Security Council demands or—more likely—with the development of an Iranian nuclear weapons capability. They will also remain regardless of what regime holds power in Tehran.

Russia's policies also reflect its greater skepticism on the effectiveness of sanctions and the threat of military force. This skepticism is not without merit: preventive military force against a nascent military program is widely viewed as unlikely to succeed, and economic sanctions frequently fail to produce positive outcomes.[76] Russia quite rationally fears that these policies could fail, leaving Russian (and Western) interests worse off than they would have been had they not been undertaken in the first place.

Because Russia's Iran policy is grounded in genuine strategic interests, many of them long-term, Moscow is likely to respond to U.S. pressure and inducements only to a limited degree. Ultimately, Russia has a great deal to lose should its relationship with Iran deteriorate. Moscow is unlikely to risk such an outcome unless it has compelling reasons to do so. Past U.S. attempts to bribe Russian cooperation on Iran through lucrative nuclear cooperation deals, or to coerce Moscow through sanctions on Russian firms or restrictions on space and nuclear threat reduction projects, have largely failed because Russia's interests in Iran go well beyond economic opportunities.

U.S. efforts to win Russian support are more likely to be successful when they address Russia's underlying strategic and economic interests in Iran. Given Russia's and Iran's shared interest in keeping the United States out of the Caucasus and Central Asia, any U.S. support for Georgian membership in NATO, a continued military presence in Central Asia, and attempts to build pipelines in the Caspian that bypass both Russian and Iranian territory are likely to only reinforce the Russian-Iranian relationship. Similarly, improvements in relations between Washington and Moscow can undermine hardliners in Moscow who argue that the expanding U.S. influence is the real danger to Russia, and could make it easier for the Kremlin to accommodate the United States on Iran and other issues.

Finally, Washington should not lose sight of that fact that Russia's position on the Iran nuclear issue is much closer to America's than it is to Iran's. The United States and Europe are far more important for Russia than Iran is, and Moscow has a genuine interest in forestalling the development of a nuclear-armed Iran, which could destabilize the region and upset the existing balance of power on Russia's southern border. Moscow's resistance to sanctions, its refusal to end its cooperation at Bushehr, and its maintenance of ties with Tehran should not be seen as "spoiler" actions against the international nonproliferation regime, but as part of a careful balancing act between upholding the regime while not jeopardizing its regional interests. From Moscow's point of view, strong support for sanctions and other coercive measures is a very risky policy course. Sanctions will likely fail. U.S. or Israeli airstrikes would be destabilizing and could fail over the long term as well. Both measures could, in fact, make a nuclear-armed Iran more likely in the end by convincing Tehran that it needs nuclear weapons to protect itself. Moscow necessarily fears that strong support for such measures could leave it facing a nuclear and hostile Iran, while sacrificing the strategic and economic gains of its existing relationship with Iran—a lose-lose situation. More than anything else, it has been Iran's increasingly confrontational behavior that has moved Russia further toward the West's position, as worsening relations between Moscow and Tehran raise the costs of the relationship while lowering the benefits. The Obama administration's policy of capitalizing on this split by holding out positive inducements for Iranian cooperation on the one hand, while working to improve the U.S.-Russian relationship on the other, should be continued.

Notes

1. See Andrei Shleifer and Daniel Treisman, "Why Moscow Says No: A Question of Russian Interests, Not Psychology," *Foreign Affairs* 90, no. 1 (2011): 122–38.

2. Daniel Treisman, *The Return: Russia's Journey from Gorbachev to Medvedev* (New York: Free Press, 2011), 340–90.

3. Vladimir A. Orlov and Alexander Vinnikov, "The Great Guessing Game: Russia and the Iranian Nuclear Issue," *Washington Quarterly* 28, no. 2 (2005): 49–66.

4. Construction of the Bushehr nuclear power station had begun in 1975 by the German joint venture Kraftwerk Union but was later abandoned before completion. Kraftwerk Union had signed a contract with Iran for two 1,200-magawatt LWRs at Bushehr. After the Iranian Revolution in 1979, Kraftwerk pulled out of the contract, leaving the two reactors only partially completed. The unfinished structures were later bombed on sev-

eral occasions by the Iraqis during the Iran-Iraq War. "Russia, China Set to Sell Iran Reactors," Associated Press, September 11, 1992; Thomas W. Lippman, "Russia-Iran Atomic Deal Irks U.S.; Sen. McCain Asks State Dept. to Act," *Washington Post*, February 11, 1995.

5. The George H.W. Bush administration had tried and failed to pressure the Russians to end the Bushehr deal. Clinton began to push the issue with Moscow immediately upon taking office. At the April 1993 Clinton-Yeltsin summit in Vancouver, Undersecretary of State Lynn Davis engaged in a frustrating back-and-forth with Minatom chief Viktor Mikhailov and suggested that financial losses from enhanced export controls could be offset by increased U.S. trade with Russia's aerospace sector, to no avail. Strobe Talbott, *The Russia Hand: A Memoir of Presidential Diplomacy* (New York: Random House, 2002); personal communication with Lynn Davis, February 2011.

6. Fred Hiatt, "U.S. Efforts to Block Iran Reactor Sale Cause Anger in Moscow," *Washington Post*, March 3, 1995.

7. More accurately, this was leaked by U.S. officials seeking to put pressure on the administration to take a harder line with Moscow. Talbott, *Russia Hand*, 169.

8. Steven Greenhouse, "U.S. Says Russia Promised Nuclear Gear to Iran," *New York Times*, April 29, 1995.

9. Yuriy Vishnevskiy, chairman of Russia's state Committee for Supervision of Nuclear and Radiation Safety (Russia's counterpart to the Nuclear Regulatory Commission), accused Minatom head Viktor Mikhailov of pushing the centrifuge deal and took a strong stance against it. Fred Hiatt, "Russia Denies Plan to Sell Gas Centrifuge to Iran," *Washington Post*, May 5, 1995; "Russian Agency Opposes Sale of Centrifuge to Iran," Interfax (in Russian, translated by BBC Monitoring), May 6, 1995. Russia's ambassador to the United States, Yuliy Vorontsov, also claimed that the centrifuge deal was brokered by Minatom and was done without the Kremlin's knowledge. "Ministry 'Engineered' Parts of Iranian Nuclear Deal-Russian Ambassador to U.S.," Interfax (in Russian, translated by BBC Monitoring), May 10, 1995. When discussing the issue with Secretary of State Warren Christopher, Russian foreign minister Kozyrev stated that Minatom's chief was "out of control" and was making deals with Iran without Yeltsin's knowledge. Talbott, *Russia Hand*, 168.

10. The Gore-Chernomyrdin Commission had been established in 1993 to discuss space, energy, and other high-technology issues between the United States and Russia. See U.S. Congress, Senate, *A Review of Gore-Chernomyrdin Diplomacy: Hearing before the Subcommittee on European Affairs and the Subcommittee on Near Eastern and South Asian Affairs of the Committee on Foreign Relations, United States Senate, One Hundred Sixth Congress, second session, October 25, 2000* (Washington, D.C.: U.S. Government Printing Office, 2001).

11. Robert J. Einhorn and Gary Samore, "Ending Russian Assistance to Iran's Nuclear Bomb," *Survival* 44, no. 2 (2002): 53.

12. Fred Wehling, "Russian Nuclear and Missile Exports to Iran," *Nonproliferation Review* 6, no. 2 (1999): 134–43.

13. Brenda Shaffer, *Partners in Need: The Strategic Relationship of Russia and Iran* (Washington, D.C.: Washington Institute for Near East Policy, 2001).

14. Most notable was the cancelation of a deal by the Russian aerospace firm NPO Trud to provide missile engine technology to Iran. Steven Erlanger, "U.S. Gets Russia's Firm Vow to Halt Missile Aid to Iran," *New York Times*, January 16, 1998; "Russia Arrests Iranian Seeking Missile Data," *New York Times*, November 15, 1997.

15. Howard Diamond, "U.S., Russia Take New Steps to Control Technology Transfers to Iran," *Arms Control Today* 28, no. 2 (1998).

16. In return for Clinton's veto of sanctions against Russia, the Kremlin agreed to intensify its efforts to reign in Russian sales of military technology to Iran. Tensions became more acute in July 1998 after Iran tested a Shahhab-3 missile. Talbott, *Russia Hand*, 273; Stephen Sestanovich, "At Odds with Iran and Iraq: Can the United States and Russia Resolve Their Differences?," Century Foundation and Stanley Foundation Joint Project on Domestic Politics and America's Russia Policy, February 2003, www.stanleyfoundation.org/publications/archive/EAIrussiaAo3p.pdf.

17. Adamov, a civilian nuclear engineer, was disfavored by hardliners in Moscow because of his focus on expanding civilian nuclear exports at the expense of the military. He did, however, prove to be very willing to aggressively and independently pursue nuclear deals with unsavory regimes and enjoyed political support in Moscow through the patronage of powerful oligarch Boris Berezovsky. Craig M. Johnson, "The Russian Federation's Ministry of Atomic Energy: Programs and Developments," Pacific Northwest National Laboratory, paper prepared for U.S. Department of Energy (PNNL-13197), February 2000.

18. Thomas W. Lippman, "2 Nuclear Accords Expected; U.S.-Russia Pact Involves Uranium Buy," *Washington Post*, March 21, 1999.

19. Anthony H. Cordesman and Adam C. Seitz, *Iranian Weapons of Mass Destruction: The Birth of a Regional Nuclear Arms Race?* (Santa Barbara, Calif.: Praeger Security International; Washington, D.C.: Center for Strategic and International Studies, 2009), 104–12.

20. Treisman, *Return*, 92–102.

21. Susan B. Glasser, "Russia, Iran Renew Alliance Meant to Boost Arms Trade; Tehran Seeking Advanced Technology; U.S. Is Concerned," *Washington Post*, March 13, 2001.

22. Dimitri K. Simes, "Losing Russia: The Cost of Renewed Confrontation," *Foreign Affairs* 86, no. 6 (2007): 36.

23. Celeste A. Wallander, "Russia's Interest in Trading with the 'Axis of Evil,'" Program on New Approaches to Russian Security (PONARS) Policy Memo 248, Center for Strategic and International Studies, October 2002, http://csis.org/files/media/csis/pubs/pm_0248.pdf.

24. Christina Chuen, "Russian Nuclear Exports to Iran: U.S. Policy Change Needed," James Martin Center for Nonproliferation Studies, March 27, 2003, http://cns.miis.edu/stories/030327.htm.

25. Simon Saradzhyan and Caroline McGregor, "Russia Hardens Stance toward Iran," *Moscow Times*, September 22, 2003.

26. "Russian Foreign Minister Calls for 'Balanced' IAEA Resolution on Iran," RIA Novosti (in Russian, translated by BBC Monitoring), November 24, 2003.

27. The Russian position was not entirely inconsistent with many other countries' positions on the issue. States in the Non-Aligned Movement (NAM) favored a similar approach. The Tehran Agreement proposed by the United Kingdom, France, and Germany (the "EU-3") offered civilian nuclear cooperation as an incentive to Iran to agree to the Additional Protocol and to freeze its enrichment activities. Similarly, Russia's decision not to support a U.S.-backed resolution in the IAEA to formally censure Iran in November 2003 was in line with the majority of the members of the IAEA Governing Council: only Canada, Australia, and Japan supported the U.S. position. David E. Sanger, "Nuclear Board Said to Rebuff Bush over Iran," *New York Times*, November 20, 2003; Felicity Barringer, "Plans by Iran for a Reactor Pose Concerns about Arms," *New York Times*, June 7, 2003; and Mark Landler, "U.S. and U.N. Agency Press Iran on Its Nuclear Program," *New York Times*, June 18, 2003.

28. Peter Baker, "Russians Pressure Iran on Weapons," *Washington Post*, June 5, 2003.

29. Andrew E. Kramer, "Russia Settles Issues on Nuclear Power Plant," *New York Times*, December 14, 2007.

30. Of course, such a deal could not only be lucrative for Moscow but would provide the Russians with substantially greater leverage over Iran. Molly Moore, "U.S. Still Short in Iran Security Council Push," *Washington Post*, January 22, 2006; Shahram Chubin, *Iran's Nuclear Ambitions* (Washington, D.C.: Carnegie Endowment for International Peace, 2006), 109–10.

31. "Russia to Supply Unique Missile Systems," Interfax (in Russian, translated by BBC Monitoring), December 2, 2005.

32. Iran would be "reported" rather than "referred" to the Security Council, a technical move that would allow additional time for negotiation. Kevin Sullivan and Dafna Linzer, "Iran to Be Reported to Security Council," *Washington Post*, January 31, 2006; Nazila Fathi, "Iran Rejects Russian Offer to Defuse Nuclear Dispute," *New York Times*, March 13, 2006.

33. Iran announced it would no longer comply with the Additional Protocol in February 2006 and by April had enriched uranium to the 3.5 percent level (low enriched uranium, or LEU) using a 164-centrifuge cascade at Natanz. That July, the Security Council passed Resolution 1696, which demanded that Iran suspend all fuel cycle activities before an August 31 deadline. Iran rejected the P5+1 inducements package in August and failed to suspend enrichment activities before the deadline.

34. Howard LaFranchi, "Will EU and US Be Tougher Now on Iran?" *Christian Science Monitor*, December 26, 2006.

35. "Russia Completes Missile Deliveries: Tass," Reuters, January 23, 2007.

36. Andrew E. Kramer, "Russia Will Slow Work on Iran's Nuclear Plant." *New York Times* February 20, 2007.

37. For example, one Russian official was quoted as saying: "We are suffering losses in terms of foreign policy and our image while they (the Iranians) stand their ground. They cannot play on our methodical good relations eternally and they need to understand that." Richard Beeston, "Iran's Nuclear Plans Hit as Russians Hold Back Fuel in Row about Money," *Times* (London), March 13, 2007. Also, European officials stated they were told by Russian foreign minister Sergei Lavrov that Russia had withheld the fuel for political reasons but would publicly maintain its reasons were purely financial. Iranian officials stated they were told the same by their Russian counterparts, and were informed that completion of the project would be conditioned upon cooperation with the IAEA. Elaine Sciolino, David E. Sanger, and Helene Cooper, "Russia Tells Iran It Must Suspend Uranium Project," *New York Times*, March 20, 2007; Helene Cooper, "Russia Delivers Its Nuclear Fuel to Plant in Iran," *New York Times*, December 18, 2007. Also suggestive is Russia's decision to ship fuel after talks were held between Putin and Supreme Leader Ali Khamenei in October 2007. Nazila Fathi, "Putin Is Said to Offer Idea on Standoff over Iran," *New York Times*, October 18, 2007.

38. Robert Bridge, "Russia Balks on Iran's Bushehr Site," *Moscow News*, March 23, 2007.

39. Peter Finn, "Russia to Suspend Compliance with Key European Pact," *Washington Post*, April 27, 2007.

40. "Russia and Arms Control: Vlad and MAD," *Economist*, June 9, 2007.

41. Nazila Fathi and C. J. Chivers, "Putin Says Caspian Area Is Off Limits to Attacks," *New York Times*, October 17, 2007; Tony Halpin, "Vladimir Putin Pledges to Complete Iranian Nuclear Reactor," *Times* (London), October 17, 2007.

42. Robert Tait, "Russia Starts Nuclear Fuel Deliveries to Iran," *Guardian*, December 18, 2007; Tony Halpin, "Defiant Russia Flexes Its Muscles with Uranium Shipment to Iran," *Times* (London), December 18, 2007.

43. Konstantin Lantratov and Alexandra Gritskova, "Iran Prikryvaet Atomnuyu Programmu Russkimi Raketami: Gotovitsiya Kontrakt na Postavku Sistem S-300," *Kommersant* (in Russian), December 27, 2007; Luke Harding, "Russia Sells Iran New Anti-Aircraft Missiles," *Guardian* (London), December 27, 2007; and "Russia Says No Plans to Sell Missile System to Iran," Reuters, December 28, 2007.

44. An unnamed U.S. official was cited by the *New York Times* as saying, "I cannot rule out that he delivered a message that we would like." Nazila Fathi, "Putin Is Said to Offer Idea on Standoff over Iran," *New York Times*, October 18, 2007.

45. Peter Finn, "U.S., Russia Sign Pact on Nuclear Cooperation," *Washington Post*, May 7, 2008.

46. Karen DeYoung, "U.S. Envoy Indicates Flexibility with Russia on Missile Defense," *Washington Post*, February 14, 2009; Ellen Barry, "Russian President Calls Obama Letter on Antimissile Plan a Welcome Signal," *New York Times*, March 4, 2009.

47. Dmitri Trenin and Alexey Malashenko, *Iran: A View from Moscow* (Washington: Carnegie Endowment for International Peace, 2010), 19–23; Helene Cooper and Mark Mazzetti, "A Cryptic Note from Tehran Ignites Days of Urgent Diplomacy," *New York Times*, September 26, 2009.

48. Helene Cooper and David E. Sanger, "Obama, at U.N., Is Backed on Iran and Arms Curbs," *New York Times*, September 24, 2009.

49. "S-300 Missiles Come under New UN Sanctions on Iran-Kremlin Source," RIA Novosti (in English), June 11, 2010, http://en.rian.ru/russia/20100611/159387435.html.

50. "Russia Steps Up Criticism of NATO Libya Campaign," Reuters, May 20, 2011.

51. David E. Sanger, "Syria, Iran, and the Obama Doctrine," *New York Times*, February 26, 2012.

52. Ellen Barry, "Russia Dismisses Calls for New U.N. Sanctions on Iran," *New York Times*, November 10, 2011; Steven Erlanger, "European Union Moves Closer to Imposing Tough Sanctions on Iran," *New York Times*, January 21, 2012.

53. Javad Heydarian, "Russia's Iran Nuclear Solution," *Diplomat*, November 16, 2011.

54. Isabel Kershner and Rick Gladstone, "Decision on Whether to Attack Iran Is 'Far Off,' Israeli Defense Minster Says," *New York Times*, January 19, 2012.

55. Helen Belopolsky, *Russia and the Challengers: Russian Alignment with China, Iran, and Iraq in the Unipolar Era* (Blasingstoke, Eng.: Palgrave Macmillan, 2009), 97–137.

56. Martin Malek, "Russia, Iran, and the Conflict in Chechnya," *Caucasian Review of International Affairs* 2, no. 1 (2008): 25–34.

57. For a discussion of Iran's pragmatic approach to foreign policy, see Ray Takeyh, *Guardians of the Revolution: Iran and the World in the Age of the Ayatollahs* (Oxford: Oxford University Press, 2009).

58. Shaffer, *Partners in Need*, 38–48.

59. Shleifer and Treisman, "Why Moscow Says No"; John W. Parker, *Persian Dreams: Moscow and Tehran since the Fall of the Shah* (Washington, D.C.: Potomac Books, 2009), 147–68.

60. Shleifer and Treisman, "Why Moscow Says No."

61. Parker, *Persian Dreams*, 295.

62. Pavel Felgenhauer, "The 'Unraveling Relationship' between Russia and Iran," BBC, July 24, 2010, www.bbc.co.uk/news/world-europe-10684110.

63. Parker, *Persian Dreams*, 211–13, 293–94.

64. Shleifer and Treisman, "Why Moscow Says No."

65. Belopolsky, *Russia and the Challengers*.

66. "Iran Hopes for Oil Partnerships with Moscow, Minister Tells Russian Agency," RIA Novosti (in Russian, translated by BBC Monitoring), September 3, 2012.

67. Shleifer and Treisman, "Why Moscow Says No."

68. Ibid.

69. Mary Beth Nikitin, *U.S.-Russian Civilian Nuclear Cooperation Agreement: Issues for Congress* (Washington, D.C.: Congressional Research Service, 2011).

70. Parker, *Persian Dreams*, 103–9, 116–17; Adam N. Stulberg, "Nuclear Regionalism in Russia: Decentralization and Control in the Nuclear Complex," *Nonproliferation Review* 9, no. 3 (2002): 31–46.

71. For example, in the early 2000s, a $1 change in the price of a barrel of oil on world markets could move Russia's GDP up or down by as much as 0.35 percent. Wallander, "Russia's Interest."

72. Lilia Shevtsova, *Putin's Russia* (Washington, D.C.: Carnegie Endowment for International Peace, 2003), 104–33; Peter Rutland, "Putin and the Oligarchs," in *Putin's Russia: Past Imperfect, Future Uncertain*, 3rd ed., ed. Dale R. Herspring (Lanham, Md.: Rowman & Littlefield, 2007); and Iulia Shevchenko. *The Central Government of Russia: From Gorbachev to Putin* (Burlington, Vt.: Ashgate, 2004), 161–79.

73. Andrew E. Kramer, "Gazprom Becomes the Bear of Russia," *New York Times*, December 27, 2005.

74. Dmitry Shlapentokh, *Russian Elite Image of Iran: From the Late Soviet Era to the Present* (Carlyle, Pa.: Strategic Studies Institute, U.S. Army War College, 2009).

75. Treisman, *Return*.

76. See Dan Reiter, *Preventive War and Its Alternatives: The Lessons of History* (Carlisle, Pa.: Strategic Studies Institute, U.S. Army War College, 2006); and Gary Clyde Hufbauer, Jeffrey J. Schott, Kimberly Ann Elliott, and Barbara Oegg, *Economic Sanctions Reconsidered*, 3rd ed. (Washington, D.C.: Peterson Institute for International Economics, 2007).

CHAPTER 8

Brazil and Mexico in the Nonproliferation Regime

Common Structures and Divergent Trajectories in Latin America

Arturo C. Sotomayor

THERE ARE MULTIPLE OPTIONS for Latin American countries to support and comply with the nuclear nonproliferation regime. At the global level, states can decide to ratify the core treaties and join their supporting institutions such as the Treaty on the Non-Proliferation of Nuclear Weapons (NPT), the International Atomic Energy Agency (IAEA), the Comprehensive Nuclear-Test-Ban Treaty (CTBT), the Nuclear Suppliers Group (NSG), the Missile Technology Control Regime, the International Convention on the Suppression of Acts of Nuclear Terrorism, and the Limited Test Ban Treaty (LTBT). At the regional level, countries in the Western Hemisphere can adhere to the Treaty for the Prohibition of Nuclear Weapons in Latin America and the Caribbean, also known as the Treaty of Tlatelolco, which in 1968 created the world's first nuclear-weapons-free zone in a densely populated region. Although the treaty is fully in force and has been ratified by all Latin American states, regional support for the nonproliferation regime has varied substantially over time, with some countries choosing to endorse the regime early on, and other states historically opposing it. Empirically and theoretically, it is worth exploring this variation in nonproliferation strategies, including questioning why some traditionally oppositional states changed their position over time.

Brazil and Mexico are regional, middle-sized powers, a category of states that have the ability and willingness to adopt an activist, initiative-oriented diplomatic approach to effectively engage the international system through international institutions and other nonmilitary means. As politically and economically significant states, they are able to pursue multilateral solutions and act as facilitators in building coalitions, managers in their own regions, and promoters/enforcers of international norms.[1] Both Brazil and Mexico share these middle power attributes, having both the region's largest military forces and its biggest economies, along with the subregional influence this grants them—Brazil in the southern cone of South America and Mexico in Central America. They are both founding members of the United Nations system and have been involved in key multilateral negotiations on issues ranging from the environment and peacekeeping to disarmament.[2] Given these similarities, both Brazil and Mexico are likely cases in Latin America for international primacy in the nonproliferation regime. However, these two middle powers have historically behaved very differently in very different international roles, implementing different foreign policies. Nowhere are these differences more evident than in the nonproliferation regime, where each country has followed separate paths.

Brazil once had a clandestine, military nuclear program and expressed strong reservations about the nonproliferation regime, including the Treaty of Tlatelolco. In fact, Brazil did not remove its reservations toward Tlatelolco until 1994 and did not sign the NPT until 1998, a latecomer to both the global and regional nonproliferation regimes. By contrast, Mexico promoted regional nonproliferation treaties and nuclear disarmament early in the 1960s. In fact, Mexico was the first Latin American country to ever sign a full safeguards agreement with the IAEA (in 1968), based on Tlatelolco, which predated the NPT. In due course, Mexico became the leading Latin American country in disarmament circles, often pushing for nuclear disarmament and nonproliferation measures in both regional and global forums. Why did these two middle powers follow such different nonproliferation approaches? Why did Mexico support the regime, while Brazil initially rejected it? Moreover, why did Brazil join the regime in the 1990s, after decades of opposition to it? Why has Mexico's support for the regime eroded in the past decade?

To examine these variations of policies toward the nonproliferation regime, this chapter assesses several hypotheses regarding the opposition to or support for nonproliferation efforts, including resource constraints and economic interests, threat perceptions, and discrimination. It concludes that several of these structural hypotheses lack sufficient comprehensive utility to explain the divergent nonproliferation strategies of Brazil and Mexico. Instead, the main argument focuses on two main, mutually reinforcing explanatory variables: U.S. influence (systemic politics) and domestic politics. Together, they account for the variation in terms of support/opposition to the nonproliferation regime. Specifically, Washington's nonproliferation policies toward Latin America alienated countries with advanced nuclear development programs, such as Brazil, demonstrating how U.S. foreign policy plays a key role in shaping policy preferences in Latin America. This is consistent with structural approaches to international relations—such as realism—which argue that major powers have an important independent effect on the behavior of states in the international system, including the structure of alliances and the balancing of coalitions, including in the developing world.[3] As noted realist Stephen M. Walt argues, "weak states are also likely to be especially sensitive to proximate power. Where great powers have both global interests and global capabilities, weak states will be concerned primarily with events in their immediate vicinity."[4] The reality is that at the international level, Latin America's security complex is largely shaped, although not fully determined, by the U.S. sphere of influence, which includes power, statecraft, and a unique geography in the Western Hemisphere.[5]

While hegemonic policies restrain or empower other countries to follow certain paths, they do not by themselves determine other states' policy decisions or outcomes. Middle powers may or may not acquiesce to the hegemon's definition of security, leading to important policy variations between states with similar structures and capabilities, which can only be explained, then, by domestic politics.[6] In Brazil and Mexico, systemic factors provide the context for the decision-making processes while domestic politics largely determine the nonproliferation policies. In particular, this chapter focuses on the relationship between civil-military relations and proliferation motivations. In Brazil, an inward-looking domestic coalition dominated by the military (especially after the 1964 coup) assumed responsibility and control over nuclear issues. In a context dominated by Cold War politics and regional rivalry, the military determined Brazil's nuclear policies and then shaped preferences toward the nonproliferation regime. By contrast, civilian authorities in Mexico opted for disarmament and support for the nonproliferation regime in part to keep the military out of politics and away from foreign policy debates. In other words, a civilian-led domestic coalition committed itself to nonproliferation efforts to increase the cost of military meddling in Mexico's security affairs.[7] Since military institutions have historically played a key political role in Latin America, it is important to understand how they grappled with their civilian counterparts for control over nuclear policy at different points in time.

In drawing these conclusions, this chapter applies international relations theorist Etel Solingen's theory of domestic coalitions to a different set of domestic actors, including the armed forces and their separate services.[8] If coalitions are "policy networks spanning state and private political actors," a domestic coalitional approach assumes that these networks have state agency, undertake projects, and affect policy, even if they are constrained by international factors.[9] As Solingen argues, "once a certain coalition prevails politically, as a function of its size, cohesiveness, and effectiveness, its grand strategy becomes *raison d'état*. Governmental policy must now reflect the essential contours of that strategy, although the institutional context can impose limits on its implementation and even doom its viability."[10] Whereas Solingen focuses her attention on how political-economy coalitions and economic strategies (inward versus outward economic policies) affect proliferation incentives, I emphasize how the armed forces and their political allies affect incentives to join or oppose the nonproliferation regime. Solingen argues that countries with inward-looking economic coalitions face stronger incentives for nuclearization and are less committed to international overtures and nonproliferation norms. By contrast, the cases analyzed in this chapter indicate that civil-military relations shape nonproliferation paths, regardless of the economic constituencies and strategies in place.

The two arguments developed in this chapter are based on two distinct levels of analysis—systemic and domestic—and can be potentially contradictory, especially when viewed through the requisite neorealist lens.[11] Nevertheless, the point is not to determine which level matters most; obviously, they both do. Instead, what is more interesting and perhaps more challenging is to determine how the two levels matter, vary from country to country, and then interact to determine policy outcomes.

Brazil and Mexico provide an ideal laboratory in which to test alternative explanations of why states choose to support or impede nonproliferation efforts. First, as previously noted, the two Latin American countries are considered middle powers and, along with Argentina, are the only states in the region to have successfully developed nuclear power plants. Given their respective regional and middle power status, their support or opposition is relevant for regional and global nonproliferation initiatives. As "nuclear threshold states—those that have chosen nuclear restraint despite having significant nuclear capabilities," they are important "partners for the reinvigorated drive toward global nuclear disarmament."[12]

Second, Brazil has modified its nuclear policy from opposition and reservation to conditional support, all while enhancing its own nuclear energy projects. Such diverse trajectories provide an invaluable opportunity to analyze variation in nonproliferation policies. Over time, important variations in the dependent variable can be observed across the region and within states, each leading to multiple observations.

Third, in Latin America, there are at least two different ways to support the nonproliferation regime, one via the NPT and the other via Tlatelolco. While both treaties reinforce each other and are mutually compatible, each provides a different set of incentives for membership (global versus regional). Finally, a historical analysis provides an ideal opportunity to use process tracing as a research method to identify the causal chain and mechanism of how and why states differ in their approach toward the regime. In that sense, this study emphasizes turning points, critical junctures, sequencing of events, and different regime trajectories to identify causal relationships.

In the following sections, I test different hypotheses about how states support or oppose the regime. I first analyze how technical and economic factors influenced nonproliferation incentives in Brazil and Mexico. The second section examines different threat perceptions and U.S. policies, focusing on how they militate against robust nonproliferation policies. The third section analyzes how domestic politics and civil-military relations shaped different nonproliferation trajectories. Finally, I conclude with a discussion of how these historical cases might shed light on current nonproliferation policies in Latin America.

HYPOTHESIS 1: RESOURCE CONSTRAINTS AND ECONOMIC INTERESTS

One theory for resistance to the nonproliferation regime is that it imposes economic and development restrictions to nonnuclear states. From this perspective, treaties such as the NPT ban not only the diffusion of nuclear weapons but also the dissemination of nuclear technology for development, even if it is for peaceful purposes. While the NPT does allow for the transfer of nuclear technology and materials for the development of civilian nuclear energy programs among signatory countries, in practice, however, most nuclear states have prevented nonnuclear weapons states from developing an indigenous mastery of nuclear technology for peaceful purposes by imposing a virtual embargo on suppliers for nuclear industries.[13]

Indeed, Brazil's initial decision not to accede to the NPT grew from its position regarding autonomous economic development. Available studies on Latin America's nuclear strategies consistently demonstrate that the discourse of self-sufficiency and policies of *desarrollismo* (or autonomous development) motivated the development of Brazilian and even Mexican nuclear policies since the 1950s.[14] The nuclear programs in Latin America were originally conceived as a means of acquiring energy resources from the atom. Both Brazil and Mexico received their initial stimulation through the Atoms for Peace Program in the 1950s—a program conceived by the Dwight D. Eisenhower administration to assist third-world countries in developing nuclear energy (mostly through technical assistance to develop research reactors). At that time, both countries had ambitious economic programs that were focused on developing and boosting their indigenous industries. As a result, the governments of both were increasingly pressured by multinational companies and local enterprises to supply sufficient energy resources to maintain a burgeoning industry. Cities like Rio de Janeiro, São Paulo, Buenos Aires, and Mexico City were heavily industrialized areas, with increasing levels of energy consumption.

The need to develop nuclear energy was reinforced by the 1973 oil crisis. In the Brazilian case, this requirement was particularly acute. It became clear that the so-called Brazilian economic miracle of the 1960s and early 1970s relied on favorable external conditions and on cheap energy consumption.[15] Solingen suggests that the nuclear project in Brazil was motivated by its inward-looking economic strategy, in the form of import substitution industrialization or ISI, an economic strategy that replaces foreign imports with domestic production, with the goal of developing technology to attain self-sufficiency.[16] As former minister of science and technology José Goldemberg later argued, Brazil sought an indigenous technological capacity, including the production of nuclear energy, which had been "presented as a miraculous source of energy in the United States, Britain, France and the Soviet Union."[17]

Brazil saw the development of nuclear energy capabilities as key to overcoming the country's underdevelopment. For instance, some Brazilians envisioned using peaceful nuclear explosives to exploit the Amazon jungle. According to Brazilian diplomats in the 1970s, peaceful nuclear explosives provided "a solution to many of the serious problems which confront Latin American countries . . . such as the digging of canals, the connection of hydrographic basins, the recovery of oil fields, the release of natural gas, etc."[18] This, in part, explains why Brazil was a strong opponent of the nonproliferation regime. Although the NPT explicitly allows the development of peaceful applications of nuclear explosions, in practice the nuclear weapons states considerably restricted technical and financial assistance for such peaceful nuclear explosive devices.[19] Hence, Brazil and its neighbor, Argentina, perceived the NPT as an impediment to their industrialization and modernization. Both states also disagreed with the discriminatory nature of a treaty that created two types of legal obligations: one for nuclear weapons states (who were not forced to immediately disarm) and another for nonnuclear countries (banned from pursuing nuclear weapons).[20]

While economic reasons provided strong disincentives for Brazil to join the NPT, it is still unclear why Brazil had so many reservations about the regional nonproliferation regime, based on the Treaty of Tlatelolco. In fact, Brazil was, along with Mexico, one of the initial supporters of the regional nonproliferation regime. In 1962, Brazilian diplomats introduced a UN General Assembly resolution to discuss the establishment of a denuclearized zone in Latin America.[21] In 1963, then-president João Goulart signed a joint declaration of agreement with five other Latin American states—Bolivia, Brazil, Chile, Ecuador, and Mexico—to continue to commit themselves to nonproliferation in multilateral negotiations. This declaration eventually led to the negotiations that created the Treaty of Tlatelolco.[22]

The Latin American nonproliferation regime complements the NPT, but it does have some important differences. For instance, Tlatelolco explicitly allows for peaceful nuclear explosions. Article 18 reads as follows: "The Contracting Parties may carry out explosions of nuclear devices for peaceful purposes—including explosions which involve devices similar to those used in nuclear weapons—or collaborate with third parties for the same purpose, provided that they do so in accordance with the provisions of this article and the other articles of the Treaty, particularly articles 1 and 5."[23]

Mexican diplomats introduced the article in question in order to incentivize Brazil and Argentina to join the emerging regional regime.[24] In spite of this enticement, Brazil—like Argentina—signed the treaty but did not ratify or adhere to it until, in Brazil's case, 1994. According to Brazilian researcher Paulo S. Wrobel, Brazilian military authorities, who effectively controlled the government after 1964, considered Tlatelolco as a regional extension of the NPT. From Brazil's perspective, the two treaties were developed in parallel and had apparently the same primary purpose: to act as a barrier to horizontal nuclear weapons proliferation.[25] Since Brazil was technically opposed to the NPT, its adherence to the regional regime had to be consistent; hence Brasilia did not become a founding member of Tlatelolco.

It thus appears that Brazil's reservations toward the regime were more technical and political than economic. Interestingly, Mexico followed a very similar autarkic economic strategy as Brazil. Like Brazil in the 1930s and 1940s, postwar governments in Mexico embarked on import substitution industrialization policies with considerable state involvement in the economy. In fact, it was the Mexican Revolution of 1910–20 and its aftermath that created a political regime with a corporatist system and strong nationalist, developmentalist, and populist orientations. The regime was authoritarian in nature and based on a system of single-party rule, sustained by a coalition dominated by unions, peasants, and national entrepreneurs. The regime survived through tariffs, quantitative restrictions to imports, and foreign direct investment, as well as nationalization of key sectors (including the oil sector). This ushered in a period of stabilization and growth, which lasted until the late 1970s, when the Mexican economy reached an impasse as a result of its macroeconomic policies.[26]

In spite of the limitations and goals of its economic strategy, Mexico was able to develop its own nuclear program while fully joining the NPT regime and leading regional nonproliferation efforts. Although less advanced and perhaps less ambitious than Brazil's nuclear capability, the Laguna Verde nuclear plant began operations in 1986, after almost four decades of nuclear research. This was only a year after Brazil opened its first nuclear plant in 1985, known as Angra 1. While many Mexican nuclear scientists received training in the United States, the IAEA provided the bulk of the technical and financial assistance to develop Mexico's nuclear capability. Surprisingly, Mexico did not develop any bilateral nuclear research agreements with Washington or any other country during the initial stage of the construction of Laguna Verde. As University of Virginia scholar John R. Redick discovered in a pioneer study of Latin America's nuclear programs, "a desire to be independent with respect to its own power supply is also noted by Mexican officials themselves as an important rationale for opting for nuclear power."[27]

The economic and technological restrictions imposed by the NPT certainly did not impede Mexican leaders from developing a peaceful nuclear capability. Moreover, Brazil and Mexico shared very similar economic patterns throughout the 1970s and 1980s, followed by economic growth, recession, foreign debt, and economic crisis. Hence, economic reasons are neither necessary nor sufficient conditions for non-accession to the regime.

HYPOTHESIS 2: THREAT CONDITIONS AND U.S. HEGEMONY

A second line of argument considers that differential threat perceptions militate against robust nonproliferation policies. Many states see nuclear proliferation as a "U.S. problem," the priority of which falls far behind the multiple security regional threats they face, none of which are addressed by the nonproliferation regime. Other states are reluctant to join these efforts, discomforted by the notion of taking political direction from Washington. In the Latin American context, the U.S. role had larger consequences on nonproliferation decisions than did differential threat perceptions.

Compared to other parts of the globe, Latin America has been relatively peaceful and exempt from external security threats. A large number of the militarized, territorial disputes in the region have rarely escalated into interstate war.[28] Instead, when crises have appeared to escalate, Latin American states tend to rely on a diplomatic culture that is normative and principled in its approach. This has resulted in a collective understanding that favors legal obligations among regional neighbors, based on the expectation and practice that countries from the Americas almost always engage in pacific settlement when a conflict emerges.[29] Given this relatively peaceful environment, realist explanations might suggest that nuclear proliferation would be a non-issue in Latin America. As one regional political observer points out, the negotiation of a nuclear-weapon-free zone in Latin America was relatively easy because it was a region that was already denuclearized.[30] In other words, Latin America appears to be an "easy case" for nonproliferation, given its nonnuclear status and the absence of malign external threats.

That at least two South American states—including Argentina and Brazil—pursued military-led nuclear programs in a relatively benign threat environment is therefore puzzling. The southern-most area of South America, often referred to as the Southern Cone, was not a contested region in contemporary international politics. While there were indeed sources of instability, these threats essentially arose from conflicts within state borders.[31] As Goldemberg explains, "Unlike Israel or India, Brazil has no political problems with its neighbors that might lead the military to seek nuclear weapons on security grounds."[32]

Most Latin American specialists agree that Brazil's nuclear aspirations were driven by its nuclear rivalry with Argentina, thus confirming realist arguments that competitive international environments motivate arms races and rivalries.[33] The Argentine-Brazilian rivalry was, for most of the nineteenth and twentieth centuries, a perennial feature of international relations in the Southern Hemisphere; their nuclear race became a subset of their larger competition for influence in the region. From a realist perspective, the nuclear competition between both countries was motivated by a desire to achieve military primacy, which would in turn allow them to exercise regional predominance. This led nuclear proliferation experts in the 1970s and 1980s to consider Argentina and Brazil as nuclear threshold states (i.e., states with the capacity to build nuclear weapons).

However, as American diplomat Mitchell Reiss points out, Argentina and Brazil were more likely to constrain their nuclear capabilities because the two countries were "rivals, but not enemies."[34] Theoretically speaking, this condition would have allowed for compliance with the regional nonproliferation regime. Argentina and Brazil indeed have an enviably limited record of going to war with each other. The last time Argentina fought against Brazil was 1825-28, during the Cisplatine War in the Banda Oriental area of present-day Uruguay. Regional threats since have not been so intense as to prompt spiraling arms races that would lead to a full rejection of the nonproliferation regime. Yet, in spite of a relatively benign threat scenario, Brazil remained opposed to the NPT and failed to adhere to the Tlatelolco Treaty for almost thirty years. Ironically, during this time, it never overtly argued that its external security environment impeded its full accession to the regime.

Brazil did, however, express concern about U.S. policies and intentions, signaling the power of U.S. policies to shape regional proliferation preferences. Historically, the United States has reacted differently to insecurity in the region, sometimes failing to intervene in regional conflicts and other times intervening with military force. As Oxford University professor Andrew Hurrell argues, "it has always been difficult to define Latin America's security complex in a way that excludes the United States. . . . The U.S. role in the security of the hemisphere provides the perfect illustration of the old adage that intervention and non-intervention are two sides of the same coin."[35]

In particular, two events affected hemispheric perceptions of the United States and shifted policies regarding nonproliferation in Latin America. First, prompted by India's 1974 nuclear test, Washington reviewed its nuclear policy regarding the transfer of sensitive nuclear material to developing countries, eventually passing the 1978 Nuclear Non-Proliferation Act, which imposed full-scope safeguards on all nuclear transfers. This contributed to a virtual embargo on suppliers for Brazilian and Argentine nuclear industries, irritating both countries in the Southern Cone and engendering suspicion in Brazil toward the United States.

The new restrictions imposed by the U.S. government specifically targeted and affected Brazil. In 1975, Brazil signed a nuclear agreement with West Germany, which would have allowed the former to explore and enrich uranium, reprocess spent fuel, and build eight nuclear plants. But Washington reacted negatively to such a nuclear deal and eventually persuaded West Germany to require full nuclear safeguards from Brazil.[36] The military then realized that belonging to the Western bloc did not imply integration with the developed world.[37] This policy strengthened Brazil's opposition to the global regime based on its discriminatory nature and reinforced its official position for non-accession to the treaty.

A second determinant event was the 1982 Falklands/Malvinas War. In more than one sense, the Malvinas crisis brought dissent to the Southern Cone, because it illustrated the symbolic irrelevance of the Inter-American Defense system, a poorly integrated collection of countries, instruments, organizations, and norms, including, inter alia, the Organization of American States, which proved completely unable to deal with the conflict. Furthermore, the dispute represented a real threat to most countries in the Southern Cone, since it was believed that British ships carried nuclear weapons into Argentine territorial waters, a clear violation of Protocol II of the Treaty of Tlatelolco, which specified that nuclear weapons states would not transfer explosive nuclear devices to the region and would not threaten to use them against the members of the treaty. (It should be noted, however, that while the United Kingdom had ratified the protocol, it did not apply to Argentina, which had not ratified the treaty.) In any case, this event also convinced Brazilian experts and military leaders that the Tlatelolco regime was, in effect, irrelevant for nuclear crises, reinforcing their reservations toward regional nonproliferation efforts.

Curiously enough, one of the most important effects of the Falklands/Malvinas war was that U.S. policies eventually freed the military establishments of Argentina and Brazil to forge closer links among themselves; Brazil recognized Argentina's sovereignty of the Falklands, and ultimately the two signed an agreement on the peaceful uses of nuclear energy, marking the beginning of the Argentine-Brazilian nuclear entente.[38] Their similar nuclear and military policies included a mutual opposition toward the global and regional nonproliferation regimes. Washington's policies gave Brazil and Argentina a common cause to oppose the regime itself. In this way, hegemonic policies affected regional alliances and provided incentives for opposition to the regime.

In clear contrast to Brazil, Mexico was the Latin American state most vulnerable to a potential nuclear threat, precisely due to its proximity to the United States. It has been widely acknowledged that the impact of the 1962 Cuban Missile Crisis made Mexico acutely aware of the risks of a nuclear war. Not only did the crisis take place in the vicinity of Mexico—and with a Mexican ally, the revolutionary regime of Cuba—but it also attracted the East-West confrontation to the hemisphere. Historical records of that period show that Mexican decision makers were shocked to learn that Fidel Castro had invited Soviet missiles into Cuban territory, especially after the Mexican regime (led by the Revolutionary Institutional Party) had invested diplomatic energy and resources in defending Cuba at the OAS, where it had been previously suspended.[39] Some scholars argue that the 1962 crisis generated widespread inhibition on the use of nuclear weapons, provided strong incentives to avoid a nuclear war, and gave rise to the prohibitionary norm of nuclear taboo, an underwritten understanding that nuclear weapons should not be used, especially against nonnuclear states.[40]

The counterargument is equally valid; the fear of annihilation could well have triggered a predisposition toward the bomb and a natural rejection toward the regime. Indeed, as a result of the crisis, Mexico discovered that it, too, was a direct target of Soviet deterrence. Soviet strategists were determined to block all economic and raw material assistance to the United States in case of a nuclear war, thus Mexican border cities and major urban metropolises (including Mexico City) were specifically targeted.[41] From a strictly security perspective, Mexico should have either developed its own nuclear capability to deter a Soviet attack or negotiated a set of explicit nuclear guarantees with its powerful neighbor. Canada followed this latter path, for example, under the nuclear umbrella offered via NATO. Mexico took neither of these two steps. Instead, it denounced the nuclear arms race and embarked on the seemingly impossible: nuclear disarmament and nonproliferation. Mexico—along with Chile, Costa Rica, Bolivia, and Brazil—first proposed a regional nonproliferation regime in the aftermath of the Cuban Missile Crisis. A series of regional negotiations and diplomatic meetings took place in Mexico City from 1964 to 1967, at the headquarters of the Ministry of Foreign Affairs, in the neighborhood of Tlatelolco. After the treaty was opened for signature in February 1967, by 1968 Mexico was the only Latin American country to ratify it; the rest—including Brazil—changed their nuclear positions or opted not to adhere to it.

But if Mexico was the most vulnerable Latin American state to a potential Soviet nuclear attack during the Cold War era because of its proximity to the United States, why did it support nonproliferation efforts? Why not request explicit nuclear guarantees from its northern neighbor? Why did it denounce U.S. nuclear strategies and then call for disarmament? If anything, Washington's nuclear policies constituted an implicit nuclear umbrella for Mexico. At best, the international system and U.S. influence provide the context under which policy decisions for and against the nonproliferation regime emerge, but they alone cannot account for policy variations between Latin America's middle powers.

HYPOTHESIS 3: CIVIL-MILITARY RELATIONS AND DOMESTIC POLITICS MOTIVATIONS

Leaving aside the reason(s) why states pursue nuclear weapons, the decision to support the nonproliferation regime (or not) can sometimes be influenced by the decision to acquire the nuclear bomb (or not). In particular, the development of nuclear power production in Latin America has often been linked to military politics—not only because most Latin American countries have experienced previous military and authoritarian regimes, but because military potential of civil nuclear power has been evident in at least two of the three countries where nuclear energy has been successfully produced, namely, Argentina and Brazil. Consequently, it is important to assess the military's support or opposition to the regime.

Historically, the influence of the military in nuclear matters in Brazil has been especially strong. The country experienced a critical juncture in 1964, when a coup ousted President Goulart and replaced him with a dictatorial military regime. This major political event modified Brazil's support for the emerging regional nonproliferation regime as the military assumed a direct role in politics and economic development. Consequently, the changing nature of civil-military relations affected nuclear incentives. The dictatorship assumed a technical approach to Brazilian problems, supporting a new coalition of apolitical technocrats that favored industrialization and modernization. It is this new political coalition, led by the military, that reassessed nuclear issues, emphasizing the use of nuclear development "to meet Brazilian energy needs and its potential to fulfill national security requirements."[42] As Columbia University professor Alfred Stepan describes, the geopolitical thinking of Brazil's armed forces developed a close interrelationship between security and national development, which contributed to the military's all-encompassing managerialism over the domestic political system. In Brazil, this form of military thinking was branded the new "national security policy." The armed forces believed that, in comparison to civilians, they knew better and had the "correct" doctrines of national security and development.[43] Nuclear policy was no exception; Brazil's nuclear energy policy was planned and controlled by the National Commission on Nuclear Energy, then a subordinate of the Ministry of Mines and Energy, all under military tutelage from 1964 to 1984.

Indeed, the dictatorship modified and adjusted Brazil's policy toward Tlatelolco and the NPT. According to Paulo S. Wrobel, Brazil had once been South America's champion of regional denuclearization efforts, but after the 1964 coup the new foreign policy prioritized the concept of national security. In practical terms, this meant that international treaties, such as Tlatelolco, had to be redone or questioned. Brazil thus became uninterested in international negotiations for nuclear disarmament and expressed strong reservations against the regional and global nonproliferation regimes, which included technical issues (dealing mostly with restrictions to peaceful nuclear explosions), legal considerations (such as when Tlatelolco would enter into force in Brazil), and political matters (focused most notably on the discriminatory nature of the NPT).[44]

In addition to developing nuclear energy, the military engaged in a parallel nuclear program, known as the Autonomous Program of Nuclear Technology (PATN), which sought to develop uranium enrichment technologies. Three branches of the military were involved: "Both the Navy and Air Force efforts were oriented toward specific military applications that fit with traditional mission orientations; the Navy sought to ensure a reliable source of fuel for nuclear-propelled submarines, while the Air Force aimed to develop a useful power supply for satellites."[45] The army was tasked with the development of a graphite reactor that would rely primarily on plutonium. Although there were many technical delays and each military branch faced considerable scientific obstacles, Brazil mastered the enrichment process by 1987. Of the three branches involved, the navy was the most successful in mastering enrichment technology.[46] The armed forces were also involved in building centrifuges to enrich uranium in an experimental center near São Paulo. Nuclear safeguards did not cover this program, which was clandestine and unknown to civilian authorities.

This in part suggests that Brazil's military services were not primarily focused on the development of nuclear weapons per se, but rather sought to have a "nuclear option" for nonweapon military applications, such as nuclear submarines and satellites.[47] Nonetheless, the armed forces established a secret project to design weapons and test devices. The Solimões Project was the code name for this secret program that included nuclear weapons design and excavation of a thousand-foot-deep shaft at a military base near Cachimbo, in the Amazon jungle, to carry out nuclear testing.[48] The activities conducted at the base were secret until the Brazilian National Congress summoned Brazil's intelligence and military officials to explain the spending of millions of dollars on secret atomic research. Senior military officials who testified in Congress repeatedly denied knowing of the existence of the nuclear weapons program. However, the report conducted by a bicameral legislative commission, which was made public a few weeks after President Fernando Collor de Mello took office in December 1990, revealed that the nation's former military rulers intended to build an atomic bomb. Indeed, according to Pedro Paulo Leoni Ramos, Collor de Mello's minister for strategic affairs, who testified in the bicameral commission:

> everything was handled in extreme secrecy, making it difficult to rescue documents; but at a historical moment, the project was conceived within the Presidency of the Republic to enhance various autonomous programs for the development of nuclear technology. Someone or some people decided to empower these installations ... to conceive the development of an artifact. Therefore, the development of an artifact would need to complete three phases: the very existence of fissile material, engineering design and field testing.[49]

José Goldemberg, who also testified as a member of the de Mello administration in his role as minister of science and technology, publicly declared to legislators that "as a result of secrecy and lack of control, clandestine activities were developed within the government, leading to the plans to build nuclear weapons."[50] The findings of the bicameral commission concluded with the following statements:

> The testimonies of your distinguished excellences Jose Goldemberg, Minister of Science and Technology, and Paulo Leoni Ramos, Minister of Strategic Affairs of the Presidency of the Republic, were exhaustive in admitting that "at a historic moment" there was the decision, taken inside the Palace of Planalto, to build a nuclear device. The drillings performed in Cachimbo would be the proving ground of these artifacts. Brazil's civil society was completely marginalized throughout this process; it was not consulted or heard, nor was Congress informed of the Nuclear Program. Therefore, it is imperative that Congress provides the legal tools necessary to monitor nuclear activity in the country.[51]

The nonproliferation regime was perceived by the armed forces as onerous and intrusive for their military ambitions, demonstrating that Brazil's initial refusal to join the nonproliferation regime(s) was not solely based on economic or technical grounds, but on military and political motivations. Neither the NPT nor the Tlatelolco treaty would have permitted the junta to develop such expertise, since the regime restrained militarized activities. The military instead opted to create, "with CNEN's [National Nuclear Energy Commission's] support . . . a clandestine program that was designed to produce highly enriched uranium or weapons-grade plutonium outside of IAEA safeguards."[52] Brazil's junta was committed to a militarized nuclear project and covertly sought the nuclear option.

The evolving nature of civil-military relations in Brazil explains why the country modified its opposition toward the regime. In fact, the democratization process that began in 1985 provided strong incentives to demilitarize Brazil's nuclear project. The leading figure in Brazil's decision to join the nonproliferation regime was President Collor de Mello, who assumed the presidency in 1990 (the first democratically elected president after 1964). A political outsider with an entrepreneurial background, Collor de Mello won the presidential election with only a slim 53 percent runoff majority against Luis Inacio da Silva (Lula).[53] The military perceived Collor with skepticism. In fact, the armed forces (along with conservative opposition members of Congress) were Collor's foremost institutional opponent. As Etel Solingen explains, Collor "slashed military budgets from 6 percent in 1989 to 2.2 in 1990, denied salary raises to 320,000 military personnel, and purged officers from important bureaucratic positions."[54] As a result, the presidency of Collor de Mello soon came under criticism from the military institution and from civilians who supported the armed forces.

Collor faced a nuclear establishment run by those in the military who still hoped to build a Brazilian bomb. A cabinet member of the Collor administration declared that the Brazilians "could in principle enrich uranium to very high levels and produce weapons-grade material. . . . That is why we are so concerned about putting government controls in place now."[55] Therefore, Collor de Mello's statements ruling out nuclear explosions were not enough; the president required other mechanisms to remove the control of nuclear programs from military hands.

It is in this context that nonproliferation became appealing to Brazil. The process began on November 28, 1990, when Presidents Carlos Saúl Menem of Argentina and Fernando Collor de Mello of Brazil met at the Iguacu Falls, which forms a common border between the two countries. There they signed an international agreement whereby they renounced the development of nuclear weapons and set forth a number of institutional mechanisms to assure one another that their nuclear establishments would live up to their international commitment. A safeguard agreement was negotiated under IAEA auspices. In 1991, the two presidents met again in Mexico, where they signed the Guadalajara Accord for the Use of Nuclear Energy for Peaceful Purposes, which laid the basis for the creation of the first bilateral institution, namely, the Argentine-Brazilian Agency for Accounting and Control of Nuclear Materials (ABACC). ABACC is currently composed of four members, which include the presidents of the respective nuclear energy commissions and two high representatives from the respective ministries of foreign affairs, plus a secretariat based in Rio de Janeiro, the secretary of which alternates yearly between a Brazilian national and an Argentine. Under ABACC, Argentina and Brazil are to submit to the bilateral agency a complete inventory of their nuclear materials, as well as thorough descriptions of their nuclear facilities. ABACC's main task is to verify, via in situ inspections, that the information provided by both governments is accurate.[56] Ultimately, this process formalized the accession of both Argentina and Brazil to the NPT and Tlatelolco. Brazil first acceded to the Tlatelolco Treaty in 1994 and then, under the administration of President Fernando Henrique Cardoso, became a full member of the NPT in 1998.

Brazil's sudden accession to the nonproliferation regime helped ensure civilian control over nuclear programs. The creation of a bilateral institution, under IAEA auspices, promised that Brazilian nuclear policies would be subject to international scrutiny, therefore rendering it the responsibility of diplomats and other civilian decision makers, rather than the armed forces. Such a policy could not have been implemented unilaterally, prompting Brazilian civilian leaders to seek international participation in the nonproliferation regime, in order to gain leverage over the militaries that they sorely distrust.[57]

Through this diplomatic maneuvering, nuclear policy was de facto transferred to the diplomatic establishment, led by the Ministry of Foreign Affairs, known as Itamaraty, a new civilian-led coalition. In the Brazilian case, Itamaraty's main role "was to soften the nationalistic stances defended by the Brazilian military."[58] This also granted the president the "power of appointment"; that is, the president could appoint civilians to key positions related to nuclear policy. This gave inspiration to what Ambassador Julio César Carasales has branded as "presidential diplomacy," whereby foreign policy reflects the interests and motivations of the executive.[59] In so doing, the president could remove the militaries from the decision making. For instance, Collor de Mello appointed José Goldemberg as his minister of science and technology, placing him in charge of the Nuclear Energy Commission. Goldemberg, a former president of the Brazilian Physics Society and of the Brazilian Society for the Progress of Science, was a leading critic of the program's secrecy and military control. It was Goldemberg who proposed the designing of a civilian-administered control system, drawing on technical assistance from the IAEA. In Goldemberg's view, "Empowered to conduct regular and random visits, Brazilian and Argentine teams would be composed of independent, civilian scientists approved by the Brazilian Senate."[60]

Brazil's full accession to the nonproliferation regime facilitated democratization by increasing civilian leverage over the military-led coalition. The election of Fernando Henrique Cardoso to the presidency in 1994 further modified the balance between civilians and the military. In 1996, Cardoso published Brazil's first National Defense Policy and in 2000 he was finally able to establish an integrated, civilian-led Ministry of Defense.[61] It is in this political context of democratic consolidation that Brazil joined the CTBT and NPT in 1998, and finally participated in a NPT Review Conference in 2000, as a nonnuclear weapons state.

Still, the path toward military reform was not without obstacles, since the military bargained for reserved domains in exchange for their return to the barracks, and some commanders opposed such measures altogether. Nevertheless, the accession of Brazil to the nonproliferation regime facilitated some level of normalization in civil-military relations and contributed to an expanded civilian-led foreign policy agenda.[62] But as is analyzed in the next section, military remnants from the dictatorial era persist in Brazil's nonproliferation strategy.

Therefore, the international nonproliferation regime became an extension of Brazilian domestic politics, in which national leaders benefited from the ability to tie their hands by creating an international commitment that increased the cost of reversing to previous military policies.[63] Transferring the policymaking process to the international level also mobilized those coalitions who had the most to gain from the norms implicit in the nonproliferation regime, such as diplomats, civilian scientists, and environmentalists.[64] In that sense, Brazil resembles other democratizing and liberalizing states that joined the regime in the early 1990s, including Argentina and South Africa. For these states, domestic considerations and civil-military relations provided strong incentives to reverse their opposition toward the regime.

If domestic politics plays such an important role in ensuring adherence to the nonproliferation regime, what domestic motivations inspired Mexico to join the regime so early in the 1960s? Why did Mexico become a leading advocate of nuclear disarmament and nonproliferation in Latin America? If Brazil's critical juncture was the 1964 military coup, Mexico's critical juncture was the 1962 Cuban Missile Crisis. As argued above, the crisis not only prompted a foreign policy dilemma with Cuba, but it also triggered a national security debate about how to react to the nearby Soviet missiles. One option included a military response, but only at the expense of inviting the armed forces to contribute to the Mexican decision-making process. This would have entailed either an agreement with the United States to obtain an explicit nuclear umbrella, a request to deploy U.S. missiles on Mexican territory to protect the country against an attack from Moscow, or the development of military nuclear capabilities. These options, however, represented too much for a political regime that had based its stability on the exclusion of the armed forces from the single-party system. Indeed, Mexico had been able to guarantee civilian rule and stable civil-military relations by co-opting the military's political behavior, in exchange for which the armed forces were given the autonomy to decide upon promotions, doctrine, strategy, and military operations. This eventually guaranteed a depoliticized military that was servant to the party.[65] The option of securitizing and militarizing nuclear issues in Mexico was thus ruled out because it was deemed to be dangerous for the internal stability of the political regime. Mexican rulers at the time were adamant about involving the military in political issues, in part because they wanted to avert an insubordination of the kind experienced in South America, in countries such as Brazil. The fear of excessive military influence prompted the early demilitarization of Mexican politics.

Consequently, an alternative plan had to be devised to deal with the consequences of the Cuban Missile Crisis. In U.S.-Soviet relations, this translated into the détente; in Mexico, the path followed was an indisputable resolution in favor of nuclear disarmament and nonproliferation. In 1963, Adolfo Lopez Mateos (Mexico's first civilian president in the postrevolutionary era) instructed Minister of Foreign Affairs Manuel Tello and his representative to Brazil, Alfonso Garcia Robles (who would later win the 1982 Nobel Peace Prize for the Tlatelolco Treaty), to immediately embark on multilateral negotiations to ban nuclear weapons in Latin American territories.[66] The decision to rely on diplomacy instead of traditional security and military policies was clearly strategic and motivated by domestic politics. Denuclearization provided an opportunity to de-secure nuclear issues by making them a feature of diplomatic and multilateral negotiations. Hence, for Mexico, nuclear proliferation became a legal issue instead of a military affair, whereby treaties, norms, and rules were political tools with which to constrain proliferation options. In making this choice, Mexican presidents delegated a sensitive security issue to its diplomatic corps, enabling civilians to insulate the military establishment from the temptations of nuclearization, while maintaining civilian supremacy and political stability in a regime that was all but democratic. This, again, reinforces the argument that transferring authority to an international regime helps diffuse certain domestic coalitions, while it mobilizes others who might share the international norms implicit in the regime or those who have a stake in global trends.

The policy embraced by Mexico was not only less costly than the alternative; it also allowed the country to maintain full civilian control of its own nuclear program, while averting any suspicion of its intentions and ambitions. Paradoxically, the move satisfied all parties involved. First, participation in arms control agreements offered Mexico a forum in which the country was free of conflict with the United States. Washington had expressed interest in and support for regional denuclearization efforts because they explicitly prohibited Soviet missiles in Latin American territory, averting a future nuclear crisis in the region. This reinforces the argument that a propitious international context and support from the United States can affect incentives among middle powers. Second, the leftist movement in Mexico was equally satisfied. Labor unions, the Communist Party, and intellectuals had developed strong ties with Cuba, but Mexico's stand on nuclear issues appeared politically neutral and even anti-American. In sum, the support for nonproliferation appeased the military, satisfied the left, and mobilized the diplomatic establishment, while portraying an international image for Mexico that was neither pro-American nor pro-Soviet.

In due course, Mexico became Latin America's norm entrepreneur in nonproliferation forums. Its position in favor of disarmament and nuclear-weapon-free zones during the Cold War era became institutionalized and embedded in Mexican diplomacy. Once this stand was taken and assumed, Mexico's support for nonproliferation became "sacred," nearly subject to path dependence, in the sense that it was almost impossible to reverse this path. Diplomats in Mexico would often refer to their nonproliferation policies as part of a legacy, which they branded as the Garcia Robles doctrine, in reference to the founding father of the Tlatelolco regime.

LESSONS FROM THE PAST, PRESENT POLICIES, AND IMPLICATIONS FOR THE FUTURE

Given the relevance of both U.S. foreign policy and civil-military relations in Latin America, what should we expect from the region in terms of support or opposition toward the nonproliferation regime today? A number of lessons can be drawn from this historical and comparative case study.

First, policies, actions, and rhetoric from nuclear states can often have unintended consequences in the Western Hemisphere. During the Cold War era, U.S. nuclear denial policies generated negative incentives for potential proliferators, such as Brazil, to join international regimes like the NPT. To date, Washington appears to be making similar mistakes as it once again provides sticks and carrots to different states with varying nuclear ambitions. In particular, the 2008 nuclear deal with India now allows the United States to sell nuclear fuel, technology, and reactors to New Delhi for peaceful energy, despite the fact that India tested nuclear bombs in 1974 and 1998 and never signed the NPT.[67] Other states will have learned the lessons from this nuclear agreement either through emulation or by socialization. And no other state in Latin America is as interested in the Indian case as Brazil.

Like India, Brazil feels entitled to international status and recognition. The U.S. endorsement of New Delhi's nuclear program and its support for a permanent seat in the UN Security Council provides strong incentives for Brazil to follow the Indian path.[68] This could lead Brazilian leaders to reverse, reconsider, or condition their country's nonnuclear status. As Brazilian scholar Diego Santos Vieira de Jesus reminds us, Brazil is using nuclear policy to promote its new role as an "emerging power" by developing close relations with other southern and nuclear partners, including India and China.[69] Hence, U.S. nonproliferation policies in India may have established a wrong precedent, since other countries will demand similar concessions to those granted to the South Asian nuclear power.

Second, while Brazil has joined the NPT and Tlatelolco regimes, and even founded its own regional inspection mechanism (ABACC), its commitment to the nonproliferation regime remains ambivalent. Brazil needs nuclear energy to deal with its own energy shortages. Blackouts caused by low rainfall and droughts in 2000 and 2001 increased the domestic demand for civilian nuclear power programs.[70] Yet, in 2004, Brasilia denied the IAEA permission to carry out inspections in its uranium enrichment plant in Resende, near Rio de Janeiro. A confidential agreement signed between Brazil and the IAEA increased the agency's access to the nuclear plant but was short of unrestricted inspections. Brazil temporarily suspended Resende's official start date in 2006 in an effort to avoid comparisons with Iran, which had also restricted inspections to its nuclear facilities.[71] Still, Brazil continued to resist efforts to increase the IAEA's inspections mandate via the Additional Protocol to the NPT.

In fact, Argentina and Brazil closed ranks again and requested a joint exception to the Additional Protocol. They argued that ABACC exempted them from making additional arrangements with the IAEA. For Buenos Aires and Brasilia,

ABACC had already reached an agreement with the IAEA in 1997, giving inspectors access to any part of the country and ensuring the absence of nondeclared nuclear materials and activities.[72] Brazil has refused to sign the IAEA's Additional Protocol, mainly because it perceives the system as intrusive and jeopardizing its ability to develop an independent and indigenous centrifuge technology.[73] Luis Pinguelli Rosa, head of Electrobras, the national electric company, declared that "there are no conceptual secrets.... But there are advanced technological solutions, such as equipment, setup and materials, that Brazil has the right to guard."[74] In 2010, Samuel Pinheiro Gimaraes, Brazil's former minister of strategic affairs under the Lula administration, denounced the Additional Protocol for allowing nuclear weapon states to have free access to the most sensitive nuclear technologies of developing states. In his view, the protocol's guidelines on nuclear technology could promote industrial espionage.[75]

Critics of the Argentine-Brazilian exception, such as Carnegie analyst Mark Hibbs, correctly point out that the Additional Protocol and the ABACC are intended to build confidence that nuclear activities are peaceful, but they are not the same. As Hibbs argues:

> The former is a legal document setting forth inspection rights and the latter is an institution. The Additional Protocol provides the IAEA specific rights to access a wealth of information that is outside the purview of standard NPT safeguards agreements, especially concerning undeclared activities. The agreement between the IAEA and ABACC, on the other hand, is similar to standard NPT safeguards agreements and does not give the IAEA rights specified by the Additional Protocol.[76]

Furthermore, the ABACC cannot move unless the governments of Argentina and Brazil, which effectively control it, move forward; so it has less political independence to autonomously assess information provided by the governments. The exception clause given to Argentina and Brazil also raises the possibility that other countries with access to sensitive nuclear material will request exceptional treatment, thus undermining the multilateral nonproliferation regime. Ironically, the ABACC concession created a similar condition to the one that Brazil had criticized for decades before joining the NPT, namely, a regime based on discrimination and exceptions with two different types of legal obligations, one for ABACC members and another for non-ABACC states.

If Brazil pursues civilian and peaceful interests, then why is it so hesitant to allow nuclear inspectors under the IAEA Additional Protocol? Again, civil-military relations offer an answer to this puzzle. While the nuclear plant is for commercial use, designed to enrich uranium to 3.5–5 percent, the navy developed its technology. Military interests are thus still very much vested in Brazil's nuclear program. The resistance to open the Resende plant for inspection is in direct response to the military's continuous involvement in nuclear policy. The Brazilian Navy had always wanted to develop a nuclear-powered submarine, for which uranium would have to be enriched to 20 percent. To date, civilian leaders appear to have conceded to this demand. In 2008, President Lula's National Defense Strategy called for the mastery of the complete nuclear fuel cycle and for the building of nuclear-powered submarines. The Brazilian government has designated its production facilities for nuclear submarine construction as restricted military areas, thus denying IAEA inspectors access to such facilities. Military politics thus continue to shape Brazil's nuclear project.[77] Moreover, according to Hibbs, if Brazil were to join the IAEA Additional Protocol, it would be obliged to render additional information about its nuclear parallel project and "disclose to the IAEA any high-level radioactive waste inventories, which would testify to historical production of undeclared nuclear material processing in the country."

Furthermore, there is strong suspicion that the technology used by the navy to build the nuclear plant was based on the design by the European enrichment consortium URENCO, which would, as it has been pointed out, "undermine Brazil's claim to indigenous development of the centrifuges, as well as [lead to] questions about how the design was acquired."[78] From a civil-military perspective, Brazil's reservation toward the IAEA inspection system is, in fact, consistent with the military's known secrecy and lack of transparency. If Brazil were to develop a nuclear program with military assistance, then such a decision would cast doubt as to the strength of regional and global nonproliferation norms, which arguably dissuade states from considering the nuclear option.

The Brazilian Constitution and the international obligations within the NPT and Tlatelolco legally forbid Brazil from acquiring a nuclear weapon, although these legal obligations have not silenced those who believe the country should develop a nuclear device. A coalition within the military and defense establishments remained skeptical about Brazil's accession to the nonproliferation regime. For example, in 2009, Vice President Jose Alencar publically declared that nuclear weapons would be a boon to the security of Brazil. Alencar, who was a former minister of defense, declared: "The nuclear weapon, used as an instrument of deterrence, is of great importance for a country that has 15,000 kilometers of border to the west and a territorial sea that contains oil reserves."[79] This was a shocking declaration coming from one of Brazil's highest public authorities. The presidential spokesman quickly dismissed Alencar's comments, which he argued "did not reflect the position of the government."[80] Still, the vice president's statements raised questions about why a peaceful country, surrounded by mostly friendly countries, would require a nuclear bomb for deterrence. Once again, the predominant view among some military strategists is that Brazil conceded too much when it joined the NPT and Tlatelolco. Reversing the decision to become nuclear is thus suggested as a means of recovering bargaining leverage and power status. On the other hand, environmental groups, scholars, diplomats, and some scientists (not military scientists) consider that such a move is fundamentally flawed because it could destabilize the region and harm Brazil's national interests. As global public policy expert Oliver Stuenkel argues, "Brazil could conceivably use its status as the only BRIC (Brazil, Russia, India, and China) member without nuclear weapons to play a leading role in the quest for global disarmament."[81]

Ultimately, this means that nuclear analysts need to pay close attention to Brazil's domestic politics, specifically to civil-military relations. Brazil has been able to achieve substantial gains in terms of democratic consolidation (especially during the Cardoso administration), but institutional civilian control remains inherently weak. The Ministry of Defense operates mostly as an administrative agency, with little impact on strategy and doctrine; congressional oversight of the armed forces is notoriously low; and the armed forces continue to operate with a degree of institutional autonomy.[82] While the military is no longer in power, it continues to exercise influence over security and nuclear issues.

This leads us to the third and final question: Which is the ideal country to help reinvigorate nuclear disarmament and nonproliferation discussions in the region? For decades, the leading Latin American partner was Mexico, the country that had chosen nuclear restraint and whose embrace of disarmament initiatives helped propel global and regional nonproliferation norms. If anything, the nonproliferation regime requires more than just solid norms and principles to work; it also needs norm entrepreneurs and leadership. As Australian National University expert Maria Rost Rublee argues, nuclear threshold states that have chosen restraint play a significant role in this regard. Their commitment to a nonnuclear status provides "a moral stance against nuclear weapons," leading to an energetic support of global disarmament."[83]

Yet, Mexico's support for the nonproliferation regime is slowly eroding, in part due to domestic politics and U.S. influence. This too can undermine both regional and global disarmament efforts. Two dynamics are in operation in Mexico. First, the traditional role of the armed forces is being revised because of the government's offensive launch against drug cartels. Increasingly, internal security has become the main issue of concern, with nuclear proliferation occupying a secondary role. Recent survey polls conducted by one of Mexico City's leading public research institutes show that Mexicans feel threatened by drug trafficking and organized crime, global warming, AIDS, food shortages, and the global economic crisis, in that order.[84] In a country that has just recently democratized, politicians and diplomats alike feel compelled to follow their constituents' wishes. In this context, the armed forces are being asked to perform policing missions, thus occupying a more active and present role in politics than in the past. Not surprisingly, Mexico's diplomatic corps pays increasing interest to promoting and establishing an international regime for small weapons and gun control, which, ironically, is inspired by the nonproliferation regime. At the same time, the shadow of the Cuban Missile Crisis has vanished, as few Mexicans seem to remember the negative consequences of nuclear proliferation. Mexico's unconditional support for the nonproliferation regime is thus in question.

The second dynamic is directly linked to Mexico's close relationship with Washington. Since the early 1990s, there has been a tendency toward bilateralism, in which the U.S. role in Mexican politics increased at the expense of multilateralism. Mexico's economic and trade policy relies heavily on the North American Free Trade Agreement (NAFTA), since more than 86 percent of its exports go to the United States and Canada.[85] With more than 70 percent of its GDP derived from trade, Mexico's bilateral relationship with Washington has a predominance that no other issue occupies in the Mexican foreign policy agenda. There is no doubt that NAFTA has made Mexico and Washington close partners. This is evident in Mexico's voting behavior in the UN General Assembly, as well as in NPT review conferences, especially since 1995, when Mexico flatly sided with Washington after decades of opposition.[86] The strong bilateral policy has affected the country's policy in the regime itself. Personnel, resources, money, and infrastructure go to fund bilateral initiatives, including consulates and support for Mexican communities in the United States. With limited diplomatic ties in Africa, the Middle East, and Asia, Mexico is at a clear disadvantage to negotiate with members of the General Assembly, the Group of 77, and the Non-Aligned Movement (made up mostly of African and Asian states), all of which are influential in the nonproliferation regime. In other words, the bilateralization of

Mexico's foreign policy has undermined its traditional leading role in the multilateral nonproliferation regime.

The findings in this chapter lead to a number of policy prescriptions. Lessons drawn from Latin America suggest that efforts should perhaps be made to promote stable civil-military relations in countries with nuclear energy programs by strengthening civilian control of them. Interestingly enough, few civil-military relations promotion programs have an interest in nuclear policy issues. They focus instead on parliamentary control, defense spending reduction, and military effectiveness. Perhaps it is time for the United States to shift its attention away from sanctions and nuclear carrots and toward consolidating civilian control of nuclear energy programs.

Notes

A version of this chapter appeared as "Brazil and Mexico in the Nonproliferation Regime: Common Structures and Divergent Trajectories in Latin America", by Arturo C. Sotomayor, *Nonproliferation Review* 20, no. 1 (2013): 81–105. Permission for use here is granted by Taylor & Francis.

1. For a review of the literature on middle powers, see Andrew F. Cooper, ed., *Niche Diplomacy: Middle Powers after the Cold War* (Houndmills, Bassingstoke, Hampshire, U.K.: Macmillan, 1997), 1–24; and Andrew Hurrell, "Some Reflections on the Role of Intermediate Powers in International Institutions," in "Paths to Power: Foreign Policy Strategies of International Studies," ed. Andrew Hurrell, Andrew F. Cooper, Guadalupe González González, Ricardo Ubiraci Sennes, and Srini Sitaraman, Working Paper no. 244, Woodrow Wilson International Center for Scholars, Washington, D.C., March 2000.

2. On Brazil and Mexico's role in the UN system, see Arturo C. Sotomayor, "Different Paths and Divergent Policies in the UN Security System: Brazil and Mexico in Comparative Perspective," *International Peacekeeping* 16, no. 3 (2009): 364–78.

3. Kenneth N. Waltz, *Theory of International Politics* (Reading, Mass.: McGraw-Hill, 1979), pp. 102–28.

4. Stephen M. Walt, *The Origins of Alliances* (Ithaca, N.Y.: Cornell University Press, 1987), 29–30.

5. For a debate on U.S. power and influence in the Western Hemisphere, see David R. Mares, "Regional Conflict Management in Latin America: Power Complemented by Diplomacy," in *Regional Orders: Building Security in a New World*, ed. David A. Lake and Patrick M. Morgan (University Park: Pennsylvania State University Press, 1997), 195–218.

6. David R. Mares, "Middle Powers under Regional Hegemony: To Challenge or Acquiesce in Hegemonic Enforcement," *International Studies Quarterly* 32, no. 4 (1998): 454.

7. I follow the insights developed by Edward D. Mansfield and Jon C. Pevehouse, "Democratization and International Organizations," *International Organization* 60, no. 1 (2006): 137–67.

8. Etel Solingen, *Regional Orders at Century's Dawn: Global and Domestic Influences on Grand Strategy* (Princeton, N.J.: Princeton University Press, 1988).

9. Ibid., 9.

10. Ibid., 10.

11. See Miriam Fendius Elman, "The Foreign Policies of Small States: Challenging Neorealism in Its Own Backyard," *British Journal of Political Science* 25, no. 2 (1995): 171–217.

12. Maria Rost Rublee, "The Nuclear Threshold States: Challenges and Opportunities Posed by Brazil and Japan," *Nonproliferation Review* 17, no. 1 (2010): 49.

13. See Treaty on the Non-Proliferation of Nuclear Weapons, March 5, 1970, Article IV, para. 1 "Nothing in this Treaty shall be interpreted as affecting the Inalienable right of all the Parties to the Treaty to develop research, production and use of nuclear energy for peaceful purposes without discrimination and in conformity with Articles I and II of this Treaty."

14. Emanuel Adler, *The Power of Ideology: The Quest for Technological Autonomy in Argentina and Brazil* (Berkeley: University of California Press, 1987).

15. Monica Serrano, "Brazil and Argentina," in *Nuclear Proliferation after the Cold War*, ed. Mitchell Reiss and Robert S. Litwak (Baltimore: Woodrow Wilson Center Press, 1994), 237.

16. Etel Solingen, "Macropolitical Consensus and Lateral Autonomy in Industrial Policy: The Nuclear Sector in Brazil and Argentina," *International Organization* 47, no. 2 (1993): 263–98; Etel Solingen, *Industrial Policy, Technology, and International Bargaining: Designing Nuclear Industries in Argentina and Brazil* (Stanford, Calif.: Stanford University Press, 1996).

17. José Goldemberg, "Brazil," in *Non-proliferation: The Why and the Wherefore*, ed. Jozef Goldblat (London: Taylor & Francis, 1985), 83.

18. John R. Redick, *Military Potential of Latin American Nuclear Energy Programs*" (Beverly Hills, Calif.: Sage, 1972), 26.

19. See Treaty on the Non-Proliferation of Nuclear Weapons, March 5, 1970, Article V.

20. See Adler, *Power of Ideology*; and Jorge A. Aja Espil, "Argentina," in Goldblat, *Non-proliferation*, 73–76.

21. See Paulo S. Wrobel, "A Diplomacia Nuclear Brasileira: A Não-Proliferação Nuclear e o Tratado de Tlatelolco" [Brazil's nuclear diplomacy: Nonproliferation and the Treaty of Tlatelolco], *Contexto Internacional* 15 (January–June 1993), 29.

22. Serrano, "Brazil and Argentina," 237.

23. Treaty for the Prohibition of Nuclear Weapons in Latin America and the Caribbean (Treaty of Tlatelolco), February 14, 1967, Article 18.

24. For a genesis of the negotiations leading to the Treaty of Tlatelolco, see Alfonso García Robles, *El Tratado de Tlatelolco: Genesis, alcance y propósitos de la proscripeión de*

las armas nucleares en la América Latina [The Treaty of Tlatelolco: Genesis, scope and purposes of the prohibition of nuclear weapons in Latin America] (Mexico City: El Colegio de México, 1967).

25. Wrobel, "Diplomacia Nuclear Brasileira," 44.

26. Jeffrey A. Frieden, *Debt, Development, and Democracy: Modern Political Economy and Latin America, 1965–1985* (Princeton, N.J.: Princeton University Press, 1991), 180–82.

27. Redick, *Military Potential*, 31.

28. For reviews on the peaceful disposition of Latin American states, see Paul R. Hensel, "Contentious Issues and World Politics: The Management of Territorial Claims in the Americas, 1816–1992," *International Studies Quarterly* 45, no. 1 (2001): 81–109; David R. Mares, *Violent Peace: Militarized Interstate Bargaining in Latin America* (New York: Columbia University Press, 2001); and Jorge I. Domínguez, David Mares, Manual Orozco, David Scott Palmer, Francisco Rojas Aravena, and Adrés Serbin, "Boundary Disputes in Latin America," Peaceworks, no. 50 (Washington, D.C.: U.S. Institute of Peace, 2003), http://www.usip.org/publications/boundary-disputes-latin-america.

29. See, for instance, Arie M. Kacowicz, *The Impact of Norms in International Society: The Latin American Experience, 1881–2001* (Notre Dame, Ind.: Notre Dame University Press, 2005); and Carolyn M. Shaw, *Cooperation, Conflict, and Consensus in the Organization of American States* (New York: Palgrave Macmillan, 2004).

30. S. E. Kenza de Garcia Robles, "Une alternative en matiere de non-proliferation: Les zones libre d'armes nucleaires" [An alternative to nonproliferation: Nuclear-free zones], *Relations Internationales et Strategiques* 17 (1995): 192–99.

31. Roberto Russell, "Conflicto y armamentismo en América Latin" [Conflict and arms build-up in Latin America], in *Desarme y Desarrollo en América Latina* [Disarmament and development in Latin America], ed. Mónica Hirst (Buenos Aires, Argentina: Fundación para la Democracia y la Paz, 1990), 61–67.

32. Goldemberg, "Brazil," 84.

33. The literature on Argentina and Brazil's nuclear quest includes Adler, *Power of Ideology*; Michael Barletta, "Democratic Security and Diversionary Peace: Nuclear Confidence-Building in Argentina and Brazil," paper delivered at the Latin American Studies Association Annual Meeting, Chicago, September 24–26, 1998; Solingen, *Industrial Policy*; Carlos Castro Madero and Esteban A. Takacs, *Política Nuclear Argentina: Avance o retroceso?* [Argentine nuclear policy: Progress or setbacks?] (Buenos Aires, Argentina: El Ateneo, 1991); Redick, *Military Potential*; Jeffrey W. Knopf, "The Importance of International Learning," *Review of International Studies* 29, no. 2 (2003): 198–207; Jack Child, *Geopolitics and Conflict in South America: Quarrels among Neighbors* (New York: Praeger; Stanford, Calif.: Hoover Institution Press, 1985).

34. Mitchell Reiss, *Bridled Ambition: Why Countries Constrain Their Nuclear Capabilities* (Washington, D.C.: Woodrow Wilson Center Press, 1995), 14.

35. Andrew Hurrell, "Security In Latin America," *International Affairs* 74, no. 3 (1998): 531.

36. On the Brazil–West Germany nuclear agreement, see Michael Barletta, "The Military Nuclear Program in Brazil," Center for International Security and Arms Control, Stanford University, August 1997.

37. See Goldemberg, "Brazil," and Espil, "Argentina."

38. The first attempt of bilateral cooperation between the Argentine and Brazilian military regimes took place during the 1970s, when they successfully resolved their dispute regarding the Itaipu dam and the use of hydroelectric power. Then, in 1980, the military governments of generals (and presidents) Jorge Videla and João Figueiredo signed an agreement on the peaceful use of nuclear energy, which marked the beginning of the Argentine-Brazilian nuclear entente. The military autocracies of Argentina and Brazil mostly cooperated via informal means. The establishment of formal institutions only took place after the two countries democratized. For more information on the Argentine-Brazilian rapprochement, see Paul L. Leventhal and Sharon Tanzer, eds., *Averting a Latin American Nuclear Arms Race: New Prospects and Challenges for Argentine-Brazil Nuclear Co-operation* (New York: St. Martin's Press; Washington, D.C: Nuclear Control Institute, 1992); Wayne A. Selcher, "Brazilian-Argentine Relations in the 1980s: From Wary Rivalry to Friendly Competition," *Journal of Interamerican Studies and World Affairs* 27, no. 2 (1985), pp. 25–53; João Resende-Santos, "The Origins of Security Cooperation in the Southern Cone," *Latin American Politics and Society* 44, no. 4 (2002): 89–126; Charles A. Kupchan, *How Enemies Become Friends: The Sources of Stable Peace* (Princeton, N.J.: Princeton University Press, 2010), 122–34; Maria Regina Soares de Lima, "The Political Economy of Brazilian Foreign Policy: Nuclear Energy, Trade, and Itaipu," PhD diss., Vanderbilt University, 1986; and Alessandro Warley Candeas, "Relaçôes Brasil-Argentina: Uma análise dos advances e recuos" [Brazil-Argentina relations: An analysis of progress and retreats], *Revista Brasilieira de Politica Interacional* 48, no. 1 (2005): 178–213.

39. Olga Pellicer de Brody, *México y la Revolución Cubana* [Mexico and the Cuban Revolution] (Mexico City: El Colegio de México, 1972); Ana Covarrubias, "Cuba and Mexico: A Case for Mutual Nonintervention," *Cuban Studies*, no. 26 (1996): 121–41.

40. T.V. Paul, *Power versus Prudence: Why Nations Forgo Nuclear Weapons* (Montreal: McGill-Queen's University Press, 2000); and Nina Tannenwald, *The Nuclear Taboo: The United States and the Non-use of Nuclear Weapons since 1945* (Cambridge: Cambridge University Press, 2007).

41. Alejandro Nadal Egea, "Trayectorias de misiles balistícos internacionales: Implicaciones para los vecinos de las superpotencias" [Trajectories of the international ballistic missiles: Implications for states neighboring superpowers], *Foro Internacional* 30 (1989): 93–114.

42. Serrano, "Brazil and Argentina," 30.

43. Alfred C. Stepan, "The New Professionalism of Internal Warfare and Military Role Expansion," in *Authoritarian Brazil: Origins, Policies, and Future*, ed. Alfred C. Stepan (New Haven, Conn.: Yale University Press, 1973), 47–65.

44. Wrobel, "Diplomacia Nuclear Brasileira."

45. Barletta, "Military Nuclear Program," 6.

46. Redick, "Military Potential," 18–29.

47. Barletta, "Military Nuclear Program," 6.

48. David Albright, "Bomb Potential for South America," *Bulletin of the Atomic Scientists* 45, no. 4 (1989): 16–20; Redick, "Military Potential"; Adler, *Power of Ideology*; Jean Krasno, "Non-proliferation: Brazil's Secret Nuclear Program," *Orbis: A Journal of World Affairs* 38, no. 3 (1994): 425–36.

49. Pedro Paulo Leoni Ramos, minister of strategic affairs, testimony, "Comissão Parlamentar Mista de Inquérito Destinada a Apurar o Programa Autônomo de Energia Nuclear, Também Conhecido como 'Programa Paralelo'" [Joint Parliamentary Inquiry Commission Intended to Investigate the Autonomous Nuclear Energy Program, also known as the "Parallel Program"], Congressional Report no. 13, November 14, 1990, 101 (personal translation).

50. José Goldemberg, minister of science and technology, testimony, "Comissão Parlamentar Mista de Inquérito Destinada a Apurar o Programa Autônomo de Energia Nuclear, Também Conhecido como 'Programa Paralelo'" [Joint Parliamentary Inquiry Commission Intended to Investigate the Autonomous Nuclear Energy Program, also known as the "Parallel Program"], Congressional Report no. 13, November 14, 1990, 88 (personal translation).

51. Conclusões [Conclusions], "Comissão Parlamentar Mista de Inquérito Destinada a Apurar o Programa Autônomo de Energia Nuclear, Também Conhecido como 'Programa Paralelo'" [Joint Parliamentary Inquiry Commission Intended to Investigate the Autonomous Nuclear Energy Program, also known as the "Parallel Program"], Congressional Report no. 13, November 14, 1990, 107 (personal translation).

52. Reiss, *Bridled Ambition*, 51.

53. On Brazil's transition to democracy, see Juan J. Linz and Alfred Stepan, *Problems of Democratic Transition and Consolidation: Southern Europe, South America, and Post-Communist Europe* (Baltimore: Johns Hopkins University Press, 1996), 166–89.

54. Solingen, *Regional Orders*, 147–48.

55. Julia Preston, "Brazil's Leader Brings Vigorous Image, Mixed Record," *Washington Post*, June 18, 1991.

56. There is a large body of literature that addresses the foundation and establishment of ABACC. See, for instance, Barletta, "Democratic Security and Diversionary Peace"; Julio César Carasales, *De Rivales a Socios: El proceso de cooperación nuclear entre Argentina y Brasil* [From rivals to partners: The process of nuclear cooperation between Ar-

gentina and Brazil] (Buenos Aires, Argentina: Grupo Editorial Latinoamericano, 1997); Javier Corrales and Richard E. Feinberg, "Regimes of Cooperation in the Western Hemisphere: Power, Interests, and Intellectual Traditions," *International Studies Quarterly* 43, no. 1 (1999): 1–36; Hurrell, "Security in Latin America; Andrew Hurrell, "Emerging Security Community in South America?," in *Security Communities*, ed. Emanuel Adler and Michael Barnett (Cambridge: Cambridge University Press, 1998), 243–45; Knopf, "The Importance of International Learning,"; John R. Redick, Julio C. Carasales, and Paulo S. Wrobel, "Nuclear Rapprochement: Argentina, Brazil, and the Nonproliferation Regime," *Washington Quarterly* 18, no. 1 (1995): 107–22; Serrano, "Brazil and Argentina,"; Arturo C. Sotomayor, "Civil-Military Affairs and Security Institutions in the Southern Cone: The Sources of Argentine-Brazilian Nuclear Cooperation," *Latin American Politics and Society* 46, no. 4 (2004): 29–60; Paulo S. Wrobel, "From Rivals to Friends: The Role of Public Declarations in Argentine-Brazilian Rapprochement," in *Declaratory Diplomacy: Rhetorical Initiatives and Confidence Building*, ed. Michael Krepon, Jenny S. Drezin, and Michael Newbill, report no. 27 (Washington, D.C.: Henry L. Stimson Center, 1999), 135–51.

57. See Sotomayor, "Civil-Military Affairs."

58. Mónica Hirst, "Security Policies, Democratization, and Regional Integration in the Southern Cone," in *International Security and Democracy: Latin America and the Caribbean in the Post–Cold War Era*, ed. Jorge I. Dominguez (Pittsburgh: University of Pittsburgh Press, 1995), 106.

59. Carasales, *De Rivales a Socios*, 116–17.

60. James Brooke, "Brazil Uncovers Plan by Military to Build Atom Bomb and Stops It," *New York Times*, October 9, 1990.

61. Eliézer Rizzo de Oliveira and Samuel Alves Soares, "Brasil: Forças Armadas, direção política e formato institucional" [Brazil: Armed forces, political direction and institutional format], in *Democracia e Forças Armadas no Cone Sul* [Democracy and Armed Forces in the Southern Cone], ed. Maria Celina D'Araujo and Celso Castro (Rio de Janeiro, RJ: Editora FGV, 2000), 112–16.

62. Sotomayor, "Civil-Military Affairs."

63. See Mansfield and Pevenhouse, "Democratization and International Organizations."

64. For a theoretical discussion on the domestic effects of international organizations see Lisa L. Martin and Beth A. Simmons, "Theories and Empirical Studies of International Institutions," *International Organization* 52, no. 4 (1998): 747–57.

65. Roderic Ai Camp, *Generals in the Palacio: The Military in Modern Mexico* (New York: Oxford University Press, 1992); Monica Serrano, "The Armed Branch of the State: Civil-Military Relations in Mexico," *Journal of Latin American Studies* 27, no. 2 (1995): 423–48; Samuel P. Huntington, *Political Order in Changing Societies* (New Haven, Conn.: Yale University Press, 1968), pp. 315–24.

66. Miguel Marín Bosch, *Alfonso Garcia Robles: Mexico, Nobel de la Paz* (Mexico City: SEP-SER, 1984); Mónica Serrano, *Common Security in Latin America: The 1967 Treaty of Tlatelolco* (London: Institute of Latin American Studies, 1992).

67. See Peter Baker, "Senate Approves Indian Nuclear Deal," *New York Times*, October 2, 2008, www.nytimes.com/2008/10/02/washington/02webnuke.html?ref=nuclearprogram.

68. See Sheryl Gay Stolberg and Jim Yardley, "Countering China, Obama Backs India for U.N. Council," *New York Times*, November 8, 2010, http://www.nytimes.com/2010/11/09/world/asia/09prexy.html.

69. Diego Santos Vieira de Jesus, "The Brazilian Way," *Nonproliferation Review* 17, no. 3 (2010): 552.

70. Ibid., 557.

71. On the nature of the Brazilian agreement with the IAEA see Etel Solingen, "Hindsight and Foresight in South American Nonproliferation Trends in Argentina, Brazil, and Venezuela," in *Over the Horizon Proliferation Threats*, ed. James J. Wirtz and Peter R. Lavoy (Stanford, Calif.: Stanford University Press, 2012), 145; and Claire Applegarth, "Brazil Permits Greater IAEA Inspection," *Arms Control Today*, November 2004, http://www.armscontrol.org/act/2004_11/Brazil.

72. See Marcos Marzo, "Additional Protocol: Logic and Impact," Brazilian-Argentine Agency for Accounting and Control of Nuclear Energy: Working Paper, Rio de Janeiro, Brazil, January 2012, http://www.abacc.org.br/wp-content/uploads/2012/01/Additional-Protocol_Marzo.pdf.

73. Vieira de Jesus, "Brazilian Way," p. 558.

74. "Scientist Says Brazil Has Right to Nuclear Secrets," *Global Security Newswire*, April 8, 2004, http://www.nti.org/gsn/article/scientist-says-brazil-has-right-to-nuclear-secrets.

75. See Mark Hibbs, "Nuclear Suppliers Group and the IAEA Additional Protocol," Carnegie Endowment for International Peace, Washington, D.C., August 18, 2010, http://www.carnegieendowment.org/2010/08/18/nuclear-suppliers-group-and-iaea-additional-protocol/ep. See also "Fighting the Nuclear Fight: When Nuclear Sheriffs Quarrel," *Economist*, October 30, 2008, http://www.economist.com/node/12516611?story_id=12516611.

76. Hibbs, "Nuclear Suppliers Group."

77. For an assessment of Brazil's nuclear program see Hans Rühle, "Nuclear Proliferation in Latin America: Is Brazil Developing the Bomb?" *Spiegel Online*, May 7, 2010, http://www.spiegel.de/international/world/0,1518,693336,00.html.

78. Rublee, "Nuclear Threshold States," 55.

79. See "Brazil Needs Nukes, VP Says," *Global Security Newswire*, September 28, 2009, http://www.nti.org/gsn/article/brazil-needs-nukes-vp-says/.

80. Ibid.

81. Oliver Stuenkel, "Brazil Should Act on Nuclear Transparency," *World Politics Review*, October 20, 2010, http://www.worldpoliticsreview.com/articles/6776/brazil-should-act-on-nuclear-transparency.

82. For an analysis of the Ministry of Defense's institutional weaknesses, see Jorge Zavarucha, "La Fragilidad del Ministerio de Defensa Brasileño" [The fragility of the defense ministry], in *Operaciones conjuntas: Civiles y militares en la política de defensa* [Joint operations: Civilians and the military in defense policy], ed. José Huerta et al. (Lima, Peru: Serie Democracia y Fuerza Armada, 2006), 51–80; and David S. Pion-Berlin, "Political Management of the Military in Latin America," *Military Review* 85, no. 1 (2005): 19–31.

83. Rublee, "Nuclear Threshold States," 49.

84. See Guadalupe González González, Ferrán Martínez, and Jorge Schiavon, *Mexico, the Americas and the World: Foreign Policy: Public and Leader Opinion 2008* (report on the results of the third biennial national survey of the Mexican general public and leaders on foreign policy and international affairs, CIDE) (Mexico City: Center for Research and Teaching in Economics, 2009, http://www.mexicoyelmundo.cide.edu/Informacion/Imgs/Report_Mexico_the_Americas_and_the_World.pdf.

85. Antonio Ortiz Mena, "Mexico," in *The World Trade Organization: A Legal, Economic, and Political Analysis*, ed. Patrick F. J. Macrory, Arthur E. Appleton, and Michael G. Plummer (New York: Springer, 2005), 217–47.

86. See, for instance, Jorge I. Domínguez and Rafael Fernández de Castro, *The United States and Mexico: Between Partnership and Conflict* (New York: Routledge, 2001), 55–58; and Arturo Sotomayor, "U.S.-Latin American Nuclear Relations: From Commitment to Defiance", PASCC Report no. 2012 013, Project on Advanced Systems and Concepts for Countering WMD, (Monterey, Calif.: U.S. Naval Postgraduate School, Center on Contemporary Conflict, September 2012).

CHAPTER 9

The Additional Protocol in the Middle East and North Africa
Explaining Lag in Adoption

Jim Walsh

VIRTUALLY ALL COUNTRIES SUPPORT the concept of nonproliferation, and yet there is a gap between those states' preferences and their actions to strengthen the regime, even when the costs of doing so are modest. This chapter attempts to conceptualize and explain this gap. In particular, it looks at the adoption of the Additional Protocol (AP) by countries in the Middle East and North Africa (MENA).

UNDERSTANDING LAG IN THE ADOPTION OF SAFEGUARDS

The history of the nonproliferation regime is one of progressive iterations in the rules and practices governments are asked to follow to ensure compliance with their nonproliferation obligations. These arrangements, or safeguards, were first established in 1961 following the creation of the International Atomic Energy Agency (IAEA). Traditionally, safeguards involve a combination of material accountancy (i.e., confirming that no nuclear material is missing from nuclear facilities), physical security, and the use of containment and surveillance techniques. Over time, safeguards have evolved—becoming stronger, wider in scope, and supported by new technologies.[1] Safeguards were first expanded following the introduction of the Treaty on the Non-Proliferation of Nuclear Weapons (NPT) in 1970. (Article III of the treaty explicitly calls on the states parties to establish safeguards arrangements with the IAEA.) Over time safeguards continued to evolve, and in the 1990s a new enhancement, the Additional Protocol (AP), was introduced in the wake of revelations about Iraq's illicit nuclear program.

The Additional Protocol, among other things, provides the IAEA with the authority to collect more information about a wider variety of nuclear activities across the fuel cycle. It also enables the agency to make use of environmental sampling and remote monitoring to confirm a state's nonproliferation *bona fides*.[2] Many of the changes introduced in the AP are intended to address the problem of undeclared facilities—a problem that Iraq's nuclear program had made evident. Since its inception, 122 countries have adopted the protocol, but another 71 (58 percent) have not.[3] In order to devise policies that will spur more rapid acceptance, it would be helpful to know why states that otherwise support nonproliferation resist measures like the Additional Protocol.

The puzzle has at least two sides. One is why some countries are slower to adopt or never adopt nonproliferation measures beyond simple NPT ratification. A second side is why other states are faster than their counterparts to take on new nonproliferation obligations. It would be tempting to think that the answer to one question (why laggards lag) would automatically provide the answer to the second, but that may not be true and in any case would risk selecting the dependent variable. We know, for example, that the reasons why some states seek or acquire nuclear weapons and the reasons other countries do not seek or even renounce nuclear weapons are not reverse mirror images of each other.[4] Some factors are common to both sets of decisions, but there are differences too. Understanding lag will necessitate understanding laggards and adopters, but as this is a preliminary inquiry into a new topic, most attention is paid to the laggards.

HYPOTHESES

Research on why governments embrace, resist, or ignore new nonproliferation measures has not been the subject of intense scholarly investigation. The more general topic of state commitments to regimes has received some recent attention, however, mostly from scholars of international relations and scholars of international law. In general, these studies offer three broad categories of hypotheses for adoption behavior. First, there are "materialist" explanations that focus on costs, threats, and related interests. In this volume, the chapters by Deepti Choubey (who highlights the costs of Additional Protocol implementation for developing countries), Lowell H. Schwartz (who considers the role of security guarantees and interests), and Jason Enia (who looks at nonadoption from a public goods perspective) all offer explanations that, at least in part, emphasize economic and security dynamics. Second, there are "institutionalist" interpretations that look to the formal and political processes by which commitments are made. Like the first set of materialist explanations, institutionalist accounts are rationalist but focus on political variables rather than economic and security factors. Third, there are "constructivist" accounts that center on normative, ideational, or psychological dynamics—represented in this volume by Nina Srinivasan Rathbun and by Maria Rost Rublee.

The broader literature on adoption has generated some interesting findings, for example, that some commitments are most likely when participating governments believe that their pledges are less likely to be enforced. Unfortunately, many of the studies appear not to translate well to the domain of nonproliferation. Some focus on areas such as human rights, European unification, or the sex trade. Others assess issues that have a much larger economic dimension, such as treaties on labor or climate change. So, for example, studies of treaty support for labor issues have found that unemployment rates and the sectoral composition of the labor market influence outcomes—a situation not obviously analogous to nonproliferation. There is also the more general problem—not irrelevant to this inquiry's method—that a commitment to a *treaty* may not be procedurally or substantively comparable to the administrative adoption of *protocols* that enforce or upgrade previously made treaty commitments.[5]

Given these concerns, it probably makes sense to begin anew and consider hypotheses that might be relevant to the particular context of nuclear nonproliferation and the Additional Protocol. Jeffrey Fields in this volume's introductory chapter has helped lay the intellectual groundwork for such an inquiry by offering a number of hypotheses.

One set of explanations relates to the presence or absence of security threats. Fields suggests an interesting paradox, namely that countries that have already committed to the NPT and perceive themselves to be in a low-threat environment have less incentive to promote nonproliferation. He also offers a corollary, namely that countries that enjoy a security guarantee, which if credible would produce the same effect as being in a low-threat environment, similarly have a lower incentive to push for nonproliferation, because they are already safe.

Fields also points to another possible explanation. When considering Japan, he observes that Tokyo has a material interest in adopting the AP and related nonproliferation measures, because it deflects attention from the fact that Japan has a latent nuclear weapons capability. Ironically, this plausibly suggests that nuclear latency would be correlated with AP adoption. On the other hand, it is easy to imagine that states with nuclear ambitions might resist upgrades to the regime. They might hope to mask their true intentions by participating in the regime but also seek to minimize their commitments to safeguards.

As hypotheses, they suggest the following:

> Hypothesis 1. A low-threat environment (including conditions in which a state enjoys a credible security guarantee) causes AP lag.
> Hypothesis 2. A near-nuclear capability (that could invite suspicion) causes AP adoption.
> Hypothesis 3. A desire to maintain a nuclear weapons option causes AP lag.

Fields also offers two hypotheses that relate to the NPT. He suggests that governments may be reluctant to adopt the AP because they do not want to validate the discriminatory norm that is embedded in the NPT, namely that some states parties are allowed to possess nuclear weapons and maintain their good standing in the treaty despite modest progress on their disarmament obligations (Article VI). Meanwhile, the nonnuclear parties are forced to take on more and more responsibilities. A separate but related hypothesis posits that the nonnuclear weapons states (NNWS) might withhold adoption as leverage for bargaining with the nuclear weapons states (NWS) to force greater progress on disarmament. This suggests two additional hypotheses:

> Hypothesis 4. Normative concerns about the NPT's unequal obligations cause AP lag.
> Hypothesis 5. A desire for bargaining leverage with NPT NWS causes AP lag.

A third set of hypotheses relates not to the treaty itself but to the costs and benefits associated with AP adoption. One is that laggards see no benefit to the AP. As Fields postulates, they may see proliferation as an "American problem" and conclude that the AP will not generate benefits for them. This is certainly plausible, but such an explanation would have to account for why these states joined the NPT and adopted a comprehensive safeguards agreement or even several iterations of safeguards agreements only to reach a breaking point with the AP. A softer formulation of the same idea is that while countries see some value to the AP, the perceived benefit is so small that the AP takes a back seat to more pressing issues demanding attention. Combining these different strands suggests a sixth hypothesis:

> Hypothesis 6. The absence of benefit causes AP lag.

It is also possible that laggards perceive benefits in the AP, but that these benefits give them reason *not* to join. As Fields also points out, there may be a free rider problem, namely that countries can enjoy the nonproliferation benefits of the AP without having to sign up to new obligations. Here again, one would have to explain why that is true of the AP but was not true for the NPT and earlier safeguards arrangements. It is worth noting that more than a dozen NNWS are party to the NPT but do not have a comprehensive safeguards agreement in force.[6] It is possible that a free rider dynamic could apply in these cases. And so, hypothesis seven:

Hypothesis 7. Free riding causes AP lag.

It is also possible that governments see benefit from the AP for nonproliferation but also see a benefit from "selling" their signature and want to maximize the price—that is, they are holding out adoption in hope of accruing greater *individual* benefit. Like Hypothesis 2, this explanation is based on bargaining, but the bargaining is not focused on the normative dimensions of the nonproliferation regime but rather on the side payments an individual country might receive (e.g., economic aid, trade concessions). In the run-up to the 1995 NPT Review and Extension Conference, the U.S. government sent diplomats across the globe to get countries to sign up to the NPT prior to the treaty conference, so that it could strengthen its position for indefinite extension of the treaty. Side payments were very much a part of those discussions.[7]

Hypothesis 8. States seeking to maximize side payments cause AP lag.

The previous three hypotheses concern benefits: the absence of a benefit, the problem of benefits that can be enjoyed without payment, and the use of AP adoption as an asset to trade for benefits. This last hypothesis focuses on cost. Japan, for example, which has had a substantial nuclear power industry, adopted the AP but has long complained about the cost of safeguards.[8] Perhaps the economic and administrative cost of new nonproliferation obligations is simply too much for some states to assume.

Hypothesis 9. The cost of adherence causes AP lag.

A final category of hypotheses focuses on the role of politics, rather than economics. These explanations suggest that adoption is less a matter of security threats, the NPT, or the costs and benefits of adoption but instead is driven by domestic and regional politics. One potential hypothesis is that domestic opposition from the general population or from important domestic constituencies prevents states from joining the AP. Additionally, it might be expected that governments involved in active nuclear disputes with the IAEA (North Korea, Iran, and Syria) might withhold AP adoption as one part of a more general response to the IAEA. A final hypothesis in this category relates to regional politics. It suggests that a country or set of countries might withhold action on the AP to improve their bargaining position on issues that concern other governments in the region. One could imagine, for example, in decades past, the countries of southern Africa withholding participation in agreements to gain regional and domestic political advantage in their campaigns against Rhodesia or South Africa. In all, there are three hypotheses on politics.

> Hypothesis 10. Domestic opposition causes AP lag.
> Hypothesis 11. Nuclear disputes with the IAEA cause AP lag.
> Hypothesis 12. A desire for bargaining leverage on regional issues causes AP lag.

Having surveyed a number of possible hypotheses, it has to be admitted that none seems especially compelling. It may be that other explanations provide a better account or that lagging is a phenomenon that involves distinct groups of countries, or that different groups lag for different reasons.

EMPIRICAL CONTEXT

This analysis focuses on the countries of the Middle East and North Africa (MENA). And while it is tempting to run straight to the data on their AP adoption, it makes sense to first describe the broader context of regime adoption and lag. There are two reasons for doing so.

First, examining the broader empirical context can help inform an analysis of MENA behavior and reduce the tendency to selection bias. Second, it is probably necessary to distinguish between normal lag and what might be called purposive lag. Lag is a ubiquitous feature of everyday life. Few items or issues can be considered and acted upon simultaneously, and what is true of individuals is even more true of institutions, where multiple players must act together in a formal process. On average, one would expect that the larger or the more formal the institution, the greater the degree of "normal" lag. If one assumes that normal and purposive lag have different causes and thus would require different kinds of remedies, then it will be useful to distinguish the circumstances under which one kind of lag operates rather than another.

So what is a normal lag for countries adopting new nonproliferation rules? One way to get at this issue is to compare NPT ratification rates and AP adop-

TABLE 9.1. NPT ratification: All states and selected states

Year	All	Select	Year	All	Select	Year	All	Select
1968	3	0	1983	1	0	1998	1	1
1969	21	5	1984	3	0	1999	0	0
1970	38	3	1985	7	1	2000	0	0
1971	5	0	1986	5	0	2001	0	0
1972	6	0	1987	1	1	2002	1	1
1973	6	1	1988	2	1	2003	1	0
1974	1	0	1989	2	0	2004	0	0
1975	15	5	1990	2	0	2005	0	0
1976	5	1	1991	5	1	2006	1	0
1977	3	1	1992	12	1	2007	0	0
1978	2	0	1993	6	0	2008	0	0
1979	6	1	1994	7	0	2009	0	0
1980	2	1	1995	9	1	2010	0	0
1981	2	1	1996	2	0	2011	0	0
1982	4	0	1997	1	0	2012	0	0

Note: This list includes North Korea, which claims it has withdrawn from the NPT, as well as Taiwan. Taiwan joined in 1968 but was later replaced by China. Safeguards are in force in Taiwan under a three-party agreement among Taiwan, the United States, and the IAEA. The coding of North Korea is somewhat complicated, as North Korea occupies a space between proliferator and full-fledged weapons state.

tion rates. This does not provide a perfect comparison insofar as 1) NPT ratification required a much larger commitment by governments (giving up nuclear weapons versus improving ways to achieve a nonproliferation commitment that a state had already made) and 2) ratification of a treaty can require approval by a national assembly, while the AP does not. Despite its shortcomings, NPT ratification is probably a better choice for comparison than other treaties or instruments that address different kinds of issues, such as human rights or the environment.

NPT Ratification

Table 9.1 follows NPT ratification by two classes of states.[9] The first class is all countries, regardless of characteristics. As one can see, there is a burst of ratification when the treaty opens, with an all-time high of forty ratifications in 1970. After that, things settle down, but there is another surge to thirteen in 1975, the year of an NPT Review Conference and following the shock of India's 1974 nuclear test. The next high-water mark is another NPT Review Conference year, 1985. One then sees a jump in the early 1990s, driven in part by the end of the Cold War, with countries from Eastern Europe and the former Soviet Union joining, as well as two weapons states, France and China. Again, high rates of ratification in 1995 appear to be associated with the watershed NPT Review and Extension Conference.[10] Following that, the numbers decline rapidly, largely because there are fewer countries left in the pool that have not joined.

Table 9.1 also codes the behavior of a second class of thirty-three states under the label of "Select." The following list is a subset of "All" and is composed of states that are more directly relevant to nonproliferation.

Algeria	Myanmar
Argentina	North Korea
Australia	Norway
Brazil	Romania
Canada	Saudi Arabia
Chile	South Africa
Cuba	South Korea
Egypt	Spain
Germany	Sweden
Greece	Switzerland
Indonesia	Syria
Iran	Taiwan
Iraq	Turkey
Italy	Ukraine
Japan	Venezuela
Libya	Yugoslavia/Serbia
Mexico	

At one end, this subset excludes the weapons states (i.e., states that have already acquired nuclear weapons), and at the other end, it excludes countries for which a nuclear weapons program is unlikely (e.g., many of the microstates and island nations). It includes countries that have at some point demonstrated an interest in or openness to acquiring nuclear weapons (e.g., Germany, Italy, and Australia) as well as others that have been accused of harboring such an interest (e.g., Saudi Arabia).

Surprisingly, the pattern of NPT ratification for these proliferation-relevant states is not dissimilar to the picture for all countries. Again, a cluster of ratifications takes place in the first couple of years when the treaty opens, and then there are higher numbers in NPT Review years. The figures for 1994–1995 stand out a bit, but 1995 is the year of the pivotal NPT Review and Extension Conference, and

TABLE 9.2. AP adoption: All states and selected states

Year	All	Select	Year	All	Select	Year	All	Select
1997	1	1	2003	9	1	2009	8	0
1998	4	0	2004	24	7	2010	11	1
1999	3	2	2005	8	1	2011	10	1
2000	4	2	2006	8	2	2012	5	1
2001	6	2	2007	11	0	2013[a]	2	0
2002	3	1	2008	5	0	Totals	122	22

Note: Taiwan's adoption of the Additional Protocol is projected here as 2001, though there is some uncertainty. The earliest reference to Taiwan and the Additional Protocol can be found at http://www.iaea.org/About/Policy/GC/GC45/Documents/gc45-23.pdf.
[a] As of June 19, 2013.

three of the governments that ratify in those years are former Soviet bloc countries that inherited nuclear assets from the USSR (Belarus, Ukraine, and Kazakhstan).

AP Adoption

Charting adoption of the Additional Protocol is a little more complicated, because there are really three types of countries: 1) those that have adopted and for whom an agreement is in force, 2) a nontrivial number that have signed the AP but have no agreement in force, and 3) those that have so far abstained from joining. For the purpose of this analysis, the second and third categories are combined; that is, either there is an agreement in force, or there is not. Table 9.2 summarizes the results to date. Once again, the column "All" accounts for every country that has joined, while "Select" refers to the thirty-three nations that are nonnuclear weapons states and whose history or situation indicates that they could be plausible candidates for proliferation.

The good news is that the twenty-two "Select" countries that have joined the AP constitute approximately 67 percent of the total target group of proliferation-relevant states. This figure is the same as the group's NPT ratification rate for the first fifteen years of the treaty.[11] Still, the result is somewhat surprising. One would have expected a substantially higher rate for adoption of the Additional Protocol compared to the NPT in a comparable time period. This expectation is based on the fact that treaty ratification is a more institutionally onerous process, and that the decision to join or not join NPT—to retain or give up a nuclear weapons option—is a larger commitment for a government than whether to administratively strengthen a commitment that had already been made.

These results suggest that there may be something beyond "normal lag" at work here. This provisional conclusion is reinforced by the fact that many of the twenty-two proliferation-relevant countries that have signed on to the AP, while qualifying for the "select" group, are not *currently* considered to be a proliferation risk.

The AP is in force in the following proliferation-relevant countries:

Australia	Mexico
Canada	Norway
Chile	Romania
Cuba	South Africa
Germany	South Korea
Greece	Spain
Indonesia	Sweden
Iraq	Switzerland
Italy	Taiwan
Japan	Turkey
Libya	Ukraine

AP adoption by several of these countries could be characterized as significant nonproliferation victories. Japan, Libya, South Korea, Taiwan, and Turkey have all been the subject of speculation regarding their nuclear intentions. A majority of countries on this list, however, are not currently on any proliferation "watch list." Instead, they are countries that may have harbored an interest in nuclear weapons at one time in their history but have since settled comfortably into their role as NNWS. This describes Canada, Germany, and Romania, among others.

The list of proliferation-relevant countries that have not adopted the Additional Protocol is smaller but contains the names of several countries that have recently been cited as proliferation concerns:

Algeria (signed but not in force)
Argentina
Brazil
Egypt
Iran (signed but not in force)
Myanmar
North Korea

Saudi Arabia
Serbia (signed but not in force)
Syria
Venezuela

In sum, when one compares the adoption rates for the NPT and the AP, it appears as if there is abnormal lag in the adoption of the Additional Protocol. The adoption rate for the AP is hardly better than that of the NPT, despite the fact that the decision to join the NPT represented a far greater commitment and entailed a more institutionally burdensome process. It also appears that many of the states that have held back are, in fact, countries of concern with respect to possible proliferation. None of this constitutes proof, but there is enough here that those with an interest in strengthening the nonproliferation regime will want to better understand the causes of lag.

THE AP IN THE MIDDLE EAST AND NORTH AFRICA

The Middle East and North Africa are strongly represented in the category of states that are proliferation-relevant but that have not yet adopted the AP, as can be seen in the following list. Indeed, of the eleven proliferation-relevant non-adopters, almost half are in the MENA.

Algeria	Signed but not in force
Bahrain	In force
Egypt	Not in force
Iran	Signed but not in force
Iraq	In force
Jordan	In force
Kuwait	In force
Lebanon	Not in force
Libya	In force
Morocco	In force
Oman	Not in force
Qatar	Not in force
Saudi	Not in force
Syria	Not in force
Tunisia	Signed but not in force
Turkey	In force

UAE	In force
Yemen	Not in force

Countries in italics are members of the proliferation-relevant group. Turkey's and Libya's adoption of the AP is noteworthy and welcome, but that still leaves five countries of proliferation relevance that have not adopted the Additional Protocol, though two of the five have signed it.

MENA: PERFORMANCE OF THE HYPOTHESES

Having now established a general empirical context for the phenomenon of lag, one can look more specifically to the MENA countries and the hypotheses. The previous discussion of possible hypotheses yielded a crop of twelve potential explanations for AP lag. They are summarized in Table 9.3. To evaluate these hypotheses, it makes sense to first step back and consider the geostrategic and political environments in which these countries operate.

The Context: Threats, Nuclear Development, and Politics in the MENA Region

The countries of the Middle East and North Africa do not lack for threats, both external and internal. The region has witnessed several major interstate wars, minor wars, and internal contestations of which the Arab Spring is only the most recent. The minor wars and internal conflicts are not wholly irrelevant to the nuclear issue, but most analysts who think about nuclear proliferation look for threats posed by an adversary's nuclear weapons, potential nuclear weapons capability, or capability to wage large-scale conventional war.[12] These kinds of threats have more often been found in the countries of the Middle East rather than North Africa. Israel possesses nuclear weapons and fought conventional wars with Arab states in 1956, 1967, 1970, and 1973.[13] Iraq under Saddam Hussein had a nuclear weapons program and fought a long and bloody war after invading Iran in 1980.

In today's Middle East, perceptions of threat revolve around two main actors: Israel and Iran. Israel has signed peace treaties with several Arab states, but relations remain difficult at best and are more uncertain in the aftermath of political upheaval in Egypt and Syria. In addition, Israel's hostile relations with the Palestinians and the Lebanese still animate the entire region. For the Persian Gulf states, however, the more acute concern is Iran and suspicions about its nuclear

TABLE 9.3. Summary of hyptheses for AP lag

No.	Hypothesis	Type
H1	Low-threat environment (including credible security guarantee) causes lag	Threat
H2	Near-nuclear capability that could invite suspicion causes AP adoption	Threat
H3	Desire to maintain a nuclear weapons option causes lag	Threat
H4	Normative concerns about the NPT cause lag	NPT
H5	Desire for bargaining leverage with NPT NWS causes lag	NPT
H6	Absence of benefit causes lag	Economics
H7	Free riding causes lag	Economics
H8	Seeking to maximize side payments causes lag	Economics
H9	Cost of adherence causes lag	Economics
H10	Domestic opposition causes lag	Politics
H11	Nuclear disputes with IAEA cause lag	Politics
H12	Desire for bargaining leverage on regional issues causes lag	Politics

program. Israel and Iran are separated by geography and lack a history of direct conflict, but Israel might launch military strikes against Iran's nuclear facilities, much as it did against Iraq in 1981 and against Syria in 2007.

With some important exceptions, the region's nuclear development—military and civilian—has been modest. Several countries have had nuclear weapons programs or otherwise expressed an interest in acquiring nuclear weapons, including Egypt, Libya, Iraq, and Turkey.[14] Others are suspected of having had nuclear ambitions, including Saudi Arabia, Syria, and Algeria. In addition, it has to be said that despite no lack of grand pronouncements and detailed plans, none of the seven countries just mentioned has a substantial or developed nuclear infrastructure. Most have ambitions to develop their nuclear capabilities, civilian or otherwise, but that has been true for a very long time and has yielded little in the way of results. Perhaps Iran's nuclear activities will be the motivational difference for these states, but so far an existing Israeli arsenal—not just a capability but actual nuclear weapons—has not pushed these nuclear aspirants into a serious, successful program. In addition, events in Libya and Iraq have led to both a neutering of their nuclear programs and new rules of transparency that will complicate any future weapons effort. Syria is essentially in the same position. Its nuclear facilities were bombed; it faces intense scrutiny from the IAEA; and it is riven by domestic turmoil and bloodshed.

By contrast, both Israel and increasingly Iran have made important advancements in their nuclear capabilities. Israel has nuclear weapons, and Iran's slow but steady progress in the field of enrichment provides it with a theoretical nuclear weapons capability.

In many MENA countries, the most pressing threats are not from foreign adversaries but from domestic opponents, a threat not well suited to nuclear deterrence. Iran has had its own internal divisions, and governments in Syria, Bahrain, Lebanon, and Jordon, among others, worry about their continued tenure. In most countries, there are grievances about economic growth, political freedoms, youth unemployment, corruption, religion, ethnic divisions, and the like.

Threat Hypotheses

The three threat hypotheses suggest that lag is a consequence of the absence of threat or the desire for a nuclear weapons option. On the other side of the ledger is the suggestion that a country's positive enthusiasm for the AP is rooted in the fact that it has a nuclear weapons capability and wants to reduce the concerns of other states about that fact. This is not a very promising set of hypotheses when applied to the MENA context. Contrary to the first hypothesis, there is an abundance of threat or at least an abundance of opportunities to perceive threats. In addition, there is very little in the way of security guarantees for this comparatively underinstitutionalized part of the world. Inconsistent with Hypothesis 2 is the situation in which the NNWs with the highest level of nuclear development—Iran—has not adopted the AP and is, in fact, the object of intense international suspicion about its nuclear intentions.

Of the three threat variants, Hypothesis 3—that nuclear weapons ambitions cause lag—appears the most promising. Still, given the historical record, it is not particularly compelling either. Egypt, for example, has been forthcoming and transparent about its nuclear activities.[15] More generally, if these countries were chomping at the bit to develop a nuclear weapons capability, they should have accomplished a lot more than they have. What is striking is how slowly these governments have moved to build their nuclear capacity, not how quickly. Nevertheless, the hypothesis cannot be ruled out (in contrast to Hypotheses 1 and 2). The absence of a serious nuclear effort does not, by definition, exclude the possibility that these states have nuclear ambitions they have not yet abandoned.

Regime Hypotheses

These hypotheses posit that lag reflects normative concerns about the discriminatory nature of the NPT or a desire to acquire bargaining leverage with the

NWS, pushing them to make deeper reductions in their arsenals consistent with their Article VI obligations. There are strong reasons to doubt both these explanations in this particular case. First, for the countries in the Middle East, international normative concerns have not been a particularly strong driver of WMD policy. It is a region where many players joined the NPT even as they developed, maintained, and sometimes used chemical weapons, for example.[16] It is also worth remembering that the region is a leader in having violated its NPT obligations (Libya, Iran, Syria, and Iraq having all violated IAEA rules at one point).

To be fair, individual states and groups such as the Arab League have called out the weapons states on their Article VI responsibilities. As recently as the May 2010 Review Conference, Arab speakers lamented the discriminatory nature of the NPT.[17] Arab states have also chastised the weapons states in meetings of the Non-Aligned Movement and Group of 77. Still, these same governments went on to officially endorse the NPT Review Conferences' final documents. Moreover, U.S. officials and others who have participated in these forums report that global disarmament has not been a central preoccupation of the states in the MENA region.

Economic Hypotheses

The economic hypotheses look at the costs and benefits of the AP. Is there a benefit? Can one get the benefit without having to do anything? Can one receive a larger individual side payment if one holds out? Does the cost of the AP outweigh its benefit?

These explanations sound reasonable, but they do not provide a good fit for this particular set of countries. Given the history of war and competition in the region, an AP that reduces the risk of proliferation would appear to be of sufficient benefit. And it would be benefit for modest cost. Most of the MENA states have minimal nuclear programs and so, unlike Japan, have little cause for complaining about the burdens of safeguards. The free rider problem appears not to be in play, because the countries of particular concern, Israel and Iran, do not participate. That leaves the side payments hypothesis. It is possible the laggards are holding out for a better deal, so the hypothesis cannot be ruled out. Still, one would have expected that these states would have *already* received very generous offers, given the salience of nuclear issues in general and Iran in particular.

Political Hypotheses

The political hypotheses come in three flavors. One contends that AP lag is a consequence of domestic opposition. Another proposes that the AP gets held hostage to other nuclear disputes with the IAEA or the international community. The third argues that lag is a result of countries attempting to use their status as leverage for regional issues outside the confines of the NPT.

One could imagine that domestic political opposition might play a role in a MENA government's approach to the AP. Egypt, for example, has been criticized at home for a situation in which Israel has been allowed to keep its nuclear weapons while the Arabs disarmed. This has both a security aspect and, perhaps as important, a status dimension. One does not have to invoke "Arab shame" to make the point that the current regional arrangement could be perceived as an example of Israeli strength and Arab weakness. That said, it seems doubtful that a country's AP status would ever rise to the level of a "bread and butter" issue or the central concern for a small but powerful political constituency. In Egypt, the Muslim Brotherhood and the old National Democratic Party (NDP) felt politically obliged to articulate a position on nuclear safeguards and the NPT, but having a position does not mean that the issue is an emotionally powerful concern that moves public opinion. When the crowds gathered in Tahrir Square, the nonproliferation regime was not a rallying cry: the killing of protesters, a lack of democracy, unemployment, food prices, and corruption were, but not the nonproliferation regime.

The remaining two political hypotheses show promise—one in a very narrow sense and the other more generally. A refusal to adopt the AP because of other nuclear disputes is, without question, in play in the cases of Syria and Iran. Perhaps neither state would have adopted the AP in the absence of their respective disputes, but the presence of these controversies means that AP adoption is unlikely without some broader settlement. In the Iranian case, the Islamic Republic did sign and begin a process of implementation of the AP before relations between Iran, the IAEA, and the "P5+1" (United Kingdom, France, the United States, Russia, China, and Germany) deteriorated. One can also see the logic of this hypothesis in the converse, namely that Libya joined the AP as part of a 2003 deal that settled its nuclear dispute with the international community.

Arguably the most persuasive and general hypothesis is the explanation concerning regional politics. Until the information regarding Iran's enrichment program came to light in 2003, the central nuclear issue in the MENA region was Israel's possession of nuclear weapons. Today, some countries are more concerned about Iran than Israel, but Israel's nuclear weapons continue to be a dominant nuclear concern.[18] Indeed, some have suggested that public opinion surveys of the Arab world that have previously shown support for Iran's program can be explained as a reaction to Israel's nuclear status, a surprise given the traditional competition between the Arab states and the largely Persian Iran.[19]

Egypt—as the largest Arab state, the principle force behind the Arab League, and a member of the special group of leading non-aligned NPT countries—has taken the leadership role on pressing for action on Israel's nuclear program. It was Egypt at the 1995 NPT Review and Extension Conference that forced a deal with the United States and other weapons states to include a formal resolution on the Middle East as part of the conference. The resolution reaffirmed the call for universal NPT adherence by all governments and a process for pursuing a nuclear-weapons-free zone in the Middle East. Both concepts were aimed directly at Israel's status as a nuclear weapons state. A decade later, in 2005, Egypt again assumed a leading role in negotiations over the agenda of the NPT Review Conference. Unhappily, this conference ended in failure. Many countries contributed to the deadlock, including Iran, the United States, and China, but Egypt's insistence that the Review Conference address Israel's nuclear weapons was one factor that contributed to the collapse of the 2005 meeting.[20]

This brings us to the Additional Protocol. In interviews with Egyptian diplomats, nuclear specialists, and staff at the Arab League, there has been a recurrent theme: Egypt and other MENA countries would refuse to adopt the AP until they saw movement on the question of Israel's nuclear weapons. Often this position was expressed with bitterness and anger. Officials wondered aloud why their governments should continue to take on new nonproliferation burdens even as the sole nuclear weapons state in the region was allowed to quietly maintain its arsenal.[21] In several discussions, officials insisted that Egypt would abide by the spirit of the AP but would not formally join unless they received consideration on the Israeli issue.[22] This is a critical point. If that offer is substantially true and applies to the other MENA countries as well, it would call into question both the threat and economic hypotheses. If Egypt abides by the AP, formally or not, then threat and cost concerns cannot be paramount. If Cairo was worried about threats or costs, it would not bother to observe the AP in the breach.

Summary of Findings

Table 9.4 summarizes the provisional results. As is often the case, it is easier to disconfirm a hypothesis than to confirm one, and given the speculative nature of several of the judgments, the results presented here are mostly phrased in terms of probability.

Hypotheses 1, 2, 6, and 7 can be rejected because they are, on their face, contradicted by the facts. The Middle East is not a low-threat environment; the two MENA countries that have a near or actual nuclear capability (Iran and Israel) have not joined the AP; an AP that reduced the risk of proliferation would be a benefit in this region more than it would be for most areas of the world; and free riding is difficult to apply in a situation where most countries in the region and the two countries of greatest concern do not participate in the arrangements that would be required to get the free ride.

Hypothesis 3, a desire for a nuclear weapons option, cannot be discounted. Still, the recent behavior of several major states in the region (e.g., Egypt, Saudi Arabia, post–Saddam Iraq) does not suggest active and committed policies in favor of a weapons option. If anything, the surprise might be that these governments have not done more to build their capacity. Of course, two countries do appear to have moved in this direction: Iran and Syria. The book is not yet closed on the Iranian story. One could imagine a scenario in which Iran settles up with the international community, joins the AP, but nevertheless maintains a basic capability, if only because of an acquired knowledge of enrichment, much like Japan. The best case for this hypothesis is Syria, where lack of participation in the AP might easily have been a consequence of having a clandestine nuclear program. It seems unlikely, however, in the aftermath of Israel's bombing of Syria's reactor, the ongoing dispute with the IAEA, intense international scrutiny, and significant problems at home and in the region, that Damascus will make much progress in the near to intermediate term.

One cannot definitively rule out hypotheses 4, 5, 8, 9, and 10, but their cases are weak. The Arab states have raised objections to the discriminatory nature of the NPT and the failure of the NWS to live up to their Article VI obligations, but they have expended no actual political capital on these grievances. Given the small size of the nuclear programs in most MENA countries, it is hard to imagine that cost is the driving factor. If anything, it is not unreasonable to speculate that the countries in question have passed on large side payments from the United States and other states that would have more than made up for the expense of

TABLE 9.4. Summary of results

No.	Hypothesis	Verdict
H1	Low-threat environment (including credible security guarantee) causes lag	Rejected
H2	Near-nuclear capability that could invite suspicion causes AP adoption	Rejected
H3	Desire to maintain a nuclear weapons option causes lag	Possible
H4	Normative concerns about the NPT cause lag	Unlikely
H5	Desire for bargaining leverage with NPT NWS causes lag	Unlikely
H6	Absence of benefit causes lag	Rejected
H7	Free riding causes lag	Rejected
H8	Seeking to maximize side payments causes lag	Unlikely
H9	Cost of adherence causes lag	Unlikely
H10	Domestic opposition causes lag	Unlikely
H11	Nuclear disputes with IAEA cause lag	Likely
H12	Desire for bargaining leverage on regional issues causes lag	Likely

signing on. Domestic political oppositions have gained new strength in the region, but they have focused on internal economic and governance issues, not international nuclear agreements.

Two political hypotheses—11 and 12—perform best. Ongoing nuclear disputes certainly cloud the future of the AP in Iran and Syria. And the use of the AP as leverage for addressing Israel's nuclear weapons status comes closest to providing a general explanation for the MENA region. It also enjoys the virtue of having an empirical record (e.g., the Arab states' actions at the NPT Review Conferences) that is easily assessed. The regional hypothesis is also intriguing, because if the MENA states are willing to abide by the AP without formally joining, it would call into question the logic of most of the other competing hypotheses. Still, one should be suspicious of political scientists who claim that political variables provide the best explanation for outcomes.

POLICY IMPLICATIONS

This analysis provides both obvious and subtle implications for policymakers hoping to promote the universality of the AP. Starting with the obvious, a substantial part of Arab objections to the AP is tied to Israel's nuclear weapons program. In the near term, it is unlikely Israel will make concessions in this area, for example, for limits or transparency. Nonproliferation advocates have a few options, however.

One is to press for adherence in the breach and to reward that adherence with side payments of whatever kinds are most attractive to the parties.

A second option is to address Arab requests that the issue of Israel's program be addressed rhetorically and politically, if not substantively. This is what the international community did in 1995 with the NPT resolution on the Middle East. Israel was unhappy, but the sky did not fall down, and those actions gave Arab states both a sense of victory and some political cover back home.

A third option is misdirection. Rather than directly confront the Arab states on a group position in which they have invested political capital, one could accept their position, set the issue aside, and then reframe and rebrand the issue. So, for example, one could acknowledge that the MENA states have legitimate grievances, that their position is understandable, and then leave it alone. This would be followed with an initiative on fissile material security or nuclear energy that might incorporate many of the same instrumentalities as the AP. The context would not be proliferation, however. Arab governments might find that they could sign on to such a program without having their opposition to Israel's nuclear program come into question.

Another obvious implication is that the AP ought to be a condition of the resolution of the Iranian and Syrian disputes, just as it was in the case of Libya. Indeed, one could make the case that getting Iran in the AP or an "AP plus" is a far more achievable goal than zero centrifuges or a multiyear suspension of enrichment, and that it actually yields a greater nonproliferation benefit. For example, it would make it more difficult for Saudi Arabia and other governments in the region to reject the AP if Iran accepted it. As it stands, Iran's rejection gives other states an excuse for recalcitrance. Iranian acceptance of the AP might not be as difficult as supposed, if only because Iran committed to it in the past.

A related but less obvious implication from the overall record of NPT ratification and AP adoption is that nonproliferation advocates should target states that have signed on in principle but that have not yet brought an agreement into force. For those countries, the force of logic and precedence might make the AP an easier sell than in cases where the countries have made no move whatsoever.

There are other lessons that come from the experience of NPT ratification. Over time, some clear patterns emerge, most having to do with the "logic of action." Action—in this case ratification—is more likely when there is a deadline, a crisis, or a change in leadership. Clearly, the pattern of NPT and AP adoption points to the NPT Review Conferences as a kind of deadline that puts the topic on government agendas and focuses the minds of policymakers. In addition, crises or external shocks can create opportunities and political will. This was the case with the 1974 Indian nuclear test. While one cannot hope that bad things will happen, nonproliferation advocates should prepare in advance and have a plan they can implement to maximize political opportunities when such opportunities present themselves. If they do not prepare, the moment may pass them by and an opportunity may be lost.

Leadership changes present another kind of opportunity. This is often the case when a governing party is replaced by its opposition. Oppositions, by definition, are inclined to think that their political adversaries have it wrong and to be open to doing things differently. In Germany and Australia, for example, elections brought oppositions to power that quickly moved to reverse their predecessors' refusal to join the NPT. In other cases, simply a change of personality or the turning of the page to new leadership, regardless of the party, creates enough political space to allow a government to make a commitment it could not make before.

Finally, as one looks back across the history of safeguards, one is struck by their iterative nature. Today's safeguards are nothing like the safeguards of the 1950s and 1960s. The AP is a product of the crisis caused by Iraq's secret nuclear program, and at some point in the future a crisis will precipitate the call for new rules and safeguard enhancements that take advantage of previously unavailable knowledge and technology. It makes sense to work on those next-generation safeguards today and to have an AP 2.0 that is a known and ready commodity, if only for discussion.[23] Some countries will complain about having a set of rules before the old ones are fully adopted, but producing the next protocol now carries advantages. It allows states to get familiar with new approaches. It provides a ready answer to the question that arises after a major crisis, "What do we do now?" and it may make adoption of the current AP easier. States that are not interested in adopting the new arrangements or are politically constrained from doing so might adopt the current AP as a way to push off having to deal with a newer version. By having the next AP in hand, nonproliferation advocates gain leverage. They can say, "Well, ok, we will not push you on this, but at least join the old AP."

If such a strategy is pursued, it may be only a matter of time before scholars will be writing on lag in the adoption of the next generation of safeguards.

Notes

The author is indebted to a number of people who read and commented on this chapter, including Jeffrey Fields, Scott Sagan, Sharon Zalkind, Jennifer Greenleaf, Corie

Walsh, Tim Donlan, and members of the workshop on Building Responsible Nonproliferation Stakeholders.

1. IAEA, "Information Circular: The Agency's Safeguards System," INCIRC/66/Rev2. 16 September 1968, http://www.iaea.org/Publications/Documents/Infcircs/Others/inf66r2.shtml (accessed June 19, 2013).

2. IAEA, "Factsheets and FAQs: IAEA Safeguards Overview: Comprehensive Safeguards Agreements and Additional Protocols," http://www.iaea.org/Publications/Factsheets/English/sg_overview.html (accessed June 19, 2013).

3. IAEA, "Status List: Conclusion of Safeguards Agreements, Additional Protocols and Small Quantities Protocols as of 7 June 2013," http://www.iaea.org/safeguards/documents/sir_table.pdf. Accessed June 19, 2013.

4. On why states pursue and abandon their nuclear ambitions, see Mitchell Reiss, *Without the Bomb: The Politics of Nuclear Nonproliferation* (New York: Columbia University Press, 1988); Mitchell Reiss, *Bridled Ambition: Why Countries Constrain Their Nuclear Capabilities* (Washington: Woodrow Wilson Center Press, 1995); Scott D. Sagan, "Why Do States Build Nuclear Weapons? Three Models in Search of a Bomb," *International Security* 21, no. 3 (1996/1997); James Joseph Walsh, "Bombs Unbuilt: Power, Ideas and Institutions in International Politics," PhD thesis, Massachusetts Institute of Technology, 2000; Jacques E. C. Hymans, *The Psychology of Nuclear Proliferation* (Cambridge: Cambridge University Press, 2006); Etel Solingen, *Nuclear Logics: Contrasting Paths in East Asia and the Middle East* (Princeton, N.J.: Princeton University Press, 2007); Maria Rost Rublee, *Nonproliferation Norms: Why States Choose Nuclear Restraint* (Athens: University of Georgia Press, 2009).

5. See, for example, Oona A. Hathaway, "The Cost of Commitment," *Stanford Law Review* 55, no. 5 (2003): 1821–62; Wade M. Cole, "Sovereignty Relinquished? Explaining Commitment to the International Human Rights Covenants, 1966–1999," *American Sociological Review* 70, no. 3 (2005): 472–95; Bernhard Bookman, "International Labour Organization Conventions by Industrialised Democracies, 1960–1996," *European Journal of Political Research* 45, no. 1 (2006): 153–80; Uta Oberdörster, "Why Ratify? Lessons from Treaty Ratification Campaigns," *Vanderbilt Law Review* 61, no, 2 (2008): 681–712.

6. The countries with no safeguards agreements include Benin, Cape Verde, Congo, Djibouti, Montenegro, Mozambique, Togo, Equatorial Guinea, Vanuatu, Eritrea, Guinea, Guinea Bissau, Liberia, Micronesia, São Tomé and Principe, Somalia, and Timor-Leste.

7. Thomas Graham Jr., *Disarmament Sketches: Three Decades of Arms Control and International Law* (Seattle: University of Washington Press, 2002).

8. Japan nevertheless did join the AP, despite complaints about the burdens of safeguards.

9. United Nations, Office for Disarmament Affairs, "Treaty of the Non-Proliferation of Nuclear Weapons," http://disarmament.un.org/treaties/t/npt (accessed June 19, 2013).

10. This conference was required under the NPT and directed the states parties to vote on whether and how the treaty should be extended. The United States wanted a vote in favor of indefinite extension of the treaty. In order to win the vote, Washington sought to gather up all the states that had not bothered to join the NPT, so that they could then attend the conference and vote for indefinite extension.

11. Table 9.2 suggests that 2004 was a particularly important year for adoption by proliferation-relevant states. On closer examination, five of the seven are European countries with little inclination to proliferation—Germany, Italy, Greece, Spain, and Sweden. The other two are Cuba and South Korea.

12. See, for example, Stephen M. Meyer, *The Dynamics of Nuclear Proliferation* (Chicago: University of Chicago Press, 1984), 56–63.

13. One might also include the 1969 War of Attrition and the 1982 conflict in Lebanon.

14. On Egypt's past and present nuclear policy, see Jim Walsh, "Egypt's Nuclear Future: Proliferation or Restraint?," in *Forecasting Proliferation in the 21st Century*, ed. William Potter (Stanford: Stanford University Press, 2010) 13–41; Jim Walsh, "Bombs Unbuilt"; Janice Gross Stein, "Egypt and Israel in the Middle East," in *The Dynamics of Middle East Nuclear Proliferation*, ed. Steven L. Spiegel, Jennifer D. Kibbe, and Elizabeth G, Matthews (Lewiston, N.Y.: E. Mellen Press, 2001), 33–58; Mark Fitzpatrick, ed., *Nuclear Programmes in the Middle East: In the Shadow of Iran* (London: International Institute for Strategic Studies, 2008), 17–34. In an interview, a former Greek official claimed both Turkey and Greece explored the possibility of acquiring nuclear weapons during their periods of military rule. (This official was asked by the government for an assessment of a potential program for weapons development.)

15. Egypt has been the subject of nuclear controversy, however. In 2004, the IAEA noticed articles published by Egyptian nuclear scientists that were based on experiments that had not been declared to the agency. A formal IAEA investigation concluded that Egypt's infractions were minor and apparently did not reflect an interest in acquiring the bomb. That finding was bolstered by the affirmative and comprehensive character of Egypt's response to IAEA requests. See IAEA, "Implementation of the NPT Safeguards Agreement in the Arab Republic of Egypt," report by the director general (Vienna: IAEA, February 14, 2005), 5–6. See also Nuclear Threat Initiative, "Egypt Profile, Nuclear Chronology 2005," February 1, 2005, (citing Note Verbal, From the Embassy of the Arab of Egypt to the International Atomic Agency," IAEA, February 1, 2005), http://www.nti.org/media/pdfs/egypt_nuclear_1.pdf?_=1316474849 (accessed January 5, 2012). This view of Egypt's compliance was been supported in interviews with two IAEA staff.

16. On Iraq, see Central Intelligence Agency CIA, "Iraq's Chemical Warfare Program," 2004, https://www.cia.gov/library/reports/general-reports-1/iraq_wmd_2004/chap5.html (accessed June 19, 2013). On the Yemen, see M. Meselson and D. E. Viney, "The

Yemen," in *CBW: Chemical and Biological Warfare*, ed. Steven P. R. Rose, 99–102 (Boston: Beacon Press, 1968); Stockholm International and Peace Research Institute (SIPRI), "The Prevention of CBW," in *The Problem of Chemical and Biological Warfare*, vol. 5 (New York: Humanities Press, 1975), 225–38. W. Andrew Terrill, "The Chemical Warfare Legacy of the Yemen War," *Comparative Strategy* 10, no. 2 (1991): 109–19. On Libya, see "Libya's PM Confirms Presence of Chemical Weapons," *USA Today*, October 31, 2011, http://usatoday30.usatoday.com/news/world/story/2011-10-30/libya-chemical-weapons-found/51009366/1 (accessed June 19, 2013). On Syria and Iran, see Richard Guthrie, John Hart, and Frida Kuhlau, "Chemical and Biological Warfare Developments and Arms Control," *SIPRI Yearbook 2005* (Stockholm: SIPRI, 2005), 603–28; CIA, "Unclassified Report to Congress on the Acquisition of Technology Relating to Weapons of Mass Destruction and Advanced Conventional Munitions, 1 January through 30 June 2001," https://www.cia.gov/library/reports/archived-reports-1/jan_jun2001.htm (accessed June 19, 2013).

17. See, for example, Beatrice Fihn and Ray Acheson, "Planning for Nuclear Disarmament Now," NPT *News in Review*, no. 6, May 10, 2010, http://www.reachingcriticalwill.org/images/documents/Disarmament-fora/npt/NIR2010/No6.pdf (accessed June 19, 2013).

18. There are also occasional intraregional arguments, e.g., over the desirability of a Gulf free zone versus a Middle East WMD free zone. See "Nuclearization in the Gulf," *Security and Terrorism Research Bulletin*, no. 7 (2007): 32–37.

19. On Arab views of Iran and its nuclear program, see Shibley Telhami, "2008 Annual Arab Public Opinion Poll," http://www.brookings.edu/~/media/events/2008/4/14%20middle%20east/0414_middle_east_telhami.pdf (accessed February 14 2014). Since 2008, Arab views have likely soured somewhat both because of Iran's 2009 disputed presidential election and the democratic wave that swept the region in 2011.

20. The author was present at the 2005 Review Conference and had the opportunity to interview both diplomats and NGO observers. See also Harald Müller, "The 2005 NPT Review Conference: Reasons and Consequences of Failure and Options for Repair," paper no. 31 (Oslo: Weapons of Mass Destruction Commission, 2005), 35–41; Rebecca Johnson, "Politics and Protection: Why the 2005 NPT Review Conference Failed," *Disarmament Diplomacy*, no. 80 (2005), http://www.acronym.org.uk/dd/dd80/80npt.htm (accessed June 19, 2013).

21. Jim Walsh, "Egypt's Nuclear Future," 13–41.

22. It has to be said that for all the complaining by American officials about Egyptian maneuvers, this is precisely what nonproliferation advocates should want. Supporters of nonproliferation should desire that states 1) give up a weapons option even as others in the region have weapons and 2) respond to their adversary's weapons status by pushing for a tougher regime. The alternative is that the country forgoes nonproliferation and opts instead for pursing nuclear weapons of its own. The Egyptian story demonstrates how an initial set of nonproliferation commitments can generate incentives for

states to strengthen the regime, which benefits all NPT members. Unfortunately, Egypt receives little but derision from American officials who apparently cannot see the forest for the trees, or who are so preoccupied with the U.S.-Israeli relationship that they take short-term positions that may have large nonproliferation costs down the road.

23. This is understandably a sensitive issue for the IAEA. The agency already has programs with individual states for development of new safeguards concepts and technologies (e.g., with Australia), but the formal preparation of a new set of safeguards arrangements would be controversial. Of course, the IAEA does not have to drive this process. States or even nonstate actors such as universities or NGOs could take up the task and develop model agreements.

CHAPTER 10

Conclusion

Jeffrey R. Fields

DIVINING STATE MOTIVATIONS for nonproliferation policies is not simply an exercise in determining a single or best causal factor, as shown by the essays in this volume, particularly the theoretical essays. Varied, interacting factors—for example, norms, security, and economics—affect state nonproliferation decision making as they do in other areas of international relations. As Jason Enia shows in the first chapter, and as the diverse issues examined in subsequent chapters highlight, the *type* of nonproliferation activity or "good" is significant. This underpins the motivation of the entire book: the regime is expansive and multifaceted. Explaining states' behavior in general is helped by examining collective action problems, threat perceptions, and notions of fairness and legitimacy. But there is also utility in better understanding the components of the regime themselves. This has been a shortcoming in the literature on nonproliferation—a tendency to view the regime solely through the lens of the NPT, something we have endeavored to avoid here.

Rigorous, systematic study of the nuclear nonproliferation regime is an area much in need of more focused attention. Theories of proliferation—that is, state decisions to pursue nuclear weapons—are now abundant. This state of affairs owes to the gravity of the nuclear balance. Yet the number of states that have pursued nuclear weapons in the past or might pursue them in the future is relatively small. By contrast the number of states comprising the nonproliferation regime is quite large. And even when parsing the regime into different sectors, the number of states that can affect a subset of related instruments by participation or nonparticipation is still substantial. The gap in the literature is bounded not only by a dearth of research on nonproliferation (regime) decision making but also by a tendency to avoid disaggregating the regime into individual components to get traction on state behavior and focus the analysis. As mentioned at the outset of this book, we still lack a comprehensive examination of why various states joined the NPT, the foundation of the nonproliferation regime.[1] The same deficiency exists for why states support nonproliferation regime components. The NPT presents a rich area for study in this regard. But so do many of the other regime instruments that center not only on regulation of technology transfers and fuel cycle issues but also on punitive measures like sanctions and norm strengthening endeavors like nuclear-weapons-free zones.

There is a gap in the security literature on state behavior within the regime, and practitioners also struggle to understand why some governments behave in ways they find confounding—for example, why would states with no interest in nuclear weapons be reluctant to do everything possible to strengthen the nonproliferation regime? As mentioned in the introduction, two senior State Department officials separately posed a version of this question to me in 2010. Thus, an opportunity exists for a research agenda to directly have an impact in the policy world.

At the beginning of this project I envisioned a work that could neatly tie together common drivers of nonproliferation policy resulting in a tight framework through which to view states' policies. What emerged was a more eclectic set of essays that demonstrate the complexity of the issue and the need for further scholarly and policy work. In this concluding note, my intention is not to recapitulate all of the theoretical propositions presented here. Rather, I briefly put them into an overall perspective that highlights the varied and sometimes disparate nature of nonproliferation efforts. The theoretical chapters especially illustrate the diversity and interconnectedness of drivers.

PERSPECTIVES ON NONPROLIFERATION

In Scott Sagan's seminal "Why Do States Build Nuclear Weapons?" the three models he refers to in the literature are posited theoretical frameworks to explain a singular outcome—state proliferation. That is, "why states decide to build or refrain from building nuclear weapons."[2] Andrew Grotto adopts the three-model framework to offer theoretical explanations of states' nonproliferation policies—"NPT plus" measures, as he characterizes them. At the outset of this project we recognized that nonproliferation is such a complex and multifaceted issue that it is not entirely satisfying to attempt an analysis as if there were one singular outcome. It is a range of activities, and the same states support some measures, hinder others, and are ambivalent about still others. At the same time those measures are equally varied. Some are punitive while some are regulatory. Because the NPT is inherently a discriminatory treaty, regulatory components

TABLE 10.1 Nonproliferation Motivators

Security/Insecurity	Resource Allocation	Fairness
Threat perception	Economics	Legitimacy
Alliance membership	Collective Action	Disarmament

may reinforce sentiments of illegitimacy among NNWS. But as the theoretical chapters in this volume demonstrate, there are several overlapping factors that influence the multitude of nonproliferation decisions that states make, and we should expect to observe a "complex, contingent decision calculus" as states navigate their own security and deal with other mitigating and domestic factors.[3] The decision to sign the CTBT and the decision to participate in the PSI (or the decision to refrain) may have different internal drivers.

If we categorize nonproliferation efforts based on broad drivers, then variation of regime behavior and variation of state support become even clearer. Framing the intraregime dynamics more broadly might help scholars and practitioners gain more awareness and get better leverage on the complexity of the issue.

Nonproliferation policies are a function of the motivators outlined in this volume and are broadly listed as shown in Table 10.1. But there is interaction among motivators, as the chapters here detail. Progress on disarmament affects not only threat perception but also notions of fairness and legitimacy. In her chapter Maria Rublee argues that even if elites within a state construct proliferation as a threat, descriptive and injunctive nonproliferation norms must work in concert to help persuade them to support robust nonproliferation measures. But as she further points out, when the United States, for example, pursues nonproliferation policies that are not even-handed and privilege certain states, descriptive norms fall out of balance. This in turn entrenches sentiments of unfairness and illegitimacy of the regime. Nina Rathbun reinforces this in her chapter, noting that at least initially, the Obama administration's nonproliferation policies, outlined most notably in his Prague speech, had a positive effect on other states especially within the NAM and NAC. Washington's new stance on the CTBT and FMCT and the 2010 Nuclear Posture Review's reduction in reliance on nuclear weapons were positively received by other states and a legitimacy-enhancing policy shift.

Jeff Knopf's chapter takes a much-needed closer look at the question of disarmament as it relates to other states' feelings of discrimination and marginalization in the regime. The disarmament-nonproliferation link is perhaps the most discussed aspect of legitimacy in nonproliferation studies and is sure to again be

TABLE 10.2 Categories of nonproliferation efforts

Measure	Examples
Punitive	Sanctions; blockades
Security	NWFZs, arms control agreements
Preventive	Export controls, interdiction, restrictive (e.g., FMCT)
Regime reinforcing	CSA, AP

a point of contention in the lead-up to and during the next NPT Revcon.[4] Both Knopf and Jim Walsh note the possible linkages in nuclear-armed states' disarmament and nonproliferation policies, though Walsh finds the case lacking in his narrower, regional focus.[5] Walsh's examination of lag in adoption of an Additional Protocol in Middle East states again shows the complexity and multiplicity of factors influencing state nonproliferation behavior. And his analysis is focused on only one specific regime instrument. Even then, the three hypotheses he deems "likely" or "possible" explanations for lag in AP adoption differ in nature—two being political and one threat-based. If we consider the hypotheses that Walsh considers "unlikely" but does not outright reject, the picture becomes even more complex.

Walsh's summary of hypothesis types is a useful construction for encapsulating the ideas in this volume and as an organizing framework. Nonproliferation efforts can be categorized by their overall purpose. Punitive measures such as economic sanctions seek to constrain a state's ability to pursue a nuclear weapons program using economic pressures or constraining access to necessary materials and technology. Measures may increase security by reducing threat perceptions and alleviate the security dilemma. Restrictive, preventive measures regulate or impede the flow of technology and materials. All of the above could be considered regime-reinforcing measures, but it is useful to highlight activities and initiatives related to codified nonproliferation efforts, such as those mandated by the NPT (see Table 10.2). These nonproliferation typologies are not meant to be definitive but rather suggestive and a way to encapsulate especially the theoretical approaches employed by the authors in this volume in this brief concluding chapter.

FURTHER RESEARCH

This volume scratches the surface of what is a rich and underexplored aspect of security studies. A better understanding of how states think about nonproliferation, the regime, and its myriad components will help policymakers strengthen the regime and build better, more vested global nonproliferation stakeholders. The research agenda can and should be approached in a number of ways. This volume is a mix of theoretical and empirical work that does not try to tease out an overarching explanatory framework. As has been noted here, there are a multiplicity of regime instruments, and they are ripe for rigorous, individual study. Too often, research on the regime fails to define what the regime is or simply reduces it to the NPT. Policy and think tank studies are often anecdotal works of advocacy. More work like RAND's 2008 monograph on participation in the Proliferation Security Initiative is in order.[6] How do the informal aspects of the regime like the Proliferation Security Initiative and other initiatives work in relation to the broader regime? Research questions like this are a good starting point to explore state orientation to specific aspects and instruments of the regime.

The empirical chapters in this volume by Deepti Choubey, Lowell Schwartz, Robert Reardon, Arturo Sotomayor, and Jim Walsh further demonstrate both the need for and the nuance necessary to approach the issue on a regional and country-specific basis. Their analyses show that much of the "conventional" thinking about states' motivations for specific aspects of nonproliferation is often incorrect. Those chapters also suggest that there exists a need for more work on the economics of nonproliferation policies. Quantitative approaches that help identify broad trends in nonproliferation policy, activities, and participation in the regime would help push forward this research agenda. We could find no comprehensive dataset of all regime instruments and states' participatory status. Finally, framing research in a way directly useful for policymakers is paramount for strengthening the regime. Scholars and researchers should directly engage policymakers and practitioners as they further explore this research agenda.

Notes

1. Scott D. Sagan, "The Causes of Nuclear Weapons Proliferation," *Annual Review of Political Science*, vol. 14 (March 2011).

2. Scott D. Sagan, "Why Do States Build Nuclear Weapons?: Three Models in Search of a Bomb," *International Security* 21, no. 3 (1996): 54–86, doi:10.2307/2539273.

3. Andrew Grotto, "Why Do States That Oppose Nuclear Proliferation Resist New Nonproliferation Obligations? Three Logics of Nonproliferation Decision-Making," draft manuscript, January 2009, http://works.bepress.com/cgi/viewcontent.cgi?article=1000&context=andrew_grotto, 52.

4. Christopher A. Ford, "Debating Disarmament: Interpreting Article VI of the Treaty on the Non-Proliferation of Nuclear Weapons," *Nonproliferation Review* 14, no. 3 (2007): 401–28, doi:10.1080/10736700701611720.

5. Walsh singles out Israel's nuclear weapons as one potential source of Arab objections to an Additional Protocol. Israel is not a signatory to the NPT.

6. This study examined five states that were reluctant to participate in PSI. See Charles Wolf Jr., Brian G. Chow, and Gregory S. Jones, *Enhancement by Enlargement: The Proliferation Security Initiative* (Santa Monica, Calif.: RAND Corporation, 2008).

BIBLIOGRAPHY

Adler, Emanuel. *The Power of Ideology: The Quest for Technological Autonomy in Argentina and Brazil*. Berkeley: University of California Press, 1987.
Adler, Emanuel, and Michael Barnett, eds. *Security Communities*. Cambridge Studies in International Relations 62. Cambridge: Cambridge University Press, 1998.
Agency for the Prohibition of Nuclear Weapons in Latin America and the Caribbean (OPANAL). "Mongolia's Nuclear-Weapon-Free Status. Accessed July 10, 2013. http://www.opanal.org/NWFZ/Mongolia/mongolia_en.htm.
Aja Espil, Jorge A. "Argentina." In *Non-proliferation: The Why and the Wherefore*, edited by Jozef Goldblat. London: Taylor & Francis, 1985.
Albin, Cecilia. *Justice and Fairness in International Negotiation*. Cambridge: Cambridge University Press, 2001.
Albright, David. "Bomb Potential for South America." *Bulletin of the Atomic Scientists* 45, no. 4 (1989): 16–20.
Albright, David, and Corey Gay. "Taiwan: Nuclear Nightmare Averted." *Bulletin of the Atomic Scientists* 54, no. 1 (1998): 54–60.
Albright, David, and Corey Hinderstein. "Unraveling the A. Q. Khan and Future Proliferation Networks." *Washington Quarterly* 28, no. 2 (2005): 111–28.
Alfonso García Robles, México, Nobel de La Paz. México, D.F: Secretaría de Educación Pública: Secretaría de Relaciones Exteriores, 1984.
Allison, Graham. *Nuclear Terrorism: The Ultimate Preventable Catastrophe*. New York: Henry Holt, 2005.
"Analysis: Brazil and Additional Protocol." UPI. Accessed July 13, 2013. http://www.upi.com/Business_News/Security-Industry/2005/07/01/Analysis-Brazil-and-additional-protocol/UPI-85051120248062/.
Applegarth, Claire. "Brazil Permits Greater IAEA Inspection." *Arms Control Today*, November 2004. http://www.armscontrol.org/act/2004_11/Brazil.
Argüello, Irma. "The Position of an Emerging Global Power: Brazilian Responses to the 2010 U.S. Nuclear Posture Review." *Nonproliferation Review* 18, no. 1 (2011): 183–200. doi:10.1080/10736700.2011.549180.
Auner, Eric. "Obama Easing Export Controls on India." *Arms Control Today* 40, no. 10 (2010): 39–41.
Axelrod, Robert. *The Evolution of Cooperation*. New York: Basic Books, 1984.

———. *The Evolution of Cooperation.* Rev. ed. New York: Basic Books, 2009.

Axelrod, Robert, and Douglas Dion. "The Further Evolution of Cooperation." *Science*, n.s., 242, no. 4884 (1988): 1385–90.

Bagnoli, Mark, and Michael McKee. "Voluntary Contribution Games: Efficient Private Provision of Public Goods." *Economic Inquiry* 29, no. 2 (1991): 351–66.

Baker, Peter. "Russians Pressure Iran on Weapons." *Washington Post*, June 5, 2003, final ed.

———. "Senate Approves Indian Nuclear Deal." *New York Times*, October 2, 2008. http://www.nytimes.com/2008/10/02/washington/02webnuke.html.

Barletta, Michael. "Democratic Security and Diversionary Peace: Nuclear Confidence-Building in Argentina and Brazil." Paper delivered at the Latin American Studies Association Annual Meeting, Chicago, September 24–26, 1998.

———. "The Military Nuclear Program in Brazil." Center for International Security and Arms Control, Stanford University, August 1997.

Barnett, Michael. "Social Constructivism." In *The Globalization of World Politics*, edited by John Baylis and Steve Smith. 3rd ed. Oxford: Oxford University Press, 2005.

Barringer, Felicity. "Plans by Iran for a Reactor Pose Concerns about Arms." *New York Times*, June 7, 2003, late ed. (East Coast).

Barry, Ellen. "Russia Dismisses Calls for New U.N. Sanctions on Iran." *New York Times*, November 10, 2011, late ed. (East Coast).

———. "Russian President Calls Obama Letter on Antimissile Plan a Welcome Signal." *New York Times*, March 4, 2009, late ed. (East Coast).

Baylis, John, Steve Smith, and Patricia Owens. *The Globalization of World Politics: An Introduction to International Relations.* New York: Oxford University Press, 2008.

Beeston, Richard. "Iran's Nuclear Plans Hit as Russians Hold Back Fuel in Row about Money." *Times* (London), March 13, 2007.

Bekoff, Marc, and Jessica Pierce. *Wild Justice: The Moral Lives of Animals.* Chicago: University of Chicago Press, 2009.

Belopolsky, Helen. *Russia and the Challengers: Russian Alignment with China, Iran, and Iraq in the Unipolar Era.* St. Antony's Series. Basingstoke, Eng.: Palgrave Macmillan, 2009.

Bergenäs, Johan. "The Slippery Slope of Rational Inaction: UN Security Council Resolution 1540 and the Tragedy of the Commons." *Nonproliferation Review* 15, no. 2 (2008): 373–80.

Bloom, Oliver. "Is a Key Element of the NPT Dead?" Center for Strategic and International Studies, July 13, 2010. http://csis.org/blog/key-element-npt-dead.

Boese, Wade. "NSG, Congress Approve Nuclear Trade with India." *Arms Control Today*, October 2008. http://www.armscontrol.org/act/2008_10/nsgapprove.

Bookman, Bernhard. "Partisan Politics and Treaty Ratification: The Acceptance of International Labour Organisation Conventions by Industrialised Democracies, 1960–1996." *European Journal of Political Research* 45, no. 1 (2006): 153–180.

Brams, Steven. *Game Theory and Politics.* New York: Macmillan, 1973.

Brasil. Congresso Nacional. Senado Federal. Comissão Parlamentar Mista de Inquérito destinada a apurar o Programa Autônomo de Energia Nuclear, também conhecido como "Programa Paralelo." "Relatório final." Brasília: Senado Federal, 1990. http://www2.senado.leg.br/bdsf/handle/id/194598.

Braun, Chaim, and Christopher F. Chyba. "Proliferation Rings: New Challenges to the Nuclear Nonproliferation Regime." *International Security* 29, no. 2 (2004): 5–49.

Braun, Frank. "Analysis: Brazil and Additional Protocol." *UPI International Intelligence*, July 1, 2005.

Braut-Hegghammer, Målfrid. "Libya's Nuclear Turnaround: Perspectives from Tripoli." *Middle East Journal* 62, no. 1 (2008): 55–72. doi:10.3751/62.1.13.

"Brazil Needs Nukes, VP Says." *Global Security Newswire*, September 28, 2009. http://www.nti.org/gsn/article/brazil-needs-nukes-vp-says/.

"Brazil Rebuffs U.S. Pressure for Iran Sanctions." BBC, March 3, 2010. http://news.bbc.co.uk/2/hi/8547150.stm.

Bridge, Robert. "Russia Balks on Iran's Bushehr Site." *Moscow News*, March 23, 2007.

Brooke, James. "Brazil Uncovers Plan by Military to Build Atom Bomb and Stops It." *New York Times*, October 9, 1990. http://www.nytimes.com/1990/10/09/world/brazil-uncovers-plan-by-military-to-build-atom-bomb-and-stops-it.html?pagewanted=all&src=pm.

Buchanan, James M. "An Economic Theory of Clubs." *Economica*, n.s., 32, no. 125 (1965): 1–14. doi:10.2307/2552442.

Bunn, George. *Arms Control by Committee: Managing Negotiations with the Russians*. Stanford, Calif.: Stanford University Press, 1992.

Bunn, George, and Jean du Preez. "More Than Words: The Value of U.S. Non-Nuclear-Use Promises." *Arms Control Today* 37, no. 6 (2007): 18.

Butera, Fabrizio, and Gabriel Mugny, eds. *Social Influence in Social Reality: Promoting Individual and Social Change*. Seattle: Hogrefe & Huber, 2001.

Camp, Roderic Ai. *Generals in the Palacio: The Military in Modern Mexico*. New York: Oxford University Press, 1992.

Candeas, Alessandro Warley. "Relações Brasil-Argentina: Uma análise dos advances e recuos" [Brazil-Argentina Relations: An Analysis of Advances and Retreats]. *Revista Brasileira de Política Internacional* 48, no. 1 (June 2005): 178–213. doi:10.1590/S0034-73292005000100007.

Carasales, Julio César. *De Rivales a Socios: El Proceso de Cooperación Nuclear Entre Argentina y Brasil*. Buenos Aires: Instituto del Servicio Exterior de la Nación, 1997.

——. "The So-Called Proliferator That Wasn't: The Story of Argentina's Nuclear Policy." *Nonproliferation Review* 6, no. 4 (1999): 51–64. doi:10.1080/10736709908436778.

Castro Madero, Carlos. *Política Nuclear Argentina: Avance o Retroceso?* Serie Sociología y Ciencias Políticas. Buenos Aires: El Ateneo, 1991.

Central Intelligence Agency. "Iraq's Chemical Warfare Program." Accessed July 10, 2013. https://www.cia.gov/library/reports/general-reports-1/iraq_wmd_2004/chap5.html.

Chayes, Abram, and Antonia Handler Chayes. *The New Sovereignty: Compliance with International Regulatory Agreements*. Cambridge, Mass: Harvard University Press, 1995.

———. "On Compliance." *International Organization* 47, no. 2 (1993): 175–205. doi:10.1017/S0020818300027910.

Child, Jack. *Geopolitics and Conflict in South America: Quarrels among Neighbors*. New York: Praeger; Stanford, Calif.: Hoover Institution Press, 1985.

Choubey, Deepti. "Are New Nuclear Bargains Attainable?" Washington, D.C.: Carnegie Endowment for International Peace, 2008. http://carnegieendowment.org/2008/10/08/are-new-nuclear-bargains-attainable/6ly.

Chubin, Shahram. *Iran's Nuclear Ambitions*. Washington, D.C: Carnegie Endowment for International Peace, 2006.

Chuen, Cristina. "Russian Nuclear Exports to Iran: U.S. Policy Change Needed." James Martin Center for Nonproliferation Studies, March 27, 2003. http://cns.miis.edu/stories/030327.htm.

Chyba, Christopher F. "Time for a Systematic Analysis: U.S. Nuclear Weapons and Nuclear Proliferation." *Arms Control Today* 38, no. 10 (2008). https://www.armscontrol.org/act/2008_12/Chyba.

Cialdini, Robert B. *Influence: Science and Practice*. 4th ed. Boston: Allyn and Bacon, 2001.

Cialdini, Robert B., Carl A. Kallgren, and Raymond R. Reno. "A Focus Theory of Normative Conduct: A Theoretical Refinement and Reevaluation of the Role of Norms in Human Behavior." *Advances in Experimental Social Psychology* 24 (1991): 201–34.

Cialdini, Robert B., and Melanie R. Trost. "Social Influence: Social Norms, Conformity and Compliance." In *The Handbook of Social Psychology*, vol. 2, 4th ed., edited by Daniel T. Gilbert, Susan T. Fiske, and Gardner Lindzey, 151–92. Boston: McGraw-Hill, 1998.

Cirincione, Joseph, ed. *Repairing the Regime: Preventing the Spread of Weapons of Mass Destruction*. New York: Routledge, 2000.

Cirincione, Joseph, Jon B. Wolfsthal, and Miriam Rajkumar. *Deadly Arsenals: Nuclear, Biological, and Chemical Threats*. 2nd ed. Washington, D.C: Carnegie Endowment for International Peace, 2005.

Cohen, Avner. *Israel and the Bomb*. New York: Columbia University Press, 1999.

Cole, Paul M. *Sweden without the Bomb: The Conduct of a Nuclear-Capable Nation without Nuclear Weapons*. Santa Monica, Calif.: RAND Corporation, 1994.

Cole, Wade M. "Sovereignty Relinquished? Explaining Commitment to the International Human Rights Covenants, 1966–1999." *American Sociological Review* 70, no. 3 (2005): 472–95. doi:10.2307/4145391.

"Communication Received from Certain Member States Regarding Guidelines for the Export of Nuclear Material, Equipment or Technology." *International Atomic Energy Agency*, February 1978. http://www.iaea.org/Publications/Documents/Infcircs/Others/infcirc254.shtml.

Comprehensive Test Ban Treaty Organization. Preparatory Commission for the Comprehensive Nuclear-Test-Ban Treaty Organization. "Status of Signature and Ratification." Accessed July 10, 2013. http://www.ctbto.org/the-treaty/status-of-signature-and-ratification/?print=1&states=4&region=63&no_cache=1&submit.x=8&submit.y=5.

Conference on Chemical and Biological Warfare, and Bernal (J. D.) Peace Library. *CBW: Chemical and Biological Warfare*. Boston: Beacon Press, 1969.

Cooper, Andrew F., ed. *Niche Diplomacy: Middle Powers after the Cold War*. Studies in Diplomacy. Houndmills, Basingstoke, Hampshire, Eng.: Macmillan; New York: St. Martin's Press, 1997.

Cooper, Helene. "Russia Delivers Its Nuclear Fuel to Plant in Iran." *New York Times*, December 18, 2007, late ed. (East Coast).

Cooper, Helen, and Mark Mazzetti. "A Cryptic Note from Tehran Ignites Days of Urgent Diplomacy." *New York Times*, September 26, 2009, late ed. (East Coast).

Cooper, Helene, and David E. Sanger. "Obama, at U.N., Is Backed on Iran and Arms Curbs." *New York Times*, September 24, 2009, late ed. (East Coast).

Cordesman, Anthony H., and Adam C. Seitz. *Iranian Weapons of Mass Destruction: The Birth of a Regional Nuclear Arms Race?* Santa Barbara, Calif.: Praeger Security International; Washington, D.C.: Center for Strategic and International Studies, 2009.

Corera, Gordon. *Shopping for Bombs: Nuclear Proliferation, Global Insecurity, and the Rise and Fall of the A.Q. Khan Network*. Oxford: Oxford University Press, 2006.

Cornes, Richard, and Todd Sandler. "Easy Riders, Joint Production, and Public Goods." *Economic Journal* 94, no. 3 (1984): 580–98.

Corrales, Javier, and Richard E. Feinberg. "Regimes of Cooperation in the Western Hemisphere: Power, Interests, and Intellectual Traditions." *International Studies Quarterly* 43, no. 1 (1999): 1–36. doi:10.1111/0020-8833.00109.

Covarrubias, Ana. "Cuba and Mexico: A Case for Mutual Nonintervention." *Cuban Studies*, no. 26 (1996): 121–41.

Crail, Peter. "IAEA Approves India Additional Protocol." *Arms Control Today* 39, no. 3 (2009): 39–40.

Crawford, Beverly. "German Policy on Non-Proliferation and Dual Use Technology. A Case of 'Embedded Hegemony'?" March 22, 2006. http://citation.allacademic.com/meta/p_mla_apa_research_citation/0/9/9/1/8/pages99184/p99184-1.php.

———. "A Teutonic Shift: The Revolution in German Policy on Non-proliferation and Dual Use Export Controls." Paper presented at 47th Annual ISA Convention, San Diego, Calif., March 22–25, 2006.

Cupitt, Richard T., Suzette Grillot, and Yuzo Murayama. "The Determinants of Non-proliferation Export Controls: A Membership-Fee Explanation." *Nonproliferation Review* 8, no. 2 (2001): 69–80. doi:10.1080/10736700108436851.

Democracia e Forças Armadas No Cone Sul. 1a. ed. Rio de Janeiro, Brasil: Editora FGV, 2000.

Denyer, Simon, and Rama Lakshmi. "U.S.-India Nuclear Deal Drifts Dangerously." *Washington Post*, July 15, 2011. http://www.washingtonpost.com/world/asia-pacific/us-india-nuclear-deal-drifts-dangerously/2011/07/07/gIQAJTbeGI_story.html.

DeYoung, Karen. "U.S. Envoy Indicates Flexibility with Russia on Missile Defense." *Washington Post*, February 14, 2009.

Dhanapala, Jayantha. "The State of the Regime." In *Repairing the Regime: Preventing the Spread of Weapons of Mass Destruction*, edited by Joseph Cirincione, 15–22. New York: Routledge, 2000.

Diamond, Howard. "U.S., Russia Take New Steps to Control Technology Transfers to Iran." *Arms Control Today* 28, no. 2 (1998): 24.

DiFilippo, Anthony. *Japan's Nuclear Disarmament Policy and the U.S. Security Umbrella*. New York: Macmillan, 2006.

Domínguez, Jorge I., ed. *International Security and Democracy: Latin America and the Caribbean in the Post–Cold War Era*. Pittsburgh: University of Pittsburgh Press, 1998.

Domínguez, Jorge I., and Rafael Fernández de Castro. *The United States and Mexico: Between Partnership and Conflict*. New York: Routledge, 2001.

Domínguez, Jorge I., David Mares, Manuel Orozco, David Scott Palmer, Francisco Rojas Aravena, and Andrés Serbin. "Boundary Disputes in Latin America." *Peaceworks*, no. 50, (United States Institute of Peace, 2013). http://www.usip.org/publications/boundary-disputes-in-latin-america.

Dunn, Lewis A. "High Noon for the NPT." *Arms Control Today* 25, no. 6 (1995): 3.

Dunn, Lewis A., Gregory Giles, Jeffrey Larsen, and Thomas Skypek. *Foreign Perspectives on the U.S. Nuclear Policy and Posture: Insights, Issues and Implications*. SAIC/and Defense Threat Reduction Agency, December 12, 2006. http://www.fas.org/irp/agency/dod/dtra/foreign-pers.pdf.

Dunn, Michael Collins. "MEJ Author Målfrid Braut-Hegghammer on Libya's Nuclear Rollback." *MEI Bulletin* 59, no. 1 (2008): 8–9.

Durkheim, Emile. *Rules of Sociological Method*. Edited by Steven Lukes; translated by W. D. Hall. New York: Free Press, 1982.

Einhorn, Robert J., and Gary Samore. "Ending Russian Assistance to Iran's Nuclear Bomb." *Survival* 44, no. 2 (2002): 51–70.

Elman, Miriam Fendius. "The Foreign Policies of Small States: Challenging Neorealism in Its Own Backyard." *British Journal of Political Science* 25, no. 2 (1995): 171–217. doi:10.1017/S0007123400007146.

Erlanger, Steven. "European Union Moves Closer to Imposing Tough Sanctions on Iran." *New York Times*, January 21, 2012, late ed. (East Coast).

———. "U.S. Gets Russia's Firm Vow to Halt Missile Aid to Iran." *New York Times*, January 16, 1998, late ed. (East Coast).

"Europe's Leaky Borders." *Bulletin of the Atomic Scientists* 49, no. 5 (1993): 27.

Fahmy, Nabil. "Mindful of the Middle East: Egypt's Reaction to the New U.S. Nuclear Posture Review." *Nonproliferation Review* 18, no. 1 (2011): 165–81. doi:10.1080/10736700.2011.549179.

Fathi, Nazila. "Iran Rejects Russian Offer to Defuse Nuclear Dispute." *New York Times*, March 13, 2006, late ed. (East Coast).

———. "Putin Is Said to Offer Idea on Standoff over Iran." *New York Times*, October 18, 2007, late ed. (East Coast).

Fathi, Nazila, and C. J. Chivers. "Putin Says Caspian Area Is Off Limits to Attacks." *New York Times*, October 17, 2007.

Felgenhauer, Pavel. "The 'Unravelling Relationship' between Russia and Iran." BBC, July 24, 2010. www.bbc.co.uk/news/world-europe-10684110.

Festinger, Leon. "A Theory of Social Comparison Processes." *Human Relations* 7, no. 2 (1954): 117–40.

Fields, Jeffrey, and Jason S. Enia. "The Health of the Nuclear Nonproliferation Regime: Returning to a Multidimensional Evaluation." *Nonproliferation Review* 16, no. 2 (2009): 173–96. doi:10.1080/10736700902969646.

"Fighting the Nuclear Fight: When Nuclear Sheriffs Quarrel." *Economist*, October 30, 2008. http://www.economist.com/node/12516611.

Fihn, Beatrice, and Ray Acheson. "Planning for Nuclear Disarmament Now." NPT *News in Review*, no. 6 (May 10, 2010). http://www.reachingcriticalwill.org/images/documents/Disarmament-fora/npt/NIR2010/No6.pdf.

Finn, Peter. "Russia to Suspend Compliance with Key European Pact." *Washington Post*, April 27, 2007.

———. "U.S., Russia Sign Pact on Nuclear Cooperation." *Washington Post*, May 7, 2008.

Fitzpatrick, Mark. *Nuclear Programmes in the Middle East: In the Shadow of Iran*. London: International Institute for Strategic Studies, 2008.

———. "U.S.-India Nuclear Cooperation Accord: Implications for the Non-proliferation Regime." *Asia-Pacific Review* 15, no. 1 (2008): 76–85. doi:10.1080/13439000802134076.

Ford, Christopher A. "Debating Disarmament: Interpreting Article VI of the Treaty on the Non-Proliferation of Nuclear Weapons." *Nonproliferation Review* 14, no. 3 (2007): 401–28. doi:10.1080/10736700701611720.

———. "Disarmament versus Nonproliferation?" Speech, sponsored by the Los Alamos National Laboratory and the Woodrow Wilson International Center for Scholars. Washington, D.C., October 28, 2010. http://www.hudson.org/index.cfm?fuseaction=publication_details&id=7472&pubType=HI_Speeches_Testimony.

———. "Nuclear Disarmament, Nonproliferation, and the 'Credibility Thesis.'" Hudson Institute Briefing Paper, September 2009. http://www.hudson.org/files/publications/Nuclear%20DisarmamentCF909.pdf.

Franck, Thomas M. *The Power of Legitimacy among Nations.* New York: Oxford University Press, 1990.

Frantz, Douglas. "Nuclear Booty: More Smugglers Use Asia Route." *New York Times,* September 11, 2001. http://www.nytimes.com/2001/09/11/world/nuclear-booty-more-smugglers-use-asia-route.html.

Frieden, Jeffry A. *Debt, Development, and Democracy: Modern Political Economy and Latin America, 1965–1985.* Princeton, N.J: Princeton University Press, 1991.

Gaddis, John Lewis, Philip H. Gordon, Ernest R. May, and Jonathan Rosenberg, eds. *Cold War Statesmen Confront the Bomb: Nuclear Diplomacy since 1945.* Oxford: Oxford University Press, 1999.

Ganguly, Šumit. "India's Pathway to Pokhran II: The Prospects and Sources of New Delhi's Nuclear Weapons Program." *International Security* 23, no. 4 (1999): 148–77.

Ganguly, Sumit, and Dinshaw Mistry. "The Case for the U.S.-India Nuclear Agreement." *World Policy Journal* 23, no. 2 (2006): 11–19. doi:10.2307/40210014.

García Robles, Alfonso. *Alfonso García Robles, México, Nobel de La Paz.* 1a ed. Frontera. México, D.F: Secretaría de Educación Pública: Secretaría de Relaciones Exteriores, 1984.

———. *El Tratado de Tlatelolco; Génesis, alcance y propósitos de la proscripeión de las armas nucleares en la América Latina.* Publicaciones Del Centro de Estudios Internacionales 4. México City: El Colegio de México, 1967.

Garcia Robles, S. E. Kenza de. "Une alternative en matiere de non-proliferation: Les zones libre d'armes nucleaires" [An alternative to nonproliferation: Nuclear-free zones]. *Relations Internationales et Strategiques* 17 (1995): 192–99.

Gartzke, Erik, and Dong-Joon Jo. "Bargaining, Nuclear Proliferation, and Interstate Disputes." *Journal of Conflict Resolution* 53, no. 2 (2009): 209–233. doi:10.1177/0022002708330289.

Gavin, Francis J. "Blasts from the Past: Proliferation Lessons from the 1960s." *International Security* 29, no. 3 (2004): 100–135.

Gay, Colin, and David Albright. "Taiwan: Nuclear Nightmare Averted." *Bulletin of the Atomic Scientists* 54, no. 1 (1998): 54–60.

Glasser, Susan B. "Russia, Iran Renew Alliance Meant to Boost Arms Trade; Tehran Seeking Advanced Technology; U.S. Is Concerned." *Washington Post,* March 13, 2001, final ed.

Goldemberg, José. "Brazil." In *Non-proliferation: The Why and the Wherefore,* edited by Jozef Goldblat. London: Taylor & Francis, 1985.

Goldgeier, J. M., and P. E. Tetlock. "Psychology and International Relations Theory." *Annual Review of Political Science* 4, no. 1 (2001): 67–92. doi:10.1146/annurev.polisci.4.1.67.

Goldmann, Kjell. "Appropriateness and Consequences: The Logic of Neo-Institutionalism." *Governance* 18, no. 1 (2005): 35–52. doi:10.1111/j.1468-0491.2004.00265.x.

Goldschmidt, Pierre. "Is the Nuclear Non-proliferation Regime in Crisis? If So, Why? Are There Remedies?" Paper delivered to the Charlottesville Committee on Foreign Relations, Charlottesville, Va., May 11, 2006.

———. "The Urgent Need to Strengthen the Nuclear Non-proliferation Regime." *Policy Outlook*, no. 25 (Carnegie Endowment for International Peace), January 10, 2006. http://carnegieendowment.org/files/PO25.Goldschmidt.Final2.pdf.

González González, Guadalupe, Ferrán Martínez, and Jorge Schiavon. *México, the Americas and the World 2008: Foreign Policy: Public and Leader Opinion*. Mexico City: CIDE, 2009.

Gordon, Philip H. "Charles de Gaulle and the Nuclear Revolution." In *Cold War Statesmen Confront the Bomb: Nuclear Diplomacy since 1945*, edited by John Lewis Gaddis, Philip H. Gordon, Ernest R. May, and Jonathan Rosenberg, 216–35. Oxford: Oxford University Press, 1999.

Gottemoeller, Rose. "The New START Treaty." Testimony before the Senate Armed Services Committee, Washington, D.C., July 29, 2010. http://www.state.gov/t/avc/rls/145336.htm.

———. "Remarks by Rose Gottemoeller at a High Level Meeting on Revitalizing the Work of the Conference on Disarmament." Speech, New York, July 27, 2011. http://usun.state.gov/briefing/statements/2011/169152.htm.

Graham, Thomas, Jr. *Disarmament Sketches: Three Decades of Arms Control and International Law*. Seattle: Institute for Global and Regional Security Studies and University of Washington Press, 2002.

———. "The Origin and Interpretation of Article VI." Statement presented at the *Nonproliferation Review* Luncheon Briefing, James Martin Center for Nonproliferation Studies, Washington, D.C., November 29, 2007. http://cns.miis.edu/activities/071129_nprbriefing.

Greenhouse, Steven. "U.S. Says Russia Promised Nuclear Gear to Iran." *New York Times*, April 29, 1995, late ed. (East Coast).

Grossman, Elaine M. "U.S. Opposes Moving Nuclear Material Talks out of Geneva: Senior Official." *Global Security Newswire*, August 4, 2011. http://www.nti.org/gsn/article/us-opposes-moving-nuclear-material-talks-out-of-geneva-senior-official/.

Grotto, Andrew. "Why Do States That Oppose Nuclear Proliferation Resist New Nonproliferation Obligations? Three Logics of Nonproliferation Decision-Making." *Cardozo Journal of International and Comparative Law* 18, no. 1 (2010): 1–43.

Grotto, Andrew, and Joe Cirincione. "Orienting the 2009 Nuclear Posture Review: A Roadmap." *Arms Control Today* 39, no. 1 (2009): 5.

Guthrie, Richard, John Hart, and Frida Kuhlau. "Chemical and Biological Warfare Developments and Arms Control." *SIPRI Yearbook 2005*, 603–28. Stockholm: SIPRI, 2005.

Haas, Ernst B. *When Knowledge Is Power: Three Models of Change in International Organizations*. Studies in International Political Economy 22. Berkeley: University of California Press, 1990.

Halpin, Tony. "Defiant Russia Flexes Its Muscles with Uranium Shipment to Iran." *Times* (London), December 18, 2007.

———. "Vladimir Putin Pledges to Complete Iranian Nuclear Reactor." *Times* (London), October 17, 2007.

Hardin, Russell. "Collective Action as an Agreeable n-Prisoner's Dilemma." *Behavioral Science* 16, no. 5 (1971): 472–81.

Harding, Luke. "Russia Sells Iran New Anti-Aircraft Missiles." *Guardian* (London), December 27, 2007.

Hasenclever, Andreas, Peter Mayer, and Volker Rittberger. *Theories of International Regimes*. Cambridge: Cambridge University Press, 1997.

Hassner, Pierre. "Who Killed Nuclear Enlightenment?" *International Affairs* 83, no. 3 (2007): 455–67. doi:10.1111/j.1468-2346.2007.00631.x.

Hathaway, Oona A. "The Cost of Commitment." *Stanford Law Review* 55, no. 5 (2003): 1821–62. doi:10.2307/1229565.

Head, John G. "Public Goods and Public Policy." *Public Finance* 17, no. 3 (1962): 197–219.

Heinrich, Mark. "IAEA's Poor Nations Split on Iran's Attack Ban Bid." Reuters. September 16, 2009. http://www.reuters.com/article/2009/09/16/us-nuclear-iran-ban-idUSTRE58F41220090916.

Helfstein, Scott, Michael J. Meese, Don Rassler, Reid Sawyer, Troy Schnack, Mathew Sheiffer, Scott Silverstone, and Scott Taylor. "White Paper Prepared for the Secretary of Defense Task Force on DoD Nuclear Weapons Management: Tradeoffs and Paradoxes: Terrorism, Deterrence and Nuclear Weapons." *Studies in Conflict & Terrorism* 32, no. 9 (2009): 776–801. doi:10.1080/10576100903124049.

Hensel, Paul R. "Contentious Issues and World Politics: The Management of Territorial Claims in the Americas, 1816–1992." *International Studies Quarterly* 45, no. 1 (2001): 81–109. doi:10.1111/0020-8833.00183.

Hersman, Rebecca K. C., and Robert Peters. "Nuclear U-Turns." *Nonproliferation Review* 13, no. 3 (2006): 539–53. doi:10.1080/10736700601071629.

Herspring, Dale R., ed. *Putin's Russia: Past Imperfect, Future Uncertain*. 3rd ed. Lanham, Md.: Rowman & Littlefield, 2007.

Heydarian, Javad. "Russia's Iran Nuclear Solution." *Diplomat*, November 16, 2011.

Hiatt, Fred. "Russia Denies Plan to Sell Gas Centrifuge to Iran." *Washington Post*, May 5, 1995.

———. "U.S. Efforts to Block Iran Reactor Sale Cause Anger in Moscow." *Washington Post*, March 3, 1995.

Hibbs, Mark. "Nuclear Suppliers Group and the IAEA Additional Protocol." Carnegie Endowment for International Peace, July 16, 2013. http://carnegieendowment.org/2010/08/18/nuclear-suppliers-group-and-iaea-additional-protocol/ep.

Hirshleifer, Jack. "From Weakest-Link to Best-Shot: The Voluntary Provision of Public Goods." *Public Choice* 41, no. 3 (1983): 371–86.

Hirst, Mónica, ed. *Desarme y Desarrollo en América Latina*. Buenos Aires, Argentina: Fundación Arturo Illia para la Democracia y la Paz, 1990.

———. "Security Policies, Democratization, and Regional Integration in the Southern Cone." In *International Security and Democracy: Latin America and the Caribbean in the Post–Cold War Era*, edited by Jorge I. Dominguez. Pittsburgh: University of Pittsburgh Press, 1995.

Horner, Daniel. "IAEA Board Approves Fuel Bank Plan." *Arms Control Today*, January/February 2011. http://www.armscontrol.org/act/2011_01-02/Fuel%20Bank.

———. "NSG Revises Rules on Sensitive Exports." *Arms Control Today* 41, no 6 (2011). https://www.armscontrol.org/act/2011_%2007-08/Nuclear_Suppliers_Group_NSG_Revises_Rules_Sensitive_Exports.

Huerta, José, et al. *Operaciones conjuntas: Civiles y militares en la política de defensa*. Lima: Instituto de Defensa Legal, 2006.

Hufbauer, Gary Clyde, Jeffrey J. Schott, Kimberly Ann Elliott, and Barbara Oegg. *Economic Sanctions Reconsidered*. 3rd ed. Washington, D.C.: Peterson Institute for International Economics, 2007.

Huntington, Samuel P. *Political Order in Changing Societies*. New Haven: Yale University Press, 1968.

Hurd, Ian. "Legitimacy and Authority in International Politics." *International Organization* 53, no. 2 (1999): 379–408. doi:10.1162/002081899550913.

———. "Legitimacy and Power in International Relations." Unpublished manuscript, n.d.

Hurrell, Andrew. "Emerging Security Community in South America?" In *Security Communities*, edited by Emanuel Adler and Michael Barnett, 228–64. Cambridge: Cambridge University Press, 1998.

———. "Security in Latin America." *International Affairs* 74, no. 3 (1998): 529–46.

Hurrell, Andrew, Andrew F. Cooper, Guadalupe González González, Ricardo Ubiraci Sennes, and Srini Sitaraman. "Paths to Power: Foreign Policy Strategies of Intermediate States." Latin American Program Working Papers. Woodrow Wilson International Center for Scholars, March 2000. http://www.wilsoncenter.org/sites/default/files/ACF14A1.pdf.

Hymans, Jacques E. C. *The Psychology of Nuclear Proliferation: Identity, Emotions, and Foreign Policy*. Cambridge: Cambridge University Press, 2006.

———. "Theories of Nuclear Proliferation: The State of the Field." *Nonproliferation Review* 13, no. 3 (2006): 455–65. doi:10.1080/10736700601071397.

"International: Vlad and MAD; Russia and Arms Control." *Economist*, June 9, 2007.

International Atomic Energy Agency. "IAEA Regular Budget for 2012." Accessed July 12, 2013. http://www.iaea.org/About/budget.html.

———. "Implementation of the NPT Safeguards Agreement in the Arab Republic of Egypt." Report by the Director General, February 14, 2005. http://www.globalsecurity.org/wmd/library/report/2005/egypt_iaea_gov-2005-9_14feb2005.pdf.

———. "International Conventions and Legal Agreements: Convention on the Physical Protection of Nuclear Material." Accessed March 14, 2014. http://www.iaea.org/Publications/Documents/Conventions/cppnm.html.

———. *Multilateral Approaches to the Nuclear Fuel Cycle: Expert Group Report to the Director General of the IAEA*. Vienna: International Atomic Energy Agency, 2005. http://www.iaea.org/Publications/Documents/Infcircs/2005/infcirc640.pdf.

———. "Nuclear Security Advisory Services." November 6, 2010. Accessed March 15, 2011. http://www-ns.iaea.org/security/advisory.asp?s=7&l=48.

———. "Safeguards Statement for 2009." December 31, 2009. Accessed February 14, 2014. http://www.iaea.org/safeguards/documents/es2009.pdf.

———. "Status List: Conclusion of Safeguards Agreements, Additional Protocols and Small Quantities Protocols as of December 20." International Atomic Energy Agency, December 20, 2010.

———. "Status List: Conclusion of Safeguards Agreements, Additional Protocols and Small Quantities Protocols as of 7 June 2013." International Atomic Energy Agency, June 7, 2013.

International Court of Justice. "Legality of the Threat or Use of Nuclear Weapons: Advisory Opinion," The Hague, July 8, 1996. *ICJ Reports 1996*, 263–64.

International Panel on Fissile Materials. *Global Fissile Material Report 2010: Balancing the Books: Production and Stocks*. IPFM, December 2010. http://fissilematerials.org/library/gfmr10.pdf.

"Iran Hopes for Oil Partnerships with Moscow, Minister Tells Russian Agency." RIA Novosti (in Russian, translated by BBC Monitoring), September 3, 2012.

Jackson, Robert H., and Carl G. Rosberg. "Why Africa's Weak States Persist: The Empirical and the Juridical in Statehood." *World Politics* 35, no. 1 (1982): 1–24. doi:10.2307/2010277.

"Japan's Long Fuse." *Christian Science Monitor*, May 9, 2003. http://www.csmonitor.com/2003/0509/p10s01-comv.html.

Jo, Dong-Joon, and Erik Gartzke. "Determinants of Nuclear Weapons Proliferation." *Journal of Conflict Resolution* 51, no. 1 (2007): 167–94. doi:10.2307/27638542.

Joffe, Josef, and James W. Davis. "Less Than Zero: Bursting the New Disarmament Bubble." *Foreign Affairs* 90, no.1 (2011). http://www.foreignaffairs.com/articles/67034/josef-joffe-and-james-w-davis/less-than-zero.

Johnson, Craig M. "The Russian Federation's Ministry of Atomic Energy: Programs and Developments." Paper prepared for the U.S. Department of Energy. Richland, Wash.: Pacific Northwest National Laboratory, February 2000.

Johnson, Rebecca. "Politics and Protection: Why the 2005 NPT Review Conference Failed." *Disarmament Diplomacy*, no. 80 (2005). Accessed July 10, 2013. http://www.acronym.org.uk/dd/dd80/80npt.htm.

———. "The 2000 NPT Review Conference: A Delicate, Hard-Won Compromise." *Disarmament Diplomacy*, no. 46 (2000). http://www.acronym.org.uk/dd/dd46/46npt.htm.

Jones, Rodney W., and Mark G. McDonough, with Toby F. Dalton and Gregory D. Koblentz. *Tracking Nuclear Proliferation: A Guide in Maps and Charts, 1998*. Washington, D.C.: Carnegie Endowment for International Peace, 1998.

Jonter, Thomas. "The United States and Swedish Plans to Build the Bomb." In *Security Assurances and Nuclear Nonproliferation*, edited by Jeffrey W. Knopf. Stanford, Calif.: Stanford University Press, 2012.

Joyner, Daniel. *Interpreting the Nuclear Non-Proliferation Treaty*. Oxford: Oxford University Press, 2011.

Jun, Bong-Geun. "U.S.-ROK Nuclear Energy Cooperation from Tutelage to Partnership: Nonproliferation Factor." U.S.-ROK Workshop on Nuclear Energy and Nonproliferation, Washington, D.C., January 20, 2010.

Kacowicz, Arie Marcelo. *The Impact of Norms in International Society: The Latin American Experience, 1881–2001*. Notre Dame, Ind: University of Notre Dame Press, 2005.

Kagan, Robert. "New START: Too Modest to Merit Partisan Bickering." *Washington Post*, July 30, 2010. http://www.washingtonpost.com/wp-dyn/content/story/2010/07/29/ST2010072905170.html?sid=ST2010072905170.

———. "Why Is the GOP Fighting This Treaty?" *Washington Post*, July 30, 2010.

Kanbur, Ravi, Todd Sandler, and Kevin Morrison. *The Future of Development Assistance: Common Pools and International Public Goods*. Washington, D.C.: Overseas Development Council, 1999.

Kaul, Inge, Isabelle Grunberg, and Marc A. Stern, eds. *Global Public Goods: International Cooperation in the 21st Century*. New York: Oxford University Press, 1999.

Keohane, Robert O. *After Hegemony: Cooperation and Discord in the World Political Economy*. Princeton, N.J.: Princeton University Press, 2005.

Kerr, Paul. "IAEA Board Closes Safeguards Loophole." *Arms Control Today* 35, no. 9 (2005): 29.

Kershner, Isabel, and Rick Gladstone. "Decision on Whether to Attack Iran Is 'Far Off,' Israeli Defense Minister Says." *New York Times*, January 19, 2012, late ed. (East Coast).

Kimball, Daryl G. "New Nuclear Suppliers Rules a Net Plus." *Arms Control Today*. July/August 2011. Accessed July 12, 2013. http://www.armscontrol.org/act/2011_0708/Focus.

Knopf, Jeffrey W. "The Importance of International Learning." *Review of International Studies* 29, no. 2 (2003): 185–207. doi:10.1017/S0260210503001852.

———. "Nuclear Disarmament and Nonproliferation: Examining the Linkage Argument." *International Security* 37, no. 3 (2012): 92–132. doi:10.1162/ISEC_a_00109.

———, ed. *Security Assurances and Nuclear Nonproliferation*. Stanford, Calif.: Stanford University Press, 2012.

Kramer, Andrew E. "Gazprom Becomes the Bear of Russia." *New York Times*, December 27, 2005, late ed. (East Coast).

———. "Russia Settles Issues on Iran Nuclear Power Plant." *New York Times*, December 14, 2007.

———. "Russia Will Slow Work on Iran's Nuclear Plant." *New York Times*, February 20, 2007.

Krasner, Stephen D., ed. *International Regimes*. Cornell Studies in Political Economy. Ithaca, N.Y.: Cornell University Press, 1983.

Krasno, Jean. "Non-proliferation: Brazil's Secret Nuclear Program." *Orbis: A Journal of World Affairs* 38, no. 3 (1994): 425–36.

Krause, Joachim. "Enlightenment and Nuclear Order." *International Affairs* 83, no. 3 (2007): 483–99. Available at Social Science Research Network. Accessed July 15, 2013. http://papers.ssrn.com/abstract=1062047.

Krepon, Michael, Jenny S. Drezin, and Michael Newbill, eds. *Declaratory Diplomacy: Rhetorical Initiatives and Confidence Building*. Report no. 27. Washington, D.C.: Henry L. Stimson Center, 1999.

Kroenig, Matthew. "Exporting the Bomb: Why States Provide Sensitive Nuclear Assistance." *American Political Science Review* 103, no. 1 (2009): 113–33. doi:10.1017/S0003055409090017.

———. "Importing the Bomb: Sensitive Nuclear Assistance and Nuclear Proliferation." *Journal of Conflict Resolution* 53, no. 2 (2009): 161–80. doi:10.1177/0022002708330287.

Kupchan, Charles A. *How Enemies Become Friends: The Sources of Stable Peace*. Princeton Studies in International History and Politics. Princeton, N.J.: Princeton University Press, 2010.

Kutchesfahani, Sara Z. "The Relevance of Historical Experience to Current Nuclear Proliferation Challenges." 2009 PONI Conference Series. Washington, D.C: Center for Strategic and International Studies, 2009. http://csis.org/images/stories/poni/110921_Kutchesfahani.pdf.

LaFranchi, Howard. "Will EU and US Be Tougher Now on Iran?" *Christian Science Monitor*, December 26, 2006.

Lake, David A., and Patrick M. Morgan, eds. *Regional Orders: Building Security in a New World*. University Park: Pennsylvania State University Press, 1997.

Landler, Mark. "U.S. and U.N. Agency Press Iran on Its Nuclear Program." *New York Times*, June 18, 2003, late ed. (East Coast).

Lantratov, Konstantin, and Alexandra Gritskova. "Iran Prikryvaet Atomnuyu Programmu Russkimi Raketami: Gotovitsiya Kontrakt Na Postavku Sistem S-300." *Kommersant*, December 27, 2007.

Leventhal, Paul L., and Sharon Tanzer, eds. *Averting a Latin American Nuclear Arms Race: New Prospects and Challenges for Argentine-Brazil Nuclear Co-operation*. New York: St. Martin's Press; Washington, D.C.: Nuclear Control Institute, 1992.

Levine, John M., and E. Tory Higgins. "Shared Reality and Social Influence in Groups and Organizations." In *Social Influence in Social Reality: Promoting Individual and Social Change*, edited by Fabrizio Butera and Gabriel Mugny, 33–52. Ashland, Ohio: Hogrefe & Huber, 2001.

Levite, Ariel E. "Never Say Never Again: Nuclear Reversal Revisited." *International Security* 27, no. 3 (2002/2003): 59–88. doi:10.1162/01622880260553633.

"Libya's PM Confirms Presence of Chemical Weapons." *USA Today*, October 31, 2011. Associated Press. Accessed July 10, 2013. http://www.usatoday.com/news/world/story/2012-10-30/libya-chemical-weapons-found/51009366/1.

Lima, Maria Regina Soares de. "The Political Economy of Brazilian Foreign Policy: Nuclear Energy, Trade, and Itaipu." PhD diss., Vanderbilt University, 1986. https://catalyst.library.jhu.edu/catalog/bib_218120.

Linz, Juan J., and Alfred Stepan. *Problems of Democratic Transition and Consolidation: Southern Europe, South America, and Post-Communist Europe*. Baltimore: Johns Hopkins University Press, 1996.

Lippman, Thomas W. "Russia-Iran Atomic Deal Irks U.S.; Sen. McCain Asks State Dept. to Act." *Washington Post*, February 11, 1995.

———. "2 Nuclear Accords Expected; U.S.-Russia Pact Involves Uranium Buy." *Washington Post*, March 21, 1999.

Lodding, Jan. *Non-proliferation of Nuclear Weapons and Nuclear Security: IAEA Safeguards Agreements and Additional Protocols*. Vienna, Austria: International Atomic Energy Agency, May 2005.

Lodgaard, Sverre. *Nuclear Disarmament and Non-proliferation: Towards a Nuclear-Weapon Free World?* Milton Park, Abingdon, Eng.: Routledge, 2012.

Lugo, Meri. "CTBT at the RevCon." Project for the Comprehensive Nuclear Test Ban Treaty. May 21, 2010. Accessed July 10, 2013. http://www.projectforthectbt.org/RevConStatements.

Macrory, Patrick F. J. Arthur E. Appleton, and Michael G. Plummer, eds. *The World Trade Organization: Legal, Economic and Political Analysis*. New York: Springer, 2005.

Maerli, Morten Bremer, and Sverre Lodgaard, eds. *Nuclear Proliferation and International Security*. New York: Routledge, 2007.

Malek, Martin. "Russia, Iran, and the Conflict in Chechnya." *Caucasian Review of International Affairs* 2, no. 1 (2008): 25–34.

Mansfield, Edward D., and Jon C. Pevehouse. "Democratization and International Organizations." *International Organization* 60, no. 1 (2006): 137–67. doi:10.1017/S002081830606005X.

March, James G., and Johan P. Olsen. *Rediscovering Institutions: The Organizational Basis of Politics*. New York: Free Press, 1989.

Mares, David R. "Middle Powers under Regional Hegemony: To Challenge or Acquiesce in Hegemonic Enforcement." *International Studies Quarterly* 32, no. 4 (1998): 453–71.

———. "Regional Conflict Management in Latin America: Power Complemented by Diplomacy." In *Regional Orders: Building Security in a New World*, edited by David A. Lake and Patrick M. Morgan, 195–218. University Park: Pennsylvania State University Press, 1997.

———. *Violent Peace: Militarized Interstate Bargaining in Latin America*. New York: Columbia University Press, 2001.

Marín Bosch, Miguel. *Alfonso Garcia Robles: Mexico, Nobel de la Paz*. Mexico City: SEPSER, 1984.

Martin, Lisa L., and Beth A. Simmons. "Theories and Empirical Studies of International Institutions." *International Organization* 52, no. 4 (1998): 729–57. doi:10.1162/002081898550734.

Marzo, Marcos. "Additional Protocol: Logic and Impact." Brazilian-Argentine Agency for Accounting and Control of Nuclear Energy: Working Paper. Rio de Janeiro, Brazil, January 2012. http://www.abacc.org.br/wp-content/uploads/2012/01/Additional-Protocol_Marzo.pdf.

Matishak, Martin. "Top Republican Remains Opposed to Nuclear Test Ban." *Global Security Newswire*, March 29, 2011. http://gsn.nti.org/gsn/nw_20110329_7806.php.

McGoldrick, Fred. *Limiting Transfers of Enrichment and Reprocessing Technology: Issues, Constraints, Options*. Project on Managing the Atom. Cambridge, Mass.: Belfer Center for Science and International Affairs, May 2011.

McGoldrick, Fred, Harold Bengelsdorf, and Lawrence Scheinman. "The U.S.-India Nuclear Deal: Taking Stock." *Arms Control Today* 35, no. 8 (2005): 6–12. http://www.armscontrol.org/act/2005_10/OCT-Cover.

Medeiros, Evan S. *China's International Behavior: Activism, Opportunism, and Diversification*. Santa Monica, Calif.: RAND Corporation, 2009. http://www.rand.org/pubs/monographs/MG850.

Mercer, Jonathan. "Emotional Beliefs." *International Organization* 64, no. 1 (2010): 1–31. doi:10.1017/S0020818309990221.

Meselson, M., and D. E. Viney. "The Yemen." In *CBW: Chemical and Biological Warfare*, edited by Steven Rose, 99–102. Boston: Beacon Press, 1969.

Meyer, Paul. " Prague One Year Later: From Words to Deeds?" *Arms Control Today* 40, no. 4 (May 2010): 64–68.

Meyer, Stephen M. *The Dynamics of Nuclear Proliferation*. Chicago: University of Chicago Press, 1984.

Miller, Steven E. "Proliferation, Disarmament, and the Future of the Non-proliferation Treaty." In *Nuclear Proliferation and International Security*, edited by Morten Bremer Maerli and Sverre Lodgaard, 50–70. New York: Routledge, 2007.

"Ministry 'Engineered' Parts of Iranian Nuclear Deal-Russian Ambassador to U.S." Interfax (in Russian, translated by BBC Monitoring), May 10, 1995.

Mitchell, Ronald B. "International Control of Nuclear Proliferation: Beyond Carrots and Sticks." *Nonproliferation Review* 5, no. 1 (1997): 40–52. doi:10.1080/10736709708436692.

Mohammed, Arshad, and Phil Stewart. "U.S. Says Nuclear Arsenal Includes 5,113 Warheads." Reuters, May 3, 2010. http://www.reuters.com/article/idUSTRE64251X 20100503.

Monroe, Kristen Renwick, Adam Martin, and Priyanka Ghosh. "Politics and an Innate Moral Sense: Scientific Evidence for an Old Theory?" *Political Research Quarterly* 62, no. 3 (2009): 614–34. doi:10.1177/1065912909336272.

Moore, Molly. "U.S. Still Short in Iran Security Council Push; Permanent Members Russia, China Favor Less Formal Action on Atomic Program." *Washington Post*, January 22, 2006.

Mueller, John. "The Essential Irrelevance of Nuclear Weapons: Stability in the Postwar World." *International Security* 13, no. 2 (1988): 55–79.

Mueller, John E. *Atomic Obsession: Nuclear Alarmism from Hiroshima to Al-Qaeda*. New York: Oxford University Press, 2009.

Müller, Harald. "Europe's Leaky Borders." *Bulletin of the Atomic Scientists* 49, no. 5 (1993): 27.

———. "The Future of Nuclear Weapons in an Interdependent World." *Washington Quarterly* 31, no. 2 (2008): 63–75.

———. "German National Identity and WMD Proliferation." *Nonproliferation Review* 10, no. 2 (2003): 1–20. doi:10.1080/10736700308436927.

———. "The Internalization of Principles, Norms, and Rules by Governments: The Case of Security Regimes." In *Regime Theory and International Relations*, edited by Volker Rittberger, 361–88. Oxford: Oxford University Press, 1993.

———. "Nuclear Disarmament and the Nonproliferation Treaty." *WMD Insights*, no. 29 (2008/2009): 2–7.

———. "A Nuclear Nonproliferation Test: Obama's Nuclear Policy and the 2010 NPT Review Conference." *Nonproliferation Review* 18, no. 1 (2011): 219–36. doi:10.1080/10736 700.2011.549182.

———. "The 2005 NPT Review Conference: Reasons and Consequences of Failure and Options for Repair." Paper no. 31. Oslo: Weapons of Mass Destruction Commission, 2005. http://www.blixassociates.com/wp-content/uploads/2011/03/No31.pdf.

Müller, Harald, David Fischer, and Wolfgang Kötter. *Nuclear Non-proliferation and Global Order*. Oxford: Oxford University Press, 1994.

Murphy, Katharine. "No to Indian Uranium Sales." *Age* (Melbourne), February 11, 2011. http://www.theage.com.au/national/no-to-indian-uranium-sales-20110210-1a00t.html.

Nadal Egea, Alejandro. "Trayectorias de misiles balísticos intercontinentales: Implicaciones para los vecinos de las superpotencias" [Trajectories of the international ballistic missiles: Implications for states neighboring superpowers]. *Foro Internacional* 30, no. 1 (1989): 93–114.

Natalegawa, H. E. Dr. R. M. Marty M. "Statement of the Republic of Indonesia at the General Debate at the 2010 NPT Review Conference." New York, May 3, 2010. http://www.un.org/en/conf/npt/2010/statements/pdf/indonesia_en.pdf.

"Nations Weigh Taking Fissile Material Talks outside Disarmament Forum." *Global Security Newswire*, May 2, 2011. http://gsn.nti.org/gsn/nw_20110516_7823.php.

Nikitin, Mary Beth. *U.S.-Russian Civilian Nuclear Cooperation Agreement: Issues for Congress*. Washington, D.C: Congressional Research Service, 2011.

Non-Aligned Movement. XV Summit of the Non-Aligned Movement. "History and Evolution of the NAM." July 11–16, 2009. http://www.namegypt.org/en/AboutName/HistoryAndEvolution/Pages/default.aspx (accessed January 14, 2011, but no longer accessible).

"Nuclearization of the Gulf." Security and Terrorism Research Bulletin, no. 7. Dubai, UAE: Gulf Research Center, 2007. Accessed July 10, 2013. http://mercury.ethz.ch/serviceengine/Files/ISN/56136/ipublicationdocument_singledocument/2883179d-5deb-4be2-9992-3d3c453ab752/en/Security+Bulletin+No+7.pdf.

Nuti, Leopoldo. "Italy's Nuclear Choices." UNISCI Discussion Papers, no. 25 (2011). http://revistas.ucm.es/cps/16962206/articulos/UNIS1111130167A.PDF.

Nye, Joseph S. "Maintaining a Nonproliferation Regime." *International Organization* 35, no. 1 (1981): 15–38.

———. "NPT: The Logic of Inequality." *Foreign Policy*, no. 59 (1985): 123–31. doi:10.2307/1148604.

Obama, Barack. "Remarks by President Barack Obama." Speech, Hradcany Square, Prague, Czech Republic, April 5, 2009. http://www.whitehouse.gov/the_press_office/Remarks-By-President-Barack-Obama-In-Prague-As-Delivered.

Oberdörster, Uta. "Why Ratify? Lessons from Treaty Ratification Campaigns." *Vanderbilt Law Review* 61, no. 2 (2008): 681–712.

Ogilvie-White, Tanya, and David Santoro. "Disarmament and Non-proliferation: Towards More Realistic Bargains." *Survival* 53, no. 3 (2011): 101–18. doi:10.1080/00396338.2011.586194.

Oliveira, Eliézer Rizzo de, and Samuel Alves Soares. "Brasil: Forças Armadas, direção política e formato institucional" [Brazil: Armed forces, political direction and institutional format]. In *Democracia e Forças Armadas no Cone Sul* [Democracy and Armed Forces in the Southern Cone], edited by Maria Celina D'Araujo and Celso Castro, 98–124. Rio de Janeiro: Editora FGV, 2000).

Olson, Mancur. *The Logic of Collective Action: Public Goods and the Theory of Groups.* Cambridge: Harvard University Press, 1965.

Olson, Mancur, and Richard J. Zeckhauser. "Collective Goods, Comparative Advantage, and Alliance Efficiency." In *Issues in Defense Economics*, edited by Roland McKean, 25–48. New York: National Bureau of Economic Research, 1967.

———. "An Economic Theory of Alliances." *Review of Economics and Statistics* 48, no. 3 (1966): 266–79. doi:10.2307/1927082.

"The Origin and Interpretation of Article VI." Printed correspondence. *Nonproliferation Review* 15, no. 1 (2008): 7–19. doi:10.1080/10736700701852878.

Orlov, Vladimir A., and Alexander Vinnikov. "The Great Guessing Game: Russia and the Iranian Nuclear Issue." *Washington Quarterly* 28, no. 2 (2005): 49–66.

Ortiz Mena, Antonio. "Mexico." In *The World Trade Organization: A Legal, Economic, and Political Analysis*, edited by Patrick F. J. Macrory, Arthur E. Appleton, and Michael G. Plummer, 217–47. New York: Springer, 2005.

Ottaway, David B. "South Africa Agrees to Treaty Curbing Nuclear Weapons; Important Gain in U.S.-Led Campaign." *Washington Post*, June 28, 1991. http://www.highbeam.com/doc/1P2-1072260.html.

"Pakistan Warns against Fissile Material Talks outside Disarmament Forum." *Global Security Newswire*, August 1, 2011. http://gsn.nti.org/gsn/nw_20110801_3303.php.

Pan, Esther. "Nonproliferation: The Pakistan Network." Council on Foreign Relations, February 12, 2004. http://www.cfr.org/background/nonpro.php.

Parker, John W. *Persian Dreams: Moscow and Tehran since the Fall of the Shah.* Washington, D.C: Potomac Books, 2009.

Parrish, Scott, and Jean du Preez. "Nuclear-Weapon-Free Zones: Still a Useful Disarmament and Nonproliferation Tool?" Weapons of Mass Destruction Commission, 2005. Accessed July 10, 2013. http://www.blixassociates.com/wp-content/uploads/2011/03/No6.pdf.

Paul, T. V. *Power versus Prudence: Why Nations Forgo Nuclear Weapons.* Foreign Policy, Security, and Strategic Studies. Montreal: McGill-Queen's University Press, 2000.

———. "The Systemic Bases of India's Challenge to the Global Nuclear Order." *Nonproliferation Review* 6, no. 1 (1998): 1–11. doi:10.1080/10736709808436731.

———. "Systemic Conditions and Security Cooperation: Explaining the Persistence of the Nuclear Non-proliferation Regime." *Cambridge Review of International Affairs* 16, no. 1 (2003): 135–54. doi:10.1080/0955757032000075753.

———. *The Tradition of Non-use of Nuclear Weapons.* Stanford, Calif: Stanford Security Studies, 2009.

———. "The U.S.-India Nuclear Accord: Implications for the Nonproliferation Regime." *International Journal* 62, no. 4 (2007): 845–61. doi:10.2307/40204340.

Payne, Keith B. "A Vision Shall Guide Them? The Strategic Risks of President Obama's Call for Nuclear Disarmament." *National Review*, November 2009.

Pellicer de Brody, Olga. *México y La Revolución Cubana*. Publicaciones Del Centro de Estudios Internacionales 7. México City: El Colegio de México, 1972.

Perkovich, George. "The End of the Nonproliferation Regime?" *Current History* 105, no. 694 (2006): 355–62.

———. *India's Nuclear Bomb: The Impact on Global Proliferation*. Berkeley: University of California Press, 2001.

———. "Toward Realistic U.S.-India Relations." Carnegie Endowment for International Peace, October 25, 2010. Accessed July 15, 2013. http://carnegieendowment.org/publications/?fa=41797.

Perloff, Richard M. *The Dynamics of Persuasion*. Communication Textbook Series. Hillsdale, N.J: Lawrence Erlbaum, 1993.

Petty, Richard E., and Duane T. Wegener. "Attitude Change: Multiple Roles for Persuasion Variables." In *The Handbook of Social Psychology*, vol. 2, 4th ed., edited by Daniel T. Gilbert, Susan T. Fiske, and Gardner Lindzey, 323-90. New York: McGraw Hill, 1998.

Pion-Berlin, David S. "Political Management of the Military in Latin America." *Military Review* 85, no. 1 (2005): 19.

Pomper, Miles A. "U.S., UAE Sign Nuclear Cooperation Pact." *Arms Control Today*, March 2009. http://www.armscontrol.org/print/3555.

Potter, William C., ed. *Forecasting Nuclear Proliferation in the 21st Century*. Stanford, Calif.: Stanford University Press, 2010.

Potter, William, Patricia Lewis, Gaukhar Mukhatzhanova, and Miles Pomper. "The 2010 NPT Review Conference: Deconstructing Consensus." James Martin Center for Nonproliferation Studies, June 17, 2010. http://cns.miis.edu/stories/pdfs/100617_npt_2010_summary.pdf.

Potter, William C., and Gaukhar Mukhatzhanova. "Divining Nuclear Intentions: A Review Essay." *International Security* 33, no. 1 (2008): 139–69. doi:10.1162/isec.2008.33.1.139.

———, eds. *Forecasting Nuclear Proliferation in the 21st Century*. Stanford, Calif: Stanford University Press, 2010.

Preez, Jean du, and William Potter. "North Korea's Withdrawal from the NPT: A Reality Check." James Martin Center for Nonproliferation Studies. Accessed July 11, 2013. http://cns.miis.edu/stories/030409.htm.

Preston, Julia. "Brazil's Leader Brings Vigorous Image, Mixed Record." *Washington Post*, June 18, 1991. http://www.highbeam.com/doc/1P2-1070580.html.

Rademaker, Stephen. "Blame America First." *Wall Street Journal*, May 7, 2007. http://online.wsj.com/article/SB117849961888494020.html.

Rathbun, Nina Srinivasan. "The Role of Legitimacy in Strengthening the Nuclear Nonproliferation Regime." *Nonproliferation Review* 13, no. 2 (2006): 227–52. doi:10.1080/10736700601012052.

Redick, John R. *Military Potential of Latin American Nuclear Energy Programs*. Beverly Hills Calif.: Sage, 1972.

Redick, John R., Julio C. Carasales, and Paulo S. Wrobel. "Nuclear Rapprochement: Argentina, Brazil, and the Nonproliferation Regime." *Washington Quarterly* 18, no. 1 (1995): 107–22. doi:10.1080/01636609509550135.

Reed, Thomas C., and Danny B. Stillman. *The Nuclear Express: A Political History of the Bomb and Its Proliferation*. Minneapolis: Zenith Press, 2010.

Reich, Jacqueline C. "Achieving the Vision of the NPT." *Nonproliferation Review* 18, no. 2 (2011): 369–87. doi:10.1080/10736700.2011.583118.

Reiss, Mitchell. *Bridled Ambition: Why Countries Constrain Their Nuclear Capabilities*. Woodrow Wilson Center Special Studies. Washington, D.C.: Woodrow Wilson Center Press, 1995.

———. *Without the Bomb: The Politics of Nuclear Nonproliferation*. New York: Columbia University Press, 1988.

Reiss, Mitchell, and Robert S. Litwak, eds. *Nuclear Proliferation after the Cold War*. Woodrow Wilson Center Special Studies. Washington, D.C.: Woodrow Wilson Center Press, 1994.

Reiter, Dan. *Preventive War and Its Alternatives: The Lessons of History*. Carlisle, Pa.: Strategic Studies Institute, U.S. Army War College, 2006.

"Report of the Secretary of Defense Task Force on DoD Nuclear Weapons Management, Phase II: Review of the DoD Nuclear Mission." Arlington, Va., December 2008.

Resende-Santos, João. "The Origins of Security Cooperation in the Southern Cone." *Latin American Politics and Society* 44, no. 4 (2002): 89–126. doi:10.2307/3176996.

Riker, William H., and Peter C. Ordeshook. *An Introduction to Positive Political Theory*. Englewood Cliffs, N.J.: Prentice Hall, 1973.

Rublee, Maria Rost. *Nonproliferation Norms: Why States Choose Nuclear Restraint*. Studies in Security and International Affairs. Athens: University of Georgia Press, 2009.

———. "The Nuclear Threshold States: Challenges and Opportunities Posed by Brazil and Japan." *Nonproliferation Review* 17, no. 1 (2010): 49–70. doi:10.1080/10736700903484660.

Ruggie, John Gerard. "Multilateralism: The Anatomy of an Institution." *International Organization* 46, no. 3 (1992): 561–98. doi:10.2307/2706989.

Rühle, Hans. "Nuclear Proliferation in Latin America: Is Brazil Developing the Bomb?" *Spiegel Online*, July 5, 2010. http:// www.spiegel.de/international/world/0,1518,693336,00.html.

Russell, Roberto. "Conflicto y armamentismo en América Latin" [Conflict and arms build-up in Latin America]. In *Desarme y Desarrollo en América Latina* [Disarmament and development in Latin America], edited by Mónica Hirst, 61–67. Buenos Aires: Fundación para la Democracia y la Paz, 1990.

"Russia, China Set to Sell Iran Reactors." Associated Press, September 11, 1992.

"Russia and Arms Control: Vlad and MAD." *Economist*, June 9, 2007.

"Russia Arrests Iranian Seeking Missile Data." *New York Times*, November 15, 1997, late ed. (East Coast).

"Russia Completes Missile Deliveries: Tass." Reuters, January 23, 2007.

"Russian Agency Opposes Sale of Centrifuge to Iran." Interfax (in Russian, translated by BBC Monitoring), May 6, 1995.

"Russian Foreign Minister Calls for 'Balanced' IAEA Resolution on Iran." RIA Novosti (in Russian, translated by BBC Monitoring), November 24, 2003.

"Russia Says No Plans to Sell Missile System to Iran." Reuters, December 28, 2007.

"Russia Steps Up Criticism of NATO Libya Campaign." Reuters, May 20, 2011.

"Russia to Supply Unique Missile Systems." Interfax (in Russian, translated by BBC Monitoring), December 2, 2005.

Rutland, Peter. "Putin and the Oligarchs." In *Putin's Russia: Past Imperfect, Future Uncertain*, 3rd ed., edited by Dale R. Herspring. Lanham, Md.: Rowman & Littlefield, 2007.

"S-300 Missiles Come under New UN Sanctions on Iran-Kremlin Source." RIA Novosti (in English), June 11, 2010. http://en.rian.ru/russia/20100611/159387435.html.

Sagan, Scott D. "The Causes of Nuclear Weapons Proliferation." *Annual Review of Political Science* 14, no. 1 (2011): 225–44. doi:10.1146/annurev-polisci-052209-131042.

———. "Shared Responsibilities for Nuclear Disarmament." *Daedalus* 138, no. 4 (2009): 157–68. doi:10.1162/daed.2009.138.4.157.

———. "Why Do States Build Nuclear Weapons? Three Models in Search of a Bomb." *International Security* 21, no. 3 (1996): 54–86. doi:10.2307/2539273.

Sagan, Scott D., and Jane Vaynman. "Conclusion: Lessons Learned from the 2010 Posture Review." "Arms, Disarmament, and Influence: International Reactions to the 2010 Nuclear Posture Review." Special issue, *Nonproliferation Review* 18, no. 1 (2011): 237–62. doi:10.1080/10736700.2011.549183.

———. "Introduction: Reviewing the Nuclear Posture Review." "Arms, Disarmament, and Influence: International Reactions to the 2010 Nuclear Posture Review." Special issue, *Nonproliferation Review* 18, no. 1 (2011): 17–37. doi:10.1080/10736700.2011.549169.

Sagan, Scott D., and Kenneth N. Waltz. *The Spread of Nuclear Weapons: A Debate Renewed*. 2nd ed. New York: W. W. Norton, 2002.

Samore, Gary. Remarks at "International Perspectives on the Nuclear Posture Review." Washington, D.C, April 22, 2010. http://carnegieendowment.org/files/0422carnegie-samore.pdf.

Sandler, Todd. *Collective Action: Theory and Applications*. Ann Arbor: University of Michigan Press, 1992.

———. *Global Collective Action*. Cambridge: Cambridge University Press, 2004.

———. "Impurity of Defense: An Application to the Economics of Alliances." *Kyklos* 30, no. 3 (1977): 443–60.

Sandler, Todd, and Daniel G. Arce M. "A Conceptual Framework for Understanding Global and Transnational Public Goods for Health." *Fiscal Studies* 23, no. 2 (2002): 195–222. doi:10.1111/j.1475-5890.2002.tb00059.x.

———. "Pure Public Goods versus Commons: Benefit-Cost Duality." *Land Economics* 79, no. 3 (2003): 355–68.

Sandler, Todd, and John F. Forbes. "Burden Sharing, Strategy, and the Design of NATO." *Economic Inquiry* 18, no. 3 (1980): 425–44.

Sandler, Todd, and Keith Hartley. "Economics of Alliances: The Lessons for Collective Action." *Journal of Economic Literature* 39, no. 3 (2001): 869–96.

Sandler, Todd, and John Tschirhart. "Club Theory: Thirty Years Later." *Public Choice* 93, no. 3/4 (1997): 335–55.

Sanger, David E. "Nuclear Board Said to Rebuff Bush over Iran." *New York Times*, November 20, 2003, late ed. (East Coast).

———. "Syria, Iran and the Obama Doctrine." *New York Times*, February 26, 2012, late ed. (East Coast).

Santos Vieira de Jesus, Diego. "The Brazilian Way." *Nonproliferation Review* 17, no. 3 (2010): 551–67. doi:10.1080/10736700.2010.517003.

Saradzhyan, Simon, and Caroline McGregor. "Russia Hardens Stance toward Iran." *Moscow Times*, September 22, 2003.

Sartori, Anne E. *Deterrence by Diplomacy*. Princeton, N.J.: Princeton University Press, 2005.

Sauer, Tom. "The Nuclear Nonproliferation Regime in Crisis." *Peace Review* 18.3 (2006), 334–35.

Saunders, Phillip C. "New Approaches to Nonproliferation: Supplementing or Supplanting the Regime?" *Nonproliferation Review* 8, no. 3 (2001): 123–36. doi:10.1080/10736700108436868.

Scheinman, Lawrence, ed. *Implementing Resolution 1540: The Role of Regional Organizations*. United Nations Institute for Disarmament Research. New York: United Nations, 2008.

———. *The International Atomic Energy Agency and World Nuclear Order*. Washington, D.C.: Resources for the Future, 1987.

Schneider, Mycle. "Nuclear France Abroad: History, Status and Prospects of French Nuclear Activities in Foreign Countries." Paris: Mycle Schneider Consulting, May 2009. http://www.nirs.org/nukerelapse/background/090502mschneidernukefrance.pdf.

Schneidmiller, Chris. "Senate Decision Key to Future of Test Ban Treaty." *Global Security Newswire*, July 18, 2011. http://gsn.nti.org/gsn/nw_20110714_9351.php.

"Scientist Says Brazil Has Right to Nuclear Secrets." *Global Security Newswire*, July 16, 2013. http://www.nti.org/gsn/article/scientist-says-brazil-has-right-to-nuclear-secrets/.

Sciolino, Elaine, David E. Sanger, and Helene Cooper. "Russia Tells Iran It Must Suspend Uranium Project." *New York Times*, March 20, 2007, late ed. (East Coast).

Searle, John R. *Construction of Social Reality*. New York: Free Press, 1995. Online e-book. Accessed July 13, 2013. http://archive.org/details/ConstructionOfSocialRealityJohn Searle.

Selcher, Wayne A. "Brazilian-Argentine Relations in the 1980s: From Wary Rivalry to Friendly Competition." *Journal of Interamerican Studies and World Affairs* 27, no. 2 (1985): 25–53. doi:10.2307/165717.

Serrano, Mónica. "The Armed Branch of the State: Civil-Military Relations in Mexico." *Journal of Latin American Studies* 27, no. 2 (1995): 423–48. doi:10.1017/S0022216 X00010816.

———. "Brazil and Argentina." In *Nuclear Proliferation after the Cold War*, edited by Mitchell Reiss and Robert S. Litwak, 231–56. Baltimore: Woodrow Wilson Center Press, 1994.

———. *Common Security in Latin America: The 1967 Treaty of Tlatelolco*. Research Papers, University of London, Institute of Latin American Studies 30. London: Institute of Latin American Studies, 1992.

Sestanovich, Stephen. "At Odds with Iran and Iraq: Can the United States and Russia Resolve Their Differences?" Century Foundation and Stanley Foundation Joint Project on Domestic Politics and America's Russia Policy, February 2003. www.stanleyfoundation .org/publications/archive/EAIrussiaA03p.pdf.

Shaffer, Brenda. *Partners in Need: The Strategic Relationship of Russia and Iran*. Policy Paper no. 57. Washington, D.C: Washington Institute for Near East Policy, 2001.

Shaker, Mohamed Ibrahim. *The Nuclear Non-Proliferation Treaty: Origin and Implementation, 1959–1979*. London: Oceana, 1980.

Shaw, Carolyn M. *Cooperation, Conflict, and Consensus in the Organization of American States*. New York: Palgrave Macmillan, 2004.

Shevchenko, Iulia. *The Central Government of Russia: From Gorbachev to Putin*. Post-Soviet Politics Series. Burlington, Vt.: Ashgate, 2004.

Shevtsova, Lilia. *Putin's Russia*. Washington, D.C: Carnegie Endowment for International Peace, 2005.

Shlapentokh, Dmitry. *Russian Elite Image of Iran: From the Late Soviet Era to the Present*. Advancing Strategic Thought Series. Carlisle, Pa.: Strategic Studies Institute, U.S. Army War College, 2009.

Shleifer, Andrei, and Daniel Treisman. "Why Moscow Says No: A Question of Russian Interests, Not Psychology." *Foreign Affairs* 90, no. 1 (2011): 122–38.

Shultz, George P., William J. Perry, Henry A. Kissinger, and Sam Nunn. "Deterrence in the Age of Nuclear Proliferation." *Wall Street Journal*, March 7, 2011. http://online.wsj .com/article/SB10001424052748703300904576178760530169414.html.

Simes, Dimitri K. "Losing Russia: The Costs of Renewed Confrontation." *Foreign Affairs* 86, no. 6 (2007): 36–52. doi:10.2307/20032507.

Simmons, Beth A. "Compliance with International Agreements." *Annual Review of Political Science* 1, no. 1 (1998): 75–93. doi:10.1146/annurev.polisci.1.1.75.

Simpson, John. "The Future of the NPT." In *Combating Weapons of Mass Destruction: The Future of International Nonproliferation Policy*, edited by Nathan E. Busch and Daniel H. Joyner, 45–73. Athens: University of Georgia Press, 2009.

———. "The Role of Security Assurances in the Nuclear Nonproliferation Regime." In *Security Assurances and Nuclear Nonproliferation*, edited by Jeffrey W. Knopf, 57–85. Stanford, Calif.: Stanford University Press, 2012.

Simpson, John, and Anthony G. McGrew, eds. *The International Nuclear Non-proliferation System: Challenges and Choices*. New York: St. Martin's Press, 1984.

Singh, Jaswant. "Against Nuclear Apartheid: The Case for India's Tests." *Foreign Affairs* 77, no. 5 (1998): 41–52. http://www.foreignaffairs.com/articles/54391/jaswant-singh/against-nuclear-apartheid.

Singh, Sonali, and Christopher R. Way. "The Correlates of Nuclear Proliferation: A Quantitative Test." *Journal of Conflict Resolution* 48, no. 6 (2004): 859–85. doi:10.2307/4149798.

Smith, Roger K. "Explaining the Non-proliferation Regime: Anomalies for Contemporary International Relations Theory." *International Organization* 41, no. 2 (1987): 253–81. doi:10.1017/S0020818300027466.

Solingen, Etel. "Hindsight and Foresight in South American Nonproliferation Trends in Argentina, Brazil, and Venezuela." In *Over the Horizon Proliferation Threats*, edited by James J. Wirtz and Peter R. Lavoy, 136–59. Stanford, Calif.: Stanford University Press, 2012.

———. *Industrial Policy, Technology, and International Bargaining: Designing Nuclear Industries in Argentina and Brazil*. Stanford, Calif.: Stanford University Press, 1996.

———. "Macropolitical Consensus and Lateral Autonomy in Industrial Policy: The Nuclear Sector in Brazil and Argentina." *International Organization* 47, no. 2 (1993): 263–98. doi:10.1017/S0020818300027946.

———. *Nuclear Logics: Contrasting Paths in East Asia and the Middle East*. Princeton Studies in International History and Politics. Princeton, N.J.: Princeton University Press, 2007.

———. *Regional Orders at Century's Dawn: Global and Domestic Influences on Grand Strategy*. Princeton Studies in International History and Politics. Princeton, N.J: Princeton University Press, 1998.

Sotomayor Velazquez, Arturo C. "Civil-Military Affairs and Security Institutions in the Southern Cone: The Sources of Argentine-Brazilian Nuclear Cooperation." *Latin American Politics and Society* 46, no. 4 (2004): 29–60.

———. "Different Paths and Divergent Policies in the UN Security System: Brazil and Mexico in Comparative Perspective." *International Peacekeeping* 16, no. 3 (2009): 364–78. doi:10.1080/13533310903036418.

———. "U.S.-Latin American Nuclear Relations: From Commitment to Defiance." PASCC Report no. 2012 013. Project on Advanced Systems and Concepts for Countering WMD. Monterey, Calif.: U.S. Naval Postgraduate School, Center on Contemporary Conflict, September 2012.

Spector, Leonard S., and Benjamin Radford. "Algeria, Emirates Plan Nonproliferation-Friendly Nuclear Programs; Egypt Keeps Fuel Cycle Options Open, Rejects Expanded IAEA Monitoring." *WMD Insights*, June 2008. http://www.wmdinsights.com/I25/I25 _ME1_AlgeriaEmirates.htm.

Spiegel, Steven L., Jennifer D. Kibbe, and Elizabeth G. Matthews, eds. *The Dynamics of Middle East Nuclear Proliferation*. Symposium Series vol. 66. Lewiston, N.Y: E. Mellen Press, 2001.

Squassoni, Sharon. "Grading Progress on 13 Steps toward Nuclear Disarmament." Carnegie Endowment for International Peace. *Policy Outlook*, April 5, 2009. http://www .carnegieendowment.org/files/13_steps.pdf.

Stein, Janice Gross. "Egypt and Israel in the Middle East." In *The Dynamics of Middle East Nuclear Proliferation*, edited by Steven L. Spiegel, Jennifer D. Kibbe, and Elizabeth G. Matthews, 33–58. Symposium Series vol. 66. Lewiston, N.Y: E. Mellen Press, 2001.

———. "The Psychology of Assurance: An Emotional Tale." In *Security Assurances and Nuclear Nonproliferation*, edited by Jeffrey W. Knopf, 35–56. Stanford, Calif.: Stanford University Press, 2012.

Stepan, Alfred C., ed. *Authoritarian Brazil: Origins, Policies, and Future*. New Haven, Conn.: Yale University Press, 1973.

———. "The New Professionalism of Internal Warfare and Military Role Expansion." In *Authoritarian Brazil: Origins, Policies, and Future*, edited by Alfred C. Stepan, 47–65. New Haven, Conn.: Yale University Press, 1973.

Stiff, James B. *Persuasive Communication*. New York: Guilford Press, 1994.

Stockholm International Peace Research Institute (SIPRI). *The Problem of Chemical and Biological Warfare: A Study of the Historical, Technical, Military, Legal and Political Aspects of CBW, and Possible Disarmament Measures*. Vol. 5. Stockholm: Almqvist & Wiksell; New York: Humanities Press, 1975.

Stolberg, Sheryl Gay, and Jim Yardley. "Countering China, Obama Backs India for U.N. Council." *New York Times*, November 8, 2010. http://www.nytimes.com/2010/11/09/ world/asia/09prexy.html.

Stott, Noel. "Motivations and Capabilities to Acquire Nuclear, Biological, or Chemical Weapons and Missiles: South Africa." In *Over the Horizon Proliferation Threats*, edited by James J. Wirtz and Peter R. Lavoy, 68–84. Stanford, Calif.: Stanford University Press, 2012.

Strulak, Tadeusz. "The Nuclear Suppliers Group." *Nonproliferation Review* 1, no. 1 (1993): 2–10. doi:10.1080/10736709308436518.

Stuenkel, Oliver. "Brazil Should Act on Nuclear Transparency." *World Politics Review*, October 20, 2010, http://www.worldpoliticsreview.com/articles/6776/brazil-should-act-on-nuclear-transparency.

Stulberg, Adam N. "Nuclear Regionalism in Russia: Decentralization and Control in the Nuclear Complex." *Nonproliferation Review* 9, no. 3 (2002): 31–46. doi:10.1080/10736700208436902.

Suchman, Mark C. "Managing Legitimacy: Strategic and Institutional Approaches." *Academy of Management Review* 20, no. 3 (1995): 571–610. doi:10.2307/258788.

Sullivan, Kevin, and Dafna Linzer. "Iran to Be Reported to Security Council; U.S. Wins Backing of Russia, China." *Washington Post*, January 31, 2006.

Tait, Robert. "Russia Starts Nuclear Fuel Deliveries to Iran." *Guardian* (London), December 18, 2007.

Takeyh, Ray. *Guardians of the Revolution: Iran and the World in the Age of the Ayatollahs*. Oxford: Oxford University Press, 2009.

Talbott, Strobe. *The Russia Hand: A Memoir of Presidential Diplomacy*. New York: Random House, 2002.

Tannenwald, Nina. *The Nuclear Taboo: The United States and the Non-use of Nuclear Weapons since 1945*. Cambridge Studies in International Relations 87. Cambridge: Cambridge University Press, 2007.

Tate, Trevor McMorris. "Regime-Building in the Non-proliferation System." *Journal of Peace Research* 27, no. 4 (1990): 399–414.

Tauscher, Ellen. "Addressing the Nuclear Fuel Cycle." Speech, Hoover Institute, Stanford University, January 19, 2010. http://www.state.gov/t/us/136426.htm.

———. "The Case for the Comprehensive Nuclear Test Ban Treaty." Speech, Arms Control Association Annual Meeting at the Carnegie Endowment for International Peace, Washington, D.C, May 10, 2011. http://www.state.gov/t/us/162963.htm.

———. "Comprehensive Nuclear Test Ban Treaty Organization Enhances Our National Security." DipNote: U.S. Department of State Official Blog, March 2, 2010. http://blogs.state.gov/stories/2010/03/02/comprehensive-nuclear-test-ban-treaty-organization-enhances-our-national-security.

———. "The Nonproliferation and Disarmament Nexus." Speech, Foundation for Strategic Research Conference, Paris, France, June 29, 2011. http://www.state.gov/t/us/167987.htm.

Taylor, Paul, and Louis Charbonneau. "EU Big Three Offered Iran Carrot for Nuclear Deal." Reuters, September 19, 2003. http://carnegieendowment.org/2003/09/19/eu-big-three-offered-iran-carrot-for-nuclear-deal/2u52.

Telhami, Shibley. "2008 Annual Arab Public Opinion Poll." Accessed February 14, 2014. http://www.brookings.edu/~/media/events/2008/4/14%20middle%20east/0414_middle_east_telhami.pdf.

Tertrais, Bruno. "Security Guarantees and Nuclear Non-Proliferation." *FRS Notes* 2011 no. 14. Paris: Fondation pour la Recherche Stratégie, 2011.

Terrill, W. Andrew. "The Chemical Warfare Legacy of the Yemen War." *Comparative Strategy* 10, no. 2 (1991): 109–19. doi:10.1080/01495939108402836.

Thibaut, John W., and Harold H. Kelley. *The Social Psychology of Groups*. New York: Wiley, 1959.

Toshiba Corporation. "Toshiba Signs Memorandum of Understanding on Cooperation in Development of Mineral Resources and Social Infrastructure with Mongolia's MNFCC." Press release, November 26, 2010. Accessed July 10, 2013. http://www.toshiba.co.jp/about/press/2010_11/pr2601.htm.

"Treaty on the Non-Proliferation of Nuclear Weapons (NPT)." *IAEA Bulletin*, July 1, 1968. http://www.iaea.org/Publications/Magazines/Bulletin/Bull104/10403501117.pdf.

Treisman, Daniel. *The Return: Russia's Journey from Gorbachev to Medvedev*. New York: Free Press, 2011.

Trenin, Dmitri, and Alexey Malashenko. *Iran: A View from Moscow*. Washington, D.C: Carnegie Endowment for International Peace, 2010.

"U.N. Chief Floats Measures to Break Conference on Disarmament Stalemate." *Global Security Newswire*, July 28, 2011. http://www.nti.org/gsn/article/un-chief-floats-measures-to-break-conference-on-disarmament-stalemate/.

United Nations. "2000 Review Conference of the Parties to the Treaty on the Non-Proliferation of Nuclear Weapons." Final document. Vol. 1, pt. 1, New York, 2000.

———. "2010 Review Conference of the Parties to the Treaty on the Non-Proliferation of Nuclear Weapons, 3–28 May 2010." Final document. Accessed July 10, 2013. http://www.un.org/en/conf/npt/2010/.

———. Office for Disarmament Affairs. "Treaty of the Non-Proliferation of Nuclear Weapons." Accessed June 19, 2013. http://disarmament.un.org/treaties/t/npt.

———. Treaty Collection. "International Convention for the Suppression of Acts of Nuclear Terrorism." April 13, 2005. Accessed March 14, 2014. http://treaties.un.org/Pages/ViewDetailsIII.aspx?&src=IND&mtdsg_no=XVIII-15&chapter=18&Temp=mtdsg3&lang=en.

U.S. Central Intelligence Agency. "Unclassified Report to Congress on the Acquisition of Technology Relating to Weapons of Mass Destruction and Advanced Conventional Munitions, 1 January through 30 June 2001." Accessed June 19, 2013. https://www.cia.gov/library/reports/archived-reports-1/jan_jun2001.htm.

U.S. Congress, Senate. *A Review of Gore-Chernomyrdin Diplomacy: Hearing before the Subcommittee on European Affairs and the Subcommittee on Near Eastern and South*

Asian Affairs of the Committee on Foreign Relations, United States Senate, One Hundred Sixth Congress, Second Session, October 25, 2000. Vol. 4. Washington, D.C.: U.S. Government Printing Office, 2001.

U.S. Department of Defense. *Nuclear Posture Review Report, 2010.* April 2010. Washington, D.C., http://www.defense.gov/npr/docs/2010%20nuclear%20posture%20review%20report.pdf.

U.S. Department of State. "Fact Sheet: United States and India: Strategic Partnership," http://georgewbush-whitehouse.archives.gov/news/releases/2006/03/20060302-13.html.

———. "Nuclear Security Summit, Seoul 2012." Bureau of International Security and Nonproliferation, March 5, 2012. http://www.state.gov/t/isn/nuclearsecuritysummit/2012/index.htm.

———. "Treaty for the Prohibition of Nuclear Weapons in Latin America and the Caribbean (Treaty of Tlatelolco)." Press release, Bureau of Western Hemisphere Affairs, February 14, 1967. http://www.state.gov/p/wha/rls/70658.htm.

———. "U.S.-Belarus Joint Statement on Nuclear Security, Human Rights." U.S.-Belarus Bilateral Meeting, December 1, 2010. Bureau of Public Affairs. http://www.state.gov/r/pa/prs/ps/2010/12/152168.htm.

U.S. Embassy, Seoul, Korea. "Presidential Visit." November 29, 2012. http://seoul.usembassy.gov/p_pv_061609b.html.

U.S. Senate. *Treaty with Russia on Measures for Further Reduction and Limitation of Strategic Offensive Arms.* 111th Cong., 2d sess., 2010, treaty doc. 111–15.

U.S. White House, Office of the Press Secretary. "Fact Sheet: An Enduring Commitment to the U.S. Nuclear Deterrent." Press release, November 17, 2010. Accessed July 14, 2013. http://www.whitehouse.gov/the-press-office/2010/11/17/fact-sheet-enduring-commitment-us-nuclear-deterrent.

———. "Joint Statement between President George W. Bush and Prime Minister Manmohan Singh," http://georgewbush-whitehouse.archives.gov/news/releases/2005/07/20050718-6.html.

———. "Joint Vision for the Alliance of the United States of America and the Republic of Korea." Press release, June 16, 2009. http://www.whitehouse.gov/the_press_office/Joint-vision-for-the-alliance-of-the-United-States-of-America-and-the-Republic-of-Korea.

Walker, William. "Nuclear Enlightenment and Counter-enlightenment." *International Affairs* 83, no. 3 (2007): 431–53. doi:10.1111/j.1468-2346.2007.00630.x.

Wallander, Celeste A. "Russia's Interest in Trading with the 'Axis of Evil.'" Program on New Approaches to Russian Security (PONARS) Policy Memo 248. Center for Strategic and International Studies, October 2002. http://csis.org/files/media/csis/pubs/pm_0248.pdf.

Walsh, James Joseph. "Bombs Unbuilt: Power, Ideas and Institutions in International Politics." PhD thesis, Massachusetts Institute of Technology, 2001. http://dspace.mit.edu/handle/1721.1/8237.

Walsh, Jim. "Egypt's Nuclear Future: Proliferation or Restraint?" In *Forecasting Nuclear Proliferation in the 21st Century*, edited by William Potter, 13–41. Stanford, Calif: Stanford University Press, 2010.

———. "Learning from Past Success: The NPT and the Future of Non-proliferation." Weapons of Mass Destruction Commission, October 2005. http://www.un.org/disarmament/education/wmdcommission/files/no41.pdf.

Walt, Stephen M. *The Origins of Alliances*. Cornell Studies in Security Affairs. Ithaca, N.Y.: Cornell University Press, 1987.

Waltz, Kenneth N. "The Spread of Nuclear Weapons: More May Be Better." *Adelphi Papers*, no. 171. London: International Institute for Strategic Studies, 1981.

———. *Theory of International Politics*. Addison-Wesley Series in Political Science. Reading, Mass: Addison-Wesley, 1979.

Way, Christopher, and Karthika Sasikumar. "Leaders and Laggards: When and Why Do Countries Sign the NPT." Research Group in International Security, working paper 16, 2007. Accessed July 11, 2013. http://academia.edu/3129184/Leaders_and_laggards_When_and_why_do_countries_sign_the_npt.

Weber, Max. *Economy and Society: An Outline of Interpretive Sociology*. Berkeley: University of California Press, 1978.

Wehling, Fred. "Russian Nuclear and Missile Exports to Iran." *Nonproliferation Review* 6, no. 2 (1999): 134–43. doi:10.1080/10736709908436756.

Weiss, Leonard. "Atoms for Peace." *Bulletin of the Atomic Scientists* 59, no. 6 (2003). http://thebulletin.org/2003/november/atoms-peace.

Welch, David A. *Justice and the Genesis of War*. Cambridge: Cambridge University Press, 1995.

Wellen, Russ. "Are Nonproliferation and Disarmament, Once Joined at the Hip, Headed for Divorce?" *Huffington Post*, December 11, 2010. Accessed July 14, 2013. http://www.huffingtonpost.com/russ-wellen/are-nonproliferation-and-_b_795302.html.

Weltman, John J. "Nuclear Revolution and World Order." *World Politics* 32 (1980): 169–93.

Williams, Joshua, and Jon B. Wolfsthal. "The NPT at 35: A Crisis of Compliance or a Crisis of Confidence?" United Nations Association of the United States of America, 2005.

Wilmshurst, M. J. "The Development of Current Non-proliferation Policies." In *The International Nuclear Non-proliferation System: Challenges and Choices*, edited by John Simpson and Anthony G. McGrew, 28–38. New York: St. Martin's Press, 1984.

Wirtz, James J., and Peter R. Lavoy, eds. *Over the Horizon Proliferation Threats*. Stanford, Calif.: Stanford Security Studies, Stanford University Press, 2012.

Wolf, Charles, Jr., Brian G. Chow, and Gregory S. Jones. *Enhancement by Enlargement: The Proliferation Security Initiative*. Santa Monica, Calif.: RAND Corporation, 2008.

Wrobel, Paulo S. "A Diplomacia Nuclear Brasileira: A Nõ-proliferaçõ Nuclear e o Tratado de Tlatelolco" [Brazil's Nuclear Diplomacy: Nonproliferation and the Treaty of Tlatelolco]. *Contexto Internacional* 15 (January–June 1993): 27–56.

———. "From Rivals to Friends: The Role of Public Declarations in Argentine-Brazilian Rapprochement." In *Declaratory Diplomacy: Rhetorical Initiatives and Confidence Building*, edited by Michael Krepon, Jenny S. Drezin, and Michael Newbill, 135–51. Report no. 27. Washington, D.C.: Henry L. Stimson Center, 1999.

Wuebbels, Mark. "Is Taiwan Getting Serious about Export Controls?" *Nonproliferation Review* 12, no. 2 (2005): 391–404.

Young, Oran R., and Marc A. Levy. "The Effectiveness of International Environmental Regimes." In *The Effectiveness of International Environmental Regimes: Causal Connections and Behavioral Mechanisms*, edited by Oran R. Young. Cambridge, Mass.: MIT Press, 1999.

Zavarucha, Jorge. "La Fragilidad del Ministerio de Defensa Brasileño" [The fragility of the defense ministry]. In *Operaciones conjuntas: Civiles y militares en la política de defensa* [Joint operations: Civilians and the military in defense policy], edited by José Huerta et al., 51–80. Lima, Peru: Serie Democracia y Fuerza Armada, 2006.

CONTRIBUTORS

DEEPTI CHOUBEY is senior director for nuclear and bio-security at the Nuclear Threat Initiative (NTI). She has a breadth of experience in transforming innovative policy into real-world results to reduce nuclear dangers, as well as in research, analysis, and commentary on global nonproliferation, nuclear security, and disarmament issues. Prior to joining NTI, she was deputy director of the Nuclear Policy Program at the Carnegie Endowment for International Peace. She holds an MA in international affairs, with a focus on South Asia security policy, from Columbia University's School of International and Public Affairs. She holds a BA in government from Harvard University.

JASON ENIA is an assistant professor of international relations in the Department of Political Science at Sam Houston State University. His research and teaching focus on the ways that institutions structure the incentives, and therefore the politics, around low-probability, high-impact events like natural disasters and the use of WMD. He holds a PhD in politics and international relations from the University of Southern California, an MA in international political economy and development from Fordham University (New York), and a BA in political science and economics from the University of Dayton (Ohio).

JEFFREY R. FIELDS is assistant professor of the practice in international relations and director of the Dornsife Washington, D.C., program at the University of Southern California. Previously he was a senior adviser with the Department of Defense focusing on nonproliferation and counterproliferation strategies. He has also served as a foreign affairs officer at the U.S. State Department and a research associate at the James Martin Center for Nonproliferation. He received his PhD from the School of International Relations at USC.

JEFFREY W. KNOPF is professor and program chair of Nonproliferation and Terrorism Studies at the Monterey Institute of International Studies. He has also taught at the Naval Postgraduate School, the University of California–Santa Cruz, and the University of Southern California. He is the author of *Domestic Society and Inter-*

national Cooperation: The Impact of Protest on US Arms Control Policy (1998), the coauthor of US Arms Exports: Policies and Contractors (1988), and the editor of Security Assurances and Nuclear Nonproliferation (2012). He is also a former editor of the Nonproliferation Review. He received a PhD in political science from Stanford University (1991) as well as an MA from Stanford and a BA from Harvard University.

NINA SRINIVASAN RATHBUN is an assistant professor, teaching international relations, at the University of Southern California. She teaches courses on global governance, globalization, and foreign policy of Eastern Europe and serves as faculty adviser for the International Relations Undergraduate Association. Her research interests include multilateral nuclear nonproliferation and counterproliferation policies, proliferation in the Indian subcontinent, democratization in post-Communist Europe, and European Union expansion. She previously served as a foreign affairs officer for the U.S. State Department on multilateral nuclear nonproliferation. She received her PhD in political science from the University of California, Berkeley.

ROBERT J. REARDON is a research fellow with the Project on Managing the Atom and the International Security Program at Harvard University's Belfer Center for Science and International Affairs. His work focuses on the proliferation of nuclear and other sensitive dual-use technologies. He is the author of Containing Iran: Strategies for Addressing the Iranian Nuclear Challenge (2012). Previously he was a Stanton Nuclear Security Fellow at RAND. He is also a member of an NSF-funded team of interdisciplinary researchers based at MIT working on the potential safety and security implications of synthetic biology. He holds a PhD in political science from MIT and has an MS in molecular biology.

MARIA ROST RUBLEE is a senior lecturer at the Australian National University. Her book, Nonproliferation Norms: Why States Choose Nuclear Restraint (University of Georgia Press, 2009), received an international award and has been positively reviewed in numerous journals, including Foreign Affairs. She has received grants from the United States Institute of Peace, the International Studies Association, the Norwegian Ministry of Foreign Affairs, the Asia New Zealand Foundation, and the Japan Foundation. Her work has been published in a variety of international journals, including International Studies Review, Comparative Political Studies, and the Nonproliferation Review. She is an editor of International Studies Perspectives and a member of the international Fissile Material Working Group. She earned her PhD in political science from George Washington University in 2004.

LOWELL H. SCHWARTZ is a political scientist at the RAND Corporation. In 2009 and 2010, he worked for the Office of the Secretary of Defense, International Security Affairs (OSD/ISA) as an adviser on arms control and European security. He has coauthored more than a dozen RAND studies including *A View from Russia: Towards a Better Understanding of Russian Foreign Policy* (2009), *Barriers to the Broad Dissemination of Creative Works in the Arab World* (2009), and *The Challenge of Nuclear Armed Regional Adversaries* (2008). He is also the author of *Political Warfare against the Kremlin* (2009). His work has appeared in a variety of journals and newspapers including the *National Interest, Bulletin of the Atomic Scientists, Los Angeles Times,* and *Baltimore Sun*. He has a PhD in war studies from King's College of London and has an MA from Johns Hopkins School of Advanced International Studies.

ARTURO C. SOTOMAYOR is assistant professor in the Department of National Security Affairs at the Naval Postgraduate School, where his research focuses on multilateral policy, with an emphasis on Latin America's involvement in United Nations peacekeeping operations; nonproliferation strategies in Latin America; and transnational security relations in Mexico. Previously, he was a postdoctoral fellow at Tulane University's Center for Interamerican and Policy Research. He was a public policy scholar in the Mexico Institute at the Woodrow Wilson Center for International Scholars in Washington, D.C. He received his PhD in political science from Columbia University. He is the author of *The Myth of the Democratic Peacekeeper: Civil-Military Relations and the United Nations* (Johns Hopkins University Press, 2014).

JIM WALSH is a research associate at the Massachusetts Institute of Technology. His research and writings focus on international security and, in particular, topics involving nuclear weapons and terrorism. He has testified before the United States Senate on the issue of nuclear terrorism and on Iran's nuclear program. He is one of a handful of Americans who has traveled to both Iran and North Korea for talks with officials about nuclear issues. Before coming to MIT, he was executive director of the Managing the Atom project at Harvard University's John F. Kennedy School of Government and a visiting scholar at the Center for Global Security Research at Lawrence Livermore National Laboratory. He has taught at both Harvard University and MIT. He received his PhD from the Massachusetts Institute of Technology.

INDEX

Additional Protocol (AP), 100, 156, 176–77; adoption of, 251–52; 259–62; Argentina and Brazil, 238–40; hypotheses for lag in adoption, 254–56
aggregation technology, 24–30, 32
Agreed Framework, 192
Ahmadinejad, Mahmoud, 87, 92; meeting with Vladimir Putin, 197–98
Algeria, 162, 261
alliances, 7; extended deterrence, 150; and security guarantees, 9, 118; United States, 157, 165
Angarsk arrangement, 58
Angra 1 nuclear plant, 225
Antiballistic Missile Treaty, 138
Arab League, 265, 267
Arak reactor, 177
Argentina, 132, 224, 226–28; and ABACC, 234, 257; stance toward Additional Protocol, 238–39
Argentine-Brazilian Agency for Accounting and Control of Nuclear Materials (ABACC), 234, 238–39
Article VI (of NPT), 62–63, 106, 109–11, 122–32; and health of nonproliferation regime, 139; lack of progress on, 268.
Atoms for Peace initiative, 47, 223
Australia, 90, 149–50, 271

Baruch Plan, 46–47, 75n23
Be Gaehung (cargo vessel), 156
Belarus, 175, 177, 182, 259
biological weapons, 68, 116, 159
Biological Weapons Convention (BWC), 48, 66
Brazil, 4, 7–8, 72; accession to NPT, 222–25; 233–35; cooperation with Germany, 160; military nuclear program, 219; nuclear energy, 223–24; policy toward Iran, 90–91, 98; rivalry with Argentina, 226–27; 2010 NPT Review Conference, 131
Bush, George W., 94
Bush administration: FMCT policy, 65; nuclear policies, 41–42; nuclear posture review, 42, 62, 68–69, 116; robust nuclear earth penetrator, 68
Bushehr nuclear power station, 192, 211, 192–99

Canada, 177, 229, 242, 258, 260
Cardoso, Fernando Henrique, 235
Castro, Fidel, 229
Central Asian Nuclear-Weapon-Free Zone, 174
Cheney, Dick, 88
China, 69, 115–16, 151, 159, 177; India relations, 116, 127; Iran's nuclear program, 196; North Korea policy, 155; Pakistan relations, 155; and Syria, 199
Clinton, Hillary, 64
Clinton administration, 69, 192–94
collective action, 20–24, 29
Collor de Mello, Fernando, 233
Comprehensive Nuclear-Test-Ban Treaty (CTBT), 32, 71; NAM position on, 175–76; and Obama administration, 64–65
Conference on Disarmament (CD), 65–67, 71
constructed threats, 85–86
Convention on the Physical Protection of Nuclear Material, 4, 21
CTBT. *See* Comprehensive Nuclear-Test-Ban Treaty
Cuban Missile Crisis, 229, 235–36

da Silva, Luiz Inacio, 90–91, 233, 239–40
disarmament, 106; and nonproliferation, 108–10; NPT Article VI, 62–63, 111
discrimination, 7, 20, 91, 133, 176; and London Group, 51–52; in the NPT, 46–50
DPRK. *See* North Korea

Egypt, 96, 164, 264; and CTBT, 65, 176–77; member of New Agenda Coalition, 72, 126; Muslim Brotherhood, 266; renewed nuclear energy plans, 91; stance on Additional Protocol, 267; 2010 NPT Revcon, 71
Eisenhower, Dwight D., 47

Enrichment and Reprocessing (ENR), 56–58
EU-3, 196
export controls, 48, 53, 60–61, 157, 160–61

Falklands/Malvinas War, 228
Fissile Material Cutoff Treaty, 59, 62, 278; negotiations, 65–67
France, 159, 161–64; cooperation with Pakistan, 162; and Iran's nuclear program, 97, 156, 196

Garcia Robles, Alfonso, 236
Germany, 159–64, 196, 228, 260
Ghana, 177
Global Initiative to Combat Nuclear Terrorism, 182
Gottemoeller, Rose, 107
Goulart, João, 224, 230
Great Britain, 71, 97
Guadalajara Accord, 234

highly enriched uranium (HEU), 177–78, 182, 192, 194
Hussein, Saddam, 262

India, 8, 115–16, 127; as nonsignatory to NPT, 8, 41, 76n38, 132–33; nuclear deal with United States, 33–34, 38n41, 58–62, 66, 122; peaceful nuclear explosive, 30, 51
Indonesia, 88, 94, 164, 170–71, 175, 179–80
International Atomic Energy Agency (IAEA), 47; Brazil inspections, 238; inspections, 32, 61, 90
International Fuel Bank, 56
International Monitoring System (IMS), 64–65
Iran, 69, 71–72, 87–92; Additional Protocol, 262–69; and CTBT, 65, 175; and Non-Aligned Movement, 177, 181–82, 184; norms, 94, 96–98; Russia's policy toward, 191–98, 200–211
Israel, 30, 101, 204–5, 262–70; objection to Middle East NWFZ, 96; participation in PSI, 32

Kazakhstan, 58, 204, 259
Khamenei, Ali, 198
Khan, A. Q., 7, 40, 53, 101, 159
Ki-Moon, Ban, 66
Kissinger, Henry, 106

legitimacy, 43–44; and effectiveness of regimes, 45

London Group, 51–52
low enriched uranium (LEU), 58, 177, 198

Mexico: nuclear energy, 223–24; nonproliferation policies, 219
Middle East, 177; adoption of Additional Protocol in, 261–69; Arab Spring, 199; Mexican relations, 242; multilateral cooperation, 139; Nuclear Weapons Free Zone, 96; Russian relations, 202; WMD free zone, 177, 267
Miniature Neutron Source Reactors, 177
Ministry for Atomic Energy (Minatom), 192–94, 209
Mongolia, 182–83
Mubarak, Gamal, 91
Myanmar, 172, 177, 183, 258, 260

Natanz facility, 195
National Nuclear Energy Commission (CNEN), 233
negative security assurance, 68–69, 150, 171
New Agenda Coalition (NAC), 126
New START, 62–65, 69, 107, 125–26; effects on nonproliferation, 107; NAM reaction to, 72; and NPT Article VI, 154; U.S. Senate ratification, 126
Non-Aligned Movement (NAM), 72; and NPT Review Conference, 71–72, 150, 169–70, 184
nonproliferation: defining, 2, 88; disarmament linkage, 91, 114–16; 119–28
nonproliferation regime, 2, 46–50; and public goods, 25
Nonproliferation Treaty (NPT), 47, 97–98; Article IV, 51–53, 109; Article VI, 62–63, 106, 109–11, 122–32; breakout from, 2; discrimination within, 11, 41, 48–49, 61, 91; entry into force, 29–31; as measure of regime health, 169, 171; negative security assurances, 150; and Non-Aligned Movement, 174–76; rate of ratification, 256–57, 261; thirteen practical steps, 138; 2010 Review Conference, 69–71, 90, 112–13, 125, 131
norms: and conflict, 100–101; descriptive, 92–93; injunctive, 93; potency, 99–100; processing, 95–99; transmission of, 92
norm transmission, 93–95
North American Free Trade Agreement (NAFTA), 242

North Korea, 100, 129, 150, 175; and Additional Protocol, 258, 260; NPT status 77n41
NPT. *See* Nonproliferation Treaty
NSG. *See* Nuclear Suppliers Group
nuclear fuel cycle, 87, 184
Nuclear Posture Review (NPR), 9, 42, 62, 122, 154; preemptive use of nuclear weapons, 116
Nuclear Security Summit, 178–79, 182
Nuclear Smuggling Outreach Initiative (NSOI), 5, 21
Nuclear Suppliers Group (NSG), 52–54; and India 58–60
Nuclear Weapons Free Zone (NWFZ), 96, 173
Nunn, Sam, 106

Obama administration: on NPT obligations, 63–64; Prague speech 42, 56, 69, 72, 154, 184; 2010 nuclear posture review, 113, 122
Organisation for Economic Co-operation and Development (OECD), 156
Organization of American States (OAS), 228–29

Pakistan, 60, 88, 116; Chinese nuclear assistance to, 155; and FMCT 66–67; and the Non-Aligned Movement, 175
peaceful nuclear explosions, 223
Perry, William, 106
P5+1, 196, 266
plutonium, 50–51, 164, 170, 177
positive security assurance, 117–18, 150
Prisoner's Dilemma game (PD), 22
Proliferation Security Initiative (PSI), 42, 156–57, 179–80; Israel's participation in, 30, 32
public goods, 20, 22–23, 25, 28, 33
Putin, Vladimir, 190, 195–98, 208

reciprocity, diffuse and specific, 49
regimes, 43
Reprocessing, 50–57, 158
Resende facility, 238, 240
Robles, Alfonso Garcia. *See* Garcia Robles, Alfonso
ROK. *See* South Korea
Russia, 12, 57; development of Iranian nuclear and missile programs, 191–94; Iran policy 194–207; and New START, 32, 63–64; policy on nonstrategic nuclear weapons, 64; reaction to 2010 NPR, 71; reset with U.S., 199

safeguards agreement, 47; full-scope safeguards, 54; U.S.–India nuclear deal, 58
security assurances, 3, 9, 27, 68–69, 109, 110, 117, 118, 142, 150
security guarantees. *See* security assurances
September 11, 2001, 2, 153
Shultz, George, 106
Small Quantities Protocol, 19, 176
South Africa, 54–55, 95, 120, 175; Additional Protocol status, 260; HEU holdings, 177
South Korea, 150–51, 157–58; six-party talks, 156; 2012 Nuclear Security Summit, 182
Soviet Union: effect of dissolution of, 151; objections to MLF, 159
spent fuel, 158, 177, 183, 192, 207
START, 32–33
Strategic Offensive Reductions Treaty (SORT), 62, 64

Taiwan, 156–57, 162
threat perception, 6–7, 152; construction of 85–88, 91
Tor-M1 missile, 196–98
Treaty of Tlatelolco, 218–19; and Brazil, 224, 227–29, 231, 241
Trigger List. *See* Zangger Committee
Turkey, 98, 166, 260–63

Ukraine, 58, 259–60
United Arab Emirates, 182
United Nations, 45, 173
UNSCR 1540, 19, 157, 170; NAM objections to, 181
uranium enrichment, 51

Vietnam, 94, 177, 195

Warsaw Pact, 150, 172
Wassenaar Arrangements, 5, 26, 60
World Trade Organization (WTO), 45

Yeltsin, Boris, 191–94
Yugoslavia, 258

Zangger Committee, 27, 75n28
Zuma, Nkosazana Dlamini, 120

www.ingramcontent.com/pod-product-compliance
Lightning Source LLC
Chambersburg PA
CBHW010719250426
43672CB00033B/2956